JEWISH DISCOVERIES

Jeff Zaremsky

TEACH Services, Inc.
PUBLISHING
www.TEACHServices.com

World rights reserved. This book or any portion thereof may not be copied or reproduced in any form or manner whatever, except as provided by law, without the written permission of the publisher, except by a reviewer who may quote brief passages in a review.

This book was written to provide truthful information in regard to the subject matter covered. The author assumes full responsibility for the accuracy of all facts and quotations as cited in this book. The opinions expressed in this book are the author's personal views and interpretation of the Bible, Spirit of Prophecy, and/or contemporary authors and do not necessarily reflect those of TEACH Services, Inc.

This book is sold with the understanding that the publisher is not engaged in giving spiritual, legal, medical, or other professional advice. If authoritative advice is needed, the reader should seek the counsel of a competent professional

---

Written by Jeff Zaremsky
Chapter Art by James Converse
Tradition Art by Alex Schussler

Copyright © 2007 **Jewish Heritage, Inc.**
Copyright © 2012 TEACH Services, Inc. and Jewish Heritage, Inc.
ISBN-13: 978-1-57258-617-8 (Paperback)
ISBN-13: 978-1-57258-965-0 (ePub)
ISBN-13: 978-1-57258-969-8 (Kindle/Mobi)
Library of Congress Control Number: 2011921827

TEACH Services, Inc.
P U B L I S H I N G
www.TEACHServices.com

Dedicated to:
Adonai Elohim, the Lord God, the Creator of the universe,
to whom all honor and glory is due.

Special appreciation:
To my wife, Barbara, who truly is the perfect, heaven-sent helpmate.
To Samuel Jacobson and Sanford Howard who lived their lives for God.
To the many people who prayed for God to guide in the writing of this book.
To Alex Schussler for his support, encouragement, advice, and art work.
To the many people who proofread this book in its various stages.
To Jim Converse for his friendship, support, and art work.
To Southern Union ASI for their financial support.

Table of Contents

INTRODUCTION	VII
1. ABRAHAM (AVRAHAM), FATHER OF OUR FAITH	1
Simcha Torah	11
2. JACOB (YA'AKOV), T'SHUVA	13
Shofar	25
3. JOSEPH (YOSEF), THE POWER OF FORGIVENESS	27
4. MOSES (MOSHE) THE DELIVERER	41
5. MOSES (MOSHE) THE TEMPLE BUILDER	49
6. THE ULTIMATE PASSOVER	63
Tu B'shevat	77
7. A NICE JEWISH BOY	79
Bar Mitzvah	85
8. MOSES (MOSHE) AND THE 10 COMMANDMENTS	87
Kiddush	100
Havdallah	102
9. MOSES (MOSHE) THE TORAH WRITER	107
Kosher	119
10. WHY DOES GOD ALLOW SUFFERING	125
Holocaust/Shoah	135
Tish B'av	136
11. DEBORAH (D'VORAH)—A MOTHER IN ISRAEL	139
Tanak	150
Shavuot	152
Magen David	154
12. KING DAVID	157
Shema	167
13. KING SOLOMON (SHLOMO)	169
Wedding	182
Mezuzah	184
14. JONAH (YONAH) THE FISHERMAN	187
15. THE YOUNGEST KING	199
Tzedakah Box	210
16. DANIEL, THE GREATEST JEWISH STATESMAN	213
Tallit	228
Western Wall	230
17. DANIEL—PROPHET OF GOD	233
T'fillin	251

18. THE ULTIMATE YOM KIPPUR	255
Kippah	273
19. THE ULTIMATE PROMISED LAND	275
Kaddish	289
Israel's Independence	290
Sukkot	291
20. THE MOST FAMOUS JEW	295
Mikvah	311
21. QUEEN ESTHER (ESTER)	315
Purim	336
22. CHANUKAH	339

INTRODUCTION

While the focus of Jewish Discoveries is the Holy Scriptures, explanations of Jewish traditions are interwoven in this book. We will be looking at some of the traditions surrounding several of the holidays and holy days, as well as traditions regarding tallits, kiddish, havdallah, kaddish, bar/bat mitzvahs, yarmulkes (kippahs), to name a few. It should be clear that there is a difference between traditions and the Scriptures. Traditions are human inventions that help us remember the principles of the Scriptures, but they are not the Scriptures. While the traditions are good, they cannot be used as a substitute for the Scriptures. Traditions help us visualize, taste, smell, and experience the principles of the Scriptures. While the truths of the Scriptures do not change, traditions change with time and circumstances. While the Scriptures are universal and are applicable to people throughout the world, traditions differ from culture to culture. We will do our best to explain the Scriptures and the traditions while trying to differentiate between the two.

Throughout the Holy Scriptures God is referred to by many names because in the Scriptures names are often a description of character. God's character traits are so enormous that there is no one word to describe them all. Thus, through this series we will be using the various names of God interchangeably. Some of God's names in the Holy Scriptures that we will be using are: God, LORD, Adonai, LORD God, Elohim, Creator, Savior, Redeemer, Immanuel. We will not be attempting to pronounce the tetragram YHVH (יהוה). When the tetragram is used in this book it is written as "LORD." You will notice that it appears in all caps to distinguish it from the use of the words "lord" or "Lord."

Unless otherwise noted all the Scriptures quoted are from the Jewish Bible, Tanakh, The Holy Scriptures by the Jewish Publishing Society, 1985. At times the verse numbers from this version are slightly different from other popular Bible versions. For example, this version counts the title of a Psalm as the first verse while some other versions do not. The chapter and verse numbers in Bibles are not a part of the original Scriptures. They are placed in Bibles to make verse identification easier.

JEWISH HERITAGE SCRIPTURE STUDIES

ABRAHAM
FATHER OF OUR FAITH

1. ABRAHAM (AVRAHAM), FATHER OF OUR FAITH

Welcome to the first lesson of the Jewish Heritage Scripture Studies. Each lesson in this series builds on the one before it and will help you get to know God better and learn to love Him and trust Him more. It is important to read the lessons in order. Jumping ahead to read a lesson with an interesting title can make those chapters hard to grasp since some of the foundation for understanding them is covered in previous chapters. Each lesson will cover the life of one of our patriarchs or matriarchs and a specific lesson we can learn from their lives. For instance, this first lesson is about Abraham, but it is also about faith. If you are well versed in the Scriptures you may be familiar with the facts about each biblical personality, but the topics, for example faith, are topics that we can never exhaust. As you apply the rich principles of these lessons to your life every day you will possess a richer, fuller walk with Adon ha-shamayim v'ha-eretz (Master of the heavens and the earth). On the other hand, if you are something of a beginner in Bible study, you will find these lessons simple to understand and follow, and you will experience a life-changing surge of freshness and newness as you come to know God through His Word. Thus, for both the beginner and for the seasoned veteran, Jewish Discoveries will prove valuable as you apply the lessons to your individual life.

In this series of lessons we will be answering such big questions as: Is God concerned for His chosen people? How do I know the Holy Scriptures can be trusted? Will God deliver us from our enemies? Can God help me overcome bad habits? Why does God permit suffering? What happens when we die? How can I have peace (shalom) in my life? How can I have truly satisfying relationships with others? What can I do about the guilt I carry for past mistakes? How can I get relief from the hurts I have experienced? Can God's Word give me financial guidance for my current situation? Does God have a plan and direction for my life?

You may have asked yourself some of these same questions when you have thought of the centuries of suffering and persecution that have affected us. Perhaps you have been tempted to give up on God altogether. We challenge you to believe that God is **REAL!** His Scriptures can be trusted. His promises will be fulfilled.

He does not forsake us in trials. We must determine to **TRUST** Him as Abraham did. God called Abraham, just as He is calling you now. God promises to honor your request for help to understand the Holy Scriptures and to have more faith in Him. He is your Creator. I encourage you to pause for a moment right now and ask God to give you wisdom and understanding as you continue to read the remainder of this lesson.

1. Who was Abraham?

   Now this is the line of Terah: <u>Terah begot Abram</u>, . . . in his native land, Ur of the Chaldeans . . . And you shall no longer be called <u>Abram</u>, but your name shall be Abraham, for I make you the <u>father of a multitude of nations</u>. Genesis 11:27, 28; 17:3,5,6

   Abraham's birth name was Abram. He originally lived in a country called Ur. Elohim changed Abram's name to Abraham, signifying that He had a special plan for Abraham's life to make him a father of a multitude of nations.

2. What did God ask Abraham to do?

   The LORD said to Abram, "<u>Go forth from your native land and from your father's house to the land that I will show you</u>." Genesis 12:1

   The LORD called Abraham to leave the home that he had known and to step out in faith and go to a land that God had not yet revealed to him.

3. How did Abraham respond to Adonai's command?

   <u>Abram went forth</u> as the LORD had commanded him... Abram was seventy-five years old when he left Haran <u>(or Ur)</u>. Gen. 12:4

   Abraham stepped out in faith. God commanded and Abraham trusted God and left his homeland even though he was seventy-five years of age. What a strong act of faith on his part! We are going to see from our study how often God has asked men and women to make difficult decisions, and they did it because they had faith in God's love for them. Do you want Adonai to give you the faith needed to make the tough decisions that face you? Are you willing to step out in faith and follow God's leading as Abraham did?

4. What powerful promise did God give to Abraham?

1. ABRAHAM (AVRAHAM), FATHER OF OUR FAITH

<u>I will make of you a great nation, and I will bless you; I will make your name great, and you shall be a blessing. I will bless those who bless you and curse him that curses you; and all the families of the earth shall bless themselves by you.</u>" Gen. 12:2,3

Note that the promise to Abraham was not just a blessing upon Abraham and the nation that would come from him, but also that all the families of the earth would be blessed by Abraham. This is really quite an amazing promise when it says "all the families of the earth." In future lessons we will see exactly how God fulfilled this promise to Abraham's offspring and to all the families of the earth, including your family.

5. Abraham knew that his wife (Sarai, later called Sarah) was too old to bear a child, yet how did he respond to this promise that Elohim would make of him a great nation? What was it about his response that was counted as "merit" or "righteousness" in God's sight?

   <u>he put his trust in the L</u>ORD<u>;</u> (God) reckoned it to his merit.
   Genesis 15:6

Abraham trusted in the LORD even though what God had promised was humanly impossible. This is what faith really is. To trust when we can see all the possibilities is not really faith; it is expectation. Real faith believes what God said just because God said it. This is the type of faith that Abraham had. God "reckoned" or "counted" this faith to Abraham's merit as a righteous action.

Not everyone has heard God speak directly to them as Abraham did, but we all have God's Word, the Bible, available to us to show us His plan for our lives. That is why we are reading His Word together right now. While it is our prayer that you are blessed by the insights brought out in this book, the only completely trustworthy source for faith is God's Holy Word.

6. After almost 12 years of waiting, how did Abraham try to fulfill Adonai's promise to make himself a father?

   And Sarai said to Abram, "Look, the Lord has kept me from bearing. Consort with my maid; perhaps I shall have a son through her." <u>And Abram heeded Sarai's request.</u> . . . <u>He cohabited with Hagar and she conceived</u>. Genesis 16:2-4

Hagar, Sarah's handmaid, gave birth to a boy and named him Ishmael. God did not accept Ishmael as the fulfillment of the promise that Abraham's seed would bless all the families of the earth. Abraham's faith slipped and he tried to fulfill God's promise in his own way, with his own plan, and through his own abilities. Abraham did not always exercise perfect faith. His faith grew and sometimes faltered, but God never gave up on Abraham and Abraham did not give up seeking God. So it is with us also. As you read this lesson and the lessons that follow, your faith will grow or may even sometimes falter, but God will never, ever give up on you. And even if you disappoint Him—as Abraham did—He will never, ever stop loving you.

Note: we never have to break one of God's commands to fulfill one of God's promises. It is not by our power or abilities that God fulfills His promises, but it is God working through us that fulfills His promises. Abraham did not have to co-habitate with Sarah's maid in order to fulfill God's promise.

7. Through whom did God say the promise would come?

   God said, "Nevertheless, Sarah your wife shall bear you a son, and you shall name him Isaac; and I will maintain My covenant with him as an everlasting covenant for his offspring to come." Genesis 17:18,19

8. What was a reality for Abraham at the time this promise was given to him?

   (Sarah) Abram's wife, had borne him no children . . . Abraham threw himself on his face and laughed, as he said to himself, "Can a child be born to a man a hundred years old, or can Sarah bear a child at ninety?" Genesis 16:1; 17:17

   Not only had Sarah not yet had a child, she was past child bearing age. It was humanly impossible for her to have a child. How has your faith stood during difficult situations you have been through?

9. What sign did Elohim give Abraham to seal their covenant?

   Such shall be the covenant between Me and you and your offspring to follow which you shall keep: every male among you shall be circumcised. You shall circumcise the flesh of your foreskin, and that shall be the sign of the covenant between Me and you. Genesis 17:10, 11

   It is interesting that circumcision was given to Abraham after he had had a child with Hagar, Sarah's handmaid. It could have been a rebuke to Abraham for having had relations with someone who was not his spouse and a reminder to him, and all his children after him, to keep the marriage covenant pure.

1. ABRAHAM (AVRAHAM), FATHER OF OUR FAITH

10. After Abraham and his household were circumcised they received three very interesting guests. Who were they and what message did they have for Abraham and Sarah?

    <u>The L<small>ORD</small> appeared to him</u> *by the terebinths of Mamre; he was sitting at the entrance of the tent . . . Looking up,* <u>he saw three men standing near him</u>*. . . . He ran . . . to greet them and, bowing to the ground, he said, ". . . let me fetch a morsel of bread that you may refresh yourselves . . ."*

    Abraham hastened into the tent to Sarah, and said, "Quick, . . . Knead and make cakes!" He took curds and milk and the calf that had been prepared and set these before them; and he waited on them under the tree as they ate.

    Then one said, "<u>I will return to you next year, and your wife Sarah shall have a son!</u>*" . . . Abraham and Sarah were old, advanced in years; Sarah had stopped having the periods of women. And Sarah laughed to herself, saying, "Now that I am withered, am I to have enjoyment—with my husband so old?" Then the L<small>ORD</small> said to Abraham, "Why did Sarah laugh . . . ?* <u>Is anything too wondrous for the L<small>ORD</small>?</u>*"* Gen. 18:1,2,5,6,8,10-14

11. What else did these visitors tell Abraham and his nephew Lot?

    The men set out from there and looked down toward Sodom, Abraham walking with them to see them off. Now the L<small>ORD</small> had said, "Shall I hide from Abraham what I am about to do, since Abraham is to become a great and populous nation and all the nations of the earth are to bless themselves by him?" Then <u>the L<small>ORD</small> said</u>*, "*<u>The outrage of Sodom and Gomorrah is so great, and their sin so grave!</u>*"*

    The men went on from there to Sodom, while Abraham remained standing before the L<small>ORD</small>. <u>The two angels arrived in Sodom</u> *in the evening, as Lot was sitting in the gate of Sodom. Then* <u>the men said to Lot, ". . . we are about to destroy this place; because the outcry against them before the L<small>ORD</small> has become so great that the L<small>ORD</small> has sent us to destroy it.</u>*"* Genesis 18:16-18,20,22; 19:1,12,13

    Elohim, in His mercy and respect for Abraham, stopped to tell Abraham and warn Lot that He was going to destroy the cities of Sodom and Gomorrah.

12. When did the promised son finally come?

    Now <u>Abraham was a hundred years old</u> *when his son Isaac was born to him.* Genesis 21:5

    God waited until Abraham realized it was impossible for him to accomplish the fulfillment of God's promise by his own efforts. God had reminded him of His power by asking, *"Is anything too wondrous for the LORD?"* Genesis 18:14

13. As Abraham neared the end of his life he faced another monumental test. Read about it in Genesis 22.

    ***Some time afterward, God put Abraham to the test. He said to him, "Abraham," and he answered, "Here I am." And He said, "Take your son, your favored one, Isaac, whom you love, and go to the land of Moriah, and offer him there as a burnt offering** on one of the heights that I will point out to you."* Genesis 22:1,2

    How could Adonai make a great nation from Abraham's offspring and bless all the families of the earth if his child is dead? Since God brought Isaac out of a barren womb, did Abraham have faith to believe that God could somehow spare the child or even raise him from the dead? These questions were the test of faith that Abraham faced. God had these events recorded in His Word so we may know that He is able to do the impossible in our daily lives.

14. As they approached Mount Moriah Isaac raised a question that Abraham must have been dreading. How did Abraham show his trust in Elohim?

    Then Isaac said to his father Abraham, "Father!" And he answered, "Yes, my son." And he said, "Here are the firestone and the wood; but where is the sheep for the burnt offering?" And Abraham said, "God will see to the sheep for His burnt offering, my son." And the two of them walked on together. Genesis 22:7,8

    During the long 3-day climb up Mount Moriah it dawned on Isaac that they had everything they needed for offering a sacrifice to God except the sheep. He asked his father the question that must have been burning in Abraham's mind since they left their tents. Abraham spoke faith even though he did not yet see any sheep. He trusted that God Himself would provide His own burnt offering. In Ur it was not uncommon for people to sacrifice their children to their gods. The people of Ur believed they had to appease their gods. Abraham had faith that the God of heaven and earth was not a god that needed to be appeased, but rather He was the Almighty God who is always able to meet the needs of His people. Abraham trusted that God would provide His own substitute for His own offering.

15. Read the next few verses and see how God miraculously met Abraham's needs.

1. ABRAHAM (AVRAHAM), FATHER OF OUR FAITH

Abraham built an altar there; he laid out the wood; he bound his son Isaac; he laid him on the altar, on top of the wood. And Abraham picked up the knife to slay his son. Then an angel of the Lord called to him from heaven: "Abraham! Abraham!" And he answered, "Here I am." And he said, "Do not raise your hand against the boy, or do anything to him. For now I know that you fear God, since you have not withheld your son, your favored one, from Me." When Abraham looked up, his eye fell upon a ram, caught in the thicket by its horns. So Abraham went and took the ram and offered it up as a burnt offering in place of his son. And Abraham named that site Adonai-yireh; whence the present saying, "On the mount of the Lord there is vision." Genesis 22:11-14

Abraham was willing to trust God even if it meant giving up his greatest treasure. Adonai tested Abraham to see who was most important to him, his son or the One who gave him his son. Who or what is the most important thing in your life? Is it your spouse, child, career, home, reputation? Are you willing to trust God with whatever is most precious to you? Are you willing to surrender it to God and let God decide if He wants you to have it?

When did Abraham see the ram that God had provided as the substitute for Isaac? It was when he looked up. When did God put the ram in the thicket, before or after Abraham raised the knife? God's provisions are there for us. It is when we look up to Him in faith that we see His provision for us. Abraham called the place Adonai-yireh, (Lord sees). It is as we spend time with the Adonai that we will have the faith to trust that He knows and sees His plans for us.

It is also worth noting that Isaac was a healthy young man at this time and could have easily gotten away from his father, who was now over 110 years of age, if he had wanted to. Isaac, Abraham's son, was willing to lay down his life to be a sacrifice.

God, Himself, provided the sacrifice. What a God we have! He simply asks us to **believe** and to **follow** His directions.

16. How did God reaffirm His promise to Abraham?

The angel of the Lord called unto Abraham out of heaven the second time, and said, "By Myself I have sworn, saith the Lord, because thou hast done this thing, and hast not withheld thy son, thine only son: That I will greatly bless thee, and will multiply thy seed as the stars of heaven, and the sands which is upon the seashore; and thy seed shall possess the gate of his enemy; and in thy seed shall

all the nations of the earth be blessed; because thou hast obeyed My voice." Genesis 22:15-18 (The Holy Scriptures, Hebrew Publishing Company, NY, 1930 version)

In the lessons that follow we will see more and more how God has fulfilled this most important promise.

The same God who loved Abraham loves you. Elohim was able to work in Abraham's life when Abraham stopped trusting in his own efforts and determined to trust totally in God's power. This same God will work in your life as you trust Him with every aspect of your life. Since nothing is too hard for the LORD, why not trust Him right now to help you with all the desires of your heart.

Phil Bova was enjoying his life to the fullest. In addition to his career as an entertainer for many years he was also a lay cantor for a large synagogue near Cleveland, Ohio. That is, until he suffered a major stroke at the age of 29 which greatly affected his speech and voice, as well as his body. He could no longer drive a car, or run across the yard, or sing, or be active in any of the ways he once was. With a whole new physical challenge he had no idea what would happen next. In spite of this experience Phil was drawn closer to God than ever before.

Joan McCallister grew up as a happy, physically healthy, energetic, little girl. She was very active in all kinds of young girl activities. That is, until she was unexpectedly diagnosed with Juvenile Rheumatoid Arthritis at the age of twelve. Her life was changed forever. Her arthritis was severe from the onset and by age fifteen she found it necessary to begin using crutches to protect her already affected hips, knees, and ankles. When Joan was only twenty she was diagnosed with Myasthenia Gravis. She had to remain in bed for the first year, which worsened the arthritis and required that she use a wheelchair the rest of her life. Her arms, hands, fingers, and legs were not able to fully develop and her height remained at 4'9". She would have great difficulty having kids or live a so-called "normal" life. Although often tempted to question God's judgment, she chose to trust Him.

Phil met Joan. Although the illnesses negatively affected most of her body, it did not remove her beaming smile or her infectious positive attitude toward God, life, and others. The two dated, fell in love, married, fostered close to 20 abused kids, adopted two, and are proud grand-parents today. Even with her

1. ABRAHAM (AVRAHAM), FATHER OF OUR FAITH

own disabilities and continual pain, Joan has worked as an Independent Living Service Provider, is a public speaker, and has traveled around the United States giving disability awareness seminars. Phil was very instrumental in the formation of a committee that has been largely responsible for the creation of this book.

In reality, their situation has been much worse than can be told here, but God has continued to hold them through it all. Joan says, "Sometimes trusting is painful. Sometimes it is hard. But trusting while experiencing our own darkness is always beneficial."

Phil's and Joan's attitudes have always been that "all things work together for good to them that love God." They have lived their whole lives around that promise. They have chosen not to harbor anger and resentment over their disabilities. Instead, they truly believe that God, in His great wisdom, has allowed them to experience tremendous trials in order to work out a bigger plan that He has for them.

True faith is trusting God knows best even when we are not able to see where His path for our life is going. Are you willing to walk with God in faith, trusting that whatever paths He takes you down He is there with you? Are you willing to continue to hold His hand and walk with Him even if the path gets dark? Even if you have to wait for years, as did Abraham and Sarah, for the fulfillment of His promises? Are you willing to walk with Him even if He leads you, as He did with Abraham, from your current comfort zone to the place He has prepared for you? Those are big questions. Ask God to give you His faith and move forward as you answer the review questions for this lesson.

REVIEW הזרה

As is stated by the word "review," these questions are not meant to "test" your mental ability or your memory, but rather, to highlight the most important issues in the lesson using a question and answer format. You may reread the lesson while answering the questions.

1. What powerful promise did God give to Abraham?
    a. A long and healthy life.
    b. All nations of the earth blessed by his offspring.
    c. Wealth.

2. Why did Abraham doubt the promise?

a. He was very old.
   b. His wife was very old.
   c. They had no children.
   d. All of the above.

3. How did Abraham try to fulfill Adonai's promise himself?
   a. He divorced Sarai.
   b. He adopted his servant
   c. He had a child with Hagar, Sarai's maid.

4. Did God accept what Abraham had done in having Ishmael as fulfillment of the promise?
   a. Yes
   b. No

5. How did God test Abraham's faith?
   a. He asked Abraham to sacrifice his son Isaac.
   b. He asked Abraham to divorce Hagar.
   c. He asked Abraham to divorce Sarah.

6. How did God provide for the burnt offering in place of Isaac?
   a. God told Abraham just to forget the whole thing.
   b. God provided a ram as a substitute in place of Abraham's son.
   c. God told Abraham to do a few mitzvahs (good deeds) and go home.

7. Has your faith been strengthened by hearing how Elohim kept true to His promises, especially after it became humanly impossible to fulfill those promises?
   a. Yes
   b. No

8. Can you trust God with the seemingly impossible situations in your life?
   a. Yes
   b. No

TRADITIONS

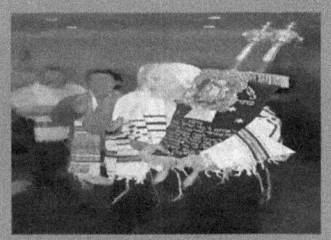

Simcha Torah

A simcha is a celebration. So if you have ever been to a wedding, birthday party, bar mitzvah, or any other celebration, you've been to a simcha. Simcha Torah celebrates the reading of the Torah, the writings of Moses. The day after Sukkot, the Feast of Tabernacles, is Simcha Torah. On Simcha Torah we start reading from the first line in the Torah. The Torah is divided up into portions or parashas to be read throughout the year. Every week a parasha of the Torah is read until we complete the cycle the following year on the last day of the Feast of Tabernacles. This is interesting because the Feast of Tabernacles reminds us of the time we spent living in tents in the wilderness after we crossed the Red Sea. It was during that time that Moses wrote the Torah. The Feast of Tabernacles also represents what our lives will be like in heaven, which is where the Holy Scriptures will find their richest fulfillment. After the reading of the last portion of the Torah, it is read all over again. It is very good for us to read these precious messages again and again. As we pray for God to show us how to apply the principles of the Scriptures to our daily lives we will find the reading alive and refreshing. I highly recommend reading the Scriptures every day on your own.

The Scriptures do not mention Simcha Torah nor do they tell us how much of the Torah to read each week or which portions to read. Certainly it is good to read the Scriptures every day throughout the year. The Torah is the first 5 books of the Bible, but the rest of the Bible is just as important. If you do not have a Bible I want to urge you to get one right away and allow Adonai to speak to you directly from His Word every day.

JEWISH HERITAGE SCRIPTURE STUDIES

JACOB T'SHUVA

2. JACOB (YA'AKOV), T'SHUVA

We often say the phrase "the God of Abraham, Isaac, and Jacob." In the last lesson we learned about Abraham and Isaac, but who was Jacob and what role did he play in establishing the nation of Israel? What lessons can we learn from Jacob's life to help us in our walk with Elohim? T'shuvah, תשובה, is a Hebrew word that means repentance. In what ways was Jacob's life a wonderful example of T'shuva? Let's look in the Torah and find out.

1. Abraham and Sarah had a miracle child, Isaac. Isaac married a beautiful girl with a lovely disposition. Her name was Rebekah. When Rebekah became pregnant with twins, they seemed to struggle in her womb. In her distress she inquired of the LORD. How did God respond?

    . . . the LORD answered her, "__Two nations are in your womb__, two separate peoples shall issue from your body; one people shall be mightier than the other, and __the older shall serve the younger__." Genesis 25:23

    The older serving the younger was totally contrary to the traditional order. Generally, in the time of our patriarchs, the first-born son was held in high esteem.

2. Who were these twin brothers? Which one was younger?

    __The first one emerged . . . Esau__. __Then his brother emerged . . . Jacob__. Genesis 25:25, 26

    Esau was named Esau because he had a lot of red hair. When Esau came out of the womb Jacob, who was still in the womb, was holding onto Esau's heel. Isaac thought this was cute so he named him Jacob, which means heal grabber, tripper, supplanter.

3. The custom of birthright gave the oldest son a double portion of the inheritance and he was assigned the spiritual leadership of the family. God had already indicated, when the children were in the womb, that Jacob would receive this birthright. What event during their lives showed Esau's passion for immediate satisfaction and Jacob's interest in the long-range benefits of

the birthright?

> *Once when Jacob was cooking a stew, Esau came in from the open, famished. And Esau said to Jacob, "Give me some of that red stuff to gulp down, for I am famished" . . . <u>Jacob said, "First sell me your birthright."</u> And <u>Esau said, "I am at the point of death, so of what use is my birthright to me?"</u> . . . Jacob then gave Esau bread and lentil stew; he ate and drank, and he rose and went away. <u>Thus did Esau spurn the birthright.</u>* Genesis 25:29-34

God did not force Esau to spurn the birthright, but because God knew in advance what Esau would choose, He prophesied that the older would serve the younger. Esau cared more about the temporal, immediate satisfaction of a bowl of soup than he did about the benefits that the birthright would give him in the future. Jacob, on the other hand, was looking for ways to fulfill God's prophecy. The account of God speaking to his mother about the older serving the younger might have been his favorite bedtime story when he was a child.

4. Disregarding God's prophecy concerning Jacob and overlooking Esau's indifference to the birthright, what did Isaac attempt to do?

> *When Isaac was old and his eyes were too dim to see, he called his older son Esau and said . . . "go out into the open and hunt me some game. Then prepare a dish . . . and bring it to me to eat, so that I may give you my innermost blessing before I die."* Genesis 27:1-4

Isaac seemed to favor Esau. Esau was his first-born. In spite of what the angel had said, Isaac determined to give his innermost blessing to Esau.

5. While Esau was out hunting, how did Rebekah encourage Jacob to deceive his father Isaac into giving him the blessing?

> *Rebekah said to her son Jacob . . . "Go to the flock and fetch me two choice kids, and I will make of them a dish for your father, such as he likes. Then take it to your father to eat, in order that he may bless you before he dies."* Genesis 27:6, 9, 10

Still holding onto the prophetic promise of many years before, Rebecca sought to fulfill Elohim's promise in her own way. In lesson 1 we saw how Abraham tried to fulfill God's promise by having an adulterous relationship with Hagar. Now we see how Rebecca tried to fulfill God's promise by lying. This is an important point to remember: we never need to break one of God's commandments (mitzvot) in order to fulfill one of God's promises.

2. JACOB (YA'AKOV), T'SHUVA

6. How did Jacob voice his resistance to his mother's plan?

   "But <u>my brother Esau is a hairy man and I am smooth-skinned</u>. If my father touches me, <u>I shall appear to him as a trickster and bring upon myself a curse, not a blessing</u>." But his mother said to him, "Your curse, my son, be upon me! Just do as I say and go fetch them for me." Genesis 27:11-13

   Jacob did not resist his mother's plan because he knew it was wrong, but because he thought it was a bad plan. He was not worried about hurting God or his father, but about being caught.

7. Jacob submitted and went along with the deception. As he brought the meal to Isaac, Isaac tested him several times to see if he was really Esau. Jacob lied each time. Isaac finally blessed Jacob, thinking he was Esau. Just as Jacob left Isaac's tent, Esau came in. When Esau found out what had happened he was so furious he threatened to kill Jacob. In her desperation, what plan did Rebekah come up with next?

   "Now, my son, listen to me. <u>Flee at once</u> to Haran, <u>to my brother Laban</u>." Genesis 27:43

   Rebecca and Jacob succeeded in getting the blessing, but they did not get it according to God's plan. There would be consequences to their lie. Rebecca proclaimed, *". . . your curse be upon me."* Rebecca never saw her son again after that fateful day. The Scriptures do not tell us how God would have stopped Isaac from giving the blessing. God could have called out from Heaven at the last second as He did when Abraham was about to sacrifice Isaac. Although we don't always know how God will fulfill His promises, we do know that He will. We see here that Jacob made the same mistake his grandfather Abraham made. He tried to fulfill God's promise in his own way. We don't have to disobey God in order to help Him fulfill His promises. We should not try to justify sinning because the end result is the fulfillment of God's plan. As we learned with Abraham, God is not always early in fulfilling His promises to us, but He is never late! He is always right on time.

8. Jacob set out for Haran. He wandered alone in the wilderness, distressed with the guilt of his deception. In what way did God give Jacob assurance of His love and mercy?

   He had a dream; a stairway was set on the ground and its top reached to the sky, and angels of God were going up and down on it. And the LORD was standing beside him and He said, "I am the LORD, *the God of your father Abraham and the God of Isaac . . . Your seed shall be as the dust of the earth . . . and <u>in thy seed shall all the families of the earth be blessed</u>. And, behold, <u>I am with you</u> . . .*" Genesis 28:12-15 (verse 14 & 15 from the Holy Scriptures, Hebrew Publishing Company, 1930 version)

Oh the mercy and love of Elohim. God did not come to Jacob with condemnation or with a load of guilt. Rather He renewed the promise that Jacob's seed, his offspring, would bless all the families of the earth. (The fulfillment of this all-important promise will be seen in the next few lessons). Like Jacob's grandfather Abraham, Jacob did not have any children when this promise was given to him.

God promised Jacob that He would be with him. Jacob was not a hunter like Esau. He was a homeboy who stayed near the camp cooking the stew. Being alone in the wilderness must have been a very frightening experience for him. As a young man, away from family and friends for the first time, uncertain of the future, it must have brought Jacob great reassurance to hear God say, "I'm going to be with you." What a loving God we have. Even when we blow it and are all alone because of our mistakes, we don't have to be afraid, because God is with us!

9. How did Jacob respond to this powerful encounter with God?

> *Jacob awoke from his sleep and said, "<u>Surely the LORD is present in this place</u>, and I did not know it!" Shaken, he said, "<u>How awesome is this place</u>! This is none other than <u>the abode of God</u>, and that is <u>the gateway to heaven</u>." . . . <u>He named that site Bethel</u> . . . Jacob then made a vow, saying, "<u>the LORD shall be my God . . . of all that You give me, I will set aside a tithe for You</u>.*" Genesis 28:16,17,19-22

Beth-El means "house of God"

Perhaps for the first time in Jacob's life he had a personal experience with Adonai. Jacob's faith and belief in what God promised him caused him to respond with praise and thanksgiving. He also determined to act upon his faith by giving back to God 10%, a tithe, of all that God would give him the ability to earn. When we have a real experience with God it will cause faith in God to well up in us and cause us to respond with praise, gratitude, and obedience.

10. Finally, after a long journey, Jacob came to a well near the land of Haran, where a group of shepherds introduced Jacob to Rachel, Laban's daughter. Jacob went to live and work with Laban's family. What did Jacob request when his uncle Laban asked him what wages he desired?

2. JACOB (YA'AKOV), T'SHUVA

***"I will serve you seven years for your younger daughter Rachel."
So Jacob served seven years for Rachel and they seemed to him but a few days because of his love for her.*** Genesis 29:18, 20

11. After waiting and working for seven long years for the love of his life Jacob was deceived by Laban, who switched his older daughter, Leah, for Rachel on the wedding night. What goes around comes around. Jacob the deceiver was deceived. When Jacob protested, Laban promised Jacob that he could have Rachel also for an additional seven years of service. Laban continually changed Jacob's wages during the twenty years Jacob worked for him. What did God instruct Jacob to do at this difficult time?

. . . the L<small>ORD</small> said to Jacob, "Return to the land of your fathers where you were born, and I will be with you." Genesis 31:3

As bad as the situation was with Laban, going home must have been a scary thought. Jacob had not seen his brother in 20 years. He must have been wondering: "Has he forgiven me? Will he accept me? Is Esau still angry? Will he try to hurt me?"

12. How did God faithfully show love and concern for Jacob and his family in their journey back to Jacob's home?

Jacob went on his way, and angels of God encountered him. When he saw them, Jacob said, "This is God's camp." Gen. 32:2

God never leaves us or forsakes us. Not ever. As the Psalmist sang, ***"the Angel of the L<small>ORD</small> encamps around about those who fear Him."*** Psalm 34:8

13. When Jacob came close to home he sent a message to Esau. What words did Jacob specifically tell his messengers to use showing that he was sorry for his past mistakes?

'To my lord Esau, thus says your servant Jacob: I stayed with Laban and remained until now . . . I send this message to my lord in the hope of gaining your favor.' Genesis 32:5, 6

Jacob could have said, "Remember, God said you would serve me. Remember, you sold me your birthright. Remember, Dad blessed me." But no, he came humbly and repentantly. What a great lesson for us to learn as we respond to those with whom we have had disagreements.

14. When Esau received the message he came after Jacob with 400 men. He was obviously still angry, even 20 years later. This frightened Jacob. He split up his camp into two parts to protect them. Then he went to pray. What did he

say to God, showing his repentance for his sin?

"... O Lord ... <u>I am unworthy</u> of all the kindness that You have so steadfastly shown Your servant: <u>with my staff alone I crossed this Jordan</u> ... <u>Deliver me, I pray</u> ..." Genesis 32:10-12

Jacob was truly repentant. He confessed his sins and surrendered himself into Adonai's hands. Jacob was not trying to hide, deny, or excuse his sins. He was determined to follow the Lord's plan, even in the face of fear and danger.

15. Jacob sent 550 animals in small groups, one after another, to Esau as a peace offering. What happened to Jacob that night that changed his life forever?

Jacob was left alone. And <u>a man wrestled with him</u> until the break of dawn. When he saw that he had not prevailed against him, he wrenched Jacob's hip at its socket, so that the socket of his hip was strained as he wrestled with him. Then (the man) *said, "Let me go, for dawn is breaking." But* <u>(Jacob) answered, "I will not let you go, unless you bless me</u>." *Said the other, "What is your name?" He replied, "Jacob." Said he, "<u>Your name shall no longer be Jacob, but Israel</u> ..."* Genesis 32:25-29

Note: Israel literally means prince with God, prevailed with God, or overcame with God.

16. With what words did God show Jacob that both God and Esau had forgiven his sin?

"<u>As a prince with God you have striven with God and man, and have prevailed</u>" Genesis 32:29 (margin)

Jacob prevailed in holding on when everything seemed against him. This actual physical wrestling match was symbolic of Jacob's inner wrestling with the guilt he bore for tricking his brother and lying to his father. He prevailed in receiving God's forgiveness through his repentance. Through God's power Jacob's character had changed from one that grabbed, tricked, and lied to one that overcame with God's power. Thus God changed his name from Jacob, which means "supplanter," to "Israel," which means "prince with God" or "one who prevails with God."

Each of us needs to have a time of "wrestling" with God. It is not wrestling against God; it is wrestling against our natural tendencies to do wrong, to think wrong, and to have wrong motives. In the "wrestling" match God is not wrestling against us—He is wrestling with us! He is on our side against our past mistakes and sins. That is why God had to dislocate Jacob's hip. Jacob had to come to the point where he realized that he could not stand on his own—He needed Elohim to hold him up. Jacob needed to understand that he could not face Esau in his own strength; he could only do it with God's help. Jacob needed to understand he could not wrestle and win against his natural tendencies to sin; he needed God to give him the victory. God is not wrestling against us, God is wrestling with us, on our side, as we wrestle with the thoughts of whether or not we can trust Him with every aspect of our lives, whether or not we should surrender to Him, whether or not we can have total faith in what the Bible says, whether or not we should follow what He says, whether or not we should get rid of things in our lives that are hindering our walk with Adonai. We need to hold onto God and not let go until we have His blessing, His assurance that we have the victory, the peace that we have made the right choices for Him.

17. Who was this "man" that Jacob wrestled with?

So Jacob named the place Peniel . . . (understood as "<u>face of God</u>.") Genesis 32:31 (margin)

God initially appeared to Jacob as a man, just as He did when He came to tell Abraham about Sodom and Gomorrah. In the dark, Jacob might have thought it was Esau or one of Esau's men. He wrestled with him. Somewhere in the struggle Jacob realized this "man" was actually God in human form and He refused to let go unless God blessed him. Jacob called the place "face of God" honoring and acknowledging that it was God who he was wrestling with, and who had blessed him, and who had changed his character and his name.

18. When Jacob again showed humility and sorrow for his sin how did Esau demonstrate his emotions?

<u>*Jacob*</u> *. . .* <u>*bowed low to the ground seven times*</u> *until he was near his brother.* <u>*Esau ran to greet him. He embraced him and, falling on his neck, he kissed him*</u>*; and* <u>*they wept.*</u> Gen. 33:1, 3, 4

This must have been a very touching moment when Esau, the big, burley warrior, cried on his brother's neck. Jacob's humility and repentance before God and Esau won his brother over. Humility and repentance before God and those you associate with can bring reconciliation to the strained relationships in your life.

19. God instructed Jacob to go back to Bethel, the place where God appeared to

him in a dream when he had fled from his brother. How did Jacob and his family respond to this call of God?

"Come, let us go up to Bethel, and <u>I will build an altar there to the God who answered me</u> when I was in distress and who has been with me wherever I have gone." <u>They gave to Jacob all the alien gods that they had, and the rings that were in their ears, and Jacob buried them.</u> Genesis 35:3, 4

As Jacob and his family grew closer to God they got rid of the things in their lives that distracted them from God. We see in Jacob's life a continual growing with God. He did not just have a once-and-for-always experience with God; he had on-going, ever deepening encounters with Him. Jacob must have heard about God from his parents. Jacob experienced God when he was alone under the stars running away from his home because of his sin. He encountered the angels of God when he was on his way back home from his Uncle Laban's house. Jacob came face to face with God as he wrestled with Him before meeting up with his brother. Then more than 20 years from his first experience at Beth-El Jacob was still drawing closer to God and getting rid of more things that drew him away from God. So should it be with us. We should not rely only on our past experience with God. We need to be continually, even daily, growing with God and having experiences with Him through prayer and the reading of His Word. Even if we have had an experience with God for 20 or more years we can still grow closer to God and even after many years of walking with God there might still be other things in our lives we should be burying or getting rid of. It might be physical things that distract you from God like Jacob got rid of or it might be a grudge or guilt or hard feelings that Elohim wants to free you from. No matter how long our walk with God may have been, we still have so much to experience about Him, so much to understand about His wonderful plan for us, so much more love to receive. Even if you have read the stories of Abraham, Isaac, and Jacob before there are still more lessons for us from their lives as we apply the biblical principles to today. As you have read this story today what have you sensed that God especially wanted to say to you? Some of the big issues we've talked about are forgiveness of others, dealing with guilt, dealing with our past mistakes, having the courage to go on even when the future seems dark and uncertain, continuing to grow with God and ridding ourselves of things that distract us from God. Do any of those hold a specific message for you today?

2. JACOB (YA'AKOV), T'SHUVA

20. In each of our lives there needs to come a day of "wrestling with God" for the forgiveness of past mistakes, as Jacob did. What assurance does God give through the Jewish prophet Jeremiah, speaking of our prevailing with God?

> **_Why have all faces turned pale? Ah, that day is awesome; there is none like it! It is a time of trouble for Jacob, but he shall be delivered from it. In that day—declares the L<small>ORD</small> of Hosts—I will break the yoke from off your neck and I will rip off your bonds_**_. . . . they shall serve the L<small>ORD</small> their God and David, the king whom I will raise up for them._ Jeremiah 30:6-9

As we face our guilt and our fears it may seem like a time of trouble, but Adonai has promised to break our bondage to sin and guilt and cause us to serve God. Israel (Jacob) did not obtain the birthright because he was perfect. It was because he was humble enough to admit his mistakes to God and to men. Israel (Jacob) overcame and prevailed, by God's power, from his wrong ways. Israel (Jacob) repented of his wrong and submitted to God's will for his life. God gave him the ability to stop doing things his own way and to start doing things God's way. God can give you this same experience. He can change your life from wrong habits, words, and actions to godly thoughts, words, and actions. Ask Him to give you a godly sorrow for your past mistakes. Then ask Him to give you a humble spirit and the courage to admit when you have been wrong. Petition Him to give you the power not to repeat those mistakes again.

Steven Wohlberg was walking along the beach with Seth, his 2-year-old son, when Seth saw some other boys throwing stones into the water. Seth picked up a stone and with all his might threw the stone into the air. The stone went backwards and hit his father right in the mouth. Taken back Steve felt to see if he had chipped any teeth. Feeling the blood coming from his lips he thought he should teach Seth a lesson about being accountable for his actions. "Seth," Steve said as his boy turned around toward him, "you hit Daddy in the mouth with that stone. Say you are sorry." His little boy just looked at him. "Seth you hit Daddy in the mouth with that stone," Steve repeated. "Say 'I'm sorry Daddy.'" Seth said, "I'm sorry Daddy," turned, and started to walk away. Steve could tell Seth was not really sorry. He was just saying it because his father told him to. As Seth was walking away from his father he stopped and turned towards his dad again. This time there were tears in his eyes as he said, "Daddy, I'm sorry." (Steve Wohlberg's life story is recorded in the book "From Hollywood to Heaven.")

There is a difference between admitting wrong and repentance. Admitting wrong comes from guilt. True godly sorrow, true repentance comes from God moving upon our hearts.

T'shuvah תשובה, is a Hebrew word that means repentance or returning. Repentance is a turning from sin to Elohim, a returning to our Creator. The Jewish month of Elul is known as the month of T'shuva as it is the month that precedes the month of Tishri, which contains the High Holy Days. (Further in the series there is a whole lesson on the High Holy Days.) T'shuva prepares our hearts to receive God's love. Jacob's life is a wonderful example of t'shuva. God changed Him from being a selfish deceiver to a prince with God, a prevailer with God and man. Jacob's name change from Jacob to Israel was an outward indication of what had happened on the inside. T'shuva is not something we can do on our own; it is a gift that Elohim gives to us. God gives us a sorrow for our sinful thoughts, actions, words, and motives. He then gives us the power to change as we invite His Spirit to work in us. Thus, as the Jewish prophet Zechariah wrote, **"Not by might, nor by power, but by My spirit—said the LORD of Hosts."** Zechariah 4:6 God changed Jacob through the gift of t'shuva and God can change you as well. God originally created man in His own image. God's desire is to return us to the original image He formed us in. God desires to have His image, His character, manifested in our lives. The beginning of this process of "returning" to the original image God created mankind with starts with t'shuva, repentance.

Jeff Persitz has always been a type-A let's go for it kind of person. From the time of his bar mitzvah being busy was a daily prerequisite. This fast paced lifestyle kept him from taking the time to truly experience the emotional part of life. It blinded him from seeing a great deal of what was taking place around him and to the reality of the downward spiral that his life would take.

In his early twenties Jeff got his dream job. He was hired as a salesman for a beer distributor. Jeff spent a great deal of time in taverns and lounges. Partying became a way of life. Alcohol became passé very quickly and Jeff was introduced to cocaine. This is just what a fast-paced out of control person craved—a powerful stimulant.

At first he only used cocaine two or three times a week in small quantities. But before he knew it, it had become a daily habit and it completely took over

2. JACOB (YA'AKOV), T'SHUVA

every aspect of his life. At this time his mother spent two years suffering with cancer before she died. Jeff found this time period very difficult to cope with. Instead of turning to God to help him he sank deeper into the pit of addiction. In the span of just a couple of years Jeff lost his family, his career, his reputation, and his friends. He used and abused everyone around him to keep his addictions fed. He was financially, physically, emotionally, and spiritually bankrupt. After his wife left him, taking their daughter with her, he sat in the empty house with nothing but a blanket to his name. At this point there seemed to be nowhere for Jeff to turn; he saw no hope and had given up thinking that his life could be restored. After three weeks of living on the streets, in cars, or at his dealer's house Jeff reached his lowest ebb and was standing on the edge of a freeway overpass ready to jump off. Right then God reached down and spoke to his heart assuring Jeff that he would be OK and that a life of love and peace would be given back to him. Jeff believed God's impression on his heart, walked off the bridge, and enrolled himself in a treatment program. Part of the Alcoholics Anonymous and Narcotics Anonymous meetings he attended included seeking a higher power. Jeff was so ashamed of his life that he was afraid to speak to God. For 45 minutes he wrestled with the thought of praying to God. When he finally gave in and closed his eyes the tears came pouring out. He pled with God never to leave him as he asked for help, guidance, and forgiveness.

Jeff has been clean and sober for almost twenty-five years and thankfully credits the victory to a loving and caring God. Because of God's love Jeff's life has been restored in every way, greater than it has ever been. God blessed Jeff by giving him back his family, his career, and a relationship with God that has grown every day.

As humans we often try to define God by our own definitions and opinions, but God is quite capable of defining Himself. We may think that God would never do such and such, or that He should be doing this and that, as if to say, "If I were God things would be different." Many times we try to base what is right and wrong on our perception of what we think should be right and wrong instead of based on what God's Word says is right or wrong. In this series of lessons we are planning on letting God define Himself so that we can be conformed and recreated into His image instead of our trying to create Him into the mental image we have of Him.

JEWISH DISCOVERIES

REVIEW הזרה

1. To whom did God indicate the birthright would be given?
   a. Rebekah.
   b. Esau.
   c. Jacob.

2. How did Jacob go about receiving the birthright?
   a. He waited upon God to reveal how it would happen.
   b. He pressured his brother and deceived his father.
   c. He killed his brother.

3. How did God react toward Jacob while he was distressed over his deception?
   a. He told Jacob how bad he was and told him he needed to give a lot of money to be forgiven.
   b. He promised to be with him and to bless all the families of the earth through his descendants.
   c. He ignored Jacob.

4. Who was the "man" that Jacob wrestled with?
   a. Isaac
   b. Laban
   c. God

5. Why did Adonai change Jacob's name to Israel?
   a. Because he prevailed with God in receiving forgiveness for his sins.
   b. Jacob wasn't a good name.
   c. So that he could hide from Esau.

6. Would you like to prevail with God and receive His forgiveness for mistakes you have made?
   a. Yes
   b. No

Israel (Jacob) eventually had twelve sons, who became the fathers of the twelve tribes of Israel. Our next lesson will look at why Joseph, one of the twelve sons, excelled despite the persecution and problems he encountered. If you have ever felt hurt, let down, or ill-treated, the life of Joseph will have deep meaning for you.

TRADITIONS

Shofar

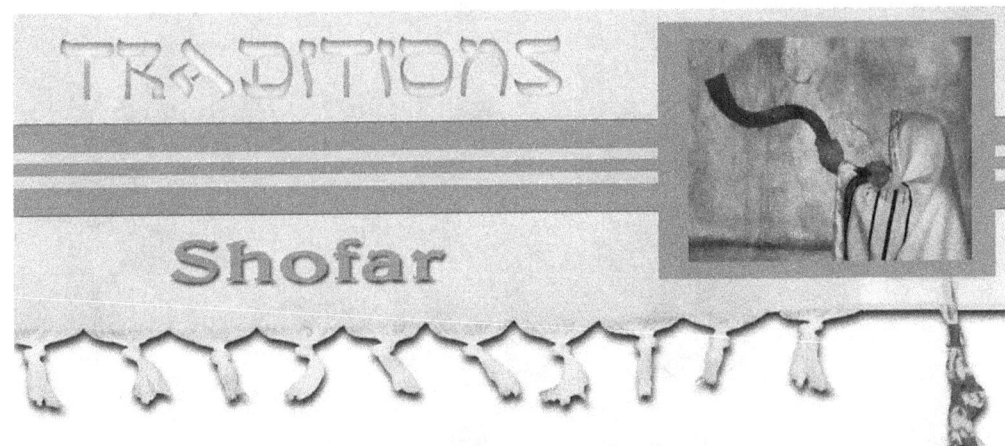

The shofar, made from a ram's horn, has been used by our people for thousands of years. The blowing of the shofar was used to call the people together for war and to call them to the Sanctuary for repentance. Both were calls for preparation and for battle. God had Joshua's men use shofars to bring down the walls of Jericho. It was shofars that Gideon used in his battle against the Midianites.

In the call to repentance, the battle is against our sinful natures and the sins we commit. God loves us and has given us t'shuva, the gift of repentance. On Rosh Hashanah the shofar is blown calling us to repent of our sins before Yom Kippur comes. Today during Rosh Hashanah the shofar is blown nearly one hundred times using four different notes: tekiah, shevarim, teruah, and tekiah gedolah.

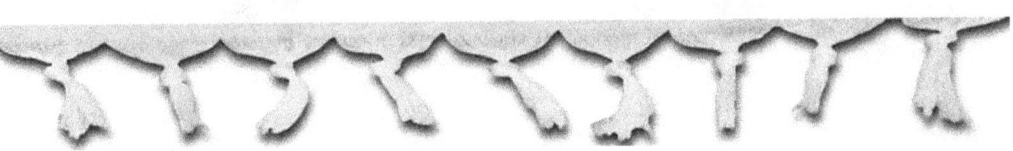

JEWISH HERITAGE
SCRIPTURE STUDIES

JOSEPH
THE POWER OF FORGIVENESS

3. JOSEPH (YOSEF), THE POWER OF FORGIVENESS

Have you ever felt alone, with no friends or family to understand what you were going through? Have you ever suffered from circumstances beyond your control? There is a story in the Torah of a man named Joseph who endured the same predicaments. Elohim carried him through some events that might have destroyed a lesser man, leading Joseph to a deeper walk with Him.

In Lesson 2 we learned that Jacob (later called Israel) had to flee from his home because he deceived his brother, Esau. After that episode Jacob married and had twelve sons and one daughter. These sons became the ancestors of the twelve tribes of Israel. Joseph was the next to youngest of the twelve. Joseph's story is one of the most touching in all the Torah. To all of us who have been let down, injured, or emotionally scarred by others, Joseph's story becomes one that we like to hear over and over again. In this lesson we will explore and find hope and courage from what happened to Joseph.

1. How did Jacob feel about Joseph, and how did he show it?

> Now <u>**Israel loved Joseph best**</u> *of all his sons, for he was the child of his old age; and* <u>**he had made him an ornamented tunic.**</u> Genesis 37:3

This just might have been a nice gift, but it also might have been Israel's way of showing that he planned to give Joseph the birthright. Even though Joseph was not Israel's first son, he was his first son from Rachel, who he loved the most.

2. What emotions were evoked toward Joseph as a result of Jacob's favoritism?

> *And when his brothers saw that their father loved him more than any of his brothers,* <u>**they hated him**</u> *so that they could not speak a friendly word to him.* Genesis 37:4

Although Jacob had grown up in a home where there was favoritism, he did not learn the hard lessons that favoritism teaches. Even though Joseph no doubt enjoyed the special attention of his father, it must have caused him untold grief to be hated by his brothers.

3. Joseph had some dreams. What was one of them, and how did his brothers react after hearing about his dream, which left Joseph even more alone and isolated from his brothers?

> *Once Joseph had a dream which he told to his brothers; and they hated him even more . . . "Hear this dream which I have dreamed: There <u>we were binding sheaves in the field, when suddenly my sheaf stood up and remained upright; then your sheaves gathered around and bowed low to my sheaf.</u>" His brothers answered, "Do you mean to reign over us?". . . And <u>they hated him even more</u> for his talk about his dream.* Genesis 37:5-8

Why would Joseph tell his brothers about his dreams? Maybe he had an inflated ego, maybe he was looking for acceptance, maybe he was just naive and didn't know it would cause them to hate him even more, or maybe God wanted the dream revealed to the brothers because of its future fulfillment.

4. While Joseph's brothers were far away tending sheep, Jacob asked Joseph to go and see how they were doing. When Joseph approached his brothers, how did they show their feelings of jealousy and anger toward him?

> *They saw him from afar, and. . . <u>They conspired to kill him</u>. . . When Joseph came up to his brothers, <u>they stripped Joseph of his tunic</u>, the ornamented tunic that he was wearing, and took him and <u>cast him into the pit</u>. . . Then they sat down to a meal. Looking up, they saw a caravan of Ishmaelites. . . They pulled Joseph up out of the pit. <u>They sold Joseph for twenty pieces of silver to the Ishmaelites</u>, who brought Joseph to Egypt*. Genesis 37:18,23-25,28.

How sad that sibling jealousy developed into hatred, which led to attempted murder and abduction. How much better it would have been for the whole family had they identified their jealous feelings as sin and surrendered them to God. God could have freed them from their angry, insecure natures, and given them love for one another and peace within themselves. Instead, they sold one of their own kin into slavery for only two silver coins each. They stooped lower into sin as they went home and lied to their father, telling him that a wild beast killed Joseph. They showed the ornamented tunic stained with blood as proof. Israel's heart was broken for much of the remainder of his life. What a sad, sad story. But wait. It's not over. It gets worse! If there are hard feelings among your family members the lesson of Joseph might be just the thing to heal the hurts and bring

3. JOSEPH (YOSEF), THE POWER OF FORGIVENESS

reconciliation.

5. Joseph was separated from his loving father and rejected by his brothers. Overnight, he went from being the favorite son of a wealthy farmer to being a slave in a foreign country. Joseph was sold to an Egyptian named Potiphar. Joseph did the best he could under what must have been very painful circumstances of being isolated and alone. He worked hard and faithfully as a foreign slave and before long was promoted by his owner to be in charge of the house. What did Potiphar see in Joseph?

> *The Lord was with Joseph, and he was a successful man; and he stayed in the house of his Egyptian master. And when <u>his master saw that the L<small>ORD</small> was with him</u> and that the L<small>ORD</small> lent success to everything he undertook, he took a liking to Joseph. He made him his personal attendant and put him in charge of his household, placing in his hands all that he owned.* Genesis 39:2-4

Joseph must have been heartbroken by what his brothers did to him. He no doubt missed his father tremendously. He must have felt alone and frightened, but he must have also trusted in the L<small>ORD</small> God and found strength and courage in Him because Elohim's inspired Word says the L<small>ORD</small> was with Joseph. Joseph must have given all his feelings of anger, revenge, hurt, and sorrow over to the L<small>ORD</small> because Potiphar saw the L<small>ORD</small> God in Joseph's life.

6. Just when Joseph's dreadfully sad life seemed to be showing some hope of better days, everything fell apart again. Potiphar's wife tried to seduce Joseph into committing adultery with her. How did Joseph respond, showing that God was first in his life?

> *He refused. He said to his master's wife, "... <u>How ... then could I do this most wicked thing, and sin before God?</u>"* Genesis 39:8,9

7. Even though Joseph did what was right he found himself falsely accused of a crime by Potiphars's wife and thrown into an Egyptian prison. Yet, in spite of all these cruel injustices, Joseph trusted in God and chose not to hold onto any feelings of anger or revenge. In spite of the rejection, injustice, and loneliness Joseph was experiencing, what brought comfort to him through these trials and how did Elohim help him?

> *But even while he was there in prison, <u>the L<small>ORD</small> was with Joseph: He extended kindness to him and disposed the chief jailer favorably toward him. The chief jailer put in Joseph's charge all the prisoners who were in the prison</u>, and he was the one to carry out everything that was done there. The chief jailer did not supervise anything that*

was in Joseph's charge, <u>because the L<small>ORD</small> was with him, and whatever he did the L<small>ORD</small> made successful.</u> Genesis 39:20-23

Do you think the chief jailer would have been favorably impressed with Joseph if Joseph had been steaming with bitterness, anger, and revengeful feelings? Do you think the chief jailer would have promoted Joseph if he was depressed and gloomy with self-pity and overwhelming sadness? After what Joseph had been through we might excuse him for some negative feelings. But remember, self-pity never helps anyone; it actually imprisons us. While Joseph was physically in prison he was not imprisoned by anger and revenge or self-pity and depression.

Even in a cold, isolated dungeon hundreds of miles from those he loved, Joseph was not alone, because God was with Him. We are never alone, no matter how lonely we feel. God has promised that He will never leave us nor forsake us, and God always keeps His promise. Circumstances may make it appear that God has forgotten us. Joseph was tempted to feel that God had forgotten him, too. The Torah reminds us that God was with Joseph even when he was rejected by his brothers, separated from his parents, all alone in a foreign land, and cruelly hurt and mistreated. God is with us even when bad things are happening to us. It was faith in this fact that kept Joseph from being depressed and bitter.

8. While in prison Joseph befriended Pharaoh's royal cupbearer, who was also in prison. Through Adonai's power, Joseph interpreted a dream the cupbearer had. What favor did Joseph ask of him in return?

   "But <u>think of me when all is well with you again, and do me the kindness of mentioning me to Pharaoh</u> so as to free me from this place . . ." Genesis 40:14

9. It took 2 years for the royal cupbearer to remember that request, yet Joseph patiently waited, trusting God in spite of another rejection. Pharaoh had some dreams that he could not understand. His wise men could not interpret them either. That is when the royal cupbearer remembered Joseph. Joseph was released, and God gave him the interpretation of those dreams. Read Pharoah's strange dream and Joseph's amazing interpretation.

   Pharaoh's dreams are one and the same: God has told Pharaoh what He is about to do . . . The <u>seven healthy cows are seven years, and the seven healthy ears (of grain) are seven years</u>; it is the same dream . . . God has revealed to Pharaoh what He is about to do. <u>Immediately ahead are seven years of great abundance in all the land of</u>

3. JOSEPH (YOSEF), THE POWER OF FORGIVENESS

Egypt. After them will come seven years of famine, and all the abundance in the land of Egypt will be forgotten . . . Accordingly, let Pharaoh find a man of discernment and wisdom, and set him over the land of Egypt . . . Let all the food of these good years that are coming be gathered, and let the grain be collected under Pharaoh's authority as food to be stored in the cities. Let that food be a reserve for the land for the seven years of famine which will come upon the land of Egypt, so that the land may not perish in the famine. Genesis 41:25-36

10. What did Pharaoh see in Joseph and what did he do for him?

And Pharaoh said . . . "Could we find another like him (Joseph), a man in whom is the spirit of God?" So Pharaoh said to Joseph, "Since God has made all this known to you, there is none so discerning and wise as you. You shall be in charge of my court, and by your command shall all my people be directed; only with respect to the throne shall I be superior to you." Genesis 41:38-40

This was an amazing turn of events. It is astounding that Pharaoh would place an imprisoned foreign slave as the second in command of the powerful nation of ancient Egypt, the most powerful nation in the world. He did it because he saw the Spirit of God in Joseph. Pharaoh would not have seen the Spirit of God in Joseph if for the last two years Joseph had been nurturing negative thoughts such as: "I can't believe the cupbearer has forgotten me. Some friend he turned out to be! After all I have done for him. I shouldn't be in this prison anyway. It's Potiphar's wife who deserves to be in this rat hole, not me. All this for following God and doing what is right. If there really was a God He certainly wouldn't allow this to happen to me. And those rotten brothers of mine. . . . If I could just get my hands on them." These are natural thoughts. These types of thoughts must have come into Joseph's mind many times over the many years he was in Egypt, but he did not entertain those negative thoughts. He continually gave them to God and put his trust in the LORD.

Joseph chose to forgive those who hurt him. He did not let their wrong actions take away his peace and Elohim's Spirit. He knew that negative thoughts would eat him away if he did not choose to forgive. Had this been a university, this class might have been called "Hard Knocks 101." This is one of the most dramatic examples of trusting God of any story in all the Holy Scriptures.

11. How old was Joseph when he was exalted to be in charge of Pharaoh's court?

__Joseph was thirty years old when he entered the service of Pharaoh king of Egypt.__ Genesis 41:46

Joseph was only seventeen when his brothers sold him as a slave (see Genesis 37:2). He had been a slave and a prisoner in Egypt for thirteen long years.

12. God had said there would be seven years of plenty followed by seven years of famine. How did God use this famine to reunite Joseph with his brothers?

    __When Jacob saw that there were food rations to be had in Egypt, he said to his sons . . . "Go down and procure rations for us there, that we may live and not die." So ten of Joseph's brothers went down to get grain rations in Egypt,__ for Jacob did not send Joseph's brother Benjamin with his brothers, since he feared that he might meet with disaster. Genesis 42:1-4

Joseph was now in a position to bring harm to his brothers who had hurt him. During all the years Joseph was apart from his family he never harbored any bitterness. He never cherished ill feelings toward his brothers who had wronged him. Not that he wasn't tempted with those feelings, but by Adonai's power, he chose not to harbor, cherish, or allow them to take root in his heart. When Joseph's brothers arrived in Egypt, Joseph recognized them, but they did not recognize him. By now Joseph was close to forty years of age. He did not disclose himself to them during their first visit to Egypt. He sent them away with food, but told them they must not come back unless they brought their youngest brother with them also. Joseph had the power to execute them all, but he had forgiven them long before he saw their faces. Because the famine was severe, his brothers eventually had to return. When they did they brought Joseph's brother Benjamin with them.

13. How does the Torah describe Joseph's reaction when he saw his brother Benjamin?

    Looking about, he saw his brother Benjamin, his mother's son, and asked, "Is this your youngest brother of whom you spoke to me?" And he went on, "May God be gracious to you, my boy." With that, Joseph hurried out, for __he was overcome with feeling toward his brother and was on the verge of tears; he went into a room and wept there__. Genesis 43:29,30

We can only imagine what a very emotional experience this was for Joseph after being separated for over twenty years from his younger brother.

3. JOSEPH (YOSEF), THE POWER OF FORGIVENESS

14. When Joseph finally revealed himself to his brothers, how did he demonstrate that he had forgiven them and that he had trusted in God during these long, difficult years?

> ***Then Joseph said to his brothers . . . <u>"I am your brother Joseph, he whom you sold into Egypt. Now, do not be distressed or reproach yourselves because you sold me hither; it was to save life that God sent me ahead of you . . . God has sent me ahead of you to ensure your survival on earth, and to save your lives in an extraordinary deliverance. So it was not you who sent me here, but God.</u>"*** Genesis 45:4-8

If Joseph had not chosen to forgive his brothers long before this he would not have been able to tell them not to reproach themselves. Joseph could now see the good that God was bringing out of all his troubles. During these hard years Joseph held on by faith that God was still in control and would eventually work it out for good. Elohim allowed Joseph to go to Egypt so that many people could be saved and the heritage of his people could be preserved.

15. Jacob and all his family moved to Egypt. Eventually Jacob died. What did Joseph's brothers fear when their father died?

> ***<u>When Joseph's brothers saw that their father was dead, they said, "What if Joseph still bears a grudge against us and pays us back for all the wrong that we did him.</u>"*** Genesis 50:15

Even after all that Joseph had done for his brothers they still didn't believe that Joseph had forgiven them. They thought he would do what they would do. Joseph's brothers hadn't received God's forgiveness so they weren't able to forgive themselves. They hadn't experienced forgiveness since they hadn't repented. Since they had not experienced forgiveness they could not imagine how Joseph could have forgiven them unconditionally. Their lack of repentance did not stop Joseph from choosing to forgive.

16. How did Joseph respond, again showing his forgiveness and trust in God to work all things together for good?

> ***But <u>Joseph said to them, "Have no fear! Am I a substitute for God? Besides, although you intended me harm, God intended it for good, so as to bring about the present result—the survival of many people. And so, fear not, I will sustain you and your children." Thus he reassured them, speaking kindly to them.</u> So Joseph and his father's household remained in Egypt.*** Genesis 50:19-22

We are never told if Joseph's brothers ever accepted his forgiveness, or if they ever asked his forgiveness, or if they ever received God's forgiveness. But regardless of how they chose to react to their own evil, Joseph chose not to hold onto any desire to bring them any harm or wish them ill. Now in a position where they could not hurt him, he chose to bless them and do good to them. If he had waited for those who hurt him to apologize he would still be waiting today. Joseph's choosing to forgive was what gave him shalom, true peace.

Joseph's brothers intended much evil toward Joseph by selling him as a slave, but Adonai overruled for the good of their family, as well as for the good of many other nations. Joseph was able to see past the evil of their betrayal and accept God's healing spirit of forgiveness toward them. Since Joseph was not harboring anger and bitterness toward those who had hurt him, and since he was choosing to allow God to fill him with a spirit of forgiveness and faith, Potiphar, the jailer, and Pharaoh all recognized God's Spirit working in Joseph.

True biblical forgiveness is not an excusing of or an ignoring of the wrongs people have done to us. We do not forgive people when they do good things to us; we only forgive people for doing bad things. By stating that we forgive someone we are not stating that everything is ok. It is saying that wrong was done and that it should not be done again. Too often we equate forgiveness with overlooking. We are not speaking about overlooking; we are talking about looking at the fault, acknowledging that wrong was done, and making it clear we do not want or expect it to happen again. Too often when someone does apologize we respond by saying "it's ok," when in reality it was not ok, it was wrong. We don't need to give a lecture or berate someone when they apologize, but it is appropriate to respond by telling them that we forgive them.

At times we need to take action to insure they are not able to do the wrong again. We may have to separate ourselves from certain people who hurt us; we might have to have them put in jail, etc. We could even, at times, expect and ask for compensation. Forgiving someone does not mean that you do not expect them to pay you what they owe you. It means they are wrong for not paying you and that you do expect your money, but at the same time you are not going to allow their wrong to destroy your peace. Biblical forgiveness is choosing not to hold onto resentful, hateful, sad, or remorseful feelings. We have chosen to not allow their wrong to effect us mentally, spiritually, or emotionally.

Others may have hurt us physically or emotionally by what they have done, but if we choose to dwell on it after the fact then we are the ones hurting our-

3. JOSEPH (YOSEF), THE POWER OF FORGIVENESS

selves. If we choose to be bitter because of their sin, then the bitterness becomes our sin, our problem. We can say we have a right to be bitter because of what they have done, but bitterness only hurts us, not them. You might say you will forgive them and let go of the bitterness when they apologize. In that case you are giving them the "remote" control over you. You are letting them decide when you are going to stop having bitterness destroy you. What if they never apologize? Then you are allowing them to dominate you the rest of your life. You may never see them again, but if you allow the situation to replay in your mind over and over again you are choosing to allow bitterness and anger to destroy you. You are choosing to hurt yourself by allowing their past wrong to continue to affect you.

Two of the ways that bitterness can manifest itself are anger and sadness. We can demonstrate the anger with hurtful words or actions, or we can hold the anger in and it can lead to sadness and depression. (This is not to say that all depression is a result of holding onto bitterness). Sadness and anger, as a result of bitterness, are two sides of the same coin. Whether you have allowed bitterness to become bursts of rage or self-pity and depression, you are the only one who can reverse the cycle by choosing to allow Elohim to give you the ability to rise above the wrong that someone else has done.

Forgiveness is the recognition that God is stronger than the people who have wounded us. Forgiveness is the recognition that God is stronger than the past. Choosing to forgive—giving the frustration, anger, and hurt over to God—brings healing to us. Joseph was deeply hurt several times by numerous people, but he chose not to live in the past; he decided to trust God, and God turned their evil into good.

We can have God's Spirit as Joseph had, and rest assured it will heal us of the unhappy, bitter feelings we have because of the wrongs we have suffered. We can accept and trust God's hand leading and guiding us through every situation in life, and God will give us the same peace Joseph had. What a wonderful gift God wants to give us!

Do you need healing from feelings of hurt, bitterness, or resentment, and acceptance of the gift of peace and trust in God right now? Just ask God to take away those harmful feelings of self-pity and sadness, or of hatred and revenge. Now choose to thank God that He has taken those hurtful feelings away. You can do this by FAITH. That means thanking God for removing those hurtful feelings whether you *feel* any different or not. (However, this does NOT mean you are saying people are right or directed by God to do evil.)

Now ask God to replace your feelings that are hurtful (that He has just taken away) with feelings of joy, peace, and contentment. Ask Him for a godly pity for those who hurt you. Also ask Him to give you faith that He will eventually work this out for good, (knowing that in His time He will bring punishment for evil). Continue to ask for this every time those sad or angry feelings come back. Eventually they *will* stop disturbing your peace, and Adonai will have full control of this area of your life. He did this for Joseph; He can do it for you. People will soon start noticing the difference God is making in your life, just as they did with Joseph.

As we stated in lesson one, these lessons have something for both those well versed in the Scriptures and those who are beginners. If you are a beginner in Bible study you probably found the life history of Joseph very fascinating and applicable to your life today. If you are well versed in the Scriptures you probably found the topic of forgiveness a topic that is either deeper than you first realized or a topic that is well worth reviewing over and over again. Because we live in a world filled with people who make mistakes, we will find it necessary to reapply the principle of forgiveness over and over again throughout our lives. There is much more to Joseph's life recorded in the Bible that we did not have room for here. We encourage you to read the full account in the Bible itself.

The Nazis arrested Corrie and the rest of the ten Boom family in Febuary 1944. Ten days after their arrest her father died. Among his last words to his family were words from Psalm 119: "You are my hiding place and my shield: I hope in your Word..." For four months Corrie was kept in solitary confinement. Eventually Corrie and her sister Betsie were sent to the notorious Ravensbruck concentration camp.

While Corrie believed in God and lived for Him, this experience tried and tested her faith to the core. As Corrie fought for the extra blanket and the crumbs of food, Betsie put other people's needs first. While Corrie manuvered herself to the inside of the morning roll call to be out of the bone-chilling wind, Betsie remained self sacrificing. Even when Betsie was cruelly beaten for not working fast enough she continued to pray for the heartless guards. Betsie even prayed for Jan Vogel the informant that turned them over to the Nazis. Corrie was filled with hatred for him. He caused her father to die and the rest of the family to

3. JOSEPH (YOSEF), THE POWER OF FORGIVENESS

go through horrible suffering. How could she ever forgive him or pray for that devil? Corrie knew in her heart that Betsie was right. Corrie hated herself for being so filled with hatred. Corrie knew that when she did the right thing, even when she did not want to do them, her heart often caught up with the actions. She did not believe it would work in this case, but she prayed for him anyway. That night, for the first time since she had learned the betrayer's identity she slept without bitterness or anger. This was a very healing experience for her. Betsie and Corrie ministered hope and encouragement to the other prisoners.

Betsie died in the concentration camp. Some of her last words to Corrie were, ". . . We must tell them that there is no pit so deep that He is not deeper still." Just a few days later Corrie's name was called. She whispered a prayer and braced herself for the worst. For some unknown reason the Nazis released her. Miraculously a clerical "error" brought her name up for release. The next week all the women her age in the camp were killed.

When the war ended Corrie opened rehabilitation centers for survivors of the Holocaust. She saw that it was those who were able to forgive who were best able to rebuild their lives. Corrie traveled to more than sixty countries sharing her experience of God's power to forgive. After a speaking engagement in Germany her testimony was put to the ultimate test. She had just finished speaking about God's power to forgive and quoting God's promise in Micah 7:19, "He will take us back in love; He will cover up our iniquities, You will hurl all our sins into the depths of the sea" when she was approached by one of the meanest guards from Ravensbruck. Although the heavy, balding man was wearing a grey overcoat all she could see in her mind was a flashback of him wearing the Nazi uniform watching her and Betsie walking before him naked. She remembered this man watching them shower. She remembered seeing Betsie's bones protruding out, covered by a thin layer of skin. She remembered how cruel he had been to people and how he had participated in their murders. He reached out his hand to her and said that he had also been at Ravensbruck and that he had asked God to forgive him for the horendous things he had done, that he had repented of his actions, that he knew God had forgiven him, but that he would like to hear it from her lips as well. Corrie's blood seemed to freeze; she could not move. She was unable to forgive, she was unable to move her hand towards his. He again reached out his hand. "Can you forgive me?" How could she? Could all that happened in that camp be erased just like that? She wrestled for a few seconds, which felt like hours. She knew it was the right thing to forgive. She knew that the angry, vengeful thoughts that boiled through her were not from God. This was the most difficult thing she was ever called to do. She prayed for God to help her. She knew that forgiveness is an act of the will, and the will can function regardless of the temperature of the heart. She still could not move. If God could forgive him so could she. She prayed again, confessing to God that she did not have the power to forgive. She cried out to Him from her heart to give her His forgiveness. She mechanically reached out her arm. Then as their hands touched a current seemed to flow down her arm to him, a warm, healing love sprang up in her heart like she never experienced before in her life. She was overwhelmed. With tears in her eyes she told this former enemy that she had forgiven him. Corrie realized that when God gives the command to love our enemies, He gives, along with the command, the love itself.

Corrie believed that forgiveness is the key that unlocks the door of resentment and the handcuffs of hate. It is a power that breaks the chains of bitterness and the shackles of selfishness. Corrie said that, "Forgiveness is setting the prisoner free, only to find out that the prisoner was me."

Corrie ten Boom has written several books, including The Hiding Place, which retells her experience in the camp. It was also made into a film and is highly recommended.

You may or may not have gone through as horrendous an experience as Corrie did, but the same God who gave her victory over bitterness, anger, self-pity, and hate can heal your heart also.

The next study in this series will be about Moses and the guidance to be found from his experiences with God. We all know that he had a crucial role in our Jewish heritage.

REVIEW הזרה

1. Why were Joseph's brothers jealous of him?
    a. Joseph was more handsome than they were.
    b. Joseph loved his father more than they did.
    c. Jacob showed more love to Joseph than to his brothers.

2. Why did the jailer treat Joseph kindly?
    a. Because Joseph gave him money.

3. JOSEPH (YOSEF), THE POWER OF FORGIVENESS

    b. Because the Lord was with Joseph giving him a peaceful spirit.
    c. Because Pharaoh told him to.

3. Why did Pharaoh make Joseph his Prime Minister?
    a. Because Joseph gave him money.
    b. Because God's Spirit was with him.
    c. Because the jailer told him to.

4. Why did Joseph forgive his brothers?
    a. They gave him money.
    b. He had God's forgiving Spirit and he trusted that God would use their evil intent to bring about good.
    c. Pharaoh told him to.

5. Would you like to have Elohim's forgiving spirit in your life, giving you peace of mind?
    a. Yes
    b. No

6. Are there people who have hurt you that you have not yet fully forgiven? Would you like God to give you the ability to forgive them and have the bitter, sad feelings replaced with peace?
    a. Yes
    b. No

JEWISH HERITAGE SCRIPTURE STUDIES

4

MOSES
THE DELIVERER

4. MOSES (MOSHE) THE DELIVERER

In lesson 3 we learned how God helped Joseph forgive his brothers. God worked through Joseph to bring his own family into Egypt. We will now discover what became of this great family, the Israelites. We will also see what inspiration awaits us from the life of one of the greatest men who ever lived—Moses.

Can you imagine being taken from your home, and then being surrounded by a completely different culture? Picture fleeing for your life because of something you did. Eventually, you come to the place where you know God is the only one who can help you.

This was the experience of Moses. In the next few lessons we will come to appreciate how Adonai used him as His temple builder, torah writer, lawgiver, health educator, and deliverer. In this lesson we will read how Moses was used to deliver God's people from Egyptian bondage. We will also see 15 points (A-O) of how Moses' life is representative of the Great Deliverer, the Messiah.

1. Many years after Joseph died a new king arose in Egypt. How did he treat the Israelites?

    Joseph died ... and all that generation. But the Israelites ... multiplied and increased very greatly ... A new king arose over Egypt who did not know Joseph ... he said "Let us deal shrewdly with them, so that they may not increase; "... <u>set taskmasters over them to oppress them</u> with forced labor ... <u>"When you deliver the Hebrew women, look at the birthstool: if it is a boy, kill him."</u> Exodus 1:6-8,10,11,16

2. Under these horrible conditions, how did God miraculously save Moses from death when he was a baby?

    <u>*The woman conceived and ... hid him for three months. When she could hide him no longer, she got a wicker basket for him ... She put the child into it and placed it among the reeds by the bank of the Nile ... the daughter of Pharaoh came down to bathe ... She spied the basket ... When she opened it, she saw that it was a child, a boy*</u>

crying. She took pity on it and said; This must be a Hebrew child." Then his sister said to Pharaoh's daughter, "Shall I go and get you a Hebrew nurse to suckle the child for you?" And Pharaoh's daughter said to her, "yes." So the girl went and called the child's mother. And Pharaoh's daughter said to her, "Take this child and nurse it for me, and I will pay your wages." So the woman took the child and nursed it. When the child grew up, she brought him to Pharaoh's daughter, who made him her son. Exodus 2:2,3,5-10

Point A: He was saved from death as a baby.

3. As Moses grew to manhood he knew that he was Jewish. How did he attempt, in his own strength, to deliver the Jewish people from bondage?

    He went out to his kinsfolk and witnessed their labors. He saw an Egyptian beating a Hebrew, one of his kinsmen. He turned this way and that and, seeing no one about, he struck down the Egyptian and hid him in the sand. Exodus 2:11-12

4. What was the result of Moses' decision to use his own strength, rather than wait for God to reveal how He was going to use Moses to deliver us?

    When Pharaoh learned of the matter, he sought to kill Moses; but Moses fled from Pharaoh. He arrived in the land of Midian. Exodus 2:15

    Moses made the same mistake that Abraham and Jacob made of trying to fulfill Elohim's will by his own power.

5. What important lesson did Moses need to learn in the wilderness before God could use him as His deliverer?

    *"**Not by might, nor by power, but by My spirit**—said the LORD of **Hosts**."* Zechariah 4:6

    It is not by our might, our power, our intellectual abilities, our talents, our skills, or our wisdom that things for God are ultimately accomplished but it is by the LORD's Spirit working through us that brings about any accomplishments, good actions, righteous deeds, mitzvahs, and acts of loving-kindness.

6. After Moses had spent 40 years in the land of Midian as a sheepherder, God spoke to him in a unique way and summoned him to deliver the children of Israel out of bondage.

    God called to him out of the bush: "Moses! . . . I am," He said, "the God of your father, the God of Abraham, the God of Isaac, and the God of Jacob . . . I have marked well the plight of My

4. MOSES (MOSHE) THE DELIVERER

people . . . yes, I am mindful of their sufferings. I have come down to rescue them . . . I will send you . . . and you shall free My people . . ." Exodus 3:4,6-8,10

Point B: God called Him to deliver His people out of bondage.

7. No longer self assertive, how did Moses humbly respond?

   Moses said to God, "Who am I that I should go . . . ?" Exodus 3:11

8. How did God respond to Moses' fear, and what did God want the children of Israel to do when we were freed?

   And He said, "<u>I will be with you</u> . . . And when you have freed the people . . . <u>you shall worship God</u> . . ." Exodus 3:12

   Point C: He led people to worship God.

9. Pharaoh refused to give the people their freedom because he didn't want to lose the free labor they had been providing. As a result, Elohim sent ten terrible plagues on Egypt. After the ten plagues fell upon Egypt the children of Israel were set free. God led us across the desert to the Red Sea. When Pharaoh's army came out after us, what did we say to Moses that revealed our lack of faith?

   "<u>Was it for want of graves in Egypt that you brought us to die in the wilderness? What have you done to us, taking us out of Egypt? Is this not the very thing we told you in Egypt, saying, 'Let us be, and we will serve the Egyptians, for it is better for us to serve the Egyptians than to die in the wilderness?</u>" Exodus 14:11,12

   Seeing miracles is not enough to give us faith to stand during times of trouble. Like Abraham, Jacob, Joseph, and Moses, we need to learn to trust God in all circumstances. When we do that, our love for Him grows.

10. What was Moses' response to the people's distrust?

    But Moses said to the people, "<u>**Have no fear! Stand by**</u>, and <u>witness the deliverance which the LORD will work for you today . . . The LORD will battle for you; you hold your peace.</u>" Exodus 14:13,14

    In the face of certain death Moses' faith stood firm because he had learned to make God his strength. God performed the miracle of parting the waters and brought the children of Israel across the Red Sea on dry land. As Pharaoh's army tried to chase down the children of Israel, God allowed the sea to return to its natural state and all of Pharaoh's soldiers drowned.

Point D: He performed miracles.

11. Soon after this powerful experience the children of Israel arrived at Mt Sinai. This is where God called Moses up to the mountain top for 40 days of fasting and communing with Him. During this time, God gave Moses the 10 commandments written on two stone tablets. What type of rebellion were the children of Israel involved in while Moses was on Mt. Sinai?

When the people saw that Moses was so long in coming down from the mountain, <u>the people gathered against Aaron and said to him, "Come, make us a God</u> who shall go before us, for that man Moses, who brought us from the land of Egypt—we do not know what has happened to him." <u>Aaron . . . cast in a mold, and made it into a molten calf.</u> Exodus 32:1,2,4

Point E: He fasted in the wilderness forty days and nights.

Point F: He was rejected by many of the people he tried to save.

Point G: He proclaimed the law of God to the people.

12. How did God test Moses' faithfulness and love for the people who doubted God's leadership?

<u>The LORD further said to Moses, "I see that this is a stiff-necked people. Now, let Me be, that My anger may blaze forth against them and that I may destroy them, and make of you a great nation."</u> Exodus 32:9,10

13. How did Moses respond when God threatened to destroy all the people? How does this demonstrate his unselfish love for Adonai and for our people during this very time when we were rejecting him? How far was Moses willing to go to rescue this rebellious crowd?

<u>I threw myself down before the LORD</u>—eating no bread and drinking no water forty days and forty nights . . . because of the great wrong you had committed . . . so <u>I . . . interceded</u> . . ." Moses implored the LORD his God, saying, "Let not Your anger, O Lord blaze forth against Your people, whom You delivered . . . Now, <u>if You will forgive their sin (well and good); but if not erase me from the record which You have written!</u>" Deuteronomy 9:18, 20 Exodus 32:11,32

Moses interceded for the people. Moses also went a step further than just interceding; he was willing to have his name taken from the book of life for the people who were rebelling against God. Moses was willing to be the substitute for sinners.

Point H: He interceded for the people's sins.

4. MOSES (MOSHE) THE DELIVERER

Point I: He was willing to die in place of those who sinned.

14. When Moses humbly asked to behold God's presence how did God reveal Himself to Moses?

The Lord passed before him and proclaimed; "The LORD! The LORD! A God compassionate and gracious, slow to anger, abounding in kindness and faithfulness, extending kindness to the thousandth generation, forgiving iniquity, transgression, and sin; yet He does not remit all punishment . . ." Exodus 34:6,7

Point J: He beheld God's presence.

15. Within the first year of traveling through the wilderness we find the children of Israel rebelling against Elohim and disobeying him. This made life extremely hard for Moses. Despite this, we see God's servant Moses continually responding with love, mercy, patience, strength, justice and obedience to God. Moses was called the humblest man on earth (Numbers 12:3). What was one of the ways Moses showed us what true humility is?

Moses said to the Lord . . . <u>"let me know Your ways, that I may know You and continue in Your favor . . . unless You go in the lead, do not make us leave this place."</u> Exodus 33:12,13,15,

Point K: He was humble.

Point L: He did God's will and not His own.

Moses lived 120 years. His life is divided into three 40-year periods. During the first 40 years Moses was everything. He was going to be the next Pharaoh and he was going to deliver the Jewish people. In the next 40 years Moses was nothing. He was a sheepherder in the wilderness. He responded to God's call by saying "who am I that I should go?" In the last 40 years of Moses' life God was everything! You and I might not be given 120 years of life. What a thrill to know that we can surrender the pride and insecurities and move to "stage 3" right now and allow God to be everything to us. Like Moses we can determine to know God, to know His ways, to walk in His favor, and to let God lead us.

16. What is one of the ways God described the Messiah to Moses?

The Lord said to me . . . <u>I will raise up a prophet for them from among their own people, like yourself. I will put My words in His mouth and He will speak to them all that I command Him, and if anybody fails to heed the words He speaks in My name, I Myself will call him to account.</u>" Deuteronomy 18:17,18,19

Point M: He was a prophet.

Point N: He spoke God's words in God's name.

Point O: People were accountable for following what he said.

17. In review, there are 15 different ways Moses' life prefigured the Messiah. What were they?

    A) Miraculously saved from death as a baby

    B) Called by God to deliver His people out of bondage

    C) Led the people to worship God

    D) Performed miracles

    E) Fasted in the wilderness forty days and nights

    F) Was rejected by many of the people he tried to save

    G) Proclaimed the law of God to the people

    H) Interceded for the people's sins

    I) Was willing to die in place of those who sinned

    J) Beheld God's presence

    K) Was humble

    L) He did God's will and not His own

    M) Was a prophet

    N) Spoke God's words in God's name

    O) People were held accountable for following what he said

These are just a few of the areas that the life of the Great Deliverer, the Messiah, is foreshadowed in the Hebrew Scriptures.

Adonai can give you the ability to be loving and courageous when facing difficult times, just as He did for Moses. Do you ever find yourself facing tough times, needing power to cope? God is that power and He makes Himself available to us through prayer. Just talk to Him as if He was a friend at your side and He will provide you with the strength that you need on a daily basis. As you draw closer to God day by day He will make Himself more and more real to you and give you humility, strength, and courage just as He gave Moses.

In our next lesson "Moses the Temple Builder" we will study about the first Jewish Temple. It was designed by God Himself and built under the leadership of Moses. With its heavenly Designer, it was no doubt the most important Temple ever designed. Most importantly, God's "Temple," like Moses' life, prefigured the work of God for us as well as the work of the Messiah.

4. MOSES (MOSHE) THE DELIVERER

REVIEW הזרה

1. Who, primarily, saved Moses' life as a child?

   a. Joseph.
   b. God.
   c. The Israelites.

2. Who called Moses to save the Israelites out of bondage?

   a. Pharaoh.
   b. God.
   c. The children of Israel.

3. Why did God use Moses to call the people out of Egypt?

   a. So they could worship God freely.
   b. So they could wander in the wilderness.
   c. So they could become doctors and lawyers.

4. When the children of Israel grumbled and rebelled against God, how did Moses respond?

   a. He yelled at them.
   b. He asked God to destroy them.
   c. He prayed and interceded for them.

5. When Adonai threatened to destroy all the rebellious Israelites and start a new nation through Moses, how did Moses respond?

   a. He shouted for joy and he started having lots of babies.
   b. He tried thinking of a new name for the new nation.
   c. He asked to be erased from God's record with the people.

6. Who did Moses prefigure?

   a. Prophet to come, Messiah.
   b. Abraham.
   c. Joseph.

7. How can you gain the strength you need to be like Moses and follow God?

JEWISH HERITAGE
BIBLE STUDIES

5

MOSES
THE TEMPLE BUILDER

5. MOSES (MOSHE) THE TEMPLE BUILDER

This lesson is about the first Jewish Temple ever built. In our last lesson we learned how the life of our great leader, Moses, prefigured, or pointed forward to the Messiah, our deliverer, in fifteen different ways (points A-O). In this lesson we will see eleven more points (P-Z) showing how the first Jewish Temple, like the life of Moses, prefigured the Messiah, the hope of Israel!

When the Jewish people left Egypt they were led to Mount Sinai. God called Moses up onto the mountain to be with Him for forty days. On Mount Sinai God gave Moses the Ten Commandments and a specific pattern for building the Temple. The Temple is also called the Sanctuary, Mishkan, or Tabernacle.

1. How did Moses know how to design and build the Sanctuary?

    The L<small>ORD</small> spoke to Moses, saying:* . . . *"Exactly as I show you—the pattern of the Tabernacle and the pattern of all its furnishings—so shall you make it." Exodus 25:1, 9

    The people built the Tabernacle but God was the architect.

2. What was this tabernacle patterned after?

    He built His Sanctuary like the heavens . . . Psalm 78:69

    As we will see in future lessons the work of the earthly Sanctuary tells us about what God is doing in heaven.

3. What was Moses to build inside this Sanctuary, or Tabernacle?

    "They shall make an <u>ark of acacia wood</u>, . . . Overlay it with pure gold." Exodus 25:10, 11

4. What was to be inside this distinctive Ark?

    "And <u>deposit in the Ark [the tablets of] the Pact which I will give you</u>" . . . ***When He finished speaking with him on Mount Sinai, He gave Moses the two tablets of the Pact, <u>stone tablets inscribed with the finger of God.</u>"*** Exodus 25:16; 31:18

    The Ten Commandments were so special they were placed inside the Ark of the Pact, the Ark of the Covenant.

5. What was one of God's purposes for His Temple or Sanctuary?

*"Make Me a Sanctuary <u>that I may dwell among them</u>."*Exodus 25:8

Elohim used the Sanctuary as a demonstration that He wants to dwell with us. What a beautiful thought, that God wants to be with us! Our God is not some far off God, but one who is close at hand. He is with us in our times of joy and laughter as well as in our times of pain and sorrow. The Hebrew term "Immanuel," "God with us" helps us experience a sense of comfort and hope. He is with you right now as you are reading this lesson. To reveal a God who is close, loving, and compassionate is one of the purposes for the Sanctuary as well as one of the purposes of the Messiah.

6. Where in this beautiful Sanctuary would God meet with us?

"<u>There I will meet with you</u>, and I will impart to you—<u>from above the cover, from between the two cherubim</u> that are <u>on top of the Ark of the Pact</u>." Exodus 25:22

This section of God's Tabernacle was called the Most Holy Place. The top part of the Ark of the Covenant was called the Mercy Seat. It was here, between two carved golden angels, that Elohim would meet with His people. God's Mercy Seat sat above His Law. In the Psalms it says "mercy & truth are met together…have kissed each other." (Psalm 85:11) It is here, in God's Most Holy Place, that mercy & truth, love & law, grace & judgment, are blended together in harmony.

7. What are the other five significant pieces of furniture that God directed Moses to build?

"You shall <u>make a table</u>…And on the table you shall set the bread of display… You shall <u>make a lampstand</u> of pure gold… Make its seven lamps… to give the light on its front side… You shall <u>make an altar for burning incense</u>. Make <u>a laver of copper</u>… for washing… Put water in it…" He made <u>the altar for burnt offering</u>. Exodus 25:23,30; 31;37; 30:18, 19; 38:1

Each piece of furniture in God's Temple was designed by God after the heavenly pattern to teach us more about God's love for us. The altar for burnt offerings was where the Israelites sacrificed animals in order to receive forgiveness of sins. (We will elaborate on this more in question 9). The laver for washing symbolized the cleansing from the guilt and defilement of sin that God does in our lives after we receive His forgiveness. The lampstand, or menorah, demonstrated Adonai's continual light shining in our lives guiding and directing us. King David referred to God's Word as a lamp for our feet. The table and the bread of display depicted God's provision for us and His desire that we absorb or internalize His truths into our lives. The altar for burning incense was where the Levites, the spiritual leaders, would pray for the children of Israel. This reminds us to be continually praying for each other.

8. Where did the materials come from to build God's Sanctuary?

Men and women, <u>all whose hearts moved them</u>, all who would make an elevation offering of gold to the L<small>ORD</small>, came <u>bringing brooches, earrings, rings, and pendants—gold objects of all kinds</u>. Exodus 35:22

Elohim designed the Temple, but we built it and paid for it from the finances God provided for us. The Egyptians gave us jewelry in their desire to get rid of us after all the plagues. We gave the jewelry to God for the building and upkeep of His Temple.

9. What was the Sanctuary primarily used for?

If any person . . . incurs guilt by doing any of the things which by the L<small>ORD</small>'s commandments ought not to be done, and he realizes his guilt—or the sin of which he is guilty . . . he shall bring a female *goat without blemish as his offering for the sin of which he is guilty. He shall lay his hand upon the head of the sin offering, and <u>the sin offering shall be slaughtered at the place of the burnt offering</u>. The priest shall take . . . some of its blood and put it on the horns of the altar of burnt offering; and all the rest of <u>its blood he shall pour out at the base of the altar</u> . . . <u>Thus the priest shall make expiation for him, and he shall be forgiven.</u>* Leviticus 4:27-31

The main daily activity that took place in the first Jewish Temple was the sacrificing of animals as substitutes for the sins of the people. We saw in lesson one, when Abraham was about to sacrifice his son Isaac, Adonai provided a ram caught in the thicket of a bush to be used as a substitute for Abraham's son. It was through the sacrificing of the animal for their sins that the Jewish people received forgiveness. It was not that God enjoyed the slaughtering of animals, but they, like the life of Moses, and the rest of the Temple, were prefiguring the life and work of the Messiah. Isaac asked his father, "Where is the sheep for the offering?" Abraham said, "God will see to the sheep for His offering." God provided His own offering by providing the Messiah for us.

10. According to Moses and the Torah is there any way to receive expiation—cleansing from and forgiveness for sins—without having to shed blood?

"The life of the flesh is in <u>the blood</u>, and <u>I have assigned it to you for making expiation for your lives</u> upon the altar; <u>it is the blood, as life, that effects expiation.</u>" Leviticus 17:11

A blood sacrifice was the only way that Elohim prescribed for us to receive forgiveness of sins. Without the shedding of blood there was no forgiveness. This was the difference between Cain's and Abel's sacrifices. Two of Adam and Eve's children were Cain and Abel. Cain offered God a sacrifice of fruits and vegetables and Abel gave God the sacrifice He had asked for, a lamb. Cain's sacrifice did not contain blood and it was not accepted, while Abel's was a blood sacrifice and God accepted it. (Again, it is not that God wants the shedding of blood, but sin is so serious that it demands death. God's law and righteousness require either the death of the sinner or an acceptable substitute that God chose). Here again we see the work of the Messiah being foreshadowed.

Point P: Messiah would die as a sacrifice for the forgiveness of our sins, symbolized by the lambs in the Sanctuary.

5. MOSES (MOSHE) THE TEMPLE BUILDER

11. According to the book of Psalms, how many of us need this expiation—cleansing from and forgiveness for sins?

> <u>*All have turned bad,*</u> *altogether foul; there is none who does good, not even one.* Psalm 14:3

Not one of us is perfect, not even one. We have all made mistakes; we all need God's forgiveness and cleansing of our records and consciences.

12. The Jewish prophet Isaiah used the illustration of the sacrifices of lambs and goats to represent the work of the Messiah being our sacrificial substitute.

> *He was despised, shunned by men, a man of suffering . . .* <u>*we held him of no account.*</u> *Yet it was our sickness that he was bearing, our suffering that he endured. We accounted him plagued, smitten and afflicted by God;* <u>*but he was wounded because of our sins, crushed because of our iniquities.*</u> *He bore the chastisement that made us whole, and by his bruises we were healed. We all went astray like sheep, each going his own way; and* <u>*the* LORD *visited upon him the guilt of all of us.*</u> *He was maltreated, yet He was submissive, He did not open his mouth;* <u>*like a sheep being led to slaughter*</u> *. . . For* <u>*He was cut off from the land of the living*</u> *through the sin of my people, who deserved the punishment. And* <u>*his grave was set among the wicked, and with the rich, in his death*</u>*—though* <u>*He had done no injustice and had spoken no falsehood*</u> *. . .* <u>*He made himself an offering for guilt, He might see offspring and have long life,*</u> *and that through him the* LORD*'s purpose might prosper. Out of his anguish He shall see it;* <u>*He shall enjoy it to the full*</u> *through His devotion. "*<u>*My righteous servant makes the many righteous, it is their punishment that He bears*</u>*; I will give Him the many as His portion, He shall receive the multitude as his spoil. For* <u>*He exposed Himself to death*</u> *and was numbered among the sinners, whereas* <u>*He bore the guilt of the many and made intercession for sinners.*</u>*"* Isaiah 53:3-12

There is a lot to digest in these verses. It would be good to reread these important verses again before we look at them point by point. Notice how often the concept of the Messiah standing as our substitute is alluded to.

Point Q: We held Him of no account; He did not receive the full honor He deserved.

Point R: His grave was with the wicked and the rich.

Point S: He would be raised from the dead to see offspring (followers) and have long life.

Point T: He would do no injustice and spoke no falsehood.

13. What incredible sign did Adonai give the prophet Isaiah to tell us about the Messiah?

> *"Assuredly, <u>my LORD will give you a sign of His own accord! Look, the young woman is with child and about to give birth to a son. Let her name him Immanuel</u>."* Isaiah 7:14

Many scholars interpret young in the sense that she was still a virgin. If the young woman mentioned here was merely a young lady giving birth to a child this would not be much of a sign from God. The Hebrew word used here is עלמה (almah). עלמה Almah is often translated as virgin instead of as young woman. (See Genesis 24:43, 16 for example). Is it possible for a virgin to give birth? Remember, God gave Abraham and Sarah a miraculous child, Isaac, after Sarah was long past childbearing age. Nothing is impossible for God.

The word "Immanuel" used in this text means "God with us." In question 5 we read that Elohim told Moses that His being with us was one of the purposes of the Sanctuary. Once again, we are shown how the Sanctuary represented the Messiah. This miraculous Son, who would be a "sign" from God, would be born of a virgin and would be known as "God with us." When the Sanctuary was originally made it was placed right in the center of all the tribes of Israel. God wants to be in the center of our lives; He wants to be with us.

Point U: Messiah would be born of a virgin as a sign from God.

Point V: Messiah would be Immanuel, "God with us."

14. What did the Jewish prophet Isaiah tell us about this extraordinary son?

> *For a child has been born to us, <u>A son has been given us</u>. And <u>authority has settled on his shoulders</u>. He has been named "<u>The Mighty God is planning grace</u>; <u>The Eternal Father, a peaceable ruler</u>"* Isaiah 9:5

15. In what town was this young woman to give birth to this remarkable child who would be "God with us"?

> *"And you, O <u>Bethlehem</u> of Ephrath, Least among the clans of Judah, <u>From you one shall come forth</u> to rule Israel for Me—<u>One whose origin is from of old</u>."* Micah 5:1

Point W: Messiah, "whose origin is from of old," would be born in the town of Bethlehem.

5. MOSES (MOSHE) THE TEMPLE BUILDER

16. Do we have other examples from the Torah where Adonai took human form and lived among us?

> *Jacob was left alone. And a man wrestled with him . . . Said the other, "What is your name?" He replied, "Jacob." Said he, "Your name shall no longer be Jacob, but Israel, for you have striven with God and man (margin), and have prevailed." . . . So Jacob named the place Peniel, meaning, "I have seen a divine being face to face, yet my life has been preserved."* Genesis 32:25,28-31

Peniel literally means face of God. Jacob wrestled face to face with God while God was veiling Himself as a man. When Jacob realized it was God he had wrestled with he called the place Peniel—face of God. Another example is when God appeared to Abraham as a man. (See Genesis 18:1,2)

Point X: He would be the Messiah, as Immanuel, God with us, yet He would dwell with us as a man.

17. In what way did the Jewish prophet Isaiah and King David prophesy that our Messiah would die?

> *"I offered my back to the floggers, and my cheeks to those who tore out my hair. I did not hide my face from insult and spittle." "My life ebbs away: all my bones are disjointed; my heart is like wax, melting within me; my vigor dries up like a shard; my tongue cleaves to my palate; You commit me to the dust of death . . . a pack of evil ones closes in on me, like lions [they maul] my hands and feet. I take the count of all my bones while they look on and gloat. They divide my clothes among themselves."* Isaiah 50:6; Psalm 22:15-19

The Messiah would be whipped and beaten. He would be insulted and spit on. He would have his hands and feet mauled while others looked on. It is amazing that King David described this form of death caused by being pierced and hung by the hands and feet. This cruel form of execution used by the Romans was not invented until hundreds of years after King David wrote this prophecy.

Point Y: In His death His bones would come out of joint.

Point Z: His hands and His feet would be mauled.

When the Messiah's hands were nailed to the wood for our sins He engraved our names upon His heart. Elohim's love for you is deep and eternal; He will never forget you. Words cannot describe a love that is greater than the love God has for you.

18. Let's review the fifteen ways Moses' life prefigured the Messiah and also look at the eleven identifying points we just read from God's Word.
    a. Like Moses the Messiah was miraculously saved from death as a baby.
    b. God called Him to deliver His people out of bondage.
    c. He led the people to worship God.
    d. He performed miracles.
    e. He fasted in the wilderness forty days and nights.
    f. He was rejected by many of the people He tried to save.
    g. He promoted the law of God to the people.
    h. He interceded for the people's sins.
    i. He was willing to die in place of those who sinned.
    j. He beheld God's presence.
    k. He was humble.
    l. He did God's will and not His own, following God's leading.
    m. He was a prophet.
    n. He spoke God's words in God's name.
    o. People were accountable for following what He said.
    p. He would die as a sacrifice for the forgiveness of our sins, symbolized by the lambs in the Sanctuary.
    q. We held Him of no account; He did not receive the full honor He deserved.
    r. His grave was with the wicked and the rich.
    s. He would be raised from the dead to see offspring (followers) and have long life.
    t. He would do no injustice and would speak no falsehood.
    u. He would be born of a virgin as a sign from God to us.
    v. He would be Immanuel "God with us."
    w. He would be born in the town of Bethlehem, even though His origin is from everlasting.
    x. He would be the Messiah, Immanuel, God with us, yet He would dwell with us as a man.
    y. In His death His bones would come out of joint.
    z. His hands and His feet would be mauled.

The chances of all 26 of these identifications, from A to Z, to be fulfilled in one individual are almost impossible. But with a little knowledge of history it can be seen that from A to Z the Jewish Messiah prophesied in the Hebrew Scriptures is Y'shua! Y'shua is the way His name is pronounced in Hebrew. It means Savior. Y'shua was how His Jewish parents referred to Him. When the name Y'shua is translated into Greek and then into English it is pronounced

5. MOSES (MOSHE) THE TEMPLE BUILDER

Jesus. Jewish people who accept that these biblical prophecies point to Y'shua as the Messiah do not stop being Jewish. They become a Jewish person who knows who his Jewish Messiah is. And then having accepted Him as your Messiah you can accept His death for the forgiveness and expiation for the sins you have committed. Y'shua becomes your substitute, carrying your burden of guilt and shame. Through His Divine forgiveness and acceptance with Adonai you have the assurance of eternal life with God. (To read how His life fulfilled these prophecies, you can examine it for yourself in the Holy Bible under the sections entitled Matthew, Mark, Luke, and John.)

Although the Messiah has been misrepresented many times by those who profess to follow Him, He is very Jewish. He was circumcised on the 8th day, kept the Passover and all the Jewish Holy Days, and He regularly attended services in the synagogues on Sabbath. He loved the God of Abraham, Isaac, and Jacob, and He kept the Ten Commandments perfectly. He never was anti-Semitic and he never encouraged anyone else to be, either. Even though He died as the sacrificial Lamb approximately 2,000 years ago, His life has been prolonged, as the Scripture in question 12 prophesied. He is alive in Heaven today and He loves you.

We must have more than just an intellectual understanding of the prophecies. You and I need to accept Him, Y'shua, as the sacrifice for our mistakes in order to receive the forgiveness of our sins for which He died.

19. Which eternal scar does God specifically mention, to remind us that God can never forget us because of the sacrifice of the Messiah as our substitute?

"I never could forget you. See, <u>I have engraved you on the palms of My hands</u> . . ." Isaiah 49:15, 16

20. How can I receive forgiveness for my sins?

    Confess my sins to the Messiah just as was done with the sheep in the Sanctuary Temple.

Barbara Gurien was working as an ultrasound technologist when she went on a date with a Jewish man who believed in Y'shua as the Messiah. Barbara was shocked. She had never met a Jewish person who believed that way. Growing up in Brooklyn everyone she knew was Jewish, including the public school teachers and the mailman. Although she never dated him again, what he said bothered her deeply. She knew that if what he said was true about the

Messiah it would greatly impact her life. What would her grandfather, the rabbi, think if he was still alive? One day a work associate gave her a Bible as a gift. She began to read the accounts of Moses and her ancestors wandering in the wilderness and the times that they did not manifest perfect faith and follow God's teachings. Barbara began to ask God if she was doing the same. Was she living up to all that He wanted for her? Was she resisting His love? About this time she received an invitation in the mail to come to some Bible meetings being held at a church called the Miami Temple. She had never been to a church in her life. She was not sure if she would be allowed in. She slipped into the back and tried to hide. Someone sat next to her. Initially she tried not to look at him but it turned out it was someone she knew from work. He quickly introduced her to two Jewish friends of his who also attended that congregation. She never promised to attend another meeting, but each night she felt drawn to attend. She was overwhelmed with the loving God she was learning about and the amazing prophecies that God had fulfilled. She cried for joy when she decided to accept Y'shua as her Messiah—but what about her parents? What would they say? Was she betraying her people? Would she ever be able to meet and marry a nice Jewish boy? She put off telling her parents for as long as she could, but when she could hold it in no longer she told them what she now believed and how much happier she was for accepting Y'shua's love. They were not happy at all. Her father threatened never to speak to her again nor attend her wedding if she ever got married. Barbara was heart broken and cried for days, but her love for Y'shua comforted her through this difficult period. Over the course of many months her family noticed how much more at peace Barbara was since she accepted Y'shua. She was much more secure and content. She had more joy and love in her heart than she ever had before. Finally, after many months, her father agreed to speak with her again. And ten years later, when Elohim brought a nice Jewish man, who believes in Y'shua, into Barbara's life, her father, Irving, walked her down the aisle and danced the hora at her wedding. (More of Barbara's story can be read in the book Twice Chosen.)

Samuel Srolovic Jacobson was born in Lithuania in a loving Orthodox Jewish home. He received religious instruction throughout his childhood and was observant in all the biblical commandments and Jewish traditions. Sam

5. MOSES (MOSHE) THE TEMPLE BUILDER

and his family attended services at their synagogue every week. Eventually the entire family moved to the Holy Land where Sam lived for four years before moving to Zimbabwe for a higher paying job. Now as an adult Sam began to read the Bible for himself for the first time in his life. He was very familiar with the commandments of what to do and what not to do as well as all the rabbinical traditions and writings, but he did not know the Holy Scriptures. Many Bible texts concerning the Messiah jumped out at him over the months that he read, prayed, and searched. Sam strongly resisted the idea that the Messiah had already come and that it was Y'shua. But the more he read and studied the harder it became to deny it. Among the many texts that stood out in his mind included Daniel 9 (which will be covered in detail later in this book), Haggai 2:9, and Genesis 49:10, all of which indicate that the Messiah would come before the second temple would be destroyed and the last king of Judah would reign. Many fears assailed Sam as he contemplated accepting Y'shua as his Messiah. Would his family reject him? Was he rejecting them? Would they be angry? Could the rabbi's be wrong? Will I still be Jewish? Will I be a traitor? As strong as those fears were Sam decided to accept what the Bible said regardless of the consequences. When Sam finally accepted Y'shua a peace filled his heart. Several people tried to persuade Sam to reject his faith in Y'shua as the Messiah. One man even offered Sam free rent for three years if he would give up his faith. But Sam's faith had become very real and precious to him and nothing was worth giving that up for. When Sam accepted Y'shua he thought he was the only Jewish person in the world who believed like he did until someone put him in contact with Frederick C. Gilbert. Gilbert wrote to Sam saying, "I was born and reared an Orthodox Jew. But how grateful I am to God that He showed me the light of the Messiah, and all through these years what a joy it has been to know that through this Messiah it is our privilege to have assurance that our sins are forgiven." Samuel's life story is recorded in the book "The Quest of a Jew."

Right now I invite you to confess your mistakes to Him; thank Him for dying for you, thank Him for giving you forgiveness. Ask Him to dwell with you, to give you peace and joy in your life. Ask Him to enter your mind, and meet your temptations in your human flesh for you! Receive His victory as your own. It will be the beginning of a whole new life for you.

JEWISH DISCOVERIES

It is through the Messiah, the seed or descendant of Abraham, Isaac, and Jacob, that all the nations of the earth have been blessed! The most famous Jewish person in history has fulfilled God's promise that all the nations of the earth would be blessed by Abraham's offspring. Every person on this earth has been blessed by the forgiveness that God has given to the world when He gave the Messiah as the lamb sacrificed for the sins of every person who will accept it.

The next two lessons will expand on the truths brought out in these last two lessons and will answer more questions that may be coming to your mind regarding the Jewishness of accepting Y'shua as the Messiah.

Passover is one of the most wonderful times of year. For many it brings back memories of family time, good cooking, and a time to reflect on our Jewish heritage. Our next lesson is entitled "The Ultimate Passover." It will answer many questions that might have come to your mind over the years, such as why do we hide the afikomen? Why are there three matzahs in the matzah covering? Why did Moses tell the people to put blood on the doorposts? What were Passovers like 2,000 years ago?

REVIEW הזרה

1. Why did God tell Moses to build a Sanctuary?
    a. To keep him busy.
    b. God likes beautiful buildings.
    c. For God to dwell with the people and to provide a way for people to receive forgiveness of sins.

2. How did people mentioned in the Bible receive God's forgiveness for their sins?
    a. By performing tashlich, throwing bread into the water.
    b. By confessing their sins to God and sacrificing a lamb.
    c. By doing good deeds (Mitzvahs) to make up for it.

3. I can receive God's forgiveness for my sins and mistakes by:
    a. Performing tashlich, throwing bread into the water.
    b. Confessing my sins to God and accepting the Messiah's death as my sacrifice.
    c. Doing good deeds (Mitzvahs) to make up for it.

5. MOSES (MOSHE) THE TEMPLE BUILDER

4. Is it clear to you that the texts in this lesson from the Hebrew Scriptures point to Y'shua as the Messiah?

   a. Yes.
   b. I still have some questions I want answered before I decide.

5. Do you want to receive God's forgiveness for past mistakes and sins by accepting the Messiah's death as your sacrifice?

   a. Yes.
   b. I still have some questions I want answered before I decide.

If you answered "b" to either of the last two questions continue on to the next two lessons asking God to answer your questions and to guide your mind and heart according to His divine will for you.

If you answered "Yes" to the last two questions—Mazel Tov! Congratulations! Your life is about to open up in some of the most amazing ways. Say a prayer to Adonai informing Him of your decision. You can say this sample prayer or you can say your own prayer in your own words. "Lord God, King of the universe, I thank You for Your love for me. I thank You for the wonderful truths I have been learning from Your Word. I want to receive forgiveness for my mistakes and be freed of my guilt, worries, and fears. I want my name written in Your book. I want eternal life with You. Never leave me or let me down. I accept your forgiveness because of the death of the Messiah and I accept His death as my substitute. Thank You for forgiving me and loving me. Come into my heart and life. In Y'shua's name, amen."

JEWISH HERITAGE SCRIPTURE STUDIES

6

ULTIMATE PASSOVER

6. THE ULTIMATE PASSOVER

For the last 3,500 years our people have been celebrating the Passover. Moses and the children of Israel gave us an example on their last day in Egypt of how it is to be kept. Moses then wrote down in the Torah God's instructions for us on how to observe the occasion in commemoration of God's great deliverance of our people. Over the last three and a half millennia a few traditions have been added to the Passover celebration, but for the most part it has remained untouched. Let's walk through a Passover Seder together and see the similarities between three Passovers—the original held in Egypt some 3,500 years ago, another held in a second floor room in Jerusalem about 2,000 years ago, and one that is typically held today in Jewish homes throughout the world.

In Exodus 12 Moses wrote down God's instructions concerning the Passover:

"Speak ye unto the congregation of Israel, saying . . . they shall take to them every man a lamb . . . <u>Your lamb shall be without blemish, a male</u> . . . kill it in the evening . . . Take a bunch of <u>hyssop</u>, and dip it in the blood that is in the basin, and strike the lintel and the two side posts with the blood that is in the basin . . . they shall eat the flesh in that night, roast with fire, and <u>unleavened bread</u>; and <u>with bitter herbs</u> they shall eat it."

"<u>Let nothing of it remain until the morning</u> . . . you shall eat it; <u>with your loins girded, your shoes on your feet, and your staff in your hand; and ye shall eat it in haste</u>: it is the L<small>ORD</small>'s Passover. For I will pass through the land of Egypt this night, and will smite all the firstborn in the land of Egypt, both man and beast; and <u>against all the gods of Egypt</u> I will execute judgment: I am the L<small>ORD</small>." KJV

Take note of the words: <u>lamb</u>, <u>unleavened bread</u>, <u>hyssop</u>, <u>bitter herbs</u>, <u>eating in haste</u>, <u>none of it remaining until morning</u>, and <u>gods of Egypt</u>. These words will be revisited later on in the Seder.

"And the blood shall be to you for a token upon the houses where ye are: and when I see the blood, I will <u>pass over you</u>, and the plague shall not be upon you to destroy you, when I smite the

land of Egypt. Seven days shall ye eat <u>unleavened bread</u>; even the first day ye shall put away leaven out of your houses."

From this verse we are able to see why the feast is called the Passover and the Feast of Unleavened Bread.

And it shall come to pass, <u>when your children shall say unto you</u>, "What mean ye by this service?" That ye shall say, it is the sacrifice of the LORD's Passover, who passed over the houses of the children of Israel in Egypt, when he smote the Egyptians, and delivered our houses. The people bowed the head and worshiped.

To ensure that the children ask questions, as is indicated from this text, four questions for the children to ask are inserted as part of the Passover Seder. We will hear these four questions later.

Chametz: The Seder starts with the father getting up from the table and sweeping some breadcrumbs off a shelf and throwing them out the door. This is symbolic of making sure that all chametz, that is leaven, is removed from the house.

Rabbi Paul of the first century compares sin to leaven because both spread and change the make-up of the item they possess. In the case of leaven it permeates and transforms the entire clump of dough; in the case of sin it permeates and destroys the person, the family, the congregation, or the society it infects. At Passover and the Feast of Unleavened Bread all leaven is removed from the home symbolizing the removing of sinful traits from our lives.

Haggada: During a traditional Seder today a haggada is used to give us the order of the service. We have been using haggadas during our Seders for many hundreds of years. There is not one haggada for all Passovers. There are several variations, but they all basically follow a similar pattern, as we will do in this lesson.

Passover plate: The Seder plate is a plate used only at Passover and there is a place on the plate for each of the different items we will be using throughout the Seder, such as the bitter herb, lamb shank bone, etc.

Last Supper: There is an immensely famous painting by Leonardo da Vinci called the Last Supper. You have no doubt seen it. It is a painting of Y'shua and His disciples eating a meal together. What is not very well known about the painting is that the supper they were eating was a Passover Seder. Amazing as that might seem to some, it is true. Y'shua, of course, was Jewish and

6. THE ULTIMATE PASSOVER

celebrated Passovers every year of His life. The painting by Leonardo da Vinci depicts Y'shua's last Passover, which turned out to be His last meal before He was killed, thus the name of the painting—the Last Supper.

Keep in mind, as we review a modern Passover Seder we will be comparing and contrasting three different Passovers. We will go back 3,500 years and look at the first Passover with Moses and the children of Israel, we will look at the Last Supper Passover which Y'shua and his friends celebrated in Jerusalem 2,000 years ago, and we will be looking at modern Passover Seders. One of the many amazing things we will learn in this lesson is that not much has changed regarding Passover Seders over the last 3,500 years.

Four cups: We traditionally drink from our cup of wine or grape juice four times. Each time a different significance is given to the drinking from the cup.

Cup of Sanctification: The first time we drink, it is called the cup of sanctification. It is Elohim who sanctifies us, sets us apart for holy use. God has sanctified, set apart, the Passover for a special purpose to remind us how He has led us in the past and to teach us important lessons regarding His love for us. The father says the blessing, "Baruch atah Adonai Elohenu melech ha'olam borei p'ri hagafen—Blessed are you O' LORD our God, King of the universe, Creator of the fruit of the vine."

During that Passover Seder 2,000 years ago, depicted in the Last Supper painting, Y'shua also picked up this first cup at this time and said, "Take this and divide it among yourselves, for I say unto you I will not drink of the fruit of the vine, until the kingdom of God shall come."

Did you notice that the words "fruit of the vine," which are used in the prayers today, were used by Y'shua 2,000 years ago. Already we are seeing that not much has changed in at least two millennia.

Urchatz: The urchatz is a ceremonial hand washing indicating our cleansing from defilement.

Y'shua took this ceremony a step further by washing not only His own hands, but by washing the feet of His followers who were with Him, showing that true leadership is in serving others, not in having others serve us.

Parsley or karpas: The parsley, or karpas, represents the hyssop, a reed that was used in Egypt as the paintbrush to put the blood on doorposts as commanded by God to avoid the tenth plague, the death of the first born. We dip the parsley in salt water, which represents the tears we shed while in slavery and the Red Sea, both of which were salty. The salt water makes the parsley sweeter to the taste; our slavery and tears were sweetened by the hope of deliverance. When we eat the parsley and salt water, we think of the sad experiences we are going through in our personal lives today, yet we are strengthened by our faith in God's love for us.

It is interesting to note that God chose the blood of a lamb to be painted on the doorpost with the hyssop. He could have said to put salt water on the doorpost or to put mezuzahs on the doorpost, but he said to place the blood of the lamb upon your home for the saving of your children. Do you think the angel of death would have passed over the homes if they had used red paint instead of the blood of the lambs when God commanded the blood of lambs to be used? Of course not. God means what He says. We cannot understate the importance of the use of the blood of lambs in God's deliverance in their lives or in ours. We will be speaking more about this a little later.

As we dip the parsley in the salt water we say the blessing; "Baruch atah Adonai Elohenu melech ha-olam borei pre ha-adamah—Blessed are you O' LORD our God, King of the universe, Creator of the fruit of the earth."

First question—matzah: As mentioned, the children, traditionally the youngest child, asks four questions. The first question is: Why is this night different from all other nights? On all other nights we eat leavened bread and unleavened bread. Why on this night do we eat only unleavened bread?

We eat only unleavened bread on Passover and throughout the Feast of Unleavened Bread, which lasts seven days, because our ancestors left Egypt in haste and did not have time to let the bread rise and because matzah was lighter to carry for our journey than whole bread.

The matzah tosh or matzah covering is a unique cover into which are placed three pieces of matzah. The matzah tosh has three compartments, with one piece of matzah in each one. The middle piece of matzah is taken out of the bag. This middle piece of matzah that has stripes on it and is pierced is then broken. Half of it is placed back in the matzah tosh and half of it is wrapped in a linen cloth and hidden away to be found later during the Seder.

Some rabbis have said the three pieces of matzah in the matzah tosh represent Abraham, Isaac, and Jacob. Others have said they represent the Levites, the

6. THE ULTIMATE PASSOVER

Cohanim, and the rest of the Israelites. It is just as valid to say they represent the oneness of Elohim. All three pieces of matzah are the same; they are kept together as one unit in one matzah tosh, and are thus united as one unit.

In many ways the matzah represents the Messiah. Matzah is unleavened, and the Messiah was unleavened—without sin. Matzah is striped; the Messiah was whipped and striped for our transgressions. The Jewish prophet Isaiah prophesied He would be "wounded because of our sins" and that He offered His "back to the floggers." The middle piece is broken and wrapped in a linen cloth and hidden away and later brought back to the father. The Messiah was broken for us. He was wrapped in a linen cloth and hidden away in the tomb until the third day when He was resurrected and brought back to the Father. The symbolism is very clear and powerful when we see the whole picture.

Before we eat a piece of matzah we say the blessing "Baruch atah Adonai Elohenu melech ha-olam ha-motsi le-chem min ha-aretz—Blessed are you O' Lord our God, King of the universe, who brings forth bread from the earth."

Second Question—bitter herbs, maror: Why is this night different from all other nights? On all other nights we eat any kind of herbs. Why on this night do we eat only bitter herbs?

The bitter herbs remind us of the bitterness of slavery. We eat the bitter herb by taking a piece of matzah and dipping it into horseradish.

Third question—dip twice: Why is this night different from all other nights? On all other nights we do not dip even once. Why on this night do we dip twice?

We dip twice because the second time we dip into the horseradish we also dip into the kharoset, a sweet mixture of apples, walnuts, and grape juice. The kharoset looks like the mortar and reminds us of the bricks we had to make for the Pharaoh in Egypt. This symbolizes how even though our slavery was a bitter experience for us it was made sweet knowing our God was going to deliver us and give us our own land.

Two thousand years ago when Y'shua was celebrating the Passover with His friends He held up this piece of matzah and said. "He who dips his hand with me in the dish, the same will betray me." If you have ever read that sentence in the gospels you may have wondered what He was dipping into. It wasn't tortilla chips in salsa, or Italian bread and tomato sauce. It wasn't even matzah ball soup. It was this very dish of horseradish and kharoset, this very one that during the Passover we ask why do we dip our bread.

Y'shua didn't just make up this dipping incident on the spot. No, He knew this part of the Passover service was coming next and He used it to teach an important lesson. Y'shua knew that one of His followers, Judas, was plotting to betray Him. Basically Y'shua was saying to Judas: "Judas, you are a very bitter person. Your life is filled with jealously, greed, selfishness, and dissatisfaction. But, Judas, I want you to know I can make your bitter life sweet if you will just let Me cover your bitterness with My sweetness just like the kharoset does to the horseradish."

By this illustration Y'shua was also saying, "Judas, in just a few hours you are going to cause me to go through a very hard bitter experience, but I want you to know that, as is prophesied in the Hebrew Scriptures, through My suffering the lives of many will be made sweet and righteous."

After Y'shua said that one of them at the table was going to betray Him a very interesting dialog took place. The followers began to ask, "Is it I? Will I be the one to betray You?" One might expect if someone says there is a betrayer in the group, that everyone will start pointing fingers. But on the contrary they did some soul searching introspection regarding themselves and asked, "Is it I?" "Is there something in my character that would cause me to fall, that would cause me to betray You?" That is a very good prayer for each of us to ask God. "Adonai, have I been betraying you by denying you? Is there bitterness or anger in my heart? Is there some unknown sin in my life? And if so, forgive me and cleanse me of it." For those who are struggling with bitterness, anger, resentment, and depression, as you think of this double dipped mixture, ask God to remove those feelings from your heart and fill you with His sweetness.

Fourth question—reclining: Why is this night different from all other nights? On all other nights we sit upright. Why on this night do we sit reclining?

During the first Passover in Egypt we were commanded by God to eat standing in preparation to flee Egypt at a moment's notice. Now we are free so we recline, proclaiming our freedom.

Not only does the account of the Passover that Y'shua had with His disciples mention matzah, juice, and dipping matzah, it also mentions reclining.

6. THE ULTIMATE PASSOVER

Today, as we invite Y'shua into our lives we have peace in our hearts. Being free in Y'shua we can rest, recline, in God's love and in His plans for our lives. If you are worried, fearful, nervous, stressed out, I encourage you to enter into Elohim's rest right now. Recline in His arms, trust in Him, give all your cares to Him because He cares for you. He loves you and He will give you peace, rest, shalom, as you give your problems to Him and trust in Him. Since we can experience that peace right now as we give our lives to Y'shua, doesn't it make sense to give your life to Him right now?

Passover story: At modern Passovers today, just before the supper, the life of Moses and the deliverance of our people out of Egypt are recounted. We saw in lesson four of this series how Moses' life as our deliverer foreshadowed the life of our Messiah our Ultimate Deliverer.

As the ten plagues are recounted we dip our fingers in our grape juice and then place a drop of grape juice onto our plates. One dip and one drop for each of the ten plagues. The ten plagues were: blood, frogs, lice, insects, diseased cattle, boils, hail, locusts, darkness, death of firstborn.

Lamb shank bone: The shank bone on the Passover plate is very important as it reminds us of the Passover lamb which we ate on our last night in Egypt and whose blood upon our doorposts saved us from the angel of death.

Before the tenth plague all the Israelites were commanded to take a lamb without blemish and to kill it and take its blood and spread it on the doorposts of their homes with the hyssop so that when the angel of death would come that night he would *"pass over"* the homes and would not kill the first born of the home.

If you were a first-born child on that fateful night and you overheard that Moses said blood of lambs had to be put on your doorpost to save the first born from the angel of death, what do you think you would say to your father when he came home? You would probably say something like, "Dad I got the lamb all ready." What if your father said, "That's nice, but we are a good family and God knows that. We have a mezuzah on the door. The angel of death will see that. He will know we are Jewish and you will be fine. Don't worry." You would still insist that as good as your family is it is not enough. Correct? What if your father said, "You are right. Moses did say lambs. But do you know how expensive they are? I got this nice pig from one of the Egyptians; it will work just as well. Blood is blood; the angel won't know the difference. Don't worry. There are many ways to be saved." Would you go for that? Certainly not! God said lambs for a reason. How insistent would you be to make sure your father did it exactly as God commanded? I know I would be very insistent to do things the way Adonai said if it was my life that was on the line that first Passover night.

The fact that God says what He means and means what He says brings up some interesting questions. Why did God say blood of a lamb? Why not just some grape juice? Why not just a mezuzah? From the very beginning of sin God has used a lamb as a substitute offering for our sin. Elohim made clothing for Adam and Eve from the first lamb offered. Abel offered up an acceptable sacrifice to God by using a lamb, while Cain was rejected because he did not use the blood of a lamb. God provided Abraham a ram as a substitute for Isaac, and in the Sanctuary service God commanded Moses and Aaron to use a lamb for the sacrifices for the forgiveness of sins. Moses wrote that *"the life of the flesh is in the blood, and I have assigned it to you for making expiation for your lives upon the altar; it is the blood, as life, that effects expiation."* Leviticus 17:11. Mitzvahs wouldn't do it; all the good deeds in the world won't do it. It is only through the shedding of blood of the prescribed sacrificial animal that forgiveness is received. The Jewish prophet Isaiah, in chapter 53, described the Messiah as coming as a lamb for the slaughter. While the shank bone on the Passover plate represents the lambs slain that Passover night it also foreshadowed that the Messiah would die on Passover as a lamb for us. The Messiah is represented in the matzah and He is also represented in the shank bone of the lamb.

Let's say your father was following what Moses said. Let's say he was using lamb's blood to cover your doorpost. I'd imagine you would still be standing by his side saying, "Dad did Moses say how much blood to use? I don't think that is enough blood Dad. I think we should put more on there. Look you missed a spot." You might say, "Dad, I was thinking that after we finish the front door we should do the back door also. And you know it would not hurt to do the windows as well. Maybe even the roof. It would probably look good in red, don't you think?" At least that is what I would be saying. If Adonai said to your father that you would die if there was not blood of a lamb on the doorpost you would want to make sure there was a lot of blood there

6. THE ULTIMATE PASSOVER

wouldn't you? A little bit of following God is not enough. We need more than just a couple of hours a week at services. We need God every day, every hour, every minute. We need His love, power, forgiveness, and grace, covering our front door, our back door, and every aspect of our lives. When it comes to God, don't settle for less.

Here is another thought for you to contemplate as we speak about the children of Israel putting the blood of lambs on their doorposts. What do you think would have happened to an Egyptian first-born child if the Egyptian family believed what Elohim said and put the blood of the lambs upon their doorposts? That is right, the angel of death would have passed over their home as well. God is no respecter of persons; He loves the Egyptians as much as He loves the Jewish people. Even as we think about the ten plagues we should view them as messages of love to the Jewish people as well as to the Egyptians. If God just wanted to bring punishment upon the Egyptians it would not have taken ten plagues to do it. God could have wiped them all out in one shot. But He didn't. He first sent nine somewhat solemn warnings to wake them up. Actually, all the plagues were about the gods of the Egyptians as we read in Exodus 12. The Egyptians worshiped the Nile, they worshiped the frogs, etc. Adonai was bringing judgment upon the things the Egyptians were worshiping to show them that He is the Only true God, the Creator of all things. Our God is a God of love; He does not desire that any should perish. That is why in mercy he sent nine plagues before anyone died. It is also why He has called us together right now, so He could speak to your heart and draw you to Himself. Do not resist His love. Accept Him into your heart and life right now. Right now invite Elohim to cover your home, your life, with the blood of the lamb, the Messiah. Ask God to forgive your mistakes, and to protect you and your family. Give God permission to be the LORD of your life.

Regarding the Passover lamb Moses commanded that none of its bones were to be broken and that none of it should remain until morning. When Y'shua was killed the Roman soldiers broke the bones of the two other men He was killed with to hasten their deaths so that their dying bodies would not remain until the morning. When they came to Y'shua to break His bones they saw that He was already dead so they did not break His bones. He was taken down that evening and buried before the day ended, just as was instructed regarding the Passover lamb, that none of its bones be broken and that it not remain until morning.

Dayenu: This is a song that goes through several choruses saying it would have been enough if God had brought us out of Egypt but did not execute judgments on the Egyptian gods. It would have been enough if He had executed judgments on the Egyptian gods but had not given us their spoils, etc. Adonai does much more for us than we deserve. He is always going beyond what is enough. We have an extremely loving, merciful God.

Second cup—the cup of judgment: The cup of judgment reminds us of the Red Sea closing in on the Egyptians, as well as the coming judgment on the world when God will destroy all who refuse His love.

Afikomen: While the family is eating supper the father hides the afikomen, the half piece of matzah from the middle of the matzah tosh that was wrapped in a linen cloth. The children look for the afikomen and when they find it the father "buys" it back from them with a gift or a coin. The father then breaks it into pieces and distributes it to everyone at the Seder.

The afikomen is unleavened matzah. It is striped, it is pierced, it looks like it has bruises on it. It is the piece of matzah that is taken from the middle of the matzah tosh and is broken. It is wrapped in a linen cloth and has been hidden away and has been brought back to the father. The afikomen beautifully and fully illustrates the life, death, and resurrection of Y'shua the Messiah who was without sin, was whipped, bruised, pierced, broken, wrapped in linen, and hidden away until He was brought back to the Father, who has bought us our salvation with the sacrifice of His Son.

During that Passover 2,000 years ago Y'shua held up this piece of matzah, the striped, bruised, pierced, broken piece, wrapped in linen, hidden away, the afikomen and said, "This is my body which is given for you: this do in remembrance of me. Take, eat." It was as if He was saying; "I am the afikomen. I was in the matzah tosh with the other two pieces of unleavened bread. I will be given over to the Romans who are going to whip me and put deep stripes into my flesh. I will be beaten and bruised. They will pierce My hands and My feet. My heart will be broken, and I will be wrapped in linen and hidden away for a time, but then I will be brought back to the Father and share with all who will invite Me into their lives." There is wonderful,

6. THE ULTIMATE PASSOVER

powerful meaning regarding the afikomen as we understand it as it applies to the Messiah. Just as the afikomen is eaten and digested we need to invite the Messiah into our hearts and allow Him to become a part of our lives.

Third cup—cup of redemption: Our God redeemed us, saved us, from Egypt, from bondage. We could not escape in our own strength or power, but only by His might and grace.

At the last supper Y'shua raised this third cup and said, "Drink ye all of it. This cup is the new covenant in my blood, which is shed for many for the remission of sins."

Elijah: At modern Passover Seders an empty seat is reserved for Elijah because the Jewish prophet Malachi prophesied saying, *"Lo, I will send the prophet Elijah to you before the coming of the awesome, fearful day of the LORD."* Malachi 3:23. The mother opens the front door of the home to invite Elijah to come in.

There is a Jewish song about Elijah coming before the Messiah. This song has been sung for thousands of years. The song is called Eliyaho Hanavi. The English translation is: Elijah the prophet, Elijah the Tishbite, Elijah from Gilead. Soon may he come, bringing with him Messiah son of David.

The disciples asked Y'shua about Elijah and Y'shua informed them that John the Immerser had the message and the spirit of Elijah and had prepared the way for Him to come. Today Elohim is filling those who believe in Him with the spirit of Elijah and has given us a message to warn the world that the Messiah is coming again, not as a meek lamb to be sacrificed, but this time as the judge, to judge the world.

It will be an awesome day of deliverance for those who have given their lives to God. It will be a fearful day of judgment for all those who resist God's love. It will be very similar to the deliverance, the plagues, and the judgment that took place when God took us out of the land of Egypt.

Fourth cup—cup of praise: We can praise God because He has saved us from the bondages of sin by giving us the Messiah.

At the end of the Seder we read Psalms 115-118 referred to as the Hallel. As is done today at Passovers around the world, it was also done in that last supper Passover 2,000 years ago. The gospel account says that after the supper they sang a song and went out. That song was the Hallel from Psalms

115-118. Let's read a few of the famous verses from the Hallel, such as "This is the day that the LORD has made; let us be glad and rejoice in it." Another one is "blessed be He who comes in the name of the LORD." This verse is also traditionally said at weddings when the bride comes to meet the groom. Y'shua said this text would be proclaimed regarding Himself just before He comes again, and here we are 2,000 years later fulfilling this prophecy. Another text reads, "The LORD has become our Salvation." Y'shua's name comes from the Hebrew word salvation.

And lastly, "The stone that the builders have rejected has become the chief corner stone." This has miraculously been fulfilled in the life of Y'shua. Thousands of Jewish people accepted Him as the Messiah, even many of the Levites, Cohanim, and other leaders. Some estimate from 25% to 50% of the population around Jerusalem accepted Him as the Messiah. Unfortunately, many of the leaders of Israel at that time, the builders, rejected Him, yet He has become the cornerstone of the most widespread religion in the world. Most countries throughout the world have their calendars, historical textbooks, and dates on their newspapers based on the dates of His life. He certainly has become, as King David prophesied regarding Him and Rabbi Paul called Him, the Chief Cornerstone. You can make Him the cornerstone of your life right now. You can let Him be the foundation, the rock you can rely on and lean on. Invite Y'shua the Messiah, the Passover lamb, the Passover matzah, the Passover afikomen, to be your Messiah, to be your Foundation Stone, your Rock, your Chief Cornerstone, so that you may say with King David, "Blessed is He who comes in the name of the LORD," and be glad and rejoice in this day that salvation has come into your life.

We traditionally say, "Next Year in Jerusalem." Even better than that, let us pray for the fulfillment of what the Jewish prophet Isaiah called the new heavens and the new earth. And so by faith we can say, "Next year in the New Jerusalem."

REVIEW הזרה

1. Y'shua's last supper was . . .
    a. A birthday party.
    b. A Christmas party.

6. THE ULTIMATE PASSOVER

    c. A Passover Seder.

2. What did Elohim require to be placed on the doorposts of the homes in order for the angel of death to "pass over" the home?
    a. A mezuzah.
    b. Blood of a lamb.
    c. Anything red.

3. Y'shua was striped, bruised, pierced, broken, wrapped in linen, and hidden away just like . . .
    a. The juice.
    b. The bitter herb.
    c. The afikomen matzah.

4. Lambs being killed during the Passover in Egypt foreshadowed . . .
    a. The Messiah being killed as an innocent lamb on Passover.
    b. The destruction of the earth.
    c. The popularity of lamb chops.

5. Y'shua used the dipping of the matzah in the bitter horseradish and the sweet kharoset together to symbolize?
    a. That God can make our bitter experiences sweet.
    b. That Judas would be the one to betray Him and that He could change Judas' bitter heart and make it sweet.
    c. That because of Y'shua's bitter experience dying for us our lives are made sweet through His salvation for us.
    d. All of the above.

6. I want the Messiah's death to cover the doorpost of my heart and home to save and protect me from sin.
    a. Yes.
    b. I still have some questions I want answered before I decide.

If you answered "b" to the last question continue on to the next lesson while praying for God to reveal His truth to you. I believe you will find the next lesson very interesting. You may pray for guidance in any way you feel comfortable, but we offer this sample prayer if you would like to make use of it. "LORD God, King of the Universe, God of Abraham, Isaac, and Jacob, reveal Yourself to me. If Y'shua is the Messiah I need to know. If not, I want to know. Give me Your wisdom and insight. Speak to my heart and mind as I continue to search Your Scriptures. Amen."

If you answered "Yes" to the last question—Mazel Tov! For the rest of your life the Passover and all the ceremonies will take on a deeper meaning for you than ever before. I would like to invite you to say a prayer to Adonai. You can say this sample prayer or you can say your own prayer in your own words. "LORD God, King of the Universe, I thank You for Your love for me. I thank You for the wonderful truths I have been learning from Your Word. Guide me and direct my paths. Hear my prayer. Speak to my heart. I want to receive forgiveness for my mistakes. I want my life sealed in Your hands. I want the angel of death to pass me by. I want to receive Your gift of eternal life. I accept Your forgiveness because of the death of the Messiah as my Passover lamb. Thank You for forgiving me and loving me. Come into my heart and life. In Y'shua's name, amen."

The Ultimate Passover has been filmed on location in Israel and Egypt. It is available for you to see and experience today. The DVD includes many extras, such as musical accompaniment played by Bill Whitman, a printable haggada, recipes, Passover jokes, and much more. You can order *The Ulimate Passover* at http://www.jewishheritage.net/

TRADITIONS

Tu B'Shevat

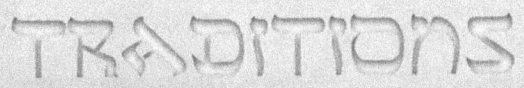

Tu'B Shevat is the 15th day of the Hebrew month of Shevat. Tu'B Shevat is when we celebrate the New Year for the trees. It is a Jewish Arbor Day and comes just at the end of the winter rainy season in Israel, which correlates to some time near February.

Trees play an important role in Jewish history. Trees are mentioned throughout the Bible, including the tree of life, the tree of the knowledge of good and evil, willow, olive, cedar, cypress, palm, fig, and many others. Although the land of Israel was very barren in 1948 when modern Israel became a nation, today it produces everything from apples to dates, including many varieties of citrus, peaches, apricots, bananas, avocados, persimmons, grapes, almonds, and many varieties of melons, to name a few. Tu'B Shevat is celebrated by planting trees and the eating of the fruit of trees.

JEWISH HERITAGE SCRIPTURE STUDIES

7

A NICE JEWISH BOY

7. A NICE JEWISH BOY

How can a nice Jewish boy from N.Y. believe that Y'shua is the Messiah? Only Elohim knows the whole story.

I grew up with my parents and two brothers in a happy Jewish home, with grandparents close by. Around the time I entered Hebrew school to prepare for my bar mitzvah I began to earnestly question whether God was real. My grandfather told me that he had an orthodox upbringing, but I could not see how it had affected his life in a positive way. Although loving and caring, he did not seem to be any different, or any more "godly" than anyone else I knew who did not claim to grow up with a religious background. It did not appear that God had deeply impacted his life. At the Hebrew school I attended I did not see anything in the lives of the teachers or rabbis that I desired. Other than their dress they did not appear to be any different from other teachers I had come in contact with. When I asked questions about the reality of God, I never received any answers that satisfied my search. The teachers seemed impatient with my questions and their answers came across as empty and without practical meaning. I was unhappy with the world around me and with the feelings inside me, and the religious people in my life were not leading me closer to Adonai.

I did not view myself as being particularly bad, but yet, at the same time I knew there were undesirable habits and traits in my character that I just could not seem to change. I would pray, almost defiantly, to God that if He was real to prove it to me. Over the years I occasionally came in contact with Christians. I enjoyed arguing with them, debating with them, and mocking their beliefs.

When I was in college my mother, Linda Brother, came in contact with some people at a Community Services Center in NYC operated by Seventh-day Adventists. They helped her through a situation she was going through and they told her that Jesus was prophesied in the Hebrew Scriptures as the Jewish Messiah. This bothered me, even to the point of determining to prove them wrong. I decided to read through the Torah (the books of Moses) and the rest of the T'nach (Jewish Bible). Elohim impressed me to read at least a little in the morning and a little before I went to sleep. The more I read the more I prayed. The more I prayed and read the more God revealed Himself to me through changes He was making in my life, giving me victory over boredom, discontentment, anger, lust, dishonesty, deceit, and insecurity. For the first time in my life God became real to me. He was no longer just a God of history or Judaism, just a dry religion of books and traditions. Adonai was revealing Himself to me through reading His words and through His created nature all around me. Life was alive with new meaning and purpose. God was real; He cared about this world, about humanity, and about me. He had a purpose for this world and a purpose for me. I was excited about reading God's word and talking with Him. Although I was still disturbed with the things my mother had learned and was sharing with me, I had not yet found anything in the Scriptures to prove her wrong.

As I read through the book of Deuteronomy, written by Moses, I noticed that God made a promise saying, ***"I will raise up a prophet for them from among their own people, like yourself: I will put My words in his mouth and he will speak to them all that I command him."*** (Chapter 18, verse 18). Proverbs chapter 30 verse 4 caught my eye, ***"Who has established all the extremities of the earth? What is his name or his son's name, if you know it?"*** I wondered and prayed, "God, what are you saying here. I really want to know. Who is the prophet like Moses? What do you mean about the Creator having a Son?" One time in particular I was driving down the road and saw a billboard that said, "Jesus is the Lord." This frustrated me to no end. I pulled off to the side of the road and cried out to God as I banged on the steering wheel, "God if this is not true, prove it wrong."

My search continued for several months. Every morning and every night I read the Bible and prayed. Page by page I was working my way through the Scriptures. Several times through the day I would talk to God as I went about my routine. When Elohim led me to read what the Jewish prophet Isaiah wrote in the book of Isaiah chapter 53, it was light shining down from Heaven. Right there in the Hebrew Scriptures it said; ***He was maltreated, yet He was submissive, He did not open his mouth; like a sheep being led to slaughter . . . He was cut off from the land of the living through the sin of my people, who de-***

*served the punishment. And His grave was set among the wicked... Though he had done no injustice... But the L*ORD *chose to crush Him... That, if He made himself an offering for guilt, He might see offspring and have long life, and that through Him the L*ORD*'s purpose might prosper. My Righteous Servant makes the many righteous, it is their punishment that he bears..."* verses 7-11.

God's Righteous Servant had to die as the lamb sacrificed for my sins! Mine! Everything began to make sense. Cain and Abel's sacrifice made sense. The sacrifices mentioned in the Torah made sense. The Sanctuary service described in the Torah made sense.

I rejoiced as the old familiar events that I learned in Hebrew school and that I had read in the Bible came to light. Abel's sacrifice was accepted and Cain's was not because Abel had a lamb to offer, a substitute, a blood sacrifice. Cain brought only fruit, no blood sacrifice. The fruit could not be slaughtered, could not bear his sins. God tested Abraham by asking him to sacrifice his son. Isaac did not have to be sacrificed because God Himself provided a sacrifice, a ram, which could be slaughtered, could shed blood, and could take his place. The blood of lambs associated with holy days all started to make sense. The reason for the blood of the lambs on the doorposts during Passover fit into place.

This was the answer to my longing, the answer to my questions. Although I thought I was basically good, I was still carrying around guilt for all my shortcomings and mistakes. From these passages I found that I had been forgiven and was released from all the guilt. I understood that God was going to send us a Jewish prophet who would be God's Son and that He would die as the sacrificial lamb for my sins. I had not known much about Y'shua other than that He was a Jewish person, that He died on a cross, and that Christians said that He died for their sins. It all came together; Y'shua is the lamb of the Jewish sacrificial offerings.

In the Jewish Sanctuary services set up during the time of Moses, people had to bring lambs to be sacrificed so that they could receive forgiveness for their sins. They would lay their hands upon the lamb, confess their sins, and symbolically the sins would be transferred to the lamb. The person would then kill his lamb. The lamb's body was burned on the altar and the blood was poured out at the base of the altar. This was the process whereby sins were removed from the people. All of this represented the work of the Messiah, God's Righteous Servant coming to die for our sins.

After reading the Hebrew Scriptures I had fears about reading the Gospels, the books that record the life of Y'shua. I was happy to find that He lived as a Jew and died as a Jew. He kept the laws of the Torah. It was His regular custom to be at services in the synagogue on Shabbat; He ate only biblically kosher foods, observed the holy days, and showed deep respect for His mother. He was a Jew through and through.

I knew in my heart that all my good deeds, all my mitzvot, could not wipe away my past sins. I needed to have my guilt removed; I needed a substitute; and I needed a blood sacrifice. And Y'shua was the one God gave to do these very things. I needed an experience like King David prayed for in Psalm 51: *"Wash me thoroughly of my iniquity, and purify me of my sin . . . Purge me with hyssop till I am pure; wash me till I am whiter than snow . . . Fashion a pure heart for me, O God; create in me a steadfast spirit."* Verses 4, 9, 12. Isaiah chapter 53, verse 6 explained it all. *"And the LORD visited upon him the guilt of all of us."*

I began to understand how all my sinful thought patterns, all my sinful habits could be taken away from me and laid on the Lamb of God, Y'shua the Messiah. What release, what joy, what freedom! The weight of guilt was removed. The feeling I had cannot be described, only experienced. Not only had Y'shua taken the record of my bad actions, motives, and intentions away, but He also had taken upon Himself all the pain and hurt that I had experienced from other people. This released me to be able to forgive those who had wronged me. As I thought of how willingly He had forgiven me for the sins I had committed against Him, it set me free to forgive those who had sinned against me. This was the biggest breakthrough in my life. Through God's power I now had the ability to forgive others and to forgive myself. This caused a great healing in my own mind and in my relationships.

At that time I realized I had forgiveness and freedom from past wrongs, and I also realized I needed a power other than myself to keep me from sinning. I was in full agreement with King David as I prayed for God to *"renew in me a right Spirit."* God also revealed this aspect of the Messiah's role in Isaiah chapter 53, verse 10, *"if he made himself an offering for guilt, He might see*

7. A NICE JEWISH BOY

offspring and have long life." After He died as an offering for my sins He was raised from the dead and had long life. Y'shua is alive, and is working in my behalf in the Sanctuary in Heaven. Because He is alive He is able to give me His power to obey. If this was just dry theory it might not mean much, but what I am saying here I have experienced, and it can be experienced by everyone. Y'shua has never let me down when I have asked Him to give me His power to obey, His power to forgive, His power to desire what is good and right and to resist what is wrong. He lived on this earth as a human, so He can relate to my needs. He is now seated at the right hand of God in Heaven making intercession for me. I am not perfect, but God is not done with me yet. He is continuing to change me back into His image, the one that He originally created humanity with.

All of the joy and liberation that I experienced did not come without some sacrifice and pain. Some of my family members and friends thought I was meshugah, (crazy). They were alarmed and tried to persuade me not to follow what I had found in the Scriptures. Some just thought it was a phase I was going through and that it would pass. As I drew nearer and nearer to God my desires for a number of the activities, conversations, and pastimes that I was involved in changed. These changes did affect some of the friendships I had with the people who I associated with who continued to practice the lifestyle that was no longer appealing to me. In the long run God has worked all things out for good. God has replaced the negative habits and lifestyles with truer, more fulfilling, and more purposeful ones. Over the many years since I accepted the Messiah into my heart my friends and family have seen the positive impact it has had on my life. God has more than abundantly replaced the old friends with truer and closer friendships. I have been able to keep in contact with some of the old friends who were willing to accept the changes God was making in my life.

Am I still a Jew? Most certainly. I am a Jew who has found the Jewish Messiah! Today I feel more Jewish than I ever did before. I am very thankful for the Jewish culture and my Jewish heritage. Today Judaism has more meaning to me than ever before. It is fuller, deeper, more practical, and more complete. I am able to follow the laws of God associated with Judaism more fully now than ever because it is not me trying to keep God's laws, it is now God working through me to keep His laws. Walking God's path is no longer a burden, it is a joy.

If you want to experience the joy of having your sins forgiven, accept Y'shua and His promise of forgiveness. If you want the power that sin has exerted over your life removed, accept Y'shua's death as your substitue. If you want to gain full victory over wrong habits, thoughts, motives, desires, and actions, accept Y'shua and His power. If you want to be able to forgive those who have hurt you, accept Y'shua and His love. If you want to have freedom from anger or sorrow and want to be filled with joy and peace instead, then accept Y'shua and His plan for your life. You can bow your head and talk to Him about it right now. Your prayer can be something like this: "Lord God, King of the Universe, God of Abraham, Isaac, and Jacob, I invite You to make Yourself real to me. Reveal Your truth, Your love, and Your plan for me. Reach down and touch my heart. My ears are open to know Your truth regarding the Messiah. I want You to guide me and direct me in Your paths. I need Your peace, Your forgiveness, Your mercy, and Your power. Come into my life and live out Your life in me and through me and for me. For Your honor and Your glory, in Your Holy Name. Amen."

Why does a nice Jewish boy from N.Y. believe that Y'shua is the Jewish Messiah? Read the Hebrew Scriptures from beginning to end, praying every day for God to lead you to the truth and you will know for yourself!

Jeff Zaremsky

TRADITIONS

Bar Mitzvah

When a young boy reaches the age of thirteen he is termed a bar mitzvah, which literally means a son of commandments or son of good deeds. For girls the term is bat mitzvah. It is at this age that the child is considered old enough to start taking part in the worship service. According to Jewish custom the parents are accountable before God for the actions of the child up to this time. But at the age of 13 children are considered old enough to answer for themselves before God in the Day of Judgment.

Traditionally on the Shabbat preceding the 13th birthday the child is called to stand in front of the congregation and read from the Torah as well as a portion from the Jewish prophets, also known as the haftarah. It was at around this age that the Messiah Y'shua went to the Temple in Jerusalem for the first time in His life.

It is good for young children to learn to be involved in the public worship service and to take responsibility for their actions. Parents with young children should realize the sacred responsibility of teaching and training their children to love and follow God with all their hearts, souls, and minds. As we teach the Scriptures and are loving examples when our children are young, as they mature they are much more likely to be so filled with God's presence that they can truly be called sons and daughters of good deeds, a bar and bat mitzvah. As King Solomon said, *"Train a lad in the way he ought to go; he will not swerve from it even in old age."* Proverbs 22:6

8. MOSES (MOSHE) AND THE 10 COMMANDMENTS

When the children of Israel wandered in the wilderness they lived in tents. Today we have steel doors and bolt locks. Why is that? Well, you say, it's because of the increase in crime. But why the increase? Why is there so much crime? It seems that people are becoming criminals at increasingly younger ages.

Society is constantly changing its moral standards. People are wearing, saying, doing, hearing, and seeing things today that would have alarmed us ten or twenty years ago. Is this good, normal or natural? Is this God's plan? What will society's standards be for future generations? Does God have standards? Are these rules stable and everlasting? Do they transcend generations, cultures, races, and nationalities? Is there one law that allows us to be individuals, yet which also binds us together, unifying us with Heaven's plan?

When we talk about rules, some people get very uncomfortable. It's a bit like taking your little sister to a party with you. Who wants to have someone looking over their shoulder to see if they're doing anything wrong? What they forget is that only when there are rules—laws, if you please—is our community a safe place to live. As we study today we will discover that God's finger wrote freedom. The greatest system of law in the history of the human race came through our people. We will see that Elohim's laws are not laws of restriction but of liberation. Elohim is not watching over our shoulder to see if we are doing anything wrong, He is living within us empowering us to do it right.

One thing that uniquely established the Jewish nation in its beginning and has helped keep it unique is the fact that God Himself directly gave us His laws to follow, but they are not just for the Jewish people. Today we will see for ourselves what the Judge of all the earth considers right and wrong. We will find His loving, divine plan for our lives! We will also find out how these laws are really laws of love, designed to benefit us.

1. How did King David feel about God's Torah?

   Happy are those who observe His decrees, who turn to Him

<u>wholeheartedly</u> . . . Would that my ways were firm in keeping Your laws; then I would not be ashamed when I regard all Your commandments . . . <u>I have turned to You with all my heart; do not let me stray from Your commandments</u> . . . Blessed are You, O L<small>ORD</small>; <u>train me in Your laws</u> . . . <u>I eagerly pursue Your commandments</u>, You broaden my understanding. <u>Teach me, O L<small>ORD</small>, the way of Your laws</u>; I will observe them to the utmost . . . <u>Lead me in the path of Your commandments, for that is my concern</u> . . . <u>I will delight in Your commandments, which I love</u> . . . <u>Your laws are a source of strength to me wherever I may dwell.</u> Psalm 119:2, 5, 6, 10, 12, 32, 33, 35, 47, and 54

Did you notice the words King David used regarding God's law, His Torah, showing how he felt about it and how it made him feel? King David used terms such as: eagerly pursue, teach me, lead me, happy, delight, love, source of strength. Are these the terms you have usually thought of when you have thought of Elohim's law, His Torah? If not, maybe we need to re-think our attitude toward God's Torah.

2. What were some of the many other things King David said about God's teachings and instructions?

The teaching of the L<small>ORD</small> is <u>perfect</u>, <u>renewing life</u>; the decrees of the L<small>ORD</small> are <u>enduring</u>, making the simple wise; The precepts of the L<small>ORD</small> are <u>just</u>, <u>rejoicing the heart</u>; the instruction of the L<small>ORD</small> is lucid, <u>making the eyes light up</u>. The fear of the L<small>ORD</small> is <u>pure</u>, <u>abiding forever</u>; the judgments of the L<small>ORD</small> are <u>true</u>, <u>righteous</u> altogether, <u>more desirable than gold</u>, than much fine gold; <u>sweeter than honey</u>, than drippings of the comb. Psalm 19:8-11

Wow! The L<small>ORD</small>'s teaching must be awesome.

3. How did Moses feel about the commandments of the L<small>ORD</small>?

Observe them faithfully, for that will be proof of your wisdom and discernment to other peoples, who on hearing of all these laws will say, "Surely, that great nation is a wise and discerning people." For what great nation is there that has a god so close at hand as is the L<small>ORD</small> our God whenever we call upon Him? Or what great nation has laws and rules as perfect as all this Teaching that I set before you this day? Deuteronomy 4:6-8

How different that is from the way our society today usually feels about rules and laws. We usually think of laws and rules as restricting annoyances. But both King David and Moses saw them as sources of wisdom and discernment,

8. MOSES (MOSHE) AND THE 10 COMMANDMENTS

more desirable than gold and sweeter than honey. These men referred to them as the cause of rejoicing and renewing. They felt the laws of Elohim were perfect, righteous, and pure and would make them the envy of other nations. We would be better off if we had their outlook towards God's laws, teachings, rules, and instructions. As you read this lesson pray that God gives you a godly outlook towards God's word just as David and Moses had.

4. The Ten Commandments are written in the Torah. Who wrote the Ten Commandments? On what did He write them, showing their everlasting validity?

<u>The Lord</u> spoke to you out of the fire . . . He declared to you the covenant that He commanded you to observe, the Ten Commandments; and <u>He inscribed them on two tablets of stone</u>. Deuteronomy 4: 12, 13

Adonai Himself wrote the Ten Commandments. That point cannot be over-emphasized. These are the only words in all the Torah that God wrote Himself. There are only four other words in the entire Bible that God Himself wrote. (Those four words are found in the book of Daniel chapter 5). These commandments must be very special and very important if God felt He needed to write them Himself. Not only are they so important that He wrote them Himself, they are so important that He wrote them in stone. Sometimes, when an agreement is not binding people will say "well, it's not written in stone." God's Ten Commandments were written in stone; they are binding, they are eternal. What God writes does not change because God does not change. *"For I am the Lord—I have not changed . . ."* (Malachi 3:6). It is popular today to abbreviate God's Ten Commandments, but Moses warned us, *"You shall not add anything to what I command you or take anything away from it, but keep the commandments of the Lord your God that I enjoin upon you."* Deuteronomy 4:2

Many people today say they believe in the Ten Commandments, yet most do not know what they are. We may think we are basically good people and are not breaking any of the "big ten," but if we don't know what they are how do we know we are not breaking them? How can we say we believe in something we do not know or do not follow? Do you believe in God's Ten Commandments? Can you quote all ten of them fully, unabbreviated? Are you now following all ten? If you answered no to any of these questions I strongly encourage you to read each one carefully. Ask God to forgive you for where you have fallen short, and ask God to write His laws on your heart and mind, and empower you to follow them.

5. What are these Ten Commandments that Adonai felt were so important that He wrote them with His own finger in stone?

God spoke all these words, saying:
1. *I the LORD am your God who brought you out of the land of Egypt, the house of bondage: You shall have no other gods besides Me.*
2. *You shall not make for yourself a sculptured image, or any likeness of what is in the heavens above, or on the earth below, or in the waters under the earth. You shall not bow down to them or serve them. For I the LORD your God am an impassioned God, visiting the guilt of the parents upon the children, upon the third and upon the fourth generations of those who reject Me, but showing kindness to the thousandth generation of those who love Me and keep My commandments.*
3. *You shall not swear falsely by the name of the LORD your God; for the LORD will not clear one who swears falsely by His name.*
4. *Remember the Sabbath day and keep it holy. Six days you shall labor and do all your work, but the Seventh Day is a Sabbath of the LORD your God: you shall not do any work—you, your son or daughter, your male or female slave, or your cattle, or the stranger who is within your settlements. For in six days the LORD made heaven and earth and sea, and all that is in them, and He rested on the Seventh Day; therefore the LORD blessed the Sabbath day and hallowed it.*
5. *Honor your father and your mother, that you may long endure on the land that the LORD your God is assigning to you.*
6. *You shall not murder.*
7. *You shall not commit adultery.*
8. *You shall not steal.*
9. *You shall not bear false witness against your neighbor.*
10. *You shall not covet your neighbor's house: you shall not covet your neighbor's wife, or his male or female slave, or his ox or his ass, or anything that is your neighbor's...*

When He finished speaking with him on Mount Sinai, He gave Moses the two tablets of the Pact, stone tablets inscribed with the finger of God. Exodus 20:1-14; 31:18

8. MOSES (MOSHE) AND THE 10 COMMANDMENTS

Now that you have read all ten, can you honestly say that all your life you have always faithfully kept all ten? Unless you want to bear false witness you will have to admit like the rest of us that you have not always been faithful in keeping all of God's laws. If we want to define God by our standards we might say, "8 or 9 out of 10 is good enough. God is very loving He won't mind." But if we allow God to define Himself we realize that He means what He says and He says what He means. He did not write them on stone for His own benefit. Fortunately, He is forgiving and even better than that, He allows us to start again and this time with His Spirit to empower us to be able to keep them.

Notice that the Ten Commandments start with the words: *I the LORD am your God who brought you out of the land of Egypt, the house of bondage.* (The abbreviated versions leave out these most important words.) We could not have gotten out of Egypt's bondage without God. He miraculously brought us out. He starts the Ten Commandments with these important words to remind us that we can no more keep the Ten Commandments by ourselves than we could get out of Egypt by ourselves. We were able to get out of Egypt by His power and we can keep the Ten Commandments by His power. It is a miracle that He performs in us that gives us the desire and the power to keep His commandments. What a loving God!

6. In which one of these loving laws did Elohim specifically use the word remember?

   Remember the Sabbath day *and keep it holy.* Exodus 20:8

   Of all ten of the commandments this is the only one in which God specifically used the word "Remember." Maybe it is because it is the one God knew many people would forget. (Sabbath is the English translation of the Hebrew word Shabbat. Throughout this book the two terms will be used interchangeably.)

7. Which day did God give us as the Sabbath day for us to enjoy?

   Six days you shall labor and do all your work, but ***the seventh day is a Sabbath of the LORD your God.*** Exodus 20:10

   God was specific. He did not say any one day in seven. He wrote, in stone, "the seventh day." God says what He means and means what He says. Do you believe that?

8. What privileges does God give us with His Sabbath day?

***Keep it holy** . . . you shall **not do any work**—you, your son or daughter, your male or female slave, or your cattle, or the stranger who is within your settlements.* Exodus 20:10

What a wonderful God! He gives us fifty-two vacation days a year! Some people think keeping God's Sabbath is a burden or work. It is just the opposite—it is rest. How hard is it to rest?

9. Why did God choose the seventh day as the special day for us to delight in with Him?

   *For in six days **the LORD made heaven and earth and sea**, and all that is in them, and He **rested on the seventh day; therefore the Lord blessed the Sabbath day and hallowed it**.* Exodus 20:11

More than any other commandment, the Sabbath commandment tells us why He has a right to be our LORD. It is because He is the Creator. He made us and He knows what is best for us. Like a loving parent He cares for us. Notice that God rested on the Sabbath. It was not because He needed to rest; it was because He wanted to stop what He was doing and spend time with us. What a loving God! That is what the Sabbath is all about, resting in God's love, spending time with Him. It is also a great time to spend enjoying God's love with other people.

10. What did Elohim specifically do regarding the seventh day, which He did not do to any other day of the week?

    ***God blessed the seventh day and declared it holy**, because on it God ceased from all the work of creation that He had done.* Genesis 2:3

The seventh day of the week is the only day in the entire Bible that God blessed and made holy. There is a special blessing in keeping the seventh day holy. Shabbat is not a burden; it is a blessing.

11. When does God's wonderful Sabbath day begin and end?

    All the days of creation start in the evening. (See Genesis 1:5-2:3 *"it was evening and morning . . ."*) Friday sunset ends the 6th day of the week; the Sabbath <u>begins at sunset Friday evening and continues until sunset Saturday evening.</u>

From the beginning God's Sabbath has been from Friday evening until Saturday evening. God does not change and neither does His Sabbath. (The history of how it has come about that some people worship God on Sunday will be covered in a later lesson).

8. MOSES (MOSHE) AND THE 10 COMMANDMENTS

12. According to King Solomon who gets to benefit from Elohim's commandments?

The sum of the matter, when all is said and done: Revere God and observe His commandments! For <u>this applies to all mankind</u>: Ecclesiastes 12:13

What a wonderful God! Not only does He want Jewish people to benefit from His loving laws and mitzvot, He wants all mankind to benefit as well.

God wrote the Ten Commandments on stone for Moses to carry down to the people. But in principle they were in existence from the beginning, in the Garden of Eden. (There was no stealing, killing, coveting, etc. allowed in the Garden of Eden. The Sabbath was also established in the Garden.) The Ten Commandments applied to the parents of mankind in the Garden of Eden and thus apply to all mankind throughout eternity. God never intended for the Jewish people to be the only ones to benefit from His loving, guiding, laws. He wants everyone to be able to benefit from His gift to humanity.

13. How long do we get to profit from God's magnificent Ten Commandments?

For <u>as the new heaven and the new earth which I will make shall endure by My will</u>—declares the L<small>ORD</small>—<u>so shall your seed and your name endure</u> . . . and <u>Sabbath after Sabbath, all flesh shall come to worship Me</u>. Isaiah 66:22,23

Even in Heaven we will be enjoying God's Shabbat. Of course we will not be killing, stealing, coveting, and lying, etc. in Heaven either. God's Ten Commandments are a package; they are one unit. They are ten individual laws but they are really one law, the law of love. As one author put it, "If you have broken one you have broken them all." They can also be summarized in two parts. One part demonstrates our love for Adonai and the other demonstrates our love for others. Keeping the first four commandments is a manifestation of loving God with all our heart, with all our soul, and with all our mind. Keeping the last six commandments is a manifestation of loving our neighbor as ourselves. If we love our neighbor as ourselves we will not kill them, steal from them, covet their stuff, or lie to them. If we love God with all our heart, soul, mind, and strength we will not use His name in vain, put other gods or things before Him, and we will rest with Him on His day of rest. Basically, God's one law of love can be subdivided into two categories with a total of ten applications. The rest of the Bible takes those ten applications and demonstrates how they apply to us.

14. According to King David how many of us have transgressed against God; how many of us have broken His law?

__All have turned bad__, altogether foul; there is none who does good, not even one. Psalm 14:3

No matter how good we are, we have all fallen short of God's ideal. We have all made mistakes and sinned. But there is hope.

15. What should you and I do when we come to realize we have broken one of God's laws?

Then I __acknowledged my sin__ to You; I did not cover up my guilt; I resolved, "I will __confess my transgressions to the__ L<small>ORD</small>," and __You forgave the guilt of my sin__. Psalm 32:5

The first step is knowing Elohim loves you. The second step is confessing where you have fallen short of His ideal for you.

16. In addition to the confession, what is needed to remove the guilt of your sins?

__If any person__ . . . __unwittingly incurs guilt__ by doing any of the things which by the L<small>ORD</small>'s commandments ought not to be done, and he realizes his guilt—or the sin of which he is guilty is brought to his knowledge—__he shall bring a female goat without blemish as his offering for the sin of which he is guilty__. He shall lay his hand upon the head of the sin offering, and the sin offering shall be slaughtered at the place of the burnt offering. The priest shall take with his finger some of its blood and put it on the horns of the altar of burnt offering; and all the rest of its blood he shall pour out at the base of the altar . . . Thus the priest shall make expiation for him, __and he shall be forgiven__. Leviticus. 4:27-31

From the beginning a blood sacrifice was required for the forgiveness of sins. This demonstrated how awful sin is in God's sight. As wonderful as God's law is, it cannot cleanse us from sin. Its purpose is to teach us right from wrong. It is a mirror showing us that we need cleansing. The mirror cannot cleanse; it can only reveal dirt. As the mirror reveals the dirt on our skin it sends us to the soap and water to be cleansed. The same is true with the law. It reveals where we have sinned, which causes us to run to God for cleansing through the Messiah. (Review lesson 5 for more on how to receive God's cleansing).

17. Who is it that willingly became our sacrificial offering, dying for our sins, and granting us forgiveness?

8. MOSES (MOSHE) AND THE 10 COMMANDMENTS

<u>Our benevolent Messiah Y'shua.</u> (See Isaiah 53 and lessons 4-7)

Sin is so horrible it requires a blood sacrifice. But our God is so loving that He provided Himself as the blood sacrifice. He Himself has taken responsibility for the sin problem even though it was not his fault.

18. Do we have the power by ourselves to just start doing what is right?

<u>Who can say, "I have cleansed my heart, I am purged of my sin"? "Can the Cushite change his skin, Or the leopard his spots? Just as much can you do good, Who are practiced in doing evil!"</u> Proverbs 20:9; Jeremiah 13:23

In our own power and strength we cannot change our ways or keep God's laws.

19. After confessing our sin and accepting the Messiah's death for the forgiveness of our sin, how can God give us the power to keep from sinning in the future?

<u>Fashion a pure heart for me, O God; create in me a steadfast spirit. Do not cast me out of Your presence, or take Your holy spirit away from me. Let me again rejoice in Your help; let a vigorous spirit sustain me</u> ... Psalm 51:12-14

<u>I will give you a new heart and put a new spirit into you: I will remove the heart of stone from your body and give you a heart of flesh; and I will put My spirit into you. Thus I will cause you to follow My laws and faithfully to observe My rules.</u> Ezekiel 36:26, 27

It is God who re-creates us. He comes inside us and changes us. He enables us to follow His laws. What a loving God! He gives us His laws for our benefit. He forgives us for where we have fallen short, and then He gives us the power not to make the same mistake again. That forgiveness and that power to overcome are ours for the asking. Why not stop right now and ask Adonai to cleanse you from all past sins and ask Him to give you His Spirit to empower you to faithfully observe His rules?

20. Now with God's Spirit working from within you, what will the results be? How will you view His Torah?

Those who love Your teaching <u>enjoy well being</u> ... O LORD; <u>I observe Your commandments</u> ... and <u>love them greatly</u>. Psalm 119:165-167

King David greatly loved God's commandments. When we have God's

Spirit living in us we will greatly love God's Torah too. As we come to fully know God and His Word we will no longer look at His laws as restricting burdens, but as liberating guides given to us by an all knowing and all loving God. We will then love His teachings and enjoy well being.

21. How often should we ask for God's Spirit?

>   *... I call to You, O L<small>ORD</small>, <u>each day</u>; I stretch out my hands to You.*
> Psalm 88:10

What we have learned here is not a once-for-all-time lesson, but something that we must experience each day.

From as early as Joshua Sink could remember he had a passion for flying. While children typically change occupational dreams a dozen times, Josh was settled from the moment he could walk that one day he would be an airline pilot. He was spellbound as he watched planes take off and land. He would spend hours just watching them soar above the sky. Getting gifts for Josh was easy—anything having to do with planes. While his sister was playing house, he was playing airport. As a young boy his dad arranged for him to see the cockpit during a flight. He was awed by the amount of gauges and controls. Throughout his schooling he was focused on getting his wings. After Josh flew his first solo flight he was determined that nothing was going to stop him from living out his dream to fly others into the heavens above the earth. He had his own private pilot's license even before he had his driver's license. Josh even married a beautiful pilot named Kelly. Almost everything in his life revolved around flying.

His training at a well-known airline company was in high gear, climbing higher and higher into the wild blue yonder, when it all seemed to stop and begin a nosedive into reality. On a Monday afternoon, during the first week of training, the director announced that a very important class was to be held the following Saturday and everyone was required to attend—if anyone missed that class, or any class for that matter, he would be cut from the roster. Before the training had begun Josh had received assurances that there were not going to be any classes on Saturday. Besides his family, there was one thing more important to Josh than flying and that was God. At an early age Josh committed his life to following God. He had more than memorized the Ten Commandments, they were written in his heart. His commitment to God and his love for flying were in line for a head on collision. The week dragged by as thoughts swirled through his head. "How could this happen? Wasn't it God who had been leading all along? Didn't

8. MOSES (MOSHE) AND THE 10 COMMANDMENTS

God open the doors for this training? God is loving and forgiving. He won't mind if I break His Sabbath this once. Besides, the circumstances are out of my control. It is just a class—it is not like it is really working." God's Word was more important to him than anything else. Josh determined that God was first and he would have no other gods before Him, including flying. Josh prayed and prayed throughout the week and sought for ways around this predicament, yet nothing seemed to open up. Five days went by and still Josh did not know what was going to happen, but come what may, God was his pilot, not his co-pilot. He was not going to ask God to follow his lead; he was going to follow God's lead and obey His orders. Friday morning the director of the program showed up to class and announced that the teacher's wife had just gone into premature labor two months before her due date and so there would not be any class on Saturday. Josh didn't know if he should rejoice that God proved faithful to His word, or be concerned for his teacher's wife and child. The director quickly announced that mother and baby were doing fine! The storm clouds had parted and Josh was now prepared for take off.

This was not the last time Josh was faced with a test of his allegiance to God and His commandments. As a commercial airline pilot Josh has seen God open the sky time and time again so that he would not have to work on God's Sabbath, His day of rest. God has promised that He will make possible whatever He commands. As with Moses at the Red Sea, sometimes the waters do not part until the last minute, but God is faithful—He has the steering column. Josh has found that even when there is turbulence during the flight of life, or when storm clouds seem ready to strike him down, God is in control when he allows Him to be the Pilot.

God's 10 commandments are more His responsibility to keep than ours. It is His Spirit that must keep them through us. If we will only allow Him to cleanse us of the sinful habits that keep us from following Him and allow Him to come into our lives and work in us and through us, He will empower us to keep His laws. Look at them as God's 10 promises or guarantees to you and me. Say to Elohim, "You promised me that I will not kill, so take this anger out of my heart and give me love and forgiveness." "You promised me that I would keep the Sabbath day holy, so help me find a job where I can have Sabbaths off." They are God's commandments, promises, guarantees, so hold Him to them! They are for you to enjoy and benefit from. God loves you.

JEWISH DISCOVERIES

REVIEW הזרה

1. Who wrote the Ten Commandments?

    a. Moses.
    b. God.
    c. Abraham.

2. On what material did Adonai write His Ten Commandments to guard against human tampering and to indicate their permanent validity?

    a. Stone.
    b. Papyrus.
    c. Sand.

3. When did people start enjoying the benefits of the Sabbath?

    a. In the Garden of Eden.
    b. When God wrote it on stone.
    c. When the Messiah died.

4. When will the privileges of Sabbath-keeping end?

    a. On Friday night.
    b. When the Messiah died.
    c. It will never stop. We will still be enjoying it in heaven.

5. As I realize that I have broken God's law I can receive forgiveness by:

    a. Performing tashlich, throwing bread in the water.
    b. Confessing my sins to God and accepting the Messiah's death as my sacrifice.
    c. Doing good deeds (Mitzvot) to make up for it.
    d. Giving money to charity.

6. I can allow God to empower me to follow His laws and to faithfully observe them by:

    a. Trying real hard.
    b. Asking Him to put His Spirit within me.
    c. Going to services a lot.

8. MOSES (MOSHE) AND THE 10 COMMANDMENTS

7. God sees His 10 Commandments as:
   a. Burdens that He unjustly allows us to bear.
   b. Impossibilities that He mistakenly gave at one time.
   c. Rules for a specific time in history.
   d. His loving promises and guarantees given to me for my benefit.

8. I choose to accept the Messiah's death for the forgiveness of my past mistakes and to allow Elohim to place His Spirit within me so that He can work from within me to empower me to keep His ways.
   a. Yes.
   b. No

TRADITIONS

Kiddush

Kiddush is from the Hebrew word for holy or sanctify, to set apart as holy. God set the Sabbath apart as holy. Saying the kiddush on Friday evening dates back about 2,500 years.

Shabbat candles are traditionally lit before the Shabbat has begun. Generally, the woman of the home lights the candles and says the candle blessing with her head covered. At least two candles are used, one for the person saying the blessing and one for God. Some families will have a candle for each member of the family. The traditional blessing says: "Baruch atah Adonai Elohenu Melech ha'olam asher kidshanu bemitzvotav vetzivanu l'hadlik ner shel Shabbat." "Blessed are you Adonai our God, King of the universe, who makes us holy with mitzvot and instructs us to kindle the lights of Shabbat."

Juice or wine is held as the kiddush is recited, "Baruch atah Adonai Elohaynu Melech ha'olam borei pri ha-gafen." "Blessed are you Adonai our God, King of the universe, who creates the fruit of the vine."

Notice the blessing is for the fruit of the vine. The picture painted is one of freshness, a gift right out of the Creator's own hand. The Sabbath is a celebration of God's creatorship. It is a memorial of His completed work. It is the weekly anniversary of creation. Thus the Sabbath is brought in with light and with life, with brightness and with joy.

In addition to the light and the juice from the vine there is the bread from the earth. All are symbols of life. You will also notice we are not asking God to bless the food—He already did that when he created it. We are blessing God, or praising God, for giving us such good food.

The hamotzi is the blessing we say for the bread. Hamotzi means "who brings forth." Challah bread is a traditional Sabbath bread. It is an egg bread that is made up of three rolls of dough braided together into one loaf. Generally two loaves are used as a reminder of the miracle of the double portion of manna that God gave to us every Friday when we were wandering in the wilderness after we left Egypt. The Torah tells us that every day, for forty years, manna came down for us to eat. Every day there was only enough for one day and any that was kept over for the next day spoiled before morning. Except on Sabbath. Every Friday a double portion came down which miraculously did not spoil that night. Even though manna came down every day throughout the week, every week, for forty years, manna never came down on the Sabbath.

Even though the manna account is recorded in the Scriptures, the Scriptures do not tell us how to bring in the Sabbath, or that there needs to be a ceremony for bringing in the Sabbath. The Scriptures do not mention the candles, or the Kiddush, or the hamotzi. They are a tradition. A beautiful and tasty tradition I might add.

Shabbat Shalom!

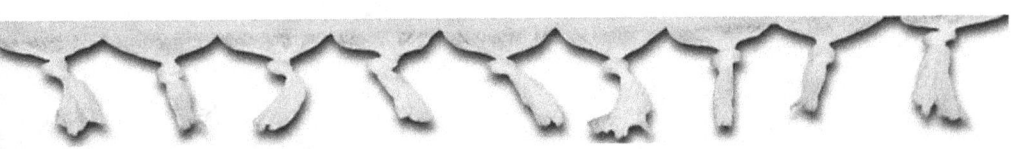

TRADITIONS

Havdallah

Havdallah means "separation" and is a service used to separate the holiness of the Sabbath from the rest of the week. It separates the day that God blessed from the regular workdays of the week. It is also a reminder to us that there is a difference between the holy and the secular. That would include time such as the difference between the Sabbath and the rest of the week, but also the difference between kinds of activities such as the difference between worship and work.

There are also sacred relationships and secular relationships such as the covenant a married couple have with each other in comparison to their relationships with others. There is a difference between the Holy Scriptures and other books. The secular is not automatically bad because it is not sacred. The six non-Sabbath days of the week are good, work is good, friendly relationships outside of marriage are good, etc., but yet they are different from the sacred.

There is also a difference between the commandments of Scripture and traditions—even godly traditions. The havdallah service is a tradition; it is not mentioned in the Scriptures. It is a beautiful service, but it is not commanded by Scripture. The Sabbath is God's sacred, set-apart, holy time. The ceremonies by which we bring in the Sabbath or close the Sabbath are traditions. There is a difference between the two, a difference between the commandments and the traditions. Often history has shown that we humans tend to lose the balance between the sacred and the tradition. We may either throw out the sacred altogether or replace it with ceremonies and traditions. In this book we are seeking to teach both the Scriptures and the traditions of our Jewish Heritage, because both are helpful. We are also attempting to reveal the difference, separation, or havdallah between the two.

Just as we bring in the Sabbath with candles and with a glass of juice from the grape (Many traditions use alcoholic wine; others use grape juice), we also close out the Sabbath in a similar way. The candles are different in the havdallah service. What is done with the juice is different, and there is an added dimension of the spice box. We exit the Sabbath, the final day of Creation, by using our sense of taste, smell, and sight. We taste the juice and smell the herbs and spices that God has created, and we look at the light, the first thing God created. The Sabbath is a memorial to the Creator and thus we bring in the Sabbath and say goodbye to the Sabbath with our senses and reminders of His Creation.

Traditionally the havdallah service does not begin until three stars can be seen in the sky bringing an end to the Sabbath.

The traditional blessing is said over the juice: "Baruch atah Adonai, Elohenu Melech ha'olam, borei p'ri hagafen." "Blessed are You, Adonai our God, Ruler of the universe, Creator of the fruit of the vine."

The juice can represent life. One of the toasts we say as we drink together is L'Chaim—to life. The Torah mentions "Shiloh" coming, a reference to the Messiah (Genesis 49:10), and Him washing His clothes in the blood of the grape. The Torah also says "the life . . . is in the blood" (Lev. 17:11). As the blood on the doorposts in Egypt gave life to the first born on the first Passover, so also the blood the Messiah shed for us gives us eternal life.

A blessing is said over the spice box (a box or jar that is filled with

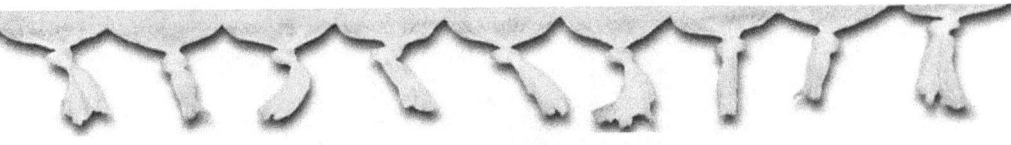

fragrant spices, clover, or herbs: "Baruch atah Adonai, Elohenu Melech ha'olam, borei minei v'samim." "Blessed are You, Adonai our God, Ruler of the universe, Creator of all kinds of spices."

The spices also remind us of our Creator, the giver of life. We sniff the spices and hold the smell in our nostrils not wanting the Sabbath to leave.

A special havdallah candle is lit. The havdallah candle consists of at least two candles woven together or braided together like the challah bread that we use at the start of the Sabbath. "Baruch atah Adonai, Elohenu Melech ha'olam, borei m'orei ha'eish." "Blessed are You, Adonai our God, Ruler of the universe, Creator of the lights of fire."

The braided havdallah candle is a wonderful symbol of unity, of oneness even in plurality, more than one candle braided as one and burning as one. It is a beautiful symbol of the oneness of Elohim. It is a beautiful symbol of the oneness He is wanting us to have with Him, a beautiful symbol of the oneness He wants us to have with each other.

Some of the juice is sipped and then the havdallah candle is extinguished in the juice. As the life of the Messiah was extinguished for a time by His death, the Sabbath light is extinguished by the juice for another week until we light it again and enter into its rest again the following Sabbath.

The song Eliyahu Hanavi is traditionally sung at the close of the Sabbath. This beautiful song, thousands of years old, calls for Elijah the prophet to come soon with the Messiah the son of David.

Eiliyahu hanavi, Eiliyahu hatishbi, Eiliyahu, Eiliyahu, Eiliyahu hagiladi. Bim'heira v'yameinu, yavo eileinu; im mashiach ben David, im mashiach ben David. Elijah the prophet, Elijah the Tishbite. Elijah the Gileadite. Soon, in our days, he will come to us with Messiah, son of David.

Shavua Tov—have a good week!

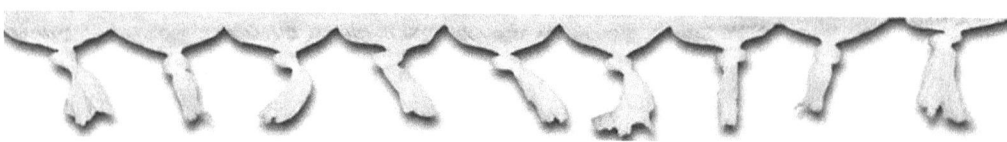

לא תרצח	אנכי יהוה
לא תנאף	לא יהיה
לא תגנב	לא תשא את
לא תענה	זכור את יום
לא תחמד	כבד את אביך

JEWISH HERITAGE SCRIPTURE STUDIES

MOSES
THE TORAH WRITER

9. MOSES (MOSHE) THE TORAH WRITER

Thus far we've read how Abraham lived a life of faith through God's power, how Jacob was able to repent and be humbly sorry for his mistakes, and how Joseph was able to forgive those who had deeply hurt him. We read how Moses' life foreshadowed the Messiah in many different ways. We also know Moses recorded the historical accounts of creation, the flood, and the experiences of Abraham, Isaac, and Jacob. We have read that Moses recorded the account of God writing the Ten Commandments and the instructions on how the Temple, or Mishkan, was to be built. It was through this Temple that God drew close to His people and granted us forgiveness. The Temple also pointed to the Messiah who would be the sacrificial lamb dying for our sins, cleansing us from guilt. Like Moses' life, the Temple, which God instructed Moses to build, foreshadowed the Messiah who was to be "Immanuel," God with us. In this lesson we will cover another fascinating and important topic written by Moses under Elohim's direction. In this lesson, Moses the Torah Writer, we will find out how to live godly lives and experience more abundant health.

Let us start by praying King David's prayer *"Teach me O LORD . . . give me understanding, that I may observe Your teaching and keep it wholeheartedly."* Amen. Psalm 119:33, 34

It is always important to start the reading of God's Word with a prayer for understanding so that we can observe and keep God's teachings. Spiritual topics found in the Bible need spiritual understanding, so we need to ask God to give us His Spirit in order to fully and correctly understand His words. We also need God's Spirit, His power, to be able to follow God's path. In Hebrew we use the word halacha (הלכה) to refer to Jewish law or teaching. Literally it comes from the root halach (הלך), which means to walk. It is not enough just to believe; our actions must follow our beliefs. In this lesson we are going to learn some of the practical areas in which Elohim calls us to walk. As we learned in the lessons building up to this one, like Abraham we need faith and like Jacob we need a willingness to allow God to change us. Are you willing to allow God to change your life so that it is in harmony with His will for you? Are you willing to allow

Him to empower you to walk the walk? I know you are, so let's get started.

1. What does God's Word, the Holy Scriptures, do for us?

    In my heart I treasure Your promise; therefore I do not sin against You* . . . *Your word is <u>a lamp to my feet, a light for my path</u>* . . . *You are <u>my protection and my shield</u>; <u>I hope</u> for Your word. Psalm 119:11, 105, 114

    As we read God's Word, the Bible, it finds lodging in our hearts and makes us strong to obey Him. It guides and directs our paths, and protects and shields us. With all these wonderful benefits it is a wonder that we do not spend more time reading the Bible.

2. It is wonderful to realize that treasuring Adonai's promises in our hearts keeps us from sinning against Him and guides our paths. How powerful is the word of God?

    For the word of the L<small>ORD</small> is <u>right</u>; His every deed is <u>faithful</u> . . . <u>By the word of the L<small>ORD</small> the heavens were made</u>, by the breath of His mouth, all their host. Psalm 33: 4, 6

    As we are reminded that Elohim created all things by His word it gives us faith that His words in the Bible will create a fresh new life within us, too. Since God's word is powerful enough to make the heavens, certainly it is powerful enough to change us and to meet our every need. The question is, are you willing to allow God to change you?

3. King David discovered how powerful the Word of God was in his life. Notice his response.

    I love Your teaching! It is my study <u>all day long</u>. Psalm 119:97

    As we draw closer to God and fall more in love with Him we will find each day that we want to spend more time with Him, even to the point as King David experienced of spending all day long with Him. Every day and all day we can meditate upon God and His Word even as we go about our everyday routines. This close of a walk with God might seem impossible for some people to even think about, but when we consider that it is God who changes us and gives us love for Him, we see that experiencing a walk with God, like David did, is a natural result of God working in our lives. Elohim does not change us in one moment. It is a gradual growing process. As with the other things we will learn in this lesson, God is pointing us toward the destination and then He walks with us

9. MOSES (MOSHE) THE TORAH WRITER

day by day, empowering us toward the goal of a happy, prosperous, healthy life.

4. As we studied in the last lesson, Adonai wrote the Ten Commandments on stone with His own finger, showing their everlasting endurance. You will recall that they were placed inside the Ark of the Covenant in the Most Holy Place of the Sanctuary. Those 10 laws are God's moral law and have a universal and everlasting purpose. Moses wrote the rest of God's instructions on either papyrus or animal skins. These laws gave instruction in civil matters, health issues, and also included the laws for the ceremonies in the Sanctuary. There are 613 laws in the Torah including the Ten Commandments. Some of these laws applied specifically to the Levites and their work in the Temple, such as laws pertaining to which animals were to be sacrificed when, etc. Some of the 613 laws have a universal and eternal application that would mean they apply to all people in all times. Some of the 613 commandments were given for a certain time period or for certain people. How can we tell which ones still apply today for everyone and which ones might not? This simple outline will show how we can tell which laws have an eternal/ universal application and which ones do not. Any law that was given to the parents of mankind before sin entered the world applies to people in all ages. Any law that was not given to the parents of mankind before sin entered the world, but was given later on, obviously could not be eternal since it was not in existence at all times, and if it was not given until sometime after Adam and Eve it certainly cannot be said that it has applied to all people. Let's look at some of the 613 laws and see which are eternal/universal and which are not.

- ♦ The Ten Commandments
    - ➢ Did God have the Ten Commandments in the Garden of Eden? Yes. Although God did not write them in stone for another 2,500 years or so they were there in the Garden. The Sabbath was established in the Garden. There was no killing, stealing, etc. allowed in the Garden. Adam and Eve were removed from the Garden of Eden for coveting and stealing the fruit they were told not to eat. They did not honor God their Father. They bore false witness and put the devil's lies before the Creator's truths. All the Ten Commandments applied to Adam and Eve and any children they would have had in the Garden had they not sinned.
- ♦ Health laws, practicing good hygiene and not eating or drinking things that God forbids.
    - ➢ Did God have dietary laws in the Garden of Eden? Yes, God told Adam and Eve what they could and could not eat.
- ♦ Civil laws, specifics on how to interact with each other, the laws of the nation.

- ➢ Did God have civil laws in the Garden of Eden? They are not mentioned one way or the other.
- ♦ Circumcision
  - ➢ Did God have circumcision in the Garden of Eden? No. The first time circumcision is mentioned is in relation to Abraham, 2,000 years after Adam and Eve.
- ♦ The seven yearly feasts
  - ➢ Did God have the annual feasts in the Garden of Eden? No, the first Passover was not instituted until 2,500 years after Adam and Eve sinned.
- ♦ Laws pertaining to sacrifices
  - ➢ Did God have sacrifices in the Garden of Eden? No, there were no sacrifices in the Garden of Eden. The first sacrifice was not until after Adam and Eve were taken out of the Garden of Eden.

We can see from those questions which of the 613 laws are universal and eternal and which ones are not. Even for those laws that are not eternal and universal, their principles still apply today. While they might not be binding, they are still beneficial for knowing about God's great love for us.

5. Elohim placed the Ten Commandments on a higher level than the rest of the 613 commandments by writing them Himself and by writing them in stone, while the rest of the laws were written by Moses. What was another way God showed that the ten laws were unique?

> ***Moses charged the Levites who carried the Ark of the Covenant of the L***ORD***, saying: Take this book of Teaching and <u>place it beside the Ark</u> of the Covenant of the L***ORD *** your God, and let it remain there as a witness against you.*** Deuteronomy 31:25,26

The Ten Commandments were written by God, on stone, and placed inside the Ark of the Covenant. The rest of the Torah was written by Moses and placed beside the Ark of the Covenant.

6. What is one example of the civil laws, which still teaches important principles of justice for today?

> ***When a man's ox injures his neighbor's ox and it dies, they shall sell the live ox and divide its price; they shall also divide the dead animal.*** Exodus 21:35

Although most of us do not have oxen today the principle of this law still applies. If my dog kills your cat, or if my vehicle hits your vehicle, it is my re-

9. MOSES (MOSHE) THE TORAH WRITER

sponsibility to make restitution.

7. What promised blessing did Adonai give for following His health laws?

And if you do obey these rules and observe them carefully, the LORD *your God will maintain faithfully for you the covenant that He made on oath with your fathers . . . <u>The* LORD *will ward off from you all sickness; He will not bring upon you any of the dreadful diseases of Egypt, about which you know.</u>* Deuteronomy 7:12, 15

Who doesn't want to avoid sickness? God's Word tells us how to avoid getting sick. Certainly a God who loves us would not want us to be sick. It is amazing how many people look at God's health laws as restrictions—dos and don'ts given by a stern taskmaster, instead of loving advice from an all-knowing God. What a wonderful God! He not only wants us to live with Him eternally, but He wants us to live healthfully now! Are you ready to start experiencing the health Elohim wants to give you?

8. Which animals did God lovingly warn us not to eat?

Any animal that has true hoofs, with clefts through the hoofs, and that chews the cud—such you may eat…The following, however, of those that either chew the cud or have true hoofs, you shall not eat: the camel—although it chews the cud, it has no true hoofs: it is unclean for you; the hare—<u>although it chews the cud, it has no true hoofs: it is unclean for you;</u> and the swine—<u>although it has true hoofs, with the hoofs cleft through, it does not chew the cud: it is unclean for you</u> . . . <u>Everything in water that has no fins and scales shall be an abomination for you</u> . . . <u>All the things that swarm upon the earth are an abomination; they shall not be eaten.</u> Leviticus 11:3,4,6,7, 12,41

It is a law for all time throughout the ages, in all your settlements: <u>you must not eat any fat or any blood.</u> Lev. 3:17

Medical science is just now catching up with what God told us thousands of years ago. The land animals not to be eaten are those that are highest in fat, cholesterol, and parasites. The most common land animal eaten today that God strictly forbids is the pig. The land animals lowest in fat, cholesterol and parasites are those that have both cleft hoofs and chew their cud, such as cows and sheep. The water animals without fins and scales, such as squid, sharks, and octopus, do not get rid of their waste as well as those that do have scales. The shellfish, such as lobsters, crabs, shrimp, clams, etc. feed at the bottom of the ocean, where all the waste in the water eventually settles. They help clean the water by consuming the waste. Everything is created good for the purpose that God created it. Some things are good for human consumption; some things are good scavengers for cleaning up waste. God promises we'll be healthier if we don't eat the waste eaters.

The bloodstream is where all the diseases travel through the body. The Bible says, ***"The blood is the life."*** (Deut. 12:23) Whatever life was in the animal comes into us when we eat it. Whatever disease and hormones the animal had come into us as we eat their blood. We literally are what we eat. How important it is that we choose what we eat based on our Creator's infinite wisdom.

Even if the shifting opinions of medical science were to declare a forbidden food healthy, or even if we fed waste-eating animals healthy diets, kept them free of parasites, and found ways to make them low in fat and cholesterol, God still warns not to eat them. We may never know all the reasons why God tells us some things are good for us and some things are not. We should be smart enough, humble enough, and obedient enough to follow His loving Word. This lesson will walk us through the steps of how to have the power to resist those things that God forbids and how to have the power to do the things God lays out for us to do.

In review, some of the things not to be eaten are:
- Land animals that do not chew the cud or have cloven hoofs such as pigs, dogs, rats, horses, etc.
- Water animals that do not have fins or scales such as squid, octopus, sharks, shellfish of all kinds including lobsters, crabs, shrimp, and clams.
- Birds that naturally eat other birds or dead flesh such as eagles, hawks, vultures, etc.
- The blood or fat of any animal.

Someone might ask, "What can I eat?"
- Sheep, cows, and deer with the blood drained and fat removed
- Birds such as turkeys and chickens
- Most fish
- The various forms of dairy products
- The dozens of different grains, including corn, wheat, barley, oats, rice, millet, etc. in all their different forms such as in pastas, breads, or just cooked
- The huge selection of fruit, including the many types of citrus fruit, the

9. MOSES (MOSHE) THE TORAH WRITER

many types of apples, the many types of melons, plums, pears, bananas, grapes, just to name a few.
- The tons of different vegetables, including squash of all kinds, carrots, broccoli, cauliflower, cabbage, and all kinds of green leafy vegetables, just to name a few.
- The wide variety of nuts and seeds including cashews, peanuts, almonds, macadamia nuts, walnuts, pecans, sesame seeds, poppy seeds, sunflower seeds, etc., etc. etc.
- The large amount of beans and peas, including pinto beans, lima beans, black beans, navy beans, garbanzo beans, cannellini beans, lentils, green peas, black eyed peas, split peas, just to name a few.

When we stop to think that most animals only eat a small variety of foods in their diet it is amazing that Elohim has given us an almost infinite number of good things to choose from. With so much variety why would we want to choose from the few that are not good for us? It is interesting to learn that in the groups who follow these simple health principles from Scripture, the members not only live 7 to 9 years longer than the average of the population, but they also suffer less from the contemporary debilitating diseases that plague our culture today.

9. Some will say that these health benefits are just for the Jewish people. But notice that Adonai differentiated between clean and unclean animals before there ever was a Jewish person.

the Lord said to Noah, "Go into the ark, with all your household, for you alone have I found righteous before Me in this generation. Of every clean animal you shall take seven pairs, males and their mates, and of every animal that is not clean, two, a male and its mate. Genesis 7:1,2

Many people think all the animals came onto the ark by twos, but the Bible says the animals that could be used as sacrifices and for food came on by sevens, and the animals that were not to be used for food or sacrifices came on by twos. The flood took place hundreds of years before there were Jewish people. Thus we see an example of God differentiating between which animal could be eaten and which ones should not be eaten even before there were Jewish people. This demonstrates that the principles of what to eat and what not to eat are for non-Jewish people as well as for Jewish people. Obviously God loves the non-Jewish people also and does not want them to be sick or diseased either so He has given the dietary principles in love to them as well. Doesn't it make sense that God would give this loving instruction to all of His children and not just to one ethnic group?

It is interesting to note that God did not give permission for humans to eat flesh of biblically clean animals until the time Noah and his family came off the ark when the flood had destroyed all the vegetation and fruit trees. That was about 1,500 years after Adam and Eve. So for the first one thousand five hundred years all humans who were following God were vegetarians. It is interesting to note that everyone in the ten-generation lineage from Adam to Noah lived over 700 years with no indication of a decline in life span. (Actually Noah's grandfather, Methuselah, lived longer than anyone before him.) After the flood the average life span steadily decreased. In the ten generations after the flood, from Noah to Abraham, the life span went from the 800's to the 100's. Elohim does permit us to eat biblically clean animals today. Yet studies do indicate that the vegetarian diet God gave to Adam and Eve, which was eaten for the first one thousand five hundred years of earth's history, and which we will eat in heaven, is still the healthiest of all diets.

10. Why did God give us these health laws?

I the L<small>ORD</small> am He who brought you up from the land of Egypt to be your God: <u>you shall be holy, for I am holy.</u> Leviticus 11:45

Following God's health laws does not make us holy, but as we allow God to come into our hearts He begins transforming us, making us holy. We cannot of ourselves make ourselves holy no matter what we do. God is holy and He makes us holy. As we surrender our sinful desires that crave things that God says are not good for us, God then changes our desires and gives us desires for things that are pure and good. In some ways, God's dietary laws are a test of our love and obedience, just as the fruit on the tree of knowldge of good and evil was a test for Adam and Eve.

11. In addition to making wise choices by eating only healthy foods and abstaining from foods and substances that harm us, what other things can we do to maintain good health?

"<u>Do not be wise in your own eyes; fear the L<small>ORD</small> and shun evil. It will be a cure for your body, a tonic for your bones."</u> "<u>A joyful heart makes for good health.</u>" Proverbs 3:7,8; 17:22

It is more than just what we put into or don't put into our bodies that gives us health. How we think also has a big impact on our health. For one thing, don't

9. MOSES (MOSHE) THE TORAH WRITER

think you know more than Elohim. Be humble, fear the LORD, and stay away from evil. Be thankful, cheerful, and merry, and it will make for good health. Best of all, God's prescriptions have no negative side effects. Because God loves us, He has given us these sensible guidelines for being healthy and happy.

12. Perhaps you have discovered some things in today's lesson where you sense God wants to see you come into closer harmony with His plan for your life. Yet making changes in our lifestyle is never easy when we try to do it in our own strength. What wonderful promise does God give us to help us make these important health saving changes?

I will give you a new heart and put a new spirit into you: I will remove the heart of stone from your body and give you a heart of flesh; and I will put My spirit into you. Thus I will cause you to follow My laws and faithfully to observe My rules. Ezekiel 36:26

What a wonderful promise! God gives us new hearts, new desires. God promises to put His Spirit into us causing us, empowering us, to change and to follow His wonderful ways. What a great God. He takes the burden of change from us and says He will make the change in us as we surrender our hearts to Him. Thinking about the changes Elohim is wanting to do in your life might seem overwhelming if you are thinking that you have to make the changes. The wonderful thing is that the same God who shows you the areas that need changing is the One who will come into your heart and mind and He will be the One who will make the changes in you. Thus it is not you that is having to make the change, but rather God who is making the change in you.

Donna Anthes is the director of nursing at Wildwood Lifestyle Center and Hospital in Wildwood, Georgia. Wildwood Lifestyle Center and Hospital encourages its patients to live their lives according to sound medical practices and to the Biblical principles of trusting in God, eating foods that are healthy, exercising, drinking enough water, avoiding harmful substances, and getting proper amounts of sunlight, fresh air, and rest. Donna remembers meeting a patient named Jill, who happened to be an operating room nurse from another hospital. When Jill came to Wildwood LSC she had high blood pressure and type II diabetes, which made her insulin dependant. Making the changes in her lifestyle was not easy for Jill, but Donna prayed with her and God gave her the victory. Within a few weeks from the time Jill came to Wildwood LSC her blood pressure returned to normal range, she was exercising, eating right, and her blood sugar levels returned to normal range. Under doctor's supervision Jill was able to greatly reduce her intake of insulin and she was well on her way to being free of insulin dependency. Donna has worked at Wildwood LSC for over 10 years and has seen hundreds of similar experiences of God working in people's lives as they allow Him to bring their lifestyles into harmony with His divine plan of healing. Donna herself experienced the benefits of using God's natural remedies in harmony with medical science to bring her weight down from 199, when she was 19 years of age, to her current weight of 135. One of Donna's favorite books on the subject of health is Ministry of Healing. God's principles for a healthy life and clear mind are the best ways to avoid sickness and the best ways to bring about healing. Why not use them yourself? (For more information about Wildwood Lifestyle Center and Hospital call 1-800-634-9355)

Take a moment now and give God permission to change any area in your life that is not in harmony with Heaven and ask Him to place His powerful Spirit in you to change your life, giving you new desires for things that are good while giving you the power to turn from those things that are hurtful to you.

REVIEW הזרה

1. God's word
    a. Guides us, protects us, and helps us find victory over sin.
    b. Is a burden.
    c. Is just a story book.

2. Elohim showed that the 10 Commandments are unique by
    a. Writing them on stone.
    b. Writing them Himself.
    c. Having them placed inside the Ark of the Covenant.
    d. All of the above.

3. Are the 10 Commandments, including the seventh-day Sabbath, still important today?
    a. Yes.
    b. No.

4. Are the health laws still helpful to us today?
    a. Yes.

9. MOSES (MOSHE) THE TORAH WRITER

    b. No.

5. Things that God forbids us to put in our body include
   a. Pigs, rats, bats, and cats.
   b. Blood and fat of any animal.
   c. Lobster, squid, shark, clam, crab, octopus.
   d. All of the above.

6. Things that God allows us to eat include
   a. Animals that chew the cud and have split hooves such as deer, cows, and sheep, with the blood drained and fat removed.
   b. Fish that have fins and scales, and chicken and turkey.
   c. Dairy products.
   d. Vegetables.
   e. Fruits.
   f. Nuts.
   g. Grains.
   h. Beans and peas
   i. All of the above.

7. God gave us his laws because
   a. He loves us.
   b. Following them will make us happier.
   c. They guide us and help us.
   d. All of the above.

8. I can make the changes in my life that need to be made by:
   a. Trying really, really hard.
   b. Doing what I have been doing and maybe one day things will be different.
   c. Inviting God to put His Spirit into my heart and giving Him permission to change me.

Sean Carney seemed destined to live the life of a drug addict. His mother died from an overdose of drugs. His father was a recovering heroin addict. Sean's father gave him drugs for his allowance instead of money. Even though Sean is Jewish he was raised as an atheist. When Sean moved out on his own his friends called his apartment the "Carney Hotel." It was a place to crash and eat vegetarian meals. Sean's favorite cookbook was called The Ten Talents, by Frank & Rosalie Hurd.

    Sean traveled to Peru, Brazil, Mexico, and around Canada and the U.S.

searching for meaning for his life. In Sean's search for truth he would pray to "God, whoever or whatever you are." The night of his cousin's bar mitzvah, Sean prayed to know the facts about this "Jesus" he had heard about. All along Sean's travels he met people who worshipped the Lord and rested on the Seventh day Shabbat, who believed in the entire Bible, in Y'shua as the Messiah, and followed what the Scriptures say regarding how to live. Sean met a college student selling a magazine called The Five Day Plan to Quit Smoking. Sean told him that if he gave Sean the book he would quit. Sean received the magazine and tossed his cigarette in a puddle. It was his last. After traveling to Osoyoos Canada he attended a Sabbath service for the first time. Several families invited Sean and his family to dinner. They accepted the first invitation and were happily surprised to see the food was what Sean loved to eat. He was amazed to find out that their favorite cookbook was also The Ten Talents. The family told Sean of a book about the greatest natural healer that ever lived. The book was "The Ministry of Healing." Sean really enjoyed the book. Sean began reading the Bible for himself. He accepted Y'shua as his Messiah, and gained the victory over drugs.

Years later, visiting the town of Osoyoos again, Sean stopped to speak to a friend who was driving a bus. They spoke for a few minutes about God. As the driver pulled away a passenger asked, "Is that Sean Carney?" She was shocked to see the dramatic changes in Sean and said, "I don't believe it! He was the wildest guy in town!" God preserved and healed Sean from being a rebellious, wild, druggie with no hope to being a computer genius. Sean worked for Apple Computer as their Internet Publishing Manager and was technical lead on the world's first 'Webcast' that was broadcast from backstage of the 1996 Grammy awards. He also worked for another company as an application engineering architect for the world's first high speed content delivery network over the cable infrastructure. Later he was the creator/founder of TAGnet, an influential web hosting company. Sean says, "if it wasn't for God I hate to think where I would be right now!"

TRADITIONS

Kosher

The word "kosher" literally means "proper." When kosher is used to describe food it refers to those foods that are proper to eat. The Bible outlines biblically kosher foods. Biblically kosher foods are described in Leviticus chapter 11.

Since the removal of all blood is one of the biblical requirements for eating animals (Lev. 3:17) there is a special procedure for slaughtering animals to ensure the draining of as much blood as possible. A kosher slaughterer is called a "Shohet." They are highly trained religious individuals. The Shohet uses a razor sharp knife known as a "chalef" that kills the animal painlessly, with a single cut along the throat severing the trachea, the esophagus, the jugular vein, and the carotid arteries.

Modern Judaism has extra restrictions that are not mentioned in the Bible. These have been added over the years. These might be termed rabbinically kosher laws or kashrut. Rabbinically kosher laws include those listed in the Scriptures but add restrictions such as not eating dairy and meat products at the same time. These extra rules have been added because of the way the rabbis have interpreted the text that says, "You shall not boil a kid in its mother's milk." Exodus 23:19. This text has been interpreted to mean that milk and meat products cannot be eaten together. More than just not eaten together, according to rabbinical Judaism, they are not even allowed in the same refrigerator, in the same restaurant, or eaten on the same plates or with the same utensils, even after those plates or utensils have been washed. Rabbinically kosher homes often have two refrigerators, two sets of dishes and utensils (sometimes more if they have special dishes and utensils for Passover), two sets of sponges and dishtowels, even two sinks and two dishwashers. If a restaurant wants to be a kosher restaurant it has to be either a dairy restaurant or a meat restaurant. It cannot sell both dairy and meat.

An entire industry has been created by the interpretation of this text. As a result of this interpretation there are dozens of kosher certification organizations that certify food products and restaurants as being kosher or not. The symbols on food products such as a "K" or a "U" in a circle or a "K" in a star, etc. are the symbols indicating which one of the various kosher certification organizations certified that product.

You may have wondered why those symbols would appear on boxes of raisins, cans of pineapple, containers of oatmeal, bags of frozen string beans, and other obviously biblically clean or kosher foods. The reason is because the certification is not only an indication that the food itself meets the biblical requirements, but that the packaging plant also meets the rabbinical kosher requirements of not packing both dairy and meat products or unclean foods from the same facility. The certifying agency also makes sure that all of the ingredients in a product meet kosher standards of not mixing meat and dairy, or containing pork, etc. as well as ensuring that only kosher ingredients are in all the other products made there as well. This requires research into all of the ingredients and all the plants where the ingredients are manufactured and packaged. The rabbinic inspector is called a mashgiach. In the U.S.A.

the kosher industry is a multi-billion dollar business annually.

As we again look at Exodus 23:19 which says, "You shall not boil a kid in its mother's milk," we notice it does not say anything about not eating meat and dairy together. It does not say anything about a need for separate restaurants, sinks, dishes, utensils, refrigerators, etc. It only says don't boil the kid in its mother's milk. Leviticus 22:28 shares a similar injunction. It says, "No animal . . . shall be slaughtered on the same day with its young." No multi-billion dollar industry has been created by this text. No unnecessary burdens have been placed on individuals and households by this text. Adonai said what he meant. If He wanted to tell us not to eat meat and dairy together he would have said so.

As a matter of biblical fact, when the Lord and two angels visited Abraham in the form of three men Abraham served them a meat and dairy meal of curds, milk, and a calf and the Bible says they ate it (See Genesis 18:8).

The Bible clearly tells us what we should do and should not do and we do not need to be adding man-made rules to the Word of God. Kosher certifying agencies have helped produce a healthier product by requiring that meat processing plants perform to a higher standard of cleanliness. And while there is nothing wrong with following the full rabbinical kosher requirements for food it is not necessary to do so in order to fulfill the Scriptural requirements.

It is very important to be able to distinguish between biblical commands from God and man-made rules. We should never confuse the commandments of God with the traditions of men.

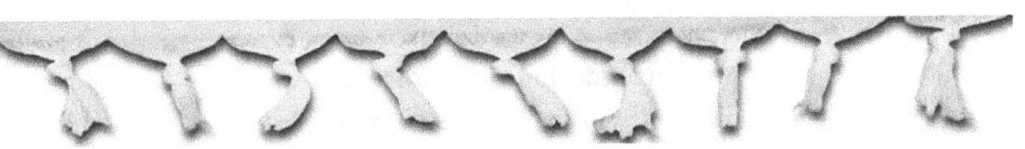

Cyril Miller has seen God answer many prayers in his life. When Cyril was about 14 years old he contracted a staph infection from a scratch on his arm. In just a few hours his body was raging with an extremely high fever. This was before penicillin was available to the public. The doctors treated him with hydrotherapy and kept his head packed in ice to avoid brain damage from the fever. His temperature was 108 degrees. The physician explained to his parents that if the infection settled in his brain, heart, or other vital organs, there would be no hope. Cyril's mother quickly called some friends in two different cities and asked them to join her in prayer. Amazingly, the next morning Cyril's temperature was normal and he continued to get better each day. His parents asked the physician, "How much do we owe you?" His reply was, "Absolutely nothing! God has healed that boy."

Another time Cyril was in a dreadful auto accident with a tractor-trailer. The impact knocked him unconscious. He awakened temporarily and found himself surrounded by people trying to pry him loose from the motor that had trapped his right foot. He heard someone say, "We're going to have to cut off his foot to get him out of here." He begged them not to cut off his foot and then he became unconscious again. The next thing he knew he was being taken by helicopter to a major trauma center where they rushed him to surgery. Cyril asked for a piece of paper and a pencil. He wrote, "Please, do not amputate my foot." He handed his note to the medic and said, "Please give this to the surgeon." Again he became unconscious and remained so for about a month. Many of his bones were broken. He got a staph infection in his wounds, developed pneumonia, and was put on a respirator. However, thank God, the surgeon was able to save his foot. One night during the 4th week of unconsciousness, the doctors told his friends he wasn't going to make it. Cyril's friends came to his bedside and offered earnest prayers for God to save his life, if it was His will, and to allow Cyril to continue his service to Him. It was a miracle! The next morning his temperature was normal and he soon became conscious and gained more and more strength every day. The Infectious Disease Specialist said with deep conviction in her voice, "there has been Divine intervention in your behalf."

God has given us much wisdom in His Word to keep us healthy. On top of that God gives us His Spirit to empower us to follow His health laws and principles. And on top of that He gives us the privelege of prayer for His

9. MOSES (MOSHE) THE TORAH WRITER

Divine intervention and healing.

God does not always heal. As we will learn in a later chapter, death is not the end. In our next chapter, Why Suffering?, we will see why God at times allows sickness and death, even when we are obedient, eat right, pray, and believe.

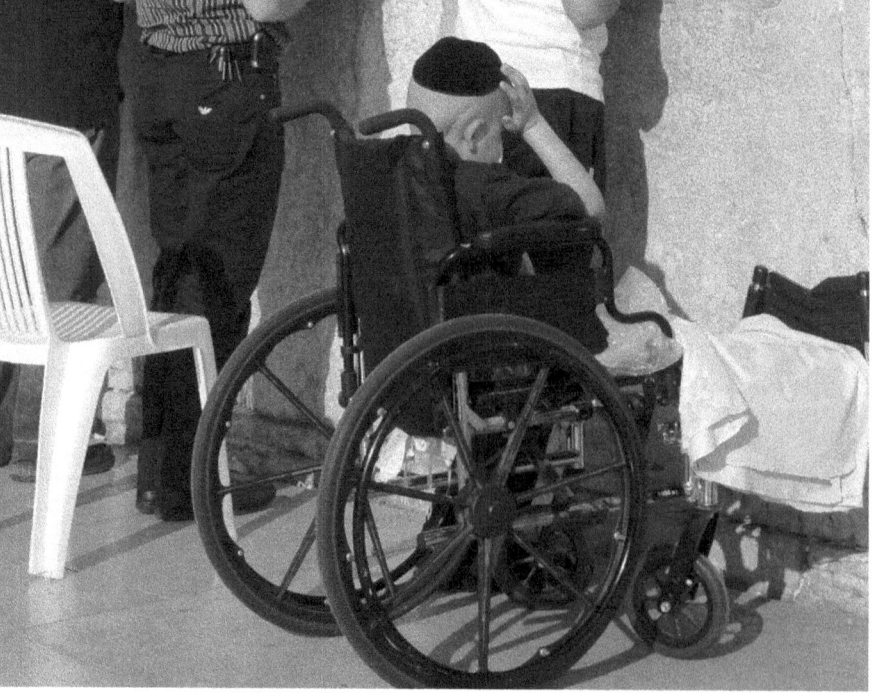

10. WHY DOES GOD ALLOW SUFFERING

In Yiddish we have many ways to express sorrow. We have words like tzuris, oy vey, oy vey is mir, oy gevalt, oy gottenyu, and even just a plain oy. Have you ever stopped to think of why we have so many sayings to express our grief? Maybe it's because we have had so many problems.

Some problems have been dumped on us by people who have treated us like chopped liver. Some problems we have brought upon ourselves. And some problems have no explanation at all.

Have you ever wondered why an all powerful and loving God allows problems, hurricanes, sickness, wars, and the death of innocent children? As we look at the big picture we will find out why. To find the real cause of suffering we must look in the book of Job. Many scholars believe that Moses wrote the book of Job.

1. What do the Scriptures tell us about this man Job?

   There was a man in the land of Uz named Job. That man was <u>blameless and upright; he feared God and shunned evil</u>. Seven sons and three daughters were born to him; his possessions were seven thousand sheep, three thousand camels, five hundred yoke of oxen and five hundred she-asses, and a very large household. That man was <u>wealthier than anyone</u> in the East . . . When a round of feast days was over, Job would send word to them to sanctify themselves, and, <u>rising early in the morning, he would make burnt offerings</u>, one for each of them; for Job thought, "Perhaps my children have sinned and blasphemed God in their thoughts." This is what Job always used to do. Job 1:1-3,5

   Job was blameless. He feared Adonai and shunned evil. Not only did he offer burnt sacrifices for forgiveness of his own sins, but he prayed and interceded for his children's sins also.

2. The real cause of suffering is exposed in the book of Job. Who is the cause of suffering? Where does he do his evil work?

   The divine beings presented themselves before the LORD, and <u>the</u>

adversary (ha-satan) *came along with them. The* LORD *said to the adversary, "Where have you been?" The adversary answered the* LORD, *"I have been roaming all over the earth."* Job 1:6,7.

Moses made it clear in the book of Job in the Hebrew Scriptures that there is a real living adversary, enemy, named Satan, (ha-satan, the Satan, in Hebrew) who roams all over the earth.

3. When God began to express his pleasure in Job's being blameless, upright and shunning evil, what evil accusation did the adversary, Satan, bring against God and Job?

The Adversary answered the LORD, *"Does Job not have good reason to fear God? Why, it is You who have fenced him round, him and his household and all that he has. You have blessed his efforts so that his possessions spread out in the land. But lay Your hand upon all that he has and he will surely blaspheme You to Your face."* Job 1:9-11

Satan's accusation against God was that the only reason Job loved God was because God was good to him. Satan was implying that Job was selfish and was not capable of manifesting real unconditional love. Satan was implying that if God took the blessings away from Job, Job would turn away from God.

4. What did Elohim allow Satan to do in order to prove him wrong to the whole universe?

So the LORD *said to the adversary (Satan), "See, he is in your power; only spare his life."* Job 2:6

Satan challenged God to take away His hand from protecting Job and remove His blessings. God did not bring suffering to Job. He did allow Satan to harass Job in order to prove Satan's lies as false.

5. Soon after this, the adversary, Satan, caused all of Job's possessions to be stolen and burned, caused all ten of his children to be killed by a windstorm that collapsed their house, and caused Job to be inflicted with a severe inflammation from head to foot. How did Job react to these terrible calamities?

Then Job arose, tore his robe, cut off his hair, and threw himself on the ground and worshiped. He said, "Naked came I out of my mother's womb, and naked shall I return there; the LORD *has given, and the* LORD *has taken away; blessed be the name of the* LORD.*" For*

10. WHY DOES GOD ALLOW SUFFERING

*all that, **Job did not sin nor did he cast reproach on God.*** Job 1:20-22

I doubt any of us have experienced suffering to the extent that Job did. To be robbed and have all your possessions destroyed is bad enough, but to also find out that all of your children have died at the same time would be more than most people could bear. On top of all that Job came down with a very severe and painful case of boils from head to foot. His wife was no support. She encouraged him to curse God and die. In spite of all these circumstances of horrendous loss, grief, and excruciating pain and suffering Job chose to love and trust God. Job did not know about the argument that was taking place between God and Satan, yet he chose, by faith, to love and trust God. That same argument is still going on today, and you and I are the ones being battled over instead of Job. We get to decide who will win the battle by either choosing to trust God through the trial or to blame God for the suffering.

It didn't seem like it could get any worse for Job, but it did. The Bible spends the next 35 chapters of this book recording how Job and some of his friends tried to figure out why these terrible things had happened to him. Job's so-called friends were no comfort. They blamed him for his suffering. Job didn't know why he was suffering and people weren't making it any easier; they were making it worse. I'm sure you can relate to how Job felt.

6. What did God say to Job, reminding us that we don't need to understand every detail and reason why and reminding us why we should trust God when we cannot see the bigger picture of the battle between God and Satan?

Where were you when I laid the earth's foundations? *Speak if you have understanding.* Job 38:4

Elohim didn't go into all the details of the battle that was taking place between Himself and Satan. Instead He reminded Job that He created everything. God sees the past and the future. He has a view and a perspective that we cannot see or understand. Even though it is beyond our full comprehension to understand all the reasons why God allows suffering in this great battle between God and Satan, we can trust that God is still in control and knows best and will work all things out together for good in the end.

7. How did Job respond to God's greatness?

I know that You can do everything, that nothing you propose is impossible for You . . . Indeed, I spoke without understanding, of

things beyond me, which I did not know ... Therefore, I recant and relent, being but dust and ashes. Job 42: 2, 3, 6.

It was Job's faith, humility, repentance, and submission to God that made him blameless in the first place. These are some of the characteristics we have seen in other people of God that we have been reading about in this series. These are the characteristics that Elohim is developing in us as we continue to read His word, pray to Him and ask Him to come and live out His life through us.

8. God and Job proved Satan wrong. They demonstrated to the universe that it is possible to love and serve God even when things are at their worst. What did God do for Job after Job's victory over the question of why suffering?

The LORD restored Job's fortunes when he prayed on behalf of his friends, and the LORD gave Job twice what he had before ... So Job died old and contented. Job 42:10, 17

Adonai restored twice as much to Job only after he prayed on behalf of his so-called friends. Not only did God give Job the characteristics of faith, humility, repentance and submission to God, God also gave him forgiveness toward his friends and enemies. Job did more than just mentally forgive them; he began praying and interceding for them. Remember, the real battle is between Elohim and Satan. We are the battleground and the people Satan uses to hurt us are being used as pawns in his hands. God is obviously pleased with us when we pray for those who have hurt us. Praying for them is truly the way to get back at Satan for using them to hurt us. If we pray for them God can move upon their hearts. With God moving on their hearts they may some day apologize. Are there some "friends" or enemies that God is bringing to your mind right now that you should be praying for? If so, pause before you read any further and pray for them right now.

We should pray for God to fill us with his patient and merciful Spirit so that we never play the part of Job's "friends" and enter into the role of condemning, criticizing, and judging others.

From the beginning Satan has been accusing God of being mean, unfair, and the cause of all suffering. God, in love and mercy to us, has not yet destroyed Satan. If God had destroyed Satan from the start God could never clear His name before the universe. There would forever be the doubt that, "maybe Satan was right." God is giving him enough opportunity to expose himself so

10. WHY DOES GOD ALLOW SUFFERING

that we can see for ourselves that Satan is the adversary who causes all suffering and that God is love, the source of all happiness. When this truth is clear to all, then Satan can be judged and destroyed, and suffering will cease.

9. Where else have we seen this adversary causing problems for Elohim's children?

> *Now the serpent was the shrewdest of all the wild beasts that the* L<small>ORD</small> *God had made. He said to the woman, "Did God really say: You shall not eat of any tree of the garden?"... And <u>the serpent said to the woman, "You are not going to die,</u>... And the* L<small>ORD</small> *God said to the woman, "What is this you have done!" <u>The woman replied, "The serpent duped me, and I ate."</u>* Gen. 3:1,4,13

Satan took the form of a serpent and talked Eve into disobeying God. God warned Eve that disobedience would cause death. Satan lied and said, "Don't worry; you will not die." (This was the very first lie that took place on earth, and it is a very dangerous one, as we will see in a future lesson on what happens after death.)

10. What curse did Adonai pronounce upon the serpent, the adversary, Satan?

> *<u>I will put enmity between you and the woman, and between your offspring and hers; They shall strike at your head, and you shall strike at their heel.</u>"* Genesis. 3:15

This promise of 'enmity' describes the great controversy between God and Satan that we experience every day. Satan tried to strike at the Messiah by having Him put to death, but God raised the Messiah back to life and took Him back to heaven. The Messiah will one day strike and crush Satan's head, destroying him. Currently Satan is striking at our heels, as Eve's children, causing problems in our lives. God can give us the faith and courage to see us through it triumphantly, like He did for Job.

The experience of Job and the behind the scene battle between God and Satan helps us to understand one of the reasons why bad things happen to good people. Yes, sometimes we bring bad results upon ourselves by our wrong choices, but sometimes bad things happen to us just because we are in the middle of a war and we are the prize being warred over. Thankfully, we are assured that if we trust in the L<small>ORD</small> our God we will be on the winning side.

11. What imagery did God use to show that He will remove our guilt and give us His righteousness while Satan is accusing us?

> (God) *further showed me Joshua, the high priest* (cohen gadol), *standing before the angel of the LORD, and the accuser standing at his right to accuse him. But [the angel of] the LORD said to the accuser, "<u>The LORD rebuke you, O accuser;</u> may the LORD who has chosen Jerusalem rebuke you! For this is a brand plucked from the fire." Now Joshua was clothed in filthy garments when he stood before the angel . . . "<u>Take the filthy garments off him!</u>" And he said to him, "<u>See, I have removed your guilt from you,</u> and <u>you shall be clothed in [priestly] robes.</u>"* Zechariah 3:1-4

After Satan entices us to disobey God, he then accuses us of our unworthiness of God's love. But God still loves us. As we accept the death of our Messiah for our sins, God removes our guilt and the power sin has had over us, and covers us in His righteousness and goodness. It is Satan who has been accusing you of your unworthiness. You can shut him up right now by claiming the Messiah's forgiveness, cleansing, and transforming power.

12. How many of us are clothed with these filthy garments needing God's cleansing and virtues?

> <u>*We have all become like an unclean thing*</u>*, and* <u>*all our virtues like a filthy rag.*</u> Isaiah 64:5

All of us have fallen for Satan's temptations and lies during our lives. We have all, at some point, doubted God's love and plan for us. We all need God's forgiveness granted us through repentance. We read in lesson 2 how Jacob repented of his mistakes. If you have not yet accepted God's forgiveness provided by the death of the Messiah, now is the time to do it. Don't put it off any longer. There is an intense battle going on between Elohim and Satan and you are the one over whom they are battling. There is a literal tug of war going on and you are the rope. The cartoon images of a good angel on one shoulder and an evil angel on the other is a reality. A thought will come into our head to do something wrong or excuses why we don't need to do something we should. At the same time thoughts will come into our mind encouraging us to do the right thing. This battle of thoughts within us is part of the very real battle that is taking place between God and Satan. Both powers are whispering in our ears to pull us to their side. Which side will we believe? Which side will we yield to? Tip the victory to God's side by surrendering to Him. God cannot win the battle for you without your consent.

10. WHY DOES GOD ALLOW SUFFERING

13. How did the Jewish prophet Ezekiel summarize for us the history and future of Satan?

> <u>You were in Eden, the garden of God</u>; *Every precious stone was your adornment . . . <u>I created you as a cherub</u> with outstretched shielding wings; and you resided on God's holy mountain . . . <u>You were blameless in your ways, from the day you were created until wrongdoing was found in you. By your far-flung commerce you were filled with lawlessness and you sinned.</u> So <u>I have struck you down from the mountain of God, and I have destroyed you</u>, O shielding cherub . . . By the greatness of your guilt, through the dishonesty of your trading, you desecrated your sanctuaries. So I made a fire issue from you, and it has devoured you; <u>I have reduced you to ashes on the ground</u>, in the sight of all who behold you. All who knew you among the peoples are appalled at your doom. <u>You have become a horror and have ceased to be forever.</u>* Ezekiel 28:13, 14, 15, 16, 18, 19

Satan was originally an angel of God named Lucifer. But because he chose to rebel against Elohim he was cast out of heaven and will soon be destroyed, turned to ashes, and will cease to be forever! Hallelujah!

You may be wondering, "If God is all-powerful, why hasn't He destroyed Satan already?" This illustration will help show why God did not just destroy Satan in the beginning. Imagine that you are at work when one of the other employees comes over to you and tells you that someone has been stealing from the company, and that the owners want to see you right away. Your boss informs you that you are the main suspect in the theft, and you will be placed on probation until a more thorough investigation is conducted. You find out that your good friend Lucy is the one who accused you. What would be the intelligent thing to do? Buy a handgun and blow Lucy away?

Is that what you would do? No, not if you ever want your name cleared. If you killed Lucy not only would you be put in prison for murder, but the authorities would be sure you were the thief and that you were trying to get rid of the witness.

You need to do more than get rid of the liar; you need to clear your name. So instead of killing Lucy you hire a detective to set some hidden cameras around the business. In three days your detective calls you and tells you someone has shown up on the camera stealing again. You watch the film and see that it's Lucy! You and the detective run to the owners, the police, and the newspapers, clearing your name and placing the blame where it belongs.

Not only has Satan, Lucifer, been causing the problems, but he has been lying to everyone trying to put the blame on God. We see Satan use humans to spread this lie when he gets people to use God's name in vain when something bad happens. Another form of this lie is when insurance companies call a natural disaster an act of God.

If God had destroyed Satan at the beginning all the angels would have believed Satan's lies. They would have thought that since God could not prove Satan's lies as false, He just destroyed him. They would no longer serve Elohim out of love, but rather out of fear. God has been giving Satan enough time to fully expose himself to everyone. God is using this earth's history as a video for the universe, exposing Satan as the real cause of suffering. When everyone, including you and me, are convinced and make our final decisions of whom we choose to follow, then God can end the battle once and for all.

One of the reasons God came to this earth as a man, Y'shua, was to fight Satan on his turf and to win back this planet from Satan. God had given dominion to Adam and Eve, but when they chose to listen to Satan and disobey the Creator they forfeited the planet to Satan. Y'shua came to defeat Satan by fully obeying Adonai while in human flesh. Another reason Y'shua came to fight Satan here was to allow it to be demonstrated to the universe what Satan's ultimate goal is—the death of God.

14. How does Adonai feel when we are troubled by Satan?

In all their troubles He was troubled . . . In His love and pity He Himself redeemed them . . . Isaiah 63:9

God is touched with the feelings of our infirmities. Every tear we shed God sheds also. Everything that hurts us hurts Him. He is as attached to us as an expectant mother is attached to her child. It is because of His great love and pity for us that He sent the Messiah to die for us to redeem us to Himself. The Messiah, who the Bible referred to as Immanuel—God with us—is indeed with us. He is always with us even through our hardest, most difficult moments. Whatever trials you are going through right now, know that God is going through them with you and will see you through. He will never leave us nor forsake us. He gives us the freedom to leave or forsake Him, just as he gave that freedom to Lucifer, but He will never leave us or forsake us. Even if we choose to leave Him, He will still have love and pity in His heart toward us.

10. WHY DOES GOD ALLOW SUFFERING

We would be mishuga (crazy) to resist and reject such love.

Rachel Hyman was a fun-loving, happy, energetic child. The more active she was, the happier she was. She looked at the world as a place full of opportunities. There were people to meet, places to go, and goals to be reached. At just seventeen years of age Rachel encountered something that would dramatically slow down her dreams. Rachel developed hypoglycemia, also known as low blood sugar. Soon Rachel wasn't able to go hiking or play soccer with her college buddies. Even though Rachel was naturally optimistic she became depressed as she saw how this disease was crippling her. For the first time in her life she couldn't concentrate and had to excuse herself from class to eat some dates. Even while socializing with her friends she would lose her train of thought. People wondered what happened to energetic, talkative Rachel who overnight became quiet and uninvolved. All of this was too much for Rachel to handle. Rachel would cry herself to sleep as she thought of all the things she was missing out on. Her active lifestyle was replaced with sitting quietly in her room with hardly any physical or mental strength. The thought occurred to Rachel to turn her solitary time into spiritual sessions with God. Instead of complaining about all of the things she was missing out on, she developed a deeper relationship with God than she ever thought possible. After spending more quality time with God and seeing how her character had become more patient, loving, self-sacrificing, and meek, she began to see how God had used her crippling illness to change her for the better. She believes God's blessings sometimes come in unexpected and unusual ways. Rachel chooses to be thankful in spite of the illness and trusts that God knows best and will work all things together for good.

In love God gave us the Garden of Eden to live in. In love God warned Adam and Eve to stay away from the tree of the knowledge of good and evil. In love God warns us to stay away from evil by giving us His Ten Commandments. In love God has given us the Messiah to die for our sins. In love God gives us His Spirit to empower us to follow His law and will. In love God strengthens us through Satan's harassment. Let's hasten Satan's judgment and bring an end to suffering by telling others about God's love. Let's stop believing Satan's lies and determine, by God's power, to follow God in every aspect of our lives.

JEWISH DISCOVERIES

After Job passed the test, Elohim gave him twice as much as he had before. Just as Job's end was better than his beginning, God has a plan for you and me.

REVIEW הזרה

1. Who caused Job's suffering?

    a. God
    b. Job
    c. Satan

2. Why did God allow Satan to cause loss and suffering to Job?

    a. Job had sinned
    b. God was being mean
    c. God needed to prove Satan's accusations were wrong

3. When Job lost all his possessions and was inflicted with a terrible sickness he:

    a. Cursed God and cried "not fair."
    b. Cursed Satan
    c. Trusted God

4. Who stands between Eve's offspring (us) and Satan?

    a. The Messiah
    b. Adam
    c. Abraham

5. When will Satan finally be destroyed?

    a. When everyone has decided whose side they are on
    b. The year 2577
    c. When God gets mad enough

6. Who do you choose to follow?

    a. God
    b. Satan

Shoah

Holocaust Remembrance Day, also known as Yom Ha-Shoah, is the 27th day of the Hebrew month of Nisan. The Holocaust, more appropriately called Shoah (Hebrew for catastrophe), is the name given to the persecution and murder of Jews under the Nazi regime in Europe during the 1930's and 40's. Historians estimate that as many as six million Jews were killed. Each year on Yom Ha-Shoah we remember the individuals who died and suffered under this atrocious pogrom and those who stood heroically in the face of it. There are several Holocaust museums around the world and they are well worth visiting.

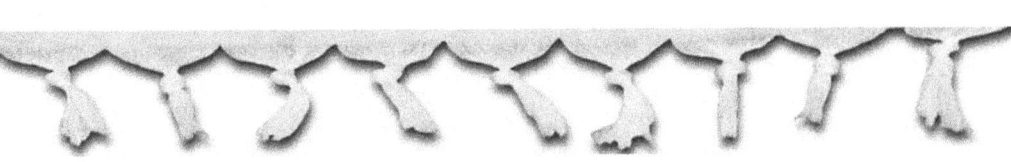

TRADITIONS

Tish B'Av

Tisha B'Av means the ninth day of the Hebrew month of Av and is traditionally a day of fasting to remember the destruction of the Temples in Jerusalem. On the ninth of Av in 586 B.C.E. the Babylonians destroyed the Temple that King Solomon had built. The Temple was rebuilt about 70 years later under the direction of Ezra and Nehemiah. 655 years after the first destruction the Romans destroyed it again on the same date, the ninth of Av, in 70 C.E. There have been several other calamities that have happened to us on the ninth of Av. In 1096 the first crusade was launched and thousands of Jewish people were murdered. On Tisha B'Av in 1290 King Edward I expelled the Jewish people from England. Sixteen years later, in 1306, France did the same thing. In 1492 King Ferdinand and Queen Isabella expelled the Jewish people from Spain on Tisha B'Av. It was at the same time Christopher Columbus left for the New World. While the Old World was closing itself off from Judaism, Adonai was opening up a whole new continent where religious freedom would eventually be granted to all people, including the Jewish people. Today on Tisha B'Av the book of Lamentations is read in the synagogue.

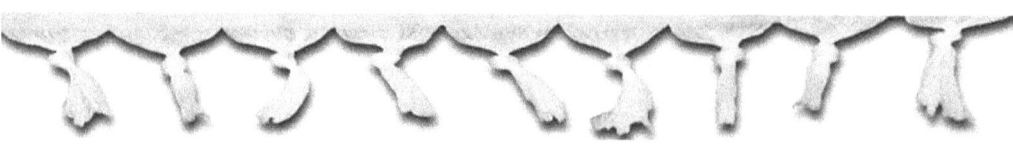

Steven Grabiner finally made it to Israel. The savings bonds that he received at his Bar Mitzvah had come to maturity and provided the fare to Israel. After a brief stay in Tel Aviv he wound up on a kibbutz in the Jezreel Valley where he could study Hebrew and religious instruction for half the day and work the other half of the day. From there he would take time out to explore the countryside, the historical sites, and his Jewish heritage. There was one ever-present question on his mind. It surfaced as he spoke with both old and young. What does it mean to be Jewish? Almost everyone Steven met in Israel was either atheistic, agnostic, or had only a vague concept of God; yet they strongly considered themselves Jewish. When asked how they could be Jewish when they didn't believe what the religion meant, there was never an adequate reply. He went to Israel in hope of finding answers to the most important questions in his life. He returned to the U.S. with more questions.

However, being in Israel did impress upon Steven the vibrancy and reality of the Scriptures. Places rich with history supported the history of the Torah. Moses actually *was* God's agent in raising a people for Himself. The people *were* delivered from their slavery and bondage. This realization helped create within Steven the desire to be liberated from habits and behaviors that bound him. Struggle as he might, there was no escape. Then a friend suggested that he simply ask God for guidance and freedom. Without fully realizing the implications, Steven asked God to reveal Himself, to show Himself. God graciously answered that prayer by instilling a distaste for those habits that had bound him. The more Steven learned of the God of Israel, the more true freedom he experienced. Steven began to read the Holy Scriptures for himself and the questions that once perplexed him have been answered. The same answers that Steven discovered are the same ones being revealed in this book.

JEWISH HERITAGE SCRIPTURE STUDIES

11

DEBORAH
A MOTHER IN ISRAEL

11. DEBORAH (D'VORAH)—A MOTHER IN ISRAEL

Just before our forefathers, the children of Israel, entered the Promised Land Moses died on Mt. Nebo. The leadership of the nation was passed on to Joshua. God used Joshua to lead the Jewish people through the Jordan River in a miraculous way by drying up the river, just as He did when they passed through the Red Sea 40 years earlier. Joshua and the Israelites circled Jericho and God caused its walls to come down. The Israelites spread through the Promised Land and prospered.

When Joshua and the other leaders passed away a void was left. It was hundreds of years before Israel had its first king. This time period is recorded in the Hebrew Scriptures in the book of Judges. It is in this book that the term "a Mother in Israel" originated. Let's open our hearts and minds, and see what Elohim wants to teach us today!

1. Who are some of the better known judges that God raised up to help Israel?

    <u>Deborah</u>, wife of Lappidoth, was <u>a prophetess</u>; she led Israel..., the men of Israel said to <u>Gideon</u>, "Rule over us..., He (<u>Samson</u>) had led Israel for twenty years. Judges 4:4; 8:22; 16:31

    Deborah, Gideon, and Samson are only three of the over twenty judges that led Israel during this time period of about 400 years.

2. What did the children of Israel do during the time of Deborah, when Israel was being ruthlessly oppressed by King Jabin of Canaan and his army commander Sisera?

    <u>The Israelites cried out to the LORD</u> Judges 4:3

3. What did Deborah, their prophetess and judge, prophesy?

    She summoned Barak... and said to him, "<u>The LORD, the God of Israel, has commanded: Go, march up to Mount Tabor, and take with you ten thousand men... And I will draw Sisera, Jabin's army commander, with his chariots and his troops, toward you... and I will deliver him into your hands."</u> Judges 4:6,7

4. How did Barak react and what second prophecy did God give the brave prophetess Deborah?

*Barak said to her, "If you will go with me, I will go; if not, I will not go." "Very well, I will go with you," she answered. "However, there will be no glory for you in the course you are taking, for then the L*ORD *will deliver Sisera into the hands of a woman." Judges 4:8, 9*

Barak, the leader of Israel's army, did not manifest a full faith in the Word of God and was only willing to go into the battle if Deborah went with him. For his lack of faith God took the glory and the honor for the victory away from him and gave it to a woman who was not even trained for battle.

5. What happened when Barak and his small army came at Sisera and the army of the Canaanites?

*Then Deborah said to Barak, "Up! This is the day on which the L*ORD *will deliver Sisera into your hands: the L*ORD *is marching before you." Barak charged down . . . All of Sisera's soldiers fell by the sword; not a man was left. Judges 4:14, 16*

6. Sisera, the Canaanite army commander, jumped out of his chariot and ran for his life. He hid himself in the tent of a lady named Jael. What did Jael do to Sisera while he was hiding in her tent, fulfilling the prophecy God gave to Deborah?

When he was fast asleep from exhaustion, she approached him stealthily and drove the pin through his temple till it went down to the ground. Thus he died. On that day God subdued King Jabin of Hazor before the Israelites. And the land was tranquil forty years. Judges 4:21, 23; 5:31

You might say "he was pinned down." God fulfilled the prophecy and gave the victory into the hand of Jael instead of Barak.

7. What was sung after the war was won, honoring the faith and courage of Deborah?

Deliverance ceased, Ceased in Israel, till you arose, O Deborah, arose, O mother, in Israel! Judges 5:7

Thus, we have the first time the term "mother in Israel" is used. Deborah judged Israel for 40 years and God gave us rest under her leadership and direction. Deborah is not the only woman mentioned in the Bible to whom God gave the gift of prophecy.

11. DEBORAH (D'VORAH)—A MOTHER IN ISRAEL

8. What was the purpose of prophets and prophetesses like Deborah?

<u>**My Lord God does nothing without having revealed His purpose to His servants the prophets.**</u> ***The spirit of <u>the Lord has spoken through me, His message</u> is on my tongue.*** *When the Lord brought Israel up from Egypt, it was through a prophet;* <u>***through a prophet they were guarded.***</u> Amos 3:7; 2 Samuel 23:2; Hosea 12:14

Adonai has given us His prophets and prophetesses to guard us and to reveal His purpose for us. How comforting to know that God does nothing without first revealing it to His prophets.

9. What will happen to us if we trust God's prophets?

Trust firmly in the Lord your God and you will stand firm; <u>***trust firmly in His prophets and you will succeed.***</u> 2 Chronicles 20:20

What a wonderful promise! As we trust the Lord we stand firm and as we trust His Word through His prophets we will succeed. True success comes from the Lord, from following His Word. There are lots of books and seminars on the market on how to be successful, but here is the simple formula for success right from God's Word: trust Him and trust His Word and we are guaranteed success. Who could ask for anything more? Do you want God's success? Are you willing to trust His prophets?

There are many who profess to hear from God, who claim to be able to tell the future, but God's Word gives us a high standard to test whether the message is actually from God or not. We will look at five tests (a-e) of a prophet of Elohim.

10. How can we know today if a prophet is a true prophet of God or not?

<u>***To the Law and to the testimony!***</u> ***If they do not speak according to this word, it is because there is no light in them. . . .*** <u>***The prophets are subject to the prophets.***</u> Isaiah 8:20; I Corin.14:32 KJV

a) They must speak according to the Law and not against or in contradiction to the Law of God.

b) They must agree with and be in harmony with all the prophets of God who have come before them.

Thus, if it appears that the writings of a prophet are contradicting a previous prophet either that person is not a true prophet of God or we are misinterpreting their writings.

11. What is another test of a true prophet of Elohim?

> *And should you ask yourselves, "How can we know that the oracle was not spoken by the LORD?"—if the prophet speaks in the name of the LORD and <u>the oracle does not come true, that oracle was not spoken by the LORD</u>; the prophet has uttered it presumptuously: do not stand in dread of him.* Deut. 18:21, 22

c) Their prophecies must come true.

This is not to say that the prophet is infallible. King David told Nathan the prophet that he wanted to build a temple to the LORD. Nathan said, **"Go and do it, the Lord is with you."** (2 Sam. 7:3) But that night God spoke to Nathan and told him to go back to David and tell him that he would not be the one to build the Temple of God. At first Nathan was not prophesying; he was just giving his personal opinion.

Also, God's prophecies are conditional upon our reaction to the prophecy. God told Jonah to tell the city of Nineveh that God was going to destroy the city. But the people repented and thus God refrained from doing what He said He would do. God's prophecies are conditional both ways. If Elohim prophesies blessings and we turn from the conditions of faith, love for Him, and obedience to Him, the prophecy will not come to pass. He will not force His prophesied blessings upon those who truly do not want Him.

12. What if their prophecy comes true but they do not love God?

> <u>*Even if the sign or portent that he named to you comes true, do not heed the words of that prophet or that dream-diviner.*</u> *For the LORD your God is testing you to see whether you really love the LORD your God with all your heart and soul.* Deut. 13:3, 4

d) A prophet or prophetess of God should be a godly person.

Their lives should be in harmony with the Word of God. This is not to say they are perfect, but they should have a heart after God. They should believe in the prophesied Messiah, and they should be striving, by God's power, to keep God's commandments.

False prophets might be able to guess or predict with some accuracy. And, as you remember from lesson 10, Satan is the master deceiver. He is very good at being able to foresee what will probably happen and communicate that through people who are under his influence, just as he spoke through a serpent to Eve to deceive her. He can take many forms and use various instruments,

11. DEBORAH (D'VORAH)—A MOTHER IN ISRAEL

even human beings unaware, to hide himself. A prophet of God must meet all the requirements, not just be correct sometimes.

13. What will the message of a true prophet of Elohim contain?

> **The L<small>ORD</small> warned** *Israel and Judah by every prophet [and] every seer, saying: "<u>Turn back from your wicked ways, and observe My commandments and My laws</u>, according to all the Teaching that I commanded your fathers and that I transmitted to you through My servants the prophets."* 2 Kings 17:13

e) True prophets will call us to turn from sin and lead us to obedience.

Notice that the text says that "every prophet" called the people to turn from their wicked ways and to observe God's commandments and laws. This is a very important test of a prophet in an age when many people are professing to hear messages from God, only to tell us who will be the next president, or what direction I should go in my life, or how many kids I am going to have. Yet, the Bible does not say that the gift of prophecy was for predictions, but for leading us to see our sins, which will lead us to the Savior, which will lead us to obedience to God's laws. Many professed "voices for God" are doing just the opposite. Some are even going so far as to say God's laws have been done away. Yet God's Word remains the same—true prophets lead us away from sin and to obedience through the Messiah.

14. What are some of the different ways Elohim speaks to and through His prophets?

> *The L<small>ORD</small> came down in a pillar of cloud . . . and He said, "Hear these My words: When a prophet of the L<small>ORD</small> arises among you, <u>I make Myself known to him in a vision, I speak with him in a dream.</u>" "<u>The L<small>ORD</small> put out His hand and touched my mouth</u>, and the L<small>ORD</small> said to me: Herewith <u>I put My words into your mouth</u>."* Numbers 12:5,6, Jeremiah 1:9

The difference between a dream and a vision is that a vision is like a dream that takes place while the person is still awake. We read in an earlier lesson about Joseph, to whom God spoke in dreams. We will see in an upcoming lesson that God spoke to Daniel in both dreams and visions.

15. What type of person does Adonai use as a prophet and until what time will He continue to have prophets?

> *I will pour out My spirit on <u>all flesh</u>; your <u>sons</u> and <u>daughters</u>*

shall prophesy; your <u>old</u> men shall dream dreams, and your <u>young</u> men shall see visions. I will even pour out My spirit upon <u>male and female</u> slaves in those days. <u>Before the great and terrible day of the L<small>ORD</small> comes</u> . . . Joel 3:1-3

God is no respecter of persons. He can work through young or old, men or women. Upon "all flesh" the text says. God can work through Jewish people and non-Jewish people. The text also says that God will give the Spirit of Prophecy before the second coming of the Messiah. God's gifts were not just for "Bible times," but for today as well.

Not all of God's prophets and prophetesses wrote books and not all of God's prophets that wrote books had their books contained in the Bible. Since God's gifts will continue until "the great and terrible day of the L<small>ORD</small>," it is important for us to be able to tell the difference between a true prophet and a false one. We don't want to miss a true Word from the L<small>ORD</small>, and we don't want to be misled by a false one. So let's review the five identifications we have discussed:

a) Will teach obedience to the words and laws of God.
b) Will be in harmony with previous prophets of God.
c) The prophecies must come true.
d) The prophet must love and follow God.
e) True prophets will call us to turn from sin, lead us to the Messiah, and to obedience.

16. To what extent does Elohim hold us accountable to read and obey His prophets?

> **"Say to them: <u>Thus said the L<small>ORD</small>: If you do not obey Me, abiding by the Teaching that I have set before you, heeding the words of My servants the prophets whom I have been sending to you persistently . . . I will make this city a curse for all the nations of earth</u>."**
> Jeremiah 26:4-6

What solemn words for us to consider. If we do not choose to obey, by God's power, and do not heed the words of the Bible, we will fall under the curse of God. This is not a popular message; it is not soothing to our ears. But a warning against upcoming danger is more valuable than smooth talk on the road to destruction.

17. To what extent does God hold His prophets accountable?

11. DEBORAH (D'VORAH)—A MOTHER IN ISRAEL

> *... the word of the LORD came to me: "O mortal, I appoint you watchman for the House of Israel; and <u>when you hear a word from My mouth, you must warn them for Me</u>. If I say to a wicked man, 'You shall die,' and you do not warn him—you do not speak to warn the wicked man of his wicked course in order to save his life—he, the wicked man, shall die for his iniquity, but <u>I will require a reckoning for his blood from you</u>. But if you do warn the wicked man, and he does not turn back from his wickedness and his wicked course, he shall die for his iniquity, but you will have saved your own life.* Ezekiel 3:16-19

Down through the ages prophets and prophetesses have not always been well received or appreciated. Being a spokesperson for God is not always an easy or pleasant position. Yet, if we do not warn others of their need for God, then according to the prophet their blood will be upon us. Most people do not want to be the bearer of bad news. Who would want to give news of cancer, or of a crime, or of death? How much worse is it to be the one to warn people of their sins? But God has called us to warn in love, with kindness, and with a true concern for the other person's best interest. We are not ready to warn others until we truly love them and like Moses are willing to say, *"if You will forgive their sin (well and good); but if not erase me from the record which You have written!"* Exodus 32:32

18. What does Adonai think of the false prophets of today who claim to be mediums, diviners, sorcerers, people who cast spells, or who consult ghosts or familiar spirits, or who inquire of the dead, or read crystal balls, palms, cards, horoscopes, and tea leaves, etc.?

> *Now, should people say to you, "<u>Inquire of the ghosts</u> and familiar <u>spirits</u> that chirp and moan; ... of <u>the dead</u> on behalf of the living—<u>for instruction and message</u>," <u>surely, for one who speaks thus there shall be no dawn ... Distress and darkness, with no daybreak; Straitness and gloom, with no dawn</u>.* Isaiah 8:19-22
>
> *<u>Let no one be found among you</u> ... who is an augur, a soothsayer, <u>a diviner, a sorcerer, one who casts spells</u>, or <u>one who consults ghosts</u> or familiar <u>spirits</u>, or <u>one who inquires of the dead. For anyone who does such things is abhorrent to the LORD</u> ... You must be wholehearted with the LORD your God. You shall not tolerate a sorceress.* Deuteronomy 18:10-12; Exodus 22:17

Palm readers, card readers, crystal ball readers, horoscopes, etc. are not from Elohim. They are false prophets. The three texts strongly warn us not to listen to instructions or messages from the dead, from ghosts, or even something that would come as a spirit of someone who is familiar to us. King Solomon wrote, *"the dead know nothing . . . they have no more share till the end of time in all that goes on under the sun."* Ecclesiastes 9:5, 6

19. How did God describe the Greatest Prophet, the Messiah, to Moses?

<u>I will raise up a prophet</u> for them <u>from among their own people, like yourself</u>: <u>I will put My words in his mouth</u> and <u>he will speak to them all that I command him</u>; and if anybody fails to heed the words he speaks in My name, I Myself will call him to account. Deuteronomy 18:18, 19

God raised up for us a Prophet like Moses, and He was even more than a prophet. God put His words in His mouth. He is the Messiah, Immanuel—God with us. We will be held to account if we fail to heed the words of love that He has for us.

20. What do we need to do to escape death and be saved in heaven as a survivor?

<u>Everyone who invokes the name of the</u> L<small>ORD</small> <u>shall escape</u>; for there shall be a remnant on Mount Zion and in Jerusalem, <u>as the</u> L<small>ORD</small> <u>promised</u>. <u>Anyone who invokes the</u> L<small>ORD</small> <u>will be among the survivors</u>. Joel 3:5

The door is open to all; the invitation says, *"everyone who invokes the name of the Lord shall escape."* Call upon the name of the L<small>ORD</small> and He will save you from your sins and mistakes.

Doug Batchelor might be the richest caveman to have ever lived. His mother was a Jewish actress and his father was a Gentile multimillionaire. Growing up among the rich and famous did not appeal to Doug. He was restless and was more comfortable hanging out with the troublemakers. At one point in his life he and his family were living on an island. The island was filled with mansions. The only way on or off the island was by private boat or security bridge. Doug and some of his friends were bored so they broke into their neighbors' homes for fun. They even began to dare each other into breaking into homes that were occupied with the lights on. The community hired a security guard to sail around the island to try to protect the homes from these criminals.

Even though Doug never got caught on any of those adventures he did get

11. DEBORAH (D'VORAH)—A MOTHER IN ISRAEL

into plenty of trouble. His parents didn't know what to do with him. After their divorce they shuttled him to one another in hopes that one of them would be able to straighten him out. They tried everything that money could buy. They sent him to fourteen different schools in nine years, including a strict military school, a lenient experimental free school, and they even tried a school that was on a yacht that sailed around the Mediterranean so these rebellious rich kids could not run away. Doug found a way to run away and he followed some friends up into the desert mountains above Palm Springs. In those mountains he found a fair sized cave with a little stream that ran in front of it. Doug decided to make this his home. He spent most of his time in the nude, except when he hiked down into the city to panhandle, shop, or visit friends. On those occasions he would put on the only clothes he chose to own, his one and only pair of overalls and boots. Doug set up his cave quite nicely with a sleeping area, a little homemade wood stove for making banana bread, and he dammed up the creek and made a swimming pool. He even had a pet cat.

But even then, freed of the materialism of this world, Doug was still not satisfied. He tried various types of drugs, had girlfriends, searched out all kinds of different religions, but nothing seemed to fill the void in his heart.

When he had moved into the cave he had noticed that he was not the first one to live there. Someone had left a Bible on a rock ledge inside the cave. Finally, he decided to read it and it began to change his life. For the first time in his life he felt that life had a purpose, that there was a reason for his existence. At first he read only from the first part of the Bible, but then, with much hesitation, he began to read the second part of the Bible including the life and teachings of Y'shua. He was surprised at how loving, caring, and forgiving Y'shua was. Doug decided Y'shua had to either be a lunatic, or a liar, or who He claimed to be, the Messiah.

As Doug continued to read he was certain that Y'shua was who He claimed to be. He knelt down in that cave and confessed his sins and invited Y'shua into his heart. Doug was filled with peace and contentment. The whole world seemed like a different place. His experience with God was so powerful as a result of reading the Bible that he prayed for God to give him more people to share his new experience with.

Just about this same time his mother had a conversation with someone who worked at NBC News. She happened to mention that her son lived in a cave. The man thought it would be a great story so he had a helicopter flown up into the mountain to interview the rich caveman. Doug was amazed at how God had answered his prayer and made sure that when the cameras were rolling he shared how reading the Bible was filling his life with true joy. A friend of Doug's, who lived in another cave on the mountain, gave Doug a few books that his mother had given him, such as The Great Controversy, Patriarchs and Prophets, and Desire of Ages. Doug started to eat up those spiritual books with a thirst for God that he never had before.

Doug is no longer living in the cave. He has since married, fathered six children, and is currently the president of Amazing Facts, a ministry that shares the love of God and the power of the Bible around the world. Doug's complete story is told in a book called "The Richest Caveman."

By giving us His prophets God has shown His love for you and me as well as His desire to help us live a life in accordance with His good plan. Many of the prophets risked their lives in writing the Scriptures for us. With these studies we are just scratching the surface of the deep, beautiful treasures of wisdom, hope, and promises of Elohim. Read the entire Word of God and your life will be richly blessed in the process.

REVIEW הזרה

1. Who can be given the Spirit of Prophecy?
    a. Men.
    b. Women.
    c. Children.
    d. All of the above.

2. A test of a true prophet is?
    a. Will teach obedience to the words and laws of God.
    b. Will be in harmony with previous prophets of God.
    c. The prophecies must come true.
    d. The prophet must love and follow God.
    e. True prophets will call us to turn from sin, lead us to the Messiah, and to obedience.
    f. All of the above.

3. Will there be true prophets of God even in the last days?
    a. Yes.

11. DEBORAH (D'VORAH)—A MOTHER IN ISRAEL

    b. No.

4. Are these from Elohim: mediums, diviners, sorcerers, people who cast spells, or who consult ghosts or familiar spirits, or who inquire of the dead, or read crystal balls, palms, cards, horoscopes, and tea leaves?

    a. Yes.
    b. No.

5. All the prophecies in the Hebrew Scriptures concerning the Messiah point to Y'shua. Y'shua's words and actions show that He loved God, His Father in Heaven, and He met all the tests of a prophet of God. Since God told Moses the Messiah would come as a Prophet, should we obey His teaching and follow Him?

    a. Yes.
    b. No.

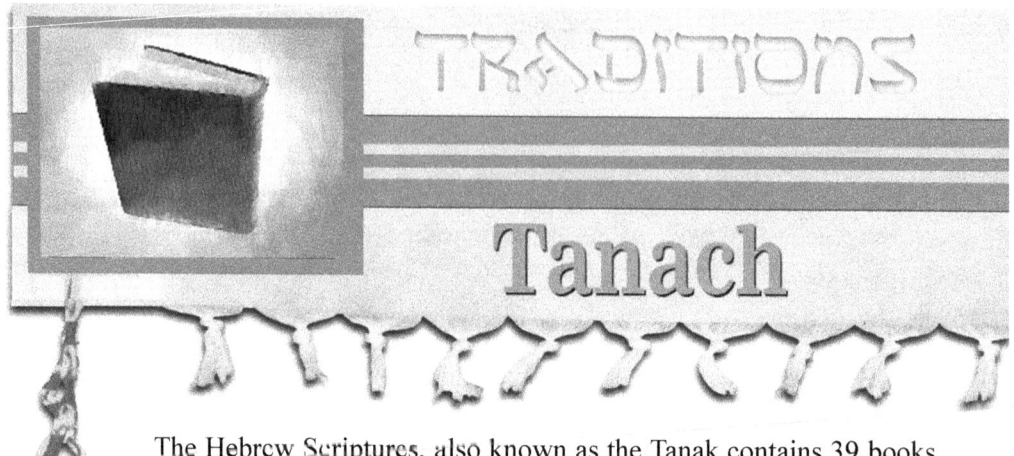

TRADITIONS
Tanach

The Hebrew Scriptures, also known as the Tanak contains 39 books divided into 3 sections. The word TaNaK is an acronym: "T" for Torah, N for navi'im, the Hebrew word for prophets, and K for k'tovim, the Hebrew word for writings.

The first section, the Torah, or in Greek the Pentateuch, was written by Moses and contains 5 books, Genesis, Exodus, Leviticus, Numbers, and Deuteronomy. The Second section is Navi'im or prophets. The Jewish prophets Isaiah, Zechariah, and Ezekiel are among the 21 books in this section. Many of these books contain prophecies concerning the Messiah. The third section, the K'tovim or writings, is comprised of 13 books. This section includes Ecclesiastes and Proverbs, written primarily by King Solomon, and the Psalms written primarily by King David. The book of Daniel, while very prophetic, also contains numerous historical accounts and is included in the "writings" section instead of the "prophets" section.

It is interesting to note that these same 39 books are the exact books used in the Christian Bible (although in a different order) usually under the title Old Testament. What is usually called the New Testament refers to 27 books written by the followers of Y'shua. These additional books are filled with quotes, illustrations, and analogies taken directly from the TaNaK. At times in this book, Jewish Discoveries, the TaNaK, or Hebrew

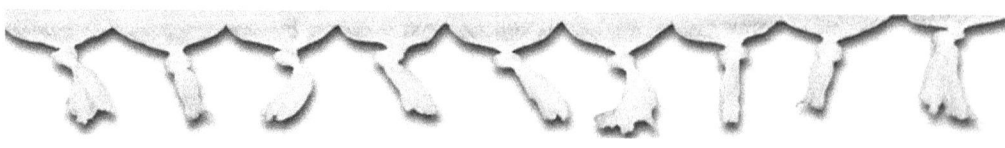

Scriptures, is referred to as the first part of the Bible while the writings of the followers of Y'shua are referred to as the second part of the Bible. If all the quotes, illustrations, and analogies from the Hebrew Scriptures were removed from the second part of the Bible there would not be much left. The Hebrew Scriptures prophesy and the second part of the Bible confirms those prophecies. If you have never read the entire Holy Scriptures, I highly recommend it. It can be purchased at many bookstores under the titles of Holy Scriptures or the Bible.

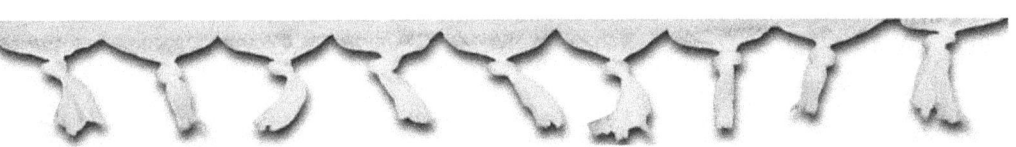

TRADITIONS

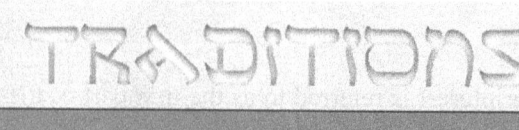

Shavuot

Shavuot means weeks and it is one of the feasts of the LORD mentioned in the Torah. The Torah does not tell us much about Shavuot other than that it comes seven weeks after the wave sheaf offering which took place on the second day of the Feast of Unleavened Bread. The wave sheaf was the first grains of the harvest. They were lifted up to heaven in a show of thanksgiving for the harvest to come. The spring harvest would then commence and last seven weeks. It is from this seven week time period that Shavuot gets its name. In Greek it is called Pentecost from the Greek word penta, meaning fifty. Seven weeks is forty-nine days; when you include the day of the wave sheaf it is fifty days. In Biblical times people came to the Temple in Jerusalem and gave the tithe and offerings of their harvest to the LORD.

Tradition tells us that it was on Shavuot that God gave Moses the Ten Commandments. Shavuot does come during the 40 days that Moses was on Mount Sinai in the presence of God. Whether or not that was the day God handed him the Ten Commandments the Scriptures do not say. In most synagogues the book of Exodus, including the Ten Commandments, is read on Shavuot. Since the biblical account of Ruth took place during the harvest season it is also customary that the book of Ruth is read from during Shavuot.

The Feast of Weeks, Shavuot, was one of the three holy days on which God commanded the men of Israel to come together before Him in Jerusalem. In the year 31 CE Y'shua was killed on Passover and was raised from the dead on the feast of the Wave Sheaf offering as a first fruit of the resurrection. On Shavuot of that year Y'shua's followers were in Jerusalem speaking to the large group of Jewish people who had gathered for the feast from various countries around Israel. God poured out His Spirit on the disciples of the Messiah and they began speaking in the native languages of the Jewish people who had gathered from the surrounding nations. The disciples shared with the people the message of a risen Messiah. As a result of their preaching 3,000 Jewish people believed in Y'shua and were immersed. (See chapter 2 of the book Acts in the Bible)

Just as Shavuot was a time of agricultural harvest, it now also became a time of spiritual harvest. Just as God poured out His Spirit on the anniversary of the giving of His royal law it reminds us of the promise that God gave to us that He would write His laws in our hearts and minds as He pours out His Spirit upon us in the last days of earth's history.

Magan David

The Magen David is the six pointed star also known as the Star of David. Magen David literally means "shield of David." It is not certain when the star became a Jewish symbol, but it was used on synagogues as far back as the fourth century as is seen in the remains of a synagogue in Capernaum, Israel. The Nazis forced Jewish people to wear yellow Jewish Star patches on their clothing. Today a blue Star of David sits in the center of the flag of Israel and a red Star of David is the symbol of Israel's first aid and relief organization called Magen David Adom. The Magen David is two triangles woven together, one triangle is pointing up to Elohim, the other pointing down to us.

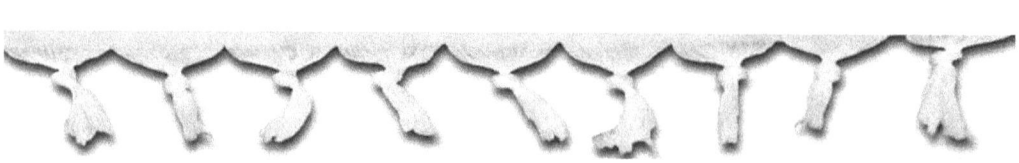

JEWISH HERITAGE
SCRIPTURE STUDIES

דוד
DAVID
KING OF ISRAEL

12. KING DAVID

David was one of the greatest kings in history —in fact, many believe he was one of the greatest men who ever lived. Elohim referred to David as a man after His own heart. We know this was not because David was perfect, but because he was quick to see his mistakes and come to God for forgiveness.

1. When Samuel was prophet and judge over Israel, what did the people ask for?

    All the elders of Israel . . . said to him, "You have grown old . . . Therefore <u>appoint a king for us</u>, to govern us like all other nations. 1 Samuel 8:4, 5

    Elohim set us apart as His special people with His directions. He was our Leader, our King. But we wanted to be like everyone else.

2. How did Samuel and Elohim feel about this request?

    Samuel was <u>displeased</u> . . . Samuel prayed to the L<small>ORD</small>, and the L<small>ORD</small> replied to Samuel . . . it is not you that they have rejected; <u>it is Me they have rejected</u> as their king. 1 Samuel 8:6, 7

    In wanting to be like everyone else we were rejecting God. God does not desire that we live just like everyone else; He has a much better plan for us. His Word gives us direction for how to live our lives and it is radically different from the rest of the world. God gives us rest, peace, joy, satisfaction, contentment, forgiveness, patience, and power over temptation that the world does not know.

3. Whom did Adonai appoint as the first king of Israel in response to the petition of His people?

    Samuel took a flask of oil and poured some on <u>Saul</u>'s head and kissed him, and said, "The L<small>ORD</small> herewith anoints you ruler over His own people." 1 Samuel 10:1

4. Saul did not follow the counsels of God. God rejected Saul, and sent Samuel to anoint David as the next king. What happened to David at that time?

*Samuel took the horn of oil and anointed him . . . **and the spirit of the LORD gripped David from that day on.*** 1 Samuel 16:13

The Spirit of the LORD gripped David. It was the Spirit of the LORD upon David that made David great. We can also have the Spirit of the LORD. As Moses said: *"Would that . . . the LORD put His Spirit upon"* everyone. (Numbers 11:29)

God allowed Saul to remain king for many years even after David was anointed to be the next king. At one time Saul had the Spirit of the LORD, but eventually he turned his back on God and rejected the Spirit. God was very merciful and long-suffering with Saul as He is with each one of us. Elohim is not wanting that any should perish, but that all would come to repentance.

5. After David was anointed to be the next king what major event in his life took place?

__Goliath, the Philistine__ . . . stepped forward . . . the men of Israel . . . fled in terror. __David said to Saul . . . Your servant will go and fight that Philistine!__ But Saul said to David, "You cannot . . . you are only a boy . . . __David replied to Saul . . . The LORD . . . will . . . save me from that Philistine."__ The Philistine . . . said to David, "Come here, and I will give your flesh to the birds . . ." __David replied to the Philistine, "You come against me with sword and spear and javelin; but I come against you in the name of the LORD of Hosts . . . the battle is the LORD's, and He will deliver you into our hands." . . . David . . . took out a stone and slung it. It struck the Philistine in the forehead; the stone sank into his forehead, and he fell face down on the ground.__ 1 Samuel 17:23,24, 32-34, 37, 44, 45, 47, 49

The Spirit of the LORD gave David the courage to fight the giant. God gave David His Spirit before He called him to go and fight against the giant. God gives us His Spirit today so we can fight against the giant issues and problems that come against us.

6. Saul became jealous of David's growing popularity. He did everything he could to destroy him. David even had to flee from Saul and live in the wilderness. When David had the opportunity to kill Saul what did he do?

Saul took three thousand picked men from all Israel and went in search of David . . . There was a cave there, and Saul went in to relieve himself. Now David and his men were sitting in the back of the cave. David's men said to him, "This is the day of which the LORD said to you, 'I will deliver your enemy into your hands . . ."

12. KING DAVID

<u>David . . . said to his men, "The L<small>ORD</small> forbid that I should do such a thing to . . . the L<small>ORD</small>'s anointed—that I should raise my hand against him; for he is the L<small>ORD</small>'s anointed." David rebuked his men and did not permit them to attack Saul.</u> 1 Samuel 24:3-8

This experience, above all others, showed David's greatness. David had already been anointed by Elohim to be the next king; Saul was acting like a lunatic by hunting David in order to kill him. David could have justifiably killed Saul and taken the throne. Nevertheless, David continued to show love and mercy toward Saul. David patiently waited many years for God's will to be made manifest. David trusted in God's timing, and God's way of dealing with the situation.

7. What are some of Saul's worst sins recorded in God's word?

    Saul died for the trespass that he had committed against the L<small>ORD</small> in <u>not having fulfilled the command of the L<small>ORD</small></u>; moreover, <u>he had consulted a ghost to seek advice</u>, and <u>did not seek advice of the L<small>ORD</small></u> . . . 1 Chronicles 10:13, 14

    Several sins are mentioned as being the cause of Saul's downfall. He did not do what Elohim commanded to be done. He did not seek God's advice. He tried to speak to the dead, and he consulted a ghost. These sins will eventually end in disaster. I pray that we are learning from these lessons to obey God, to do what He commands, to read His word, the Bible, and follow its advice, and not try to communicate with the dead.

8. After 39 years as Israel's first king, Saul's life ended tragically. David mourned greatly for his enemy. David had not held onto a grudge or anger at Saul even though Saul continually tried to kill David and made his life extremely difficult. David became king and Israel prospered. After many years of faithful service, David fell into sin also. But here is the difference between David's sin and Saul's. David repented and Saul did not. How did David express his sorrow for his sins? What specifically did David ask to not be taken away from him?

    "Have mercy upon me, O God, as befits Your faithfulness; in keeping with Your abundant compassion, blot out my transgressions. Wash me thoroughly of my iniquity, and purify me of my sin; for I recognize my transgressions, and am ever conscious of my sin. Purge me with hyssop till I am pure; wash me till I am whiter than snow. Hide Your face from my sins; blot out all my iniquities. Fashion a pure heart for me, O God; create in me a steadfast spirit. <u>Do</u>

not cast me out of Your presence, or take Your holy spirit away from me. Let me again rejoice in Your help; let a vigorous spirit sustain me. I will teach transgressors Your ways, that sinners may return to You." Psalm 51:3-5, 9, 11-15

When David prayed to be *"purged with hyssop till I am pure"* he was referring to the blood of the lambs that were placed on the doorposts with hyssop during the first Passover. The blood of those lambs, like the blood of the lambs in the Sanctuary service, represented the death of the Messiah washing away our sins, protecting us from eternal death. In no less manner, God has made provision for our sins to be purged and removed from us by the death of the Messiah.

David prayed that Elohim would not take His Holy Spirit, Ruach HaKodesh, away from him because of his sin. David received the Holy Spirit when Samuel anointed him. It was the Holy Spirit that brought the conviction of David's sin to his heart. It was the Holy Spirit that gave David courage and humility.

9. The Bible says that the Messiah would come from the lineage of David. How did the Scriptures refer to the Messiah, who would show grace, mercy and peace to His enemies as David did?

For <u>a child</u> has been born to us, <u>A son</u> has been given us. And authority has settled on his shoulders. He has been <u>named "The Mighty God is planning grace; The Eternal Father, a peaceable ruler"</u>—In token of abundant <u>authority and of peace without limit</u> upon David's throne and kingdom . . . Isaiah 9:5, 6

The Messiah would come as a child and yet would be known as "the Mighty God."

10. Are there other places in the Scriptures where God is referred to as coming to earth as a child?

"Listen, House of David," [Isaiah] retorted, "is it not enough for you to treat men as helpless that you also treat my God as helpless? Assuredly, my Lord will give you a sign of His own accord! Look, <u>the young woman is with child and about to give birth to a son. Let her name him Immanuel.</u> Isaiah 7:13, 14

Immanuel means "with us is God." Would it still be a miracle if the mother of this child was just a young married woman giving birth to a son? She is specifically referred to as young because she is a virgin. The child is referred to as Immanuel because He is God with us, God manifested as a human. The Messiah was not a man who became God; He is God who became a man.

11. What are some other times when God came to earth as a man?

<u>**The Lord appeared to . . . (Abraham)**</u>; *he was sitting at the entrance of the tent . . . Looking up,* <u>**he saw three men**</u> *standing near him. . . . He ran . . . to greet them and, bowing to the ground, he said, ". . . let me fetch a morsel of bread that you may refresh yourselves . . ."* Genesis 18:1,2,5

<u>**Jacob was left alone.**</u> *And* <u>**a man wrestled with him**</u> *until the break of dawn . . . Said the other, "What is your name?" He replied, "Jacob." Said he, "Your name shall no longer be Jacob, but Israel, for you have striven with God and man, and have prevailed." . . . So* <u>**Jacob named the place Peniel**</u> *. . ."* Gen. 32:25-31

Peniel literally means face of God.

12. Do the Hebrew Scriptures teach that God has a Son?

Nor do I possess knowledge of the Holy One. Who has ascended heaven and come down? . . . Who has established all the extremities of the earth? <u>**What is his name or his son's name**</u>*, if you know it?* Proverbs 30:3, 4

Amazing as it might seem, the Jewish Scriptures say that God has a Son. They are one family; they are one unit. There is only one God family.

13. Are there other places where our God family refers to themselves in the plural form?

God said, "Let <u>**us**</u> *make man in* <u>**our**</u> *image, after* <u>**our**</u> *likeness . . . the Lord God said, "Now that the man has become like one of* <u>**us**</u> *. . ."* Genesis 1:26; 3:22

This might seem shocking at first, but it is in the first chapter of the Torah, the very beginning of the entire Jewish Scriptures. The plural words "us" or "our" are used four different times showing how this one God family communicated with each other right from the beginning in the first book of the Torah.

14. Where does Elohim give us an example in His Scriptures of more than one individual still being considered as one?

Hence <u>**a man**</u> *leaves his father and mother and* <u>**clings to his wife**</u>*, so that* <u>**they become one flesh**</u>*. The* <u>**two of them**</u> *. . . the man and his wife.* Genesis 2:24, 25

In the second chapter of the Torah, after God created two individual people, Adam and Eve, and brought them together as husband and wife, He tells us that when men and women marry the two people become one flesh. How is it to be understood that a husband and wife become one flesh? Certainly they don't physically become one flesh with one head, one mouth, one nose, etc. But they are one in heart, one in spirit, one in purpose. They are to be united in their goals and plans, walking and working together as one unit. This is what it means in the Shema when it says that God is one. God is one in the same way a family is one, even if it has three people in the one family. God, the Holy Spirit, and God the Messiah are <u>one God family</u> even though they each have different responsibilities. They are united as one. They work together as having one mind, one desire, one plan, one purpose, one goal. One rope has three strands, but it is still one rope.

15. Are these three individuals in the one God family mentioned in the Hebrew Scriptures?

    <u>"From the time anything existed, I was there</u>. "And now the <u>Lord God</u> has sent <u>me</u>, and <u>His Spirit</u>." Isaiah 48:16 (margin)

    All three are clearly mentioned in this text by the Jewish prophet Isaiah. There is the ***"Lord God,"*** there is the ***"Me,"*** who was there ***"from the time anything existed,"*** and there is ***"His Spirit."*** These are the ***"us"*** mentioned in Genesis 1:26. The Scriptures are not talking about 3 different gods. It is one unified God family. If we were to speak of the Cohen family, for example, we would say they are one family. There may be three individuals, Alan, Ellen, & Leah, but they are all Cohens; they are all one family. God is one God even though the Scriptures talk of three individuals in that one God family. Challah bread is one loaf although it is made up of three braids of dough. A havdallah candle is a single candle even though it is made up of several wicks. A Passover matzah cover is one matzah tosh even though it has three compartments containing three pieces of matzah.

16. God's name reveals that God is a plural unity. The Hebrew word "El" means God singular, as it is used in the words: "Beth-el," which means "House of God," and "Peniel," meaning "face of God." In Hebrew, when we want to make a masculine word plural we add the Hebrew letters "yod and final mem" (pronounced "eem") onto the end, just as in English we add an "s" to the end of words to make them plural. The Hebrew word most used in the Hebrew Scriptures for the name of God is אלהים and is pronounced El-o-

heem. The "eem" sound on the end makes the name of God plural. Even in God's name, Elohim, we see the plurality of the single God family.

We often use the word "one" in the plural sense. We say: "one family," "one flock of geese," "one cluster of grapes." These are examples of several objects being considered one as they are united together as one unit. The United States of America is comprised of many states yet it is one nation. One baseball team has at least nine players yet it is still one team. God is not three different gods competing against each other as in Greek mythology. God is one God comprised of three individual Beings working together as one unit as the words "Eloheem," "us," and "our" indicate in Genesis chapter one of the Torah.

We have been taught for so long that God is singular that these texts from the Torah and other parts of the Bible might seem hard to understand. If this concept of God being one family is new to you, pray and ask God for wisdom, then read questions 8-16 again.

17. What other names of God are found in Scripture that signify His relationship to humanity?

I the L<small>ORD</small> am your <u>Savior</u>, I, The <u>Mighty One of Jacob</u>, am <u>your Redeemer</u>. Isaiah 60:16

Note: The name Savior is from the word Salvation, in Hebrew it is ישוע and is pronounced Ye-shoo-ah. That was the Messiah's name when He walked this earth.

18. In His first advent, what did the Messiah redeem us from?

He shall come as redeemer to Zion, to those in Jacob who turn back <u>from sin</u>. Isaiah 59:20

The biggest problem in this world and in our lives is the sin problem, the problem that the Messiah came to redeem us from.

19. How did He save or redeem us from our sins?

If any person . . . incurs guilt by doing any of the things which by the L<small>ORD</small>'<small>S</small> commandments ought not to be done, and he realizes his guilt—or the sin of which he is guilty is brought to his knowledge . . . <u>the sin offering shall be slaughtered</u> . . . <u>and he shall be forgiven.</u> In all their troubles He was troubled . . . In His love and pity <u>He Himself redeemed them</u> . . . Lev. 4:27-31; Isaiah 63:9

God the Messiah Himself redeemed us by becoming the sin offering for us. The Messiah came in His first advent to redeem us from our sins by dying for those sins. He will come in His second advent to redeem us from the wicked who will be causing a time of trouble that is worse than anything that has been seen before.

You may have made mistakes like David did, but you can be a person after God's own heart as David was, by being quick to confess your mistakes to God and by submitting to His leadership.

King David's experiences and writings are mentioned in at least five different books in the Bible. We certainly could not cover it all here. I encourage you to read all the accounts of his life from the Scriptures themselves along with the psalms that he wrote.

Sidney Robboy was born in Russia during the cruel anti-Semitic pogroms of the Czars. When Sidney was a young boy his family escaped from Russia by walking all night and hiding under barns during the day. Eventually Sidney moved to the United States, married, had children, and started his own business, but he never forgot the faithfulness of his parents. He and his wife retired in a community in Florida where his wife passed away. He met a widow named Ginney from the same development at the community pool.

A few years later they decided to date and get married, but who could perform the wedding and where would they worship? Sidney was Jewish and Ginney was Christian. They decided to visit the Beth-El Shalom Congregation in St. Petersburg, Florida. Sidney enjoyed the Friday night Shabbat services, being called up to the bimah, and chanting the Torah blessing. Ginney was thankful for the congregation's faith in Y'shua as the Messiah. Sidney and Ginney began studying the Jewish Discoveries with a Bible instructor from the congregation. Sidney enjoyed and looked forward to the studies each week even though he struggled with the thought of accepting Y'shua as his Messiah. One day Sidney became very ill and had to be hospitalized for a couple of months. It did not look like Sidney was going to recover and his daughter began making arrangements for him to come live by her in a nursing home. Sidney did not want to move back north. He did not want to leave Ginney. And he did not want to live in a nursing home. Ginney, her friends, and the entire Beth-El Shalom congregation began to pray earnestly for God to work a mira-

12. KING DAVID

cle in Sidney's behalf. The Bible teacher visited Sidney in the hospital several times to comfort and pray with him. He asked Sidney if he had any questions regarding the topics they had studied together. Sidney responded by saying everything was very clear but that he couldn't accept Y'shua as the Messiah. The teacher asked a few more questions. "Were your parents religious?" "Yes," Sidney replied. "Did they love God?" "Yes, very much so." "If they had had the opportunity to study these lessons like you have, and they saw all of the Bible texts that point to Y'shua as the Messiah as you have seen, do you think they would have accepted Him as their Messiah?" Sidney paused, "Yes, I think they would." The teacher continued, "Since they would have accepted Y'shua as the Messiah if they knew what you know, do you think you should accept Him as well?" Sidney answered, "Yes, I think I should." They prayed together and Sidney invited Y'shua into his heart. Sidney's recovery was remarkable and shocked his doctors and daughter. Sidney and Ginney married and lived happily ever after until Sidney's death several years later.

REVIEW הזרה

1. David showed the greatness of the Spirit of God working through him when he:
   a. Chose not to harm Saul even when Saul tried to kill him.
   b. Was willing to stand up for God when Goliath cursed God.
   c. Repented from his sins.
   d. All of the above.

2. Both Saul and David were anointed by God to be king; both made mistakes and sinned. God rejected Saul and David remained accepted. What made the difference?
   a. David repented and Saul did not.
   b. David was more handsome.
   c. Saul's sins were bigger.

3. God's Son, the Messiah, was to come from David's lineage:
   a. In a miraculous way, as a human, a child, to be God on earth, bringing a message of peace.
   b. As the prime minister of Israel.
   c. As the pope.

4. For what reason did the Messiah come the first time?

a. To be Immanuel, God with us.
   b. To be our Savior and Redeemer.
   c. To be our sacrificial offering, dying for our sins.
   d. All of the above.

5. God the Father in heaven, the Messiah, and God's Holy Spirit can all be one in the same way as:
   a. A man and a woman become one flesh when they marry.
   b. One family can have three people in it.
   c. One rope is made up of three strands.
   d. One nation can have many states.
   e. One flock of geese can have many geese in it.
   f. One loaf of challah is made of three pieces of dough.
   g. One havdallah candle has several wicks.
   h. One Passover matzah tosh has three compartments.
   i. All of the above.

6. Even though this lesson might have presented some new concepts to you that are hard to grasp and understand, are you willing to accept what the Scriptures say regarding the plural oneness of the God family?
   a. Yes
   b. I would like to re-read this lesson and the Scripture texts mentioned before making a decision.

7. Would you like to join David and have your sins forgiven and be empowered by Elohim's spirit?
   a. Yes.
   b. No.

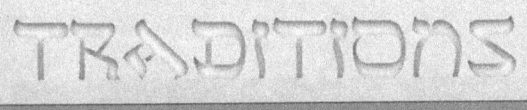

Shema

"Shema Yisrael, Adonai Elohenu, Adonai Echad." These words are the first words in every mezuzah. They are written in every tefillin and are recited every day by some Jewish people. They are considered the watchwords of Judaism. They are translated, **"Hear O Israel, the Lord our God, the Lord is one."**

The word Echad, אחד, translated one, is often used in the Scriptures denoting a plural one such as in Genesis 2:24 when Elohim said the man and the woman, the two, would be one flesh. (Other examples include two nations becoming one people, and two sticks becoming one stick—see Genesis 34:16,22 and Ezekiel 37:17). When the Scriptures refer to a specifically singular one and only one, it uses the Hebrew word Yachid, יחיד. An example of this is seen in the Torah in Genesis 22:2,12,16, when God refers to Isaac as Abraham and Sarah's one and only son. (Other examples of this include: Judges 11:34; Proverbs 4:3; Jeremiah 6:26; Amos 8:10; Zechariah 12:10). Yachid, one and only singular one, is never used to describe God in the Scriptures. When Moses quoted God, reciting the Shema in Deuteronomy 6:4, he did not use the singular "one and only" adjective Yachid. Rather he used Echad, which can be either singular or plural.

JEWISH HERITAGE
SCRIPTURE STUDIES

SOLOMON
THE WISE MAN

13. KING SOLOMON (SHLOMO)

Solomon's life clearly reveals God's mercy and God's willingness to work all things for good concerning us. God can turn the most horrible situation into a blessing for those who love God.

Bathsheba was Solomon's mother. Her first husband, Uriah, was a soldier in King David's army. David slept with Bathsheba while Uriah was in battle and she became pregnant. David eventually arranged it so that Uriah would die in battle. David then took Bathsheba as his wife, but the child of their illicit relationship died. Elohim continued to speak to David's heart until he finally confessed his sins. Adonai graciously forgave David. David and Bathsheba had a second child and they named him Solomon. It was under these circumstances that Solomon came into the world and later became the next King of Israel.

1. How did David express his sorrow for the sins he committed against Solomon's mother Bathsheba? We have visited this text several times before, but it is so good it cannot be reviewed too often. It certainly fits here, as this was the prayer that David prayed when he came under conviction for committing adultery and for having Uriah killed. It is one of the most beautiful and sincere prayers of repentance. It would be good if our prayers of repentance were modeled (not copied) after it.

> *"Have mercy upon me, O God, as befits Your faithfulness; in keeping with Your abundant compassion, blot out my transgressions. Wash me thoroughly of my iniquity, and purify me of my sin; for I recognize my transgressions, and am ever conscious of my sin. Purge me with hyssop till I am pure; wash me till I am whiter than snow. Hide Your face from my sins; blot out all my iniquities. Fashion a pure heart for me, O God; create in me a steadfast spirit. Do not cast me out of Your presence, or take Your Holy Spirit away from me. Let me again rejoice in Your help; let a vigorous spirit sustain me. I will teach transgressors Your ways, that sinners may return to You."* Psalm 51:3-5, 9-15

King Solomon is known as the wisest man who ever lived. He wrote hundreds of wise sayings recorded in the book of Proverbs in the Scriptures. In this lesson we will find out what we can gain for our lives today from listening to wise King Solomon.

2. What instructions did David give Solomon before David died?

> *"I am going the way of all the earth; be strong and show yourself a man.* <u>*Keep the charge of the* LORD *your God, walking in His ways and following His laws, His commandments, His rules, and His admonitions as recorded in the Teaching of Moses, in order that you may succeed in whatever you undertake and wherever you turn*</u>*.*
> 1 Kings 2:2, 3

There are many books on the market teaching various ways to become successful. David recommended one book, the Bible, to his son Solomon that promised him success if he followed its instructions. David told his son Solomon that true success comes from walking in God's ways, following His laws, His rules, His commandments, and His admonitions. The same is true for us today. If we apply the advice David gave to Solomon in our lives, we can claim the promise of success. It is interesting that David, a man after God's own heart, equated being "strong and showing yourself as a man," with keeping God's commandments and following God. Real men and women keep God's commandments and follow God. This is the formula for success in life.

3. When Solomon became King, what did he ask of Elohim, showing His devotion to his people?

> *The* LORD *appeared to Solomon in a dream . . ."what shall I grant you?" Solomon said . . .* <u>*an understanding mind to judge Your people, to distinguish between good and bad.*</u> 1 Kings 3:5, 6, 9

What would you ask for if the Ruler of the universe, who owns everything and is all-powerful, asked you what you wanted? Solomon wanted to be able to help people and to live for God. What a noble request that Solomon would ask for wisdom to help other people and the ability to tell right from wrong.

Solomon did not rely on his own wisdom. Instead he asked God to give him discernment and an understanding mind. True wisdom, understanding, and discernment come as a gift from God. Since this gift comes only from Elohim it is important for us to pray for it before we read the Bible, this book, or any book, or do anything. If you have not prayed before reading this lesson, pause and do so.

4. How did God respond to Solomon's unselfish request?

13. KING SOLOMON (SHLOMO)

*"**The LORD was pleased** . . . And God said to him, "Because you asked for this—**you did not ask for long life, you did not ask for riches, you did not ask for the life of your enemies, but you asked for discernment in dispensing justice**—I now do as you have spoken. **I grant you a wise and discerning mind; there has never been anyone like you before, nor will anyone like you arise again. And I also grant you what you did not ask for—both riches and glory all your life—the like of which no king has ever had. And I will further grant you long life, if you will walk in My ways and observe My laws and commandments.**"* 1 Kings 3:10-14

If we put God and others first God will be pleased and will more than take care of us. *"**Humble yourself in the sight of the LORD and He will lift you up.**"*

5. Solomon built the Temple of the LORD, which was fashioned after the manner of the Temple Moses built in the wilderness. Solomon's Temple was larger, more permanent. When the Queen of Sheba visited Solomon what did she observe?

*When the queen of Sheba observed all of **Solomon's wisdom**, and **the palace** he had built, **the fare of his table**, **the seating of his courtiers**, **the service** and **attire of his attendants**, and **his wine service**, and **the burnt offerings** that he offered at **the House of the LORD**, she was left breathless.* 1 King 10:4, 5

There were several specific things that impressed the Queen of Sheba. She observed the wisdom that Elohim had given Solomon and the beauty of his palace. She also noticed what Solomon ate. No doubt it was only "biblically kosher" healthy foods. She saw that the servants were happy to serve their king and they were treated decently. The queen took note of what the attendants were wearing. It may have been much more modest than she was used to. Solomon did not neglect to show her the most important thing—the way to receive forgiveness—the burnt offering.

6. In the proverbs of wise King Solomon what did he tell us about alcoholic wine?

*"**Wine is a scoffer, strong drink a roisterer; He who is muddled by them will not grow wise. Do not be of those who guzzle wine. Who cries, "Woe!" who, "Alas!" Who has quarrels, who complaints; Who has wounds without cause; Who has bleary eyes? Those whom wine keeps till the small hours, Those who gather to drain the cups. Do not ogle that red wine As it lends its color to the cup, As it flows on smoothly; In the end, it bites like a snake**".* Proverbs 20:1; 23:20,

29-32

King Solomon himself told us not to even ogle or look at alcohol. The wine service that the Queen of Sheba was impressed by must have been unfermented wine, grape juice.

7. What is one way Adonai's word differentiates between alcoholic wine, which is not good, and grape juice?

"Honor the L*ORD* *with your wealth, with the best of all your income, And your barns will be filled with grain, Your vats will burst with* <u>*new wine*</u>*."* Proverbs 3:9, 10

New wine gives the impression of newly or freshly squeezed grape juice. But grape juice, as used in the Bible does not always have the word "new" next to it. Sometimes it just says "wine." In the Scriptures sometimes the word wine means grape juice and sometimes it means fermented alcohol. We can tell which one the Scriptures are referring to by how it is used in context. In the Scriptures fermented alcoholic wine always has a negative connotation associated with it, while unfermented wine, fresh grape juice, is always associated with a blessing. Grape juice that becomes alcohol has gone through a fermenting process, a spoiling or rotting process. This process did not happen in the Garden of Eden nor will it happen in Heaven. Alcohol is not part of God's original plan, His eternal plan, nor is it His plan for us today.

8. What principle did King Solomon give us regarding all brain harming drugs like alcohol, tobacco, marijuana, cocaine, etc.?

"More than all that you guard, <u>*guard your mind*</u>*,* <u>*for it is the source of life*</u>*."* Proverbs 4:23

Adonai speaks to us through our mind, which receives His impressions and comprehends His written Word. Our brain is the most important part of our body as it is the only one of our senses through which God communicates His love to us. We can't taste God, or smell Him, or see Him, but He can communicate with us through our minds. Alcohol of all kinds and illegal drugs kill brain cells. It is vitally important that we keep our brains as healthy as possible so we can hear God's voice speaking to us. Since the Bible tells us to *"***guard the mind***"* why would we want to destroy the most important part of our body with even moderate drinking?

The principle is to guard the mind. The principle is the spirit of the law. The letter of the law is the exact dos and don'ts. The spirit of the law takes it

13. KING SOLOMON (SHLOMO)

a step further and says, "in addition to the things the word of God mentions avoiding, guard your mind against any mind destroying drugs that will ever be invented." This principle would include other mind and body altering drugs such as crack, cocaine, nicotine, caffeine, etc.

Since the principle is to take care of the mind and body that God has given us, the principle allows for the use of medicinal drugs for the healing of the body and mind.

9. In addition to eating only healthy foods and abstaining from foods and substances that harm us, what is another thing that we can do to maintain good health?

Do not be wise in your own eyes; fear the L<small>ORD</small> *and shun evil. It will be a cure for your body, a tonic for your bones.*
A joyful heart makes for good health. Proverbs 3:7,8; 17:22

Being humble, respecting God, avoiding sin, and choosing to be thankful are all health enhancing attitudes we can have as we invite Elohim into our hearts and minds.

10. Gambling is another vice that God hates, along with alcohol and drugs. What did the Jewish prophet Isaiah have to say about gambling?

"*. . . you who forsake the* L<small>ORD</small> *. . . who set a table for Luck And fill a mixing bowl for Destiny: I will destine you for the sword, you will all kneel down, to be slaughtered—because, when I called, you did not answer, when I spoke, you would not listen. You did what I hold evil.*" Isaiah 65:11,12

Gambling works on the premise of greed and laziness. It is trying to get rich without earning it. It is based on getting something at the expense of someone else's loss. Selfishness, greed, and laziness are not healthy characteristics. If a plumber fixes your sink you get a service performed for you and he gets money—both of you benefit. If you buy something, you get an item and the seller gets money—both of you benefit. In gambling one person loses and the other wins. Really, both lose because gambling becomes addictive and destructive because of the evil characteristics it encourages and feeds on. Gambling of all sorts, including lotteries, should be avoided.

11. What advice did King Solomon, the wisest and richest king of Israel, give us concerning money?

Wealth is of no avail on the day of wrath, but righteousness saves from death.

He who is generous to the poor makes a loan to the LORD; He will repay him his due.

Better is a poor man who lives blamelessly than a rich man whose ways are crooked.

The LORD will not let the righteous go hungry . . . Negligent hands cause poverty, but diligent hands enrich. Proverbs 11:4; 19:17; 28:6; 10:3, 4

In contrast to the desires associated with gambling Solomon encourages righteousness, generosity, contentment, and hard work.

12. What did wise King Solomon warn us about being in debt?

. . . the borrower is a slave to the lender. Proverbs 22:7

Who would choose to be a slave? Amazingly, millions of people today voluntarily become slaves to credit card companies and loan agencies. We should avoid debt like we would avoid a plague. If we have any debt we should focus all our energy into becoming debt free. Debt could be defined as owing more on an item than its value. Note that Solomon is not saying that being in debt is a sin, but he is warning us that it is a form of voluntary slavery.

13. What counsel did King Solomon give about having a happy, successful marriage?

Let your fountain be blessed; <u>find joy in the wife of your youth</u>— A loving doe, a graceful mountain goat. Let her breasts satisfy you at all times; <u>be infatuated with love of her always</u>. Why be infatuated, my son, with a forbidden woman? Why clasp the bosom of an alien woman? Proverbs 5:19- 20

Solomon told us to "find" joy in the spouse of our youth. Stay with your first spouse even if you have to search to find the joy in the relationship. Every successfully happy marriage takes work. To be infatuated with love for your spouse has more to do with you than it does with them. To be "infatuated with" means you choose to be infatuated with your spouse. It does not mean that when they change and become infatuating you will then be infatuated with them. It means that you love them the way they are. If you married them the way they are then continue to love them the way they are. Love is more of a choice than it is a feeling. Solomon is telling us to choose to love, choose to be infatuated with your spouse. People talk about falling out of love; the only way to do this is to choose not to love. When we start choosing to look and dwell on the shortcomings of our spouse and choose not to love them the way they are, we are in danger of falling for the forbidden woman or the forbidden man. Find joy—even if you have to search for it—in the spouse that you have.

14. Where should we go to find a good spouse?

... an efficient wife comes from <u>the Lord</u>. Proverbs 19:14

If you do not have a spouse from the Lord, choose to be content with the choice you made. If you are not married yet, settle for nothing less than a spouse from the Lord. A spouse from the Lord is someone who loves the Lord, who reads His Word, who follows His instructions, who is active in the house of the Lord. Before we can expect the Lord to give us a spouse we should be a person of the Lord. We should be a person who loves the Lord, reads His Word, follows His instructions, and is active in the house of the Lord.

15. What type of spouse might we end up with if we do not go to the Lord?

The <u>nagging</u> of a wife is like the endless dripping of water. Dwelling in the corner of a roof is better than a <u>contentious</u> wife in a spacious house. Proverbs 19:13; 21:9

If you have a nagging, contentious spouse choose to be content with the choice you made (Of course in certain abusive situations a person should protect themselves and separate. This is the kind of circumstance when you would be well advised to seek guidance from a godly counselor.) If you are not married yet, remember that the loneliest people in the world are not single people, but people who are married but not matched. Choose well. Choose carefully. Choose a spouse from the Lord or you may end up with a nagging, contentious spouse. Take your time when choosing a spouse to unite your life with. Spend much time talking together. Save the physical intimacy for marriage, and counsel with many people.

16. How is a capable wife described in the Holy Scriptures?

What a rare find is a capable wife! Her worth is far beyond that of rubies. Her husband puts his confidence in her, and lacks no good thing. She is good to him, never bad, all the days of her life. She rises while it is still night, and supplies provisions for her household, she girds herself with strength, and performs her tasks with vigor. She gives generously to the poor; her hands are stretched out to the needy. She is clothed with strength and splendor; she looks to the future cheerfully. Her mouth is full of wisdom, her tongue with kindly teaching. She oversees the activities of her household and never eats the bread of idleness. Her children declare her happy; her husband praises her, Grace is deceptive, Beauty is illusory; it is for her fear of the LORD *that a woman is to be praised.* Proverbs 31:10-12,15,17, 20, 25-28, 30

These texts apply to being a capable husband as well. There are only a few things better than being the right spouse and having the right spouse. Solomon says they are a rare find so choose carefully. God hates divorce. Marriage should be for life. To have a happy marriage it takes love from God, continual surrender to God and to each other, continual choices of contentment, patience, forgiveness, unselfishness, and work. A happy marriage starts with being a capable spouse as described in this text. It takes God in our hearts to make us and keep us as a capable spouse.

Solomon said it is not beauty or graces that cause a spouse to be worthy of praise but rather it is a fear of the LORD that is deserving of praises. What do you focus most of your time, money, and energy on—how you look or storing up God in your heart? God is so big that if He is really in us, He will stick out everywhere. When people see you, do they see you or do they see God in you? Are you focused more on your outer beauty or your inner beauty?

17. What advice about choosing friends did King Solomon give?

<u>*Do not associate with an irascible man, or go about with one who is hot-tempered*</u>*, lest you learn his ways and find yourself ensnared. Do not envy* <u>*evil men; do not desire to be with them*</u>*; for their hearts talk violence, and their lips speak mischief. Do not envy sinners in your heart, but* <u>*only God-fearing men, at all times*</u>*, for then you will have a future, and your hope will never fail. For* <u>*the commandment is a lamp*</u>*, the teaching is a light, and the way to life is the rebuke that disciplines.* <u>*It will keep you from an evil woman, from the smooth tongue of a forbidden woman.*</u> Proverbs 22:24, 25; 24:1, 2; 23: 17, 18; 6:23, 24

These are clear words about choosing friends. Evil associations corrupt good morals. Be friendly to everyone but choose only friends from people who love God. Make acquaintances with everyone else and encourage them to come to know the LORD.

There is an important lesson here about dating. Do not date someone who does not know the LORD and who does not believe as you believe. One way to make sure you never marry someone who does not believe the way you do is to

13. KING SOLOMON (SHLOMO)

never date someone who does not believe like you do. It is very hard to marry someone you have not dated. You can be guaranteed not to marry the wrong person if you do not date the wrong person.

18. What did King Solomon tell us about dealing with enemies?

If your enemy is hungry, <u>give him bread to eat</u>; if he is thirsty, <u>give him water to drink</u>. You will be heaping live coals on his head, and the L<small>ORD</small> will reward you. <u>Do not say, "I will requite evil"; put your hope in the L<small>ORD</small> and He will deliver you</u>. He who seeks love <u>overlooks faults</u>, but he who harps on a matter alienates his friend. Proverbs 25:21, 22; 20:22; 17:9

It is not possible to love our enemies in our own power. We need to call on Elohim to give us this love. There are lessons here for marriages, family relationships, work associations, and relationships of all kinds. If we harp on a matter we will alienate. If we overlook faults we will be seeking an awakening of love. As we learned from Joseph, forgiveness is not ignoring a fault or wrong someone did to us, it is overlooking—looking over and beyond the wrong that was done. It is choosing to rise above the wrong doer and show God's love in return for evil. If you are still struggling with being able to forgive someone re-read the proverbs quoted in this question and look at the promises of God for us when we choose to forgive. God will reward you. God will deliver you. If you are still struggling with forgiveness, re-read lesson 3 on the life of Joseph.

19. How can we have wisdom like King Solomon?

<u>The beginning of wisdom is fear of the L<small>ORD</small>, and knowledge of the Holy One is understanding. Listen to advice and accept discipline</u> in order that you may be wise in the end. Proverbs 9:10; 19:20

Wisdom, knowledge, and understanding come from the L<small>ORD</small>. This is one of the reasons it is important to spend time every day in prayer and in reading the Bible. We need God's wisdom to understand His Word. Wisdom and understanding of God's Word gives us knowledge and wisdom, not only on theology, but also in every aspect of our lives. Whether it is financial matters, interpersonal associations, family concerns, work habits, food and clothing choices, or personal issues, God is the source of wisdom.

Clifford Goldstein will tell you that his family tree is full of typewriters, pens, and books. His blood is 50% hemoglobin and 50% ink. In the late 1970's

Cliff was traveling the world writing his novel. Cliff ate, drank, and dreamt about his book. It was his life. He was sure it was going to catapult him into the Barnes and Nobel hall of fame.

While Cliff was traveling he spent some time on a kibbutz in Israel where he ran into a group of people who believed that Y'shua is the Messiah. Cliff had met Christians in the USA but he never expected to meet some on a kibbutz in Israel. During Cliff's college days there was a street preacher that Cliff became so proficient at mocking that his friends called him Heckle. Cliff started to use his heckle routine on this group that were staying at the kibbutz. These guys were different. They were nice. They did not condemn Cliff to an eternity in a tar pit. They were friendly to him. To all his abuses they responded with kindness and love, so much so that Cliff's arguments against Y'shua were melted away and Cliff accepted Y'shua as his Messiah.

Cliff moved to Florida and was selling colored ice to sugar craving kids in order to support his writing habit. Every night he would type away. One night he felt a strong urge that God wanted him to give up his book. No way, was his immediate response. It could not be God that would ask him to give up the book, but Cliff knew the book had become his idol, his god. He had spent two years on his book. There was nothing obscene or anti-God about the book— Cliff debated back and forth. Cliff knew in his heart that it stood between him and God. He had been playing with God. A little prayer here and there, a few minutes with the Bible every so often. But the book was his love; it got all the time and attention. Cliff walked through the night, but the conviction followed him - if he was going to get serious with God the book had to go. Finally he stopped and prayed, "I want you more than I want the book, but I don't have it in me to burn it. If you want it you are going to have to do it Yourself." Immediately a weight was lifted off his shoulders and a surge of excitement ran through him. All the worries, fears, and anxieties about what would happen to his life if he gave up the book disappeared. No bolt of lightning flew through the window to burn the stack of pages on the desk. A few minutes earlier if anyone would have tried to take the manuscript it would have cost him his life, but now Cliff was placing his life's dream on an electric hot plate. For two minutes nothing happened. No flame jumped from the pile of paper, nor did an angel from heaven stay Cliff's hand and tell him he passed the test. Eventually gray smoke began to ascend and the papers smoldered away for an hour before they were completely ashes. That night Cliff slept the sweet sleep of

13. KING SOLOMON (SHLOMO)

contentment.

It didn't happen overnight, but when it was clear that God was Cliff's first love, God blessed his writing career. He has written several books, many articles for periodicals, and has been the editor of Shabbat Shalom and Liberty magazines and a quarterly Bible study guide called The Sabbath School Quarterly.

20. At the end of King Solomon's life how did he sum up all his observations?

The sum of the matter, when all is said and done: <u>Revere God and observe His commandments!</u> For this applies to all mankind: that God will call every creature to account for everything unknown, be it good or bad. Ecclesiastes 12:13,14

For everyone on this earth the sum of the matter, the bottom line in life, is loving and respecting Adonai and keeping His commandments.

21. Through Solomon God has given us some high morals to follow. How can we live by these standards?

<u>Trust in the L</u><small>ORD</small> <u>with all your heart, and do not rely on your own understanding. In all your ways acknowledge Him, and He will make your paths smooth.</u> Proverbs 3:5, 6

It starts with trusting in the L<small>ORD</small>. If we trust in what He says, not in what we think, and if we trust in His power, not our power, to live these standards in our lives He will make our ups and downs smooth. This does not mean there will not be bumps or potholes in the road, but God's shock absorbers will keep our emotions smooth.

You shall sanctify yourselves and be holy, for I the L<small>ORD</small> am your God. You shall faithfully observe My laws: <u>I the L</u><small>ORD</small> <u>make you holy. I the L</u><small>ORD</small> <u>who sanctify you am holy</u>. Leviticus 20:7, 8; 21:8

What a powerful promise. God makes us holy! It is not us making ourselves holy, but it is allowing God to make us holy. God is all-powerful and all loving. He knows your past and your weaknesses. God is able to transform you in spite of the past. He is holy and can make your life holy, if you allow Him to work upon your heart. Accept Messiah Y'shua's death for the forgiveness of your shortcomings and for the Holy Spirit to live God's life through you. Isn't this what David's prayer quoted in the beginning of this lesson was all about?

The high standards on the many different topics Solomon has outlined for us might seem overwhelming to us. But really they are not hard to reach—they are impossible, in our own strength and power. But with God's power, God's

JEWISH DISCOVERIES

Holy Spirit, working in us and through us, He will empower us to reach and live these high standards. In our food, drink, and dress choices, and in our attitudes regarding finances, work, and relationships, God is able to give us His desires, His thoughts, His actions as we surrender each area to Him. Now that you are a child of the King, the King will transform you to live like a prince or princess for Him.

Are you willing to allow Elohim to work in you to reach the high and holy standard He is calling you to?

Your next lesson is entitled "Jonah the fisherman." Whether you enjoy fishing or not, you will find this next lesson very interesting.

REVIEW הזרה

1. What did Solomon ask the LORD for?
   a. Riches.
   b. Wisdom to judge the people.
   c. Long life.

2. What were some of the things that impressed the Queen of Sheba?
   a. Solomon's wisdom.
   b. What he ate and drank.
   c. How his servants were dressed.
   d. The sacrifices in the Temple.
   e. All of the above.

3. The reason for abstaining from all alcohol and illegal drugs is:
   a. The Bible says so.
   b. To guard the mind God has given me.
   c. God is pure and Holy and He is making me pure and Holy.
   d. All of the above.

4. God considers those things that have to do with luck, chance, destiny, and other forms of gambling as:
   a. Evil.
   b. Good moneymakers.
   c. Harmless.

5. Where does a good spouse come from?
   a. Singles clubs.
   b. Matchmakers.

13. KING SOLOMON (SHLOMO)

    c. The LORD.

6. In regard to work and finances, Elohim calls us to be:
   a. Rich
   b. Lazy
   c. Righteous, blameless, generous
   d. Lucky

7. Being in debt is being:
   a. Normal
   b. Wise
   c. A slave

8. How can you accept God's power to help you to follow the principles outlined in the Holy Scriptures?
   a. Trust in the LORD with all my heart.
   b. Have a Holy fear or reverence for the LORD.
   c. Ask the Messiah to wash my sinful tendencies away by the power of His death for me; allow Him to live out His life within me through His Holy Spirit.
   d. All of the above.

9. In what ways have you grown spiritually by reading these lessons?

TRADITIONS

Wedding

A chupah is a large covering that is often used at weddings to cover the bride and groom. It can be constructed with four vertical poles with a prayer shawl or similar cloth draped over them. This canopy represents God's protection and blessing over the couple.

As the bride enters the hall the rabbi announces, "Baruch habah beshem Adonai, (ברוך הבא בשם יי) blessed is the one who comes in the name of the LORD." Traditionally the bride will circle the groom, reminiscent of the text in Jeremiah 31:22 that says, "A woman shall court (go around) a man" and Hosea 2:19,20; "I will betroth you unto me . . ." Seven blessings are usually recited, including the kiddish and quotes from Jeremiah 33:11.

During the wedding ceremony, the rabbi will usually read the ketubah, the Jewish marriage covenant that is signed by the bride (kallah), groom (chatan), and witnesses. Toward the end of the ceremony the groom will break a glass with his right foot. Some say this is a reminder that our Temple in Jerusalem is still in ruins. Others say it symbolizes that all other relationships are broken and now the bride is the only woman for him and that just as the broken glass is an irrevocable act so is his commitment to her.

As beautiful as the wedding traditions are it is God that makes a marriage successful. We need God's covering, not just over our wedding but also over our entire marriage. Just as a chupah represents God's protection over us, we should do all we can to protect the feelings of our loved ones. Elohim places His righteousness and His law in our hearts, which will cause our homes to be constantly filled with acts of righteousness and order. As we appreciate how God loves us just as we are, we are able to love our spouses just as they are. We need God's faithfulness and His forgiveness covering our lives to have a happy life. So also we need to allow God to make us faithful and forgiving in order to have a happy home.

TRADITIONS

Mezuzah

A mezuzah is a little box that is nailed to the doorpost of a Jewish home. The Hebrew word mezuzah means doorpost. It is generally placed on the right side of the door about one quarter of the way from the top of the door, and the top of the mezuzah is tilted inwardly at an angle. On the outside of the mezuzah the Hebrew letter shin (ש) is generally shown. The shin is the first letter in the word shema, which means hear or listen, and is the first word on the scroll that is in the mezuzah. Shin is also the first letter for the word Shadai, which means almighty, a reference to God.

Inside the mezuzah there is a little piece of rolled up parchment containing verses from the book of Deuteronomy chapters 6 and 11 starting with the shema which says *"Hear O Israel: The LORD our God is one LORD. You shall love the LORD your God with all your heart, and with all your soul, and with all your might. And these words which I command you this day shall be in your heart."* The *"words that I command you this day"* are the Ten Commandments, which are recorded in the previous chapter of Deuteronomy, chapter 5. Yet it is not the Ten Commandments that are written in the mezuzahs, but rather it is the instructions about writing the Ten Commandments on your heart, doors, etc. that is written in the mezuzah.

The Lord says these commandments need to be in our hearts. In other words, they should become a part of our lives. Our lifeblood should pulsate with their principles. The text then continues by saying, *"**You shall teach them diligently unto your children, and shall talk of them when you sit in your house, and when you walk by the way and when you lie down and when you rise up.**"* We are being told here that God's holy law, His Ten Commandments, need to be incorporated into everything that we do 24 hours a day seven days a week. Their principles need to be lived out in our lives and taught to our children. Then in verse 9 Moses states, *"**You shall write them upon the posts of your house and on your gates.**"*

Tradition takes these words literally and thus we have the words written on the scroll, put in boxes, and nailed to the doorpost. But if this part is to be taken literally it would stand to reason that the verse that says write them on the heart should also be taken literally. Should we have a surgeon place a scroll inside our chest? Obviously not. The Jewish prophet Jeremiah wrote in chapter 31:33, *"**Declares the Lord, I will put my teaching into their inmost being, and inscribe it upon their hearts . . .**"* Here God is saying He will write His law in our hearts. Of course, God is not talking about physically writing words inside our chests. He is saying that obedience will spring forth out of our lives because of the love God has instilled in our hearts and minds. While having a mezuzah on the doorpost might be a nice reminder of the importance to live godly lives in our homes, merely having mezuzahs on our doors will not make us children of God. Rather than calling for physical mezuzahs on our doorposts Elohim is inviting us to live out His love and His law in our homes.

JEWISH HERITAGE SCRIPTURE STUDIES  14

JONAH
THE FISHERMAN

14. JONAH (YONAH) THE FISHERMAN

Jonah was not exactly a fisherman; he was more like the bait. He did not catch the fish but the fish caught him. Yet his experience teaches us a great lesson. The wonderful truth we want to explore today is just how eager God is for all the world to hear the story of His love.

1. What did Adonai ask Jonah to proclaim for Him?

    The word of the LORD came to Jonah . . . <u>Go at once to Nineveh, that great city, and proclaim judgment upon it</u>; for their wickedness has come before Me. Jonah 1:1, 2

2. What did Jonah do in response to God's request?

    <u>Jonah, however, started out to</u> flee to Tarshish from the LORD's service. He went down to Joppa and found a ship going to Tarshish. He paid the fare and went aboard <u>. . . away from the service of the LORD</u>. Jonah 1:3

    Not only did Jonah go away from the service of the LORD, he went 180 degrees in the opposite direction of Nineveh. We might be able to understand Jonah's fear. Nineveh was a great city, a large city, and a wicked city. Nineveh was not even in the land of Israel. Actually it is quite far from Israel. Nineveh is still in existence today in the country of Iraq. It was not a Jewish city, and the inhabitants were goyim, Gentiles. Jonah would be a foreigner with no national protection. He would be proclaiming to a city that did not believe in his God that his God was going to destroy them. Jonah was called to a very dangerous assignment. You can probably think of some cities in the world that would fit this description. What would you do if God called you to go to one of them and tell them your God said they were going to be destroyed?

3. Instead of allowing Jonah to just run away from the Lord's service, what did God do for Jonah?

    <u>The LORD cast a mighty wind upon the sea</u>, and such a great tempest came upon the sea that the ship was in danger of breaking

up. Jonah 1:4

Certainly Elohim could have found someone else just as willing, or unwilling, as Jonah to go to Nineveh. This assignment was as much for Jonah's benefit as it was for Nineveh, and God, in His love for Jonah, was not going to let him out of this.

4. In their fear of sinking what did the sailors do?

<u>*In their fright, the sailors cried out, each to his own god; and they flung the ship's cargo overboard to make it lighter for them* ... *The men said to one another, "Let us cast lots and find out on whose account this misfortune has come upon us." They cast lots and the lot fell on Jonah. They said to him, "Tell us, you who have brought this misfortune upon us, what is your business? Where have you come from? What is your country, and of what people are you?"*</u> Jonah 1:5, 7, 8

5. How did Jonah respond to the sailors' questions?

<u>*I am a Hebrew*," he replied. "*I worship the* L<small>ORD</small>, *the God of Heaven, who made both sea and land.*</u>" Jonah 1:9

Did Jonah tell them the truth? Yes and no. Yes, he was a Hebrew, or what we would refer to today as Jewish. Yes, the L<small>ORD</small>, the God of Heaven, made both the sea and the land. But no, Jonah was not worshipping Him. It is not possible to worship God and disobey Him at the same time. That applies to us as well. You may be praying, you may be reading the Bible, you may be singing songs of praise to God, you may be attending services, but if you are just going through the motions—you are not worshipping Him. Obeying Him would include allowing Him to live in your life to empower you to live the life you have been learning about in this series of Bible studies. I know you have been gratified and enriched as you have seen Him bringing your life into harmony with the great teachings of Scripture. Seeing Him at work within us draws forth an attitude of worship.

Worshipping God also includes sharing God's love with someone else. God has called all of us to share His love with others. We become His hands to help, His feet to go, His mouth to share, His heart to love and care. We become His representatives, His ambassadors. What a privilege it is to be a representative of the L<small>ORD</small>, the God of Heaven, the Creator of the sea and the earth!

14. JONAH (YONAH) THE FISHERMAN

6. When Jonah told them he was running away from Elohim the sailors asked him what they could do to calm the storm. How did Jonah respond, showing that he had not yet experienced God's mercy and forgiveness?

    He answered, "<u>Heave me overboard</u>, and the sea will calm down for you; for I know that this terrible storm came upon you on my account." Jonah 1:12

    Jonah seemed to have forgotten the accounts of Joseph and Job and that in every calamity God has a purpose planned. Because he did not remember these things, Jonah didn't realize that this storm was actually for his good. Jonah must have forgotten how God accepted Jacob's, Moses', and David's repentance. He seemed to think the only way to stop the storm was by his death. God did not want Jonah to die. He wanted him to repent of his sin and receive God's forgiveness through the sacrifices offered in the Temple representing the Messiah's death. God wanted Jonah to accept the power of the Ruach HaKodesh (the Holy Spirit) to take away his fear and cause him to be obedient to God's will for his life.

7. The sailors resisted such an extreme solution, so they continued to do everything they could to save the boat, but as things continued to get worse these heathen sailors pleaded with God not to hold this act against them, and they heaved Jonah overboard. Immediately the sea became calm. How did these non-Jewish, Goyim (Gentiles), react to this experience?

    <u>The men feared the L</u><u>ORD</u><u> greatly; they offered a sacrifice to the L</u><u>ORD</u><u> and they made vows</u>. Jonah 1:16

    These Gentile sailors became more receptive to God than Jonah had been. They tried everything they could to avoid throwing him overboard and when the storm calmed they worshipped Elohim, offered a sacrifice, and decided to follow the LORD. Sometimes it is the other way around. People will fear God, offer God everything, and make every kind of promise to God when they are going through a difficult time. But then, after the danger has passed, they forget God and take back their pledges and their promises. Which scenario has been more common in your past? Which scenario has been more common since you have been regularly studying God's Word?

8. What did Adonai do next to show Jonah that He still loved him and that He still wanted the heathen Gentiles of Nineveh to know about Him?

    <u>The L</u><u>ORD</u><u> provided a huge fish to swallow Jonah</u>; and Jonah re-

mained in the fish's belly three days and three nights. Jonah prayed to the LORD his God from the belly of the fish. He said: In my trouble I called to the LORD, and He answered me…my prayer came before You, Into Your holy Temple. <u>The LORD commanded the fish, and it spewed Jonah out upon dry land. The word of the LORD came to Jonah a second time: "Go at once to Nineveh, that great city, and proclaim to it what I tell you.</u>" Jonah 2:1-3, 8, 11; 3:1, 2

God did not let Jonah off the hook; He used a fish to catch Jonah. This is not your typical fishing trip, yet Jonah certainly had a whopper of a fish story to tell! God loves us even when we are being disobedient and running away from Him. God did not give up on Jonah or Nineveh and He will not give up on you or me or any of our loved ones.

9. Jonah went to the large, wicked city of Nineveh with the warning that the city would be destroyed within forty days. What did these godless Gentiles of Nineveh do in response to Elohim's message through Jonah?

<u>The people of Nineveh believed God. They proclaimed a fast, and great and small alike put on sackcloth . . . (saying) "Who knows but that God may turn and relent? He may turn back from His wrath, so that we do not perish.</u>" Jonah 3:5, 9

The Spirit of God softened the Ninevites' hearts and they truly repented of their sins. What a powerful experience, and to think that Jonah was reluctant to go! Maybe there is someone you are fearful of sharing God's love with. You may be thinking, "They are not interested in God. Their life is so far from what the Bible says, they will not accept the truth if I share it with them. They may even get mad at me and reject me if I say anything." We never know how people will react. God may be moving upon their hearts before you even say a word. If God could turn wicked Nineveh because of the words of fearful, faithless Jonah, certainly He can use you and me.

10. Did the God of Israel show love and mercy to the Gentile people of Nineveh and spare them of the destruction He had pronounced upon them?

<u>God saw what they did, how they were turning back from their evil ways. And God renounced the punishment He had planned to bring upon them, and did not carry it out.</u> Jonah 3:10

What a God of love we serve. His love is for all the earth.

There is more to the account of Jonah. I encourage you to read all of it in the Bible (in the book of Jonah).

14. JONAH (YONAH) THE FISHERMAN

11. Are there other Gentiles recorded in the first part of the Bible who became believers in the only true God because of the witnessing or proselytizing of Jewish people? Yes. Notice these examples:

    - Egyptians who left Egypt with the Israelites during the exodus. Exodus 12:38
    - Rahab, an inhabitant of the city of Jericho, who protected the Israelite spies. Joshua 6:25
    - The Gibeonites, shortly after the children of Israel crossed the Jordan River into the land of Canaan. Joshua 9:24
    - Ruth, a Moabite, was King David's great grandmother, making her an ancestor of the Messiah. Ruth 4:13-18
    - King Nebuchadnezzar, King of Babylon, who was greatly influenced by the Jewish prophet Daniel. Daniel 4:34

From the beginning Elohim has showed His love and compassion for all people of the earth. God had Noah warn the world for 120 years before the flood came. God allowed the people of Sodom and Gomorrah to come in contact with Abraham and even sent two angels to the city before they were destroyed. God used Moses to give warnings to the Egyptians and God mercifully gave them 9 demonstrations of His power before even one Egyptian died. And God has placed you and me in contact with people whom He wants to know about His love.

12. How many nations were to be blessed by the seed of Abraham?

    All the nations (Goyim ***) of the earth shall bless themselves by your descendants, because you have obeyed My command."*** Genesis 22:18

All the nations of the earth are blessed by the seed of Abraham? Certainly as a people we have made our contributions to society as a whole, but all the nations of the earth blessed? How can this be? It is through the promised seed, the promised child of the lineage of Abraham, the Messiah, God's servant, His chosen One. Through the Messiah's death for the sins of the entire world everyone who has ever lived has had forgiveness of sins available to them. All the inhabitants of the world, including you and me, have been blessed because of the intercession of the Messiah, whether they realize it or not.

God calls us to continue to bless all the nations of the earth by sharing His message of love with every person on earth. That might seem like an impossible task for you and me, but we will see in lesson 20 how that is possible.

13. In what way would Abraham's descendants, especially the Messiah, bless the other nations?

>   *This is <u>My servant</u>, whom I uphold, <u>My chosen one</u>, in whom I delight. <u>I have put My spirit upon him</u>, <u>He shall teach the true way to the nations</u>* (Goyim). Isaiah 42:1
>
>   <u>the Lord God will make Victory and renown shoot up in the presence of all the nations</u> (Goyim). Isaiah 61:11
>
>   For I am a great King—said the Lord of Hosts—and <u>My name is revered among the nations</u> (Goyim). Malachi 1:14
>
>   <u>I will also make you a light of nations</u> (Goyim), <u>that My salvation may reach the ends of the earth</u>." Isaiah 49:6

Note: The word salvation in the last verse has the same Hebrew root as the Messiah's name. The Hebrew letters for both the word and the name is ישוע. The name is pronounced Ye-shoo-ah (Y'shua) in Hebrew or Jesus in English. God's salvation has reached the ends of the earth through His Messiah, the Seed of Abraham, Y'shua! Remember in lesson one and two we learned that God promised that all the nations of the world would be blessed by Abraham's and Jacob's offspring? God loves every person on this planet and He sent the Messiah, Y'shua, from the lineage of Abraham, to die not only for the sins of Jewish people but also for every person on this planet. All the nations of the earth have been blessed because of Abraham's descendant Y'shua. Y'shua's death, as the sacrificial lamb, gives every person on this earth the gift of salvation. When we receive His sacrifice for our sins we receive this gift that He has given us.

14. What special promises did Elohim have for foreigners who attached themselves to the Lord?

>   *Thus said the Lord: Observe what is right and do what is just; For soon <u>My salvation shall come</u>, And my deliverance be revealed. <u>Happy is the man who does this</u>, The man who holds fast to it: <u>Who keeps the sabbath</u> and does not profane it, And stays his hand from doing any evil. Let not <u>the foreigner</u> say, Who has attached himself to the Lord, "The Lord will keep me apart from His people . . . For thus said the Lord: <u>I will give them an everlasting name which shall not perish</u>. As for <u>the foreigners who attach themselves to the Lord, to minister to Him, and to love the name of the Lord, to be His servants—All who keep the sabbath</u> and do not profane it, and <u>who hold fast to My covenant—I will bring them to My sacred mount</u>*

14. JONAH (YONAH) THE FISHERMAN

<u>*and let them rejoice in My house of prayer. Their burnt offerings and sacrifices shall be welcome on My altar; for My House shall be called A house of prayer for all peoples.*</u>*"* Isaiah 56:1-7

What an interesting promise in the Jewish Bible. *"My salvation shall come,"* again the root word ישוע , Y'shua, the Messiah's name, is used. Isaiah, the Jewish prophet, says *"Happy is . . . the foreigner* (a Gentile) *. . . who keeps the Sabbath . . . who attaches themselves to the* LORD *. . . to be His servants."* They have an *"everlasting name,"* they will *"not perish,"* they will be brought to God's *"sacred mount,"* into God's *"house of prayer."* This is why God's house is called *"a house of prayer for all peoples."* God is an inclusive God; He wants us all to be united in Him. He desires that we become as one. The only way this can happen is if we allow God to use us to share His love with others, especially those who we are not currently united to.

15. In David's great prayer of repentance what did he promise to do for transgressors after he himself had been purged with hyssop and filled with God's Spirit? This purging with hyssop represented the blood of the lambs placed with hyssop on the doorposts during the Passover in Egypt. Those lambs represented the death of the Messiah, who shed His blood for our sins.

> *"Have mercy upon me, O God, as befits Your faithfulness; in keeping with Your abundant compassion, blot out my transgressions. Wash me thoroughly of my iniquity, and purify me of my sin; for I recognize my transgressions, and am ever conscious of my sin. Purge me with hyssop till I am pure; wash me till I am whiter than snow. Hide Your face from my sins; blot out all my iniquities. Fashion a pure heart for me, O God; create in me a steadfast spirit. Do not cast me out of Your presence, or take Your Holy Spirit away from me. Let me again rejoice in Your help; <u>let a vigorous spirit sustain me. I will teach transgressors Your ways, that sinners may return to You.</u>"* Psalm 51:3-5, 9-15

We have looked at this text several times throughout these lessons. It is a powerful text. Each time we have read it we have focused on a different aspect. In one lesson we focused on the cleansing of our guilt and sin through the blood of the lambs. Another time we focused on the Holy Spirit. This time we want to focus on David's assertion that after he was forgiven of his sins and had God's Spirit empowering Him, he would teach other sinners how to receive forgiveness. Telling others about God's Messiah and forgiveness is a very Jewish thing to do. It was done by King David, Abraham, Moses, Jonah, Isaiah, and has been done by Jewish people throughout Jewish history.

16. How many of us have sinned against Adonai?

*<u>**All have turned bad**</u>, altogether foul; there is <u>**none who does good, not even one**</u>.* Psalm 14:3

Everyone needs forgiveness. Everyone needs the Messiah. God needs us to share His love with those who are not yet experiencing His forgiveness.

17. Can people, as transgressors of God's ways, just turn from sin on their own strength?

*<u>**Who can say, "I have cleansed my heart, I am purged of my sin"? "Can the Cushite change his skin, Or the leopard his spots? Just as much can you do good, Who are practiced in doing evil**</u>!"* Proverbs 20:9; Jeremiah 13:23

We cannot purge ourselves of our fear of sharing God's love with others any more than a leopard can change his spots. But God can change us. He can remove the fear and give us His boldness and love for others that will compel us to want to share with others. It is impossible to fully experience God's love and salvation in our own life and not have a burden to share it with others.

Just as you and I don't have the ability to change without God's Spirit in our lives, neither does anyone else. How, then, can we expect people to be good, kind, and fair, when they do not even know about our merciful God's power to set them free from their sins? Just think, if we as a people had done more in sharing God's love over the last 6,000 years with people who do not know of His forgiveness and power to transform their lives, there would be much less crime, violence, and immorality today. All the nations of the earth were to be blessed by Abraham's seed. They were to be blessed with knowledge of and experience with the God of Abraham. If we do not teach others about the power of God to change their lives, who will? If all the nations were like the "happy foreigners" that "keep the Sabbath" and worship together with us in "God's house of prayer for all nations" which Isaiah talks about in Isaiah 56 (question 14), then we would not have had all the persecution that we have had all these years. How will they learn about our God who loves them and can change them if we do not tell them about Him?

18. What did Elohim say about those who tell others of His love?

14. JONAH (YONAH) THE FISHERMAN

<u>How welcome on the mountain are the footsteps of the herald</u> announcing happiness, heralding good (news), announcing victory, telling Zion, "Your God is King!" Isaiah 52:7

When you are experiencing freedom from guilt and are having victory over sin, it is just so exciting that it is impossible to keep it in. You want everyone to know what God has done in your life, and you want them to be as happy as you are. Chances are your family and friends are already noticing the positive changes taking place in your life and are wondering how it can happen for them also. Don't be afraid to tell them. God did not call Jonah to be a fisherman; He called him to be a fisher of men. He is calling you and me to do the same.

Sydell Greenberg grew up in a wonderful Jewish home in Brooklyn, New York. As a result of a rough period in her life she started searching for God. Shortly thereafter she accepted Y'shua as her Messiah. Her mother, Ann, despised the idea of Sydell accepting Y'shua as the Messiah and for the next 20 years tried to make Sydell regret her decision.

Sydell eventually moved to Florida and joined a congregation called Temple of the Advent Hope in Hollywood, Florida. There she met Curtis Jones. Despite their differences in upbringing they hit it off and had the common bonds of faith in Y'shua and love for people. After Curtis and Sydell married they started the Ariel Congregation in Lake Worth, Florida.

When Curtis was young he loved to sing Christian music. As a teenager he sang in the youth choir. When he grew older he was a prominent singer in the adult choir. Over the years he sang with quartets and was regularly asked to sing solos for different occasions, such as weddings. But the most memorable song of his life was when he was singing Hevenu Shalom Alechem while painting the apartment of his mother-in-law, Ann Greenberg.

Ann asked him where he learned the song. Curtis told her that it was one of the many Jewish melodies that he sang at the Friday night Shabbat service. The idea of a goy singing Jewish melodies touched her heart. She even accepted Curtis' invitation to start attending services with him and her daughter Sydell. Sydell couldn't believe it. She had tried for over 20 years to lead her mother to a knowledge and acceptance of Y'shua but had never gotten a good response. Now her mother was attending services with them and learning how much Y'shua loved her. To keep a wonderful story brief Ann Greenberg accepted Y'shua as her messiah at age 91 and was immersed by her son-in-law. Something as simple as a Jewish melody may be the opening to a person's heart.

REVIEW הזרה

1. Did Jonah want to go to Nineveh to warn the wicked people?

   a. Yes
   b. No

2. When Jonah got on the boat for Tarshish, was he experiencing the love of God in his life and worshipping God?

   a. Appears to be yes
   b. Appears to be no

3. According to Isaiah 56:1-7 (question 14) God wants:

   a. Jewish people and Gentile people to rejoice together in worship in God's house of prayer on His Sabbath.
   b. Jewish people to worship God on Sabbath and Gentile people to worship God on Sunday
   c. Foreigners to stay out of His house of prayer

4. When we are experiencing the joy of having our guilt purged from us by the blood of the Messiah and are filled with God's Spirit, giving us power over sin, the natural result will be:

   a. Sharing God's love with others.
   b. Keeping it a secret just for us.
   c. Boasting that we are better than everyone else.

5. Can you think of someone who needs you to share the love of God with them? And are you willing to let God help you do it?

   a. Yes
   b. No

Do you know who the youngest king of Israel was? In our next lesson we will learn about him, how to get hold of one of the most important areas of your life, and how to excel in it.

Tanya grew up in an Orthodox Jewish home in the Soviet Union. Her family's tea business was beginning to flourish when Stalin began his purges. When Tanya was 17, her father was taken by the secret police and shot in the head. During the Second World War her brother, sister, and husband were killed. She lost everyone closest to her in a two-year span.

Tanya struggled with depression. Although she advanced in educational and diplomatic circles, she always sensed that something was missing. She could never come to terms with all the suffering her family had experienced. She couldn't accept the terrible finality of their cruel deaths.

One day Tanya passed the Moscow Olympic Stadium and saw a sign proclaiming "The Bible Way to New Life." Mark Finley was holding a series of meetings covering the same Bible topics in this book.

Tanya was deeply moved as she heard the Bible come alive. She accepted Y'shua as her Messiah and was filled with the hope of heaven and of being reunited with her loved ones forever. She moved beyond her past and looked forward to a glorious future.

On February 3, 1943 a torpedo struck the S.S. Dorchester. Chaos reigned on board as the boat filed with water. Men rushed around in a panic. Many had run up from the hold without life jackets. Overcrowded lifeboats capsized; rafts drifted away before anyone could reach them. Survivors testified that there seemed only one little island of order in all the confusion—the spot where four chaplains stood on the steeply sloping starboard side.

Alexander David Goode, a rabbi, George Lansing Fox, a pastor, Clark Poling, a minister, and John Washington, a priest, calmly guided men to their boat stations. They distributed life jackets from a storage locker and then helped men frozen with fear over the side. Hundreds of men were crying, pleading, praying, and swearing. But through it all, the chaplains spoke words of courage and confidence. "Their voices were the only thing that kept me going," one survivor recalled. When the supply of life jackets was gone, the four chaplains gave away their own. As the water flooded the deck the chaplains remained standing firm, arms linked; their voices could be heard across the waters praying in Hebrew, Latin, and English. God will give you the power to stand firm in the face of the storms of life. He will give you His peace as you trust in Him.

(The stories of Tanya and of the chaplains are adapted from the book Solid Ground by Mark Finley and published by Review and Herald 2003, used with permission.)

JEWISH HERITAGE SCRIPTURE STUDIES

THE YOUNGEST KING OF ISRAEL

15. THE YOUNGEST KING

Stop and visualize a seven-year-old child you know. Maybe he's a child of yours, a niece, nephew, or grandchild. Now try to imagine that child being the current Prime Minister of Israel or the President of your country. Now that is a shocking thought, isn't it, seven years old and head of our nation? Yet at one time Israel was ruled by a seven-year-old boy king; his name was Joash. (He is also sometimes known in the Scriptures as Jehoash.)

The Bible tells us that when Joash was only one year old his father, King Ahaziah, was killed. Joash's wicked grandmother, Athaliah, decided to take this opportunity to rule the nation. Athaliah was the daughter of two of the most wicked rulers of the Jewish people, King Ahab and Queen Jezebel. Athaliah began her rule by ordering that all of the royal line be killed, which meant the killing of all her children and grandchildren. Joash was the only one of the royal line that survived. Joash survived because his aunt hid him in the Temple. He remained there for six years while his grandmother, Athaliah, ruled over the land. When Joash turned seven all of Judah united with the cohen gadol (the high priest) and the Levites in crowning and anointing Joash as king. They held a grand celebration proclaiming him their king. And "they clapped their hands and shouted, "Long live the king!" 2 Kings 11:12. When Queen Athaliah heard this she cried out, "Treason, Treason!" Athaliah and her followers were slain. Thus, our youngest king, Joash, began his reign at seven years of age.

1. What did the cohen gadol do after making Joash king?

   ***Solemnized a covenant* between himself and the people and the king *that they should be the people of the* L<small>ORD</small>.** 2 Chron. 23:16

   First the people committed themselves to the L<small>ORD</small>. This is what we have been doing as we have been studying the Scriptures together. Committing our lives to the L<small>ORD</small> is the first thing we should do. Before we try to overcome any habits or change anything in our lives it all must start with first committing our lives to the L<small>ORD</small>. Committing ourselves to the L<small>ORD</small> is not a one-time decision.

It is how every day should begin. If you have never committed your life to the LORD, don't read any further. Stop right now and surrender your heart to Him in prayer. If you have committed your life to the LORD in the past but have not yet today recommitted your life to Him, stop right now and make that recommitment.

2. What was one of the good things Joash did as king?

Joash decided to renovate the House of the LORD. 2 Chron. 24:4

He could have decided to renovate the king's palace or his gardens or his stables, but he chose to renovate the House of the LORD.

3. Where did the money come from to renovate the Temple?

*The king ordered that a chest be made and placed on the outside of the gate of the House of the LORD . . . **all the people gladly brought it** and threw it into the chest till it was full. They did this day by day, and much money was collected.* 2 Chronicles 24:8, 10,11

This was a free will offering. People gave freely as Elohim moved their hearts. The funds did not come from taxes or state dollars. They came from the people. The people brought the money gladly because they had first committed their hearts to the LORD. When God has our hearts and His Spirit is living in us obedience and giving become a joy. Obedient joyous giving is a miracle that happens when God is in our lives.

4. During the time of Moses where did the money come from to build the first Temple?

*Everyone who excelled in ability and everyone whose spirit moved him came, bringing to the LORD his offering for the work of the Tent of Meeting and for all its service.... Men and women, **all whose hearts moved them**, all who would make an elevation offering of gold to the LORD, came **bringing brooches, earrings, rings, and pendants— gold objects of all kinds.*** Exodus 35:21,22

From the first Jewish Temple until now God expects His people to participate in the physical work of building up, maintaining, and funding the work of the LORD. In this first example people gave from their hearts and they gave up the ornaments of the world. Instead of decorating themselves they committed to decorating God's house.

5. What do the Scriptures call it when we give financially out of the goodness

15. THE YOUNGEST KING

of our hearts?

> *Offering your <u>freewill contribution</u> according as the LORD your God has blessed you. Then Hezekiah said, "Now you have consecrated yourselves to the LORD; come, <u>bring sacrifices of well-being and thanksgiving</u> to the House of the LORD.* Deuteronomy 16:10; 2 Chronicles 29:31

Again we see the proper order demonstrated. After we have consecrated ourselves to the LORD contributions will freely and thankfully come forth from our hearts for the House of the LORD.

6. According to the Psalms why would anyone want to freely give money away?

> *<u>I love the LORD</u> for <u>He hears my voice, my pleas</u>; for <u>He turns His ear to me whenever I call</u> . . . I invoked the name of the LORD, "O LORD, save my life!" <u>The LORD is gracious and beneficent</u>; our <u>God is compassionate. The LORD protects</u> . . . <u>He saved me</u>. Be at rest, once again, O my soul, for <u>the LORD has been good</u> to you. <u>You have delivered me from death</u>, my eyes <u>from tears</u>, my feet <u>from stumbling</u>. <u>I shall walk before the LORD in the lands of the living</u>. <u>I trust [in the LORD]</u> . . . <u>How can I repay the LORD</u> for all His bounties to me? I raise the cup of deliverance and invoke the name of the LORD. <u>I will pay my vows to the LORD in the presence of all His people</u>. O LORD, I am Your servant, Your servant . . . <u>You have undone the cords that bound me. I will sacrifice a thank offering to You</u> and invoke the name of the LORD. <u>I will pay my vows to the LORD in the presence of all His people, in the courts of the house of the LORD</u>, in the midst of Jerusalem. Hallelujah.* Psalm 116:1-10, 12-14, 16-18

Several reasons are listed in this text for wanting to give to the LORD. The first reason listed is because we love the LORD. This should be our main reason. The psalm also mentions that we give as a symbol of our gratitude, as a sign of our thankfulness that God hears our voice, that He turns His ear to us, and is gracious, beneficent, and compassionate. He protects us, saves us, and is good to us. He delivers us from death, crying, and stumbling. He promises everlasting life in Heaven. With such a great God as this how could we hold back from wanting to give him our hearts and our offerings, especially when those gifts will be used in building up His house so that others can come to know of His great love?

7. How is it that we have been able to acquire any money at all?

> *Remember that it is <u>the LORD your God who gives you the power</u>*

to get wealth. Deuteronomy 8:18

It is not our talents, wisdom, diplomas, or skills that get us wealth; it is the LORD our God who gives us the power to use the talents, wisdom, education, and skills that He has given us. It is God who gave us a mind to get the diplomas. It is God who gave us hands, feet, eyes, and skills to use them. In a moment, during a disaster or horrendous accident, all our own abilities can be removed from us. All that we are able to do is because Elohim has given us the ability to do it. Thus, He really is the One who has given us the power to earn money. Moses tells us to remember this.

8. Since it is God who gives me the ability to acquire wealth, what would be the logical response of thanks that I should show for all the wonderful things God has done for me?

Honor the LORD with your wealth, with the best of all your income, And your barns will be filled with grain. Proverbs 3:9,10

We should give God the best, or first, of our income, not what is left over, not used stuff that we don't want anymore. God has given us His best. He deserves our best.

9. Follow the order here: God gives me the power to get money. Then I show my appreciation by giving back the best, or first, of that income. The Bible calls it the "first fruits." How does God then promise to respond?

Honor the LORD with your wealth, with the best of all your income, and your barns will be filled with grain. Proverbs 3:9,10

Bring the full tithe into the storehouse, and let there be food in My House, and thus put Me to the test—said the LORD of Hosts. I will surely open the floodgates of the sky for you and pour down blessings on you. Malachi 3:10

God gives, we give back, then God gives again, and so on. The only ones who can break the cycle are you and me. The Sea of Galilee, in Israel, is full of fish and life. The Jordan River flows in and flows out. Yet the Dead Sea, down river from Galilee, is dead. The Jordan River flows in but the Dead Sea does not let any water flow out. It tries to keep it all to itself. If we do not allow God's blessings to flow through us eventually our hearts grow stagnant and die. If we are not thankful and responsive to that thankfulness in blessing others the end result is death.

10. How did Abraham show his appreciation for God's goodness?

15. THE YOUNGEST KING

[Abram] gave him a tenth of everything. Genesis 14:20

Abraham gave ten percent of all that he had to Melchisedec, the minister of God.

11. How did Jacob show his appreciation for God's goodness?

"the Lord shall be my God . . . and of all that You give me, I will set aside a tithe for You." Genesis 28:21, 22

Jacob, like Abraham, set aside a tithe or ten percent for God.

12. What did Elohim specifically tell Moses concerning the tithe?

All tithes . . . are the Lord's; they are holy to the Lord. Lev. 27:30

The tithe, or first ten percent, of all that God has given to us is holy to the Lord. It is set apart specifically for God's ministers. The tithe is different from the freewill offering that helped build the Temple. The freewill offerings are over and above the ten percent and are used for the building and congregational expenses.

13. What does God call it when we do not give Him back the 10% tithe and the freewill thank offerings?

Ought man to defraud God? Yet you are defrauding Me. And you ask, "How have we been defrauding You?" In tithe and contribution. You are suffering under a curse, yet you go on defrauding Me. Malachi 3:8, 9

Here again we see a distinction between the tithe (first 10%) and freewill offerings or contributions. If we are stingy in either of these areas God says we are defrauding or stealing from Him and that we are under a curse. Pretty strong words from God! Stealing is a bad enough sin, stealing from God clearly shows if we have committed ourselves to Him or not. All the things we have been learning in Jewish Discoveries demonstrate whether or not we have surrendered our hearts to God and if we are allowing Him to be the Lord of our lives. How willingly and cheerfully you give of your finances is one indicator God has given so that you can tell who is most important to you, God or yourself.

14. According to King David, who really owns everything?

The earth is the Lord's and all that it holds, the world and its inhabitants. Psalm 24:1

God owns the world, and everything we have. He has given us the ability to get wealth, so He really is the owner of it all. He lets us manage it. God requires we return 10% of what is really His and then He allows us to choose what percentage we want to give Him as a freewill offering out of the 90% he leaves for us to manage and use.

If your neighbor lends you his lawn mower and you return it to him are you doing any great deed? No, you are just doing what is right; you are returning what belongs to your neighbor. If you gave him a gift of appreciation then you are doing something extra that he did not ask for. When we return God's tithe to Him we are just giving Him back what He tells us is His. We start being generous when we give freewill offerings on top of the ten percent.

Returning God's ten percent tests our obedience and trust. Freewill offerings above the tithe demonstrate our love and thankfulness to God.

15. What is life like for someone who refuses to allow Adonai to give him a generous heart?

> ***Thus said the L<small>ORD</small> . . . : Consider how you have been faring! You have <u>sowed much and brought in little; you eat without being satisfied; you drink without getting your fill; you clothe yourselves, but no one gets warm; and he who earns anything earns it for a leaky purse . . . Because of My House which lies in ruins, while you all hurry to your own houses!</u>*** Haggai 1:5,6, 9

Do you sometimes feel this way? Do you sometimes feel like you have been working a lot and getting a little, or that you are never satisfied with what you have, or that you never seem to have enough? Does it ever seem like what you earn just leaks out as if there is a hole in your pocket? Could it be because you have not understood how God's arithmetic works? Have you been trying to put yourself first and God second? If your way is not working, if you are still a slave to debt and each month you are living from paycheck to paycheck, try God's way. Don't wait until you have enough left over to give to God; you never will. Give to God first and watch Him stretch the rest of the money in ways you never thought possible. Step out in faith; trust Him.

Everything we have God has given us the ability to get. He really has given to us first, and He instructs us to put Him first with the money He has given us the ability to get. Y'shua gave a wonderful promise: ***"Give, and it shall be given unto you; good measure, pressed down, and shaken together, and running over . . ."*** Luke 6:38 KJV.

15. THE YOUNGEST KING

16. According to Moses, how important is this topic?

    When you make a vow to the L<small>ORD</small> your God, <u>do not put off fulfilling it</u>, for <u>the L<small>ORD</small> your God will require it of you, and you will have incurred guilt.</u> Deuteronomy 23:22

17. If you are afraid that you could not make it financially if you willingly gave back to God what is His, you can surrender these fears to God and He will give you faith. If you realize that you are at heart selfish and do not want to give what you feel you have earned, you can surrender those feelings to God also and He will give you His generous righteous Spirit. Remember how He changed Jacob to Israel? He is still in the heart-changing business. That is why the Messiah died, to take away our guilt, our selfishness, our fears. Listen again to how David prayed for forgiveness and transformation.

    "Indeed <u>I was born with iniquity</u> . . . Have mercy upon me, O God, as befits Your faithfulness; in keeping with Your abundant compassion, <u>blot out my transgressions. Wash me thoroughly of my iniquity, and purify me of my sin;</u> for I recognize my transgressions, and am ever conscious of my sin. <u>Purge me with hyssop till I am pure; wash me till I am whiter than snow.</u> Hide Your face from my sins; <u>blot out all my iniquities. Fashion a pure heart for me, O God; create in me a steadfast spirit.</u> Do not cast me out of Your presence, or take Your holy spirit away from me. Let me again rejoice in Your help; <u>let a vigorous spirit sustain me.</u> I will teach transgressors Your ways, that sinners may return to You." Psalm 51:7, 3, 4, 9-15

    This prayer is a perfect example for us to use as a model for our prayers of confession. Put the prayer into your own words and tell Elohim your specific area of need, whether selfishness, fear, greed, etc. and ask Him to give you His pure generous spirit.

18. What does David tell us will be the result of giving Y'shua our fears, guilt, and selfishness and accepting His righteousness?

    <u>The righteous is generous and keeps giving. Those blessed by Him shall inherit the land</u> . . . Though he stumbles, he does not fall down, for the L<small>ORD</small> gives him support. I have been young and am now old, but <u>I have never seen a righteous man abandoned, or his children seeking bread. He is always generous, and lends, and his children are held blessed.</u> Shun evil and do good, and you shall abide forever. For <u>the L<small>ORD</small> loves what is right, He does not abandon His faithful ones. They are preserved forever</u> . . . <u>The righteous shall inherit the land, and abide forever in it.</u> Psalm 37:21-29

God makes us righteous by His transforming power. Part of being made righteous is being made generous. The righteous are not only generous, but they keep on giving. Those who allow God to transform their hearts to make them righteous and generous will inherit the land—the heavenly land with no mortgage and no taxes! In Judaism the term tzedakah indicates generosity, but the word also translates as righteousness. Righteousness, generosity, love, and charity are not separable characteristics. Each of these characteristics becomes ours as God fills us with His Spirit.

In putting God first we set aside the tithe before we consider our own needs or expenses. God's 10% comes out of our increase. God's portion comes first. God comes before taxes, God comes before the country we live in. God comes before bills, God comes before wants, and God comes before needs. As we put God first He will make sure the rest is taken care of. He will not abandon us. He will take care of us. Putting Him first takes faith. That is why our first lesson, on Abraham, was on faith. It is faith in the beginning and faith all the way through that leads us to Heaven. God will give us the faith we need as we ask Him for it.

19. There is an old saying: you cannot serve two masters; you cannot serve God and money. Where your treasure is, there shall your heart be also. Who did Joshua decide to serve?

   "Now, therefore, <u>revere the LORD and serve Him with undivided loyalty</u> . . . and serve the LORD. Or, if you are loath to serve the LORD, choose this day which ones you are going to serve . . . but <u>I and my household will serve the LORD</u>." Joshua 24:14,15

   Do you want to serve God with an undivided loyalty? Are you willing to serve Him with every aspect of your life, including your finances? I know those are the decisions you have been making as we have studied God's Word.

   Imagine that you have been out of work for some time and your financial situation is getting really rough. You finally find a job as a hired hand on a large farm owned by a nice man named Ivan Canaday. He has good equipment and teaches you how to use the high tech irrigation system he has. After many days of long hours and hard work you harvest his crop and bring it into his silos. The next day Mr. Canaday invites you to come to the market with him. On the way back he asks you to count up the money. It comes to $60,000. Mr. Canaday asks you to separate $6,000 to give back to him and tells you to keep the remaining $54,000. You exclaim, "It's a deal."

15. THE YOUNGEST KING

Would you be happy with that arrangement? Of course you would. It is really no different than what God does with us. God gives us minds, talents, and muscles as tools to get wealth. He allows us to work on His land (He owns everything), and then he lets us keep 90% of all that He helps us acquire. That's a deal!

Allow God to quietly speak to you for a minute. Where is your heart, where is your treasure, where are your loyalties? Are they caught up in getting money and getting the things that money buys? Or is God most important to you. Think about these questions personally. Where are my thoughts primarily focused? Where do I use the time God has entrusted to me? How do I use the money that God has given me the power to get? Who do I really love the most, myself or God? Who do I put first with my finances, myself or God? Who will I choose to serve today?

Elohim is passionate about seeing the good news of His love told everywhere. Since it costs for that to happen, He has chosen to finance the project by putting resources in the hands of His people. As we give joyously, we demonstrate that our hearts beat in tune with His . . . our goals are the same as His. Those are the kinds of people He can safely trust with eternal life.

Jeff and Barbara met and fell in love. Both were native New Yorkers. Both were Jewish and believed in Y'shua as the Messiah. Both kept the Sabbath holy and all of the Ten Commandments. Both were vegetarians. Both were active in ministry for God. A real match made in heaven. Both had experienced the emotional roller coaster and heartache associated with physical attachments during the dating period. So both decided to not even hold hands until Jeff asked for Barbara's hand in marriage, and not to kiss until the minister said, "You may now kiss the bride." This gave them plenty of time to get to know each other and talk about the important issues that hold a marriage together.

Finances being one of the most important areas of marriage, they decided to find out how compatible they were in this area. It turns out that both had already been giving a full twenty percent (ten percent for tithe, ten percent for offering) of their gross income to the LORD. Even though they were both volunteers, earning just a small stipend at the time, they always had enough. As plans of a wedding were birthed they wondered how they could give tithes and offerings on their wedding gifts. How do you give twenty percent of a blender? Most of their friends did not earn much more than they did and they were expecting mostly home made afghans for gifts. They decided that they would figure out how much the value of the physical gifts were and then give the appropriate amount in cash, and if they did not have enough cash they would have to return a blender or something so they would have enough cash. When they finally opened all their presents they not only had enough cash gifts to cover their tithe and offerings on all their gifts, both cash and physical gifts, they had enough to cover the cost for their whole two week honeymoon, including airfare, rental car, and hotels. In addition to the cash they also received more than needed for furnishing their new apartment. And there was even a little money left over to put in the bank. Weeks after their honeymoon they took a class on how to set up a spending plan that has kept them out of debt (other than their mortgage) and has helped them to buy the things that they really need and often want.

For more than nineteen years of marriage Jeff and Barbara have never lacked for anything they really needed nor have they even questioned whether they could afford to give twenty percent back to the Lord. Actually they decided they could not afford not to and increased their percentage over the years. God has always been faithful and Jeff and Barbara have always had more than enough.

REVIEW הזרה

1. How much of what is in this world rightfully belongs to God?
   a. Only wild animals
   b. Everything
   c. Nothing

2. Where does the ability to get wealth come from?
   a. My college education
   b. My own hard work
   c. God gives me the ability to think and work hard

3. According to King David (question 17, Psalm 51:7), are we born with a generous spirit or with a selfish disposition?
   a. Born with iniquity (Sinfulness)
   b. Born good, righteous, and generous

15. THE YOUNGEST KING

4. Even though we are born selfish, how can we change?
    a. Try really hard
    b. Think positively
    c. Ask the Messiah to cleanse me of my selfish heart and ask Him to give me a generous heart.

5. I want to serve God with all my heart, soul, and might, including my finances. I choose to put God first by giving God His ten percent and free will offerings.
    a. Yes, how could I do anything less?
    b. No yet, I want to reread this lesson.

TRADITIONS

Tzedakah

Tzedakah is from the word meaning righteousness. A tzadek is a righteous person. The term is used to describe the act of charity or giving. Tzedakah boxes are used for collecting donations. The Yiddish word for a tzedakah box is pushke. A tzedakah box or a pushke can be made from anything and can be used in the home to store up the money or in the synagogue.

Helping someone to become self-sufficient is considered the highest form of tzedakah. The reasoning is similar to the saying that if you give someone a fish you helped him for a day; if you teach him how to fish you have fed him for a lifetime.

Tzedakah is more than just giving a donation. Tzedakah is a life of caring and the giving of one's self in order to help humanity. Since God is the giver of all things we give to others out of our gratitude to Him. Being a tzadek, a righteous person, and doing mitzvahs (good deeds) and giving tzedakah go hand in hand.

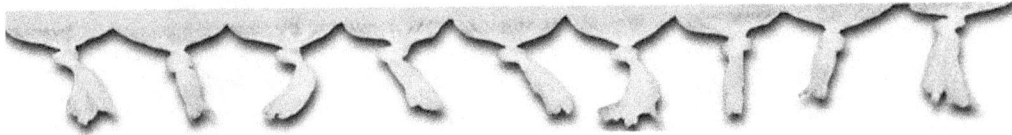

16. DANIEL, THE GREATEST JEWISH STATESMAN

Certainly calling Daniel the "greatest" Jewish statesman can be debated, since there have been many great Jewish statesmen throughout history, including Joseph, King David, King Solomon, Don Isaac Abrabanel, Benjamin Disraeli, Theodor Herzl, Ben Gurion, Chaim Weitzman, and Abba Eban, just to name a few. Daniel's political career spanned more than half a century. Interestingly, not only did Daniel hold the highest position, next to the king, in the empire of Babylon, but he also became the president, second only to the ruler, of the Medo-Persian Empire, which had overthrown Babylon.

The Jewish prophet Daniel lived during a very tragic time in Israel's history. When Daniel was still a teenager, King Nebuchadnezzar, King of Babylon, sent his army to the city of Jerusalem. Babylon's army destroyed Jerusalem and the beautiful Temple that King Solomon had built. Most of the Jewish people were either killed or taken captive. Daniel was taken as a captive to Babylon. Elohim gave the prophet Jeremiah a message that the Jewish people would remain in exile for 70 years. Exactly 70 years later God's prophecy came true, just as Jeremiah had said. Daniel lived through those years and saw this prophecy fulfilled.

One thing that characterized Daniel's life of trials and successes was his habit of immediately bringing every situation to God through prayer.

1. With what other famous people did the Jewish prophet Ezekiel classify Daniel while Daniel was still alive?

    If a land were to sin against Me and commit a trespass, and I stretched out My hand against it ... even if these three men—<u>Noah, Daniel, and Job</u>—should be in it, they would by their righteousness save only themselves—declares the L<small>ORD</small> God. Ezekiel 14:13, 14

    This is an amazing honor. It is one thing for a person to be exalted and remembered after they die, but while Daniel was still alive he was grouped with Noah and Job, two men whom the Bible described as righteous and upright. Can you imagine someone comparing you with Noah and Job? How would you feel if it was the LORD God who was the One comparing you with Noah and Job? It would leave you with a high expectation to live up to wouldn't it? I'm sure it was quite a humbling experience for Daniel as he realized there was no way he could live up to that expectation without God's power.

2. King Nebuchadnezzar wished to take advantage of some of Israel's brightest minds, so Daniel and some of the other Jewish captives were offered positions in the king's service. Daniel's first test of loyalty to God came when the king graciously offered them a special gift. What did he offer?

<u>The king allotted daily rations to them from the king's food and from the wine he drank.</u> Daniel 1:5

It was a high honor to be offered the same food that was served to the king, but it was a problem for those who wanted to follow God with all their hearts, all their souls, and all their minds. The animals were most probably among the ones God had commanded not to eat. The wine that was served was probably alcoholic wine and not grape juice.

3. What did Daniel and his three friends, Hananiah, Mishael, and Azariah, resolve to do about this unhealthy diet, even if it meant death?

<u>Daniel resolved not to defile himself with the king's food or the wine he drank. So he sought permission of the chief officer not to defile himself, and God disposed the chief officer to be kind and compassionate toward Daniel. "Please test your servants . . . giving us legumes to eat and water to drink."</u> Daniel 1:8, 9, 12

Daniel and his friends chose water and a vegetarian diet instead of alcohol that destroys brain cells and makes us more susceptible to temptations, and the meat of animals that God said not to eat.

Daniel and his three friends could have tried to justify their disobedience to Adonai. They were away from their homeland, their parents were probably dead, and they had no choice in the food that was given them. They could be killed for disobeying, and it would be disrespectful and improper to refuse such a generous offer given with good intentions from their host. They may have also reasoned that since God did not protect their city, their parents, or them why should they obey His laws. Even with all of these reasons and peer pressure they resolved, determined, decided to follow God all the way, no matter what the consequences. Have you been using some of these same excuses

16. DANIEL, THE GREATEST JEWISH STATESMAN

for your disobedience to God? If so, you can surrender those excuses and allow God to bring your life in harmony with His will.

God was first in their lives and that was what was most important, even more important than life itself. They believed they were in God's hands and if God wanted to protect them He would. They believed it was not their job to protect their lives. They believed that was God's job. They believed it was their responsibility to obey God and leave the rest with Him. Now you can see why Daniel was compared with Noah and Job. It reminds us of the statements by Job: *"the LORD gives and the LORD takes away—blessed be the name of the LORD." "Though He slay me, yet will I trust in Him."*

4. How did Elohim bless His faithful servants in the outcome of this test?

    <u>*God made all four of these young men intelligent and proficient in all writings and wisdom, and Daniel had understanding of visions and dreams of all kinds. The king spoke with them, and of them all none was equal to Daniel, Hananiah, Mishael and Azariah; so these entered the king's service.*</u> *Daniel 1:17, 19*

    God blessed their obedience and made them healthier and wiser than all the rest of the people in the king's court. Faith is learning to put God first and trusting the results with Him.

5. The next challenge Daniel faced was when King Nebuchadnezzar had a dream. When he awoke, he couldn't remember what the dream was about, only that he was profoundly shaken by it. None of his advisors—magicians, sorcerers, enchanters, mediums, astrologers, etc. could interpret the dream, either. How did the king react?

    Whereupon the king flew into a violent rage, and gave an order to do away with all the wise men of Babylon. Daniel 2:12

6. What did Daniel do in this difficult situation?

    <u>*Daniel went to his house*</u> *and informed his companions, Hananiah, Mishael, and Azariah, of the matter,* <u>*that they might implore the God of Heaven for help*</u> *regarding this mystery, so that Daniel and his colleagues would not be put to death . . . Daniel 2:17, 18*

    In everything Daniel prayed. Prayer, obedience, and trust in Adonai characterized the life of Daniel.

7. How did God answer their prayers and how did Daniel respond back to God?

> *The mystery was revealed to Daniel in a night vision; then Daniel blessed the God of Heaven . . . and said: . . . He gives the wise their wisdom and knowledge to those who know.* Daniel 2:19, 21

God gave Daniel, like Joseph before him, the interpretation to the king's dream. Daniel, like Joseph, gave God the praise and credit for the wisdom given him. Another characteristic of Daniel's life was humility before God. All of these things that characterized Daniel's life—prayer, obedience, trust, & humility—are available to each of us. All we have to do is ask Adonai to live these characteristics out in our lives.

8. What did Daniel tell the king about this mysterious dream?

> But <u>there is a God in heaven who reveals mysteries</u>, and <u>He has made known</u> to King Nebuchadnezzar <u>what is to be at the end of days</u> . . . <u>The great God has made known to the king what will happen in the future</u>. Daniel 2:28, 45

Elohim had given King Nebuchadnezzar a dream that would reveal what would happen in the future, even to "the end of days." This prophetic dream is very important because it lays the foundation for the rest of the prophecies in the biblical books of Daniel and Revelation. God uses this time line as an outline of biblical prophecy and then each successive prophecy adds flesh and skin to the skeleton.

9. What was the dream that God gave the king, as recorded in Daniel chapter 2?

> *"O king . . . there appeared a great statue. This statue . . . was awesome. The head . . . was of fine gold; its breast . . . were of silver; its belly and thighs, of bronze; its legs were of iron, and its feet part iron and part clay . . . a stone was hewn out, not by hands, and struck the statue on its feet of iron and clay and crushed them . . . a wind carried them off until no trace of them was left. But the stone that struck the statue became a great mountain and filled the whole earth . . .*
>
> *You, O king . . . are the head of gold. But another kingdom will arise after you, inferior to yours; then yet a third kingdom, of bronze . . . But the fourth kingdom will be as strong as iron . . . You saw the feet and the toes, part potter's clay and part iron . . . it will be a divided kingdom . . . part strong and in part brittle . . . they shall intermingle . . . but shall not hold together, just as iron does not mix with clay. And in the time of those kings, the God of Heaven will establish a kingdom that shall never be destroyed . . . but shall . . . last forever—just as you saw how a stone was hewn from the mountain,*

16. DANIEL, THE GREATEST JEWISH STATESMAN

not by hands, and crushed the iron, bronze, clay, silver, and gold. The great God has made known to the king what will happen in the future. Daniel 2:31-45

History shows us that these successive world kingdoms were:
a. Babylon as the head of gold,
b. Persia as the chest of silver,
c. Greece as the belly and thighs of bronze,
d. Rome as the legs of iron,
e. Europe as the divided kingdoms represented by iron and clay, which is part strong, part weak, and has never joined together.
f. Messiah's second coming as the stone that destroys all earthly kingdoms.

We are now living in the time of the end, as depicted by the toes of the statue. Europe is being accurately described in this prophecy. It is at this time that the prophecy says that the Messiah will come again, as the stone, and will destroy the kingdoms of this earth and start over with *"a new heaven and a new earth."* Isaiah 65:17. God later gave Daniel other visions with more detail about the same time periods covered in this dream, which we will be covering in the next few lessons.

The Bible prophecies in the books of Daniel and Revelation work on a principle of repetition and expansion. It is similar to a child studying history in a classroom in the United States. The first year the child will learn very rudimentary history of the 200 plus years of United States history. The next year he will learn about the same 200-year period, but with more information about the history of the USA, such as learning the names of famous people. The following year the student will again cover the same 200-year time period, possibly learning about important wars and years of important events. This pattern of repetition and expansion will continue throughout the student's years in school. The same is true with the study of Daniel and Revelation; each chapter repeats and expands on the ones before it.

Remember this time line of Daniel 2, as this is the framework upon which all the rest of the prophecies of Daniel and Revelation will build. This is not to say that countries such as China, Russia, Japan, African nations, etc. are not important to God. The political powers that are listed in this prophecy and the ones to follow are not listed because they are more important than other nations, but because these are the primary ones that directly affected people who were studying the Scriptures and following God. The primary focus of the entire Bible is God's interaction with people who choose to follow Him. As was stated earlier, this first prophecy is just a foundation; more will be added as we continue. Even though more will be added as we continue it will be added to the original foundation. To try to understand the other prophecies of Daniel and Revelation outside of this foundation prophecy will be like trying to build a house off of the poured foundation. Thus, any interpretation that takes you off the foundation would be an error. As we follow each successive prophecy in Daniel and Revelation we will see them staying within the framework of the nations mentioned in Daniel 2.

Notice that although there are 5 time periods depicted before the Messiah's second coming, there are only 4 metals representing only 4 powers that would rule from the time of Daniel until the second advent of the Messiah. The fourth metal, iron, is mentioned in the fourth and fifth time periods of the prophecy, both in the legs and in the feet and toes. Thus, Rome was to have an influence in history from the time of Rome replacing Greece in the year 168 BCE, until the Messiah comes again.

10. Because Daniel was able to interpret Nebuchadnezzar's dream, the king praised the God of Daniel. But sometime later he had a change of heart and made a statue of solid gold more than ten stories tall, in defiance of the dream God had given him. Evidently, the king did not like the idea that his kingdom, represented in the dream as "the kingdom of gold," was going to be replaced by another kingdom, represented by the silver chest. The king of Babylon wanted Babylon to rule forever. He did not want his kingdom to be replaced. He did not accept the prophecy that there were going to be successive kingdoms. So instead of creating a statue made of 4 metals in 5 sections, he made a statue that was solid gold—solidly Babylonian from head to toe.

When the statue was completed an unveiling ceremony was scheduled and all government officials were told to attend. Apparently Daniel was away in another part of the kingdom at the time, but his three friends were among those invited. What did the king command at this ceremony, and what was the king told when the unveiling took place?

__Whoever will not fall down and worship shall at once be thrown into a burning fiery furnace.__" . . . certain Chaldeans came forward to slander the Jews. They spoke up and said to King Nebuchadnezzar

16. DANIEL, THE GREATEST JEWISH STATESMAN

... __There are certain Jews whom you appointed to administer the province of Babylon . . . those men . . . do not . . . worship the statue__ . . ." Daniel 3:6, 8, 12

These faithful young Jewish men chose to obey God, although it meant almost certain death to defy the king. They did not bow down and worship Nebuchadnezzar's statue. By choosing to follow God in the daily issues, such as what they ate, they were strengthened morally to take a stand when they were confronted with this issue. They could have knelt down and made it look as though they were worshiping and yet not worship the statue, but they did not want to even give the appearance that they were being disloyal to the LORD God of heaven and earth. Their reputation as followers of the only true God was more important to them than life on this earth. There is a good lesson for us in their example. We should avoid being in situations or participating in activities that even give the appearance of doing evil.

11. The king called them forward and gave them another chance to bow down to the image, warning them of the fire. How did they respond, showing their utter trust and love for God, whether God delivered them or not?

__Our God whom we serve is able to save us__ from the burning fiery furnace, __and He will save us__ from your power, O king. __But even if He does not__, be it known to you, O king, that __we will not . . . worship the statue of gold.__ Daniel 3:17, 18

Even with a second chance they still refused to compromise. What a beautiful answer they gave. They had faith that God was able to save them from death, but they allowed God to be sovereign. If God knew it would be best for them to die at this point they were more willing to die with the promise of heaven than to disobey God and live. Do we love God that much? Is what God says and commands more important than life on this earth to you? When it comes to a choice of obeying man-made laws or God's laws, which will you choose? As we will see in the next few lessons, we will be tested down to the very end of time on this issue of deciding whether to follow God and His laws or man-made laws that are in opposition to God's laws.

12. The king became so angry at their act of defiance that he had the furnace heated up seven times hotter than usual and had Hananiah, Mishael, and Azariah thrown into the furnace. The furnace was so hot it killed the soldiers that threw the three Jewish men into it. What did the king see in

the furnace after the three men were thrown in?

"I see <u>four men walking about unbound and unharmed in the fire</u>". Daniel 3:25

13. Whom did the king say the fourth man looked like?

". . . the fourth looks like <u>a divine being</u>." Daniel 3:25

Here is another time when God took the form of a man. We read about Him coming to Abraham and Jacob as well as the prophecies that the Messiah would come to earth the first time as a man.

14. When the king called Daniel's three friends out of the furnace, how had Elohim proved His protection?

<u>The fire had had no effect, the hair of whose heads had not been singed, whose shirts looked no different, to whom not even the odor of fire clung.</u> Daniel 3:27

Hananiah, Mishael and Azariah were standing in a fire that was so hot it killed the soldiers who came close to the furnace, yet the fire did not even singe their hair or clothing. They didn't even smell of smoke. God will stand by you as you put Him first in your life. Are you going through a fiery ordeal right now? Trust the LORD. He is standing with you right now and will see you through.

15. For a time the king again praised the Most High God, but soon pride crept back into his heart and God humbled this powerful man again. At the end of the final experience recorded in Scripture about King Nebuchadnezzar, what did he say regarding God, showing the positive influence that Daniel, his friends, and God's Spirit had had upon him?

"<u>I, Nebuchadnezzar, praise, exalt, and glorify the King of Heaven, all of whose works are just and whose ways are right, and who is able to humble those who behave arrogantly.</u>" Daniel 4:34

What a powerful testimony to the pure lives of Daniel, Hananiah, Mishael, and Azariah. If they had compromised on any of the teachings of Scripture they believed, or had let their minds and convictions become dulled with alcohol, or if they had obeyed man's laws over God's laws, this king of the most powerful nation on the earth at the time would probably never have surrendered himself to the God of Heaven.

It is interesting that the times before this, when Nebuchadnezzar was convinced of God's power but not totally changed in heart, he made religious laws

16. DANIEL, THE GREATEST JEWISH STATESMAN

to enforce worship of the God of Daniel. He was trying to use man-made laws to force people to love God. But that is not how it works with God. It is God's love that awakens in us a love for Him. When the king was fully changed in heart he no longer made laws enforcing faith; he only gave his testimony.

16. Approximately twenty-four years after Nebuchadnezzar's death, the kingdom of Babylon was taken over by Persia, just as God had revealed to Daniel in the king's dream of the statue. Quickly seeing the extraordinary spirit that Daniel manifested, the new king, Darius, appointed Daniel, now in his 80's, over the whole kingdom. The other political leaders in the realm did not like this, but could find nothing in Daniel's life to accuse him of. They came up with a plan to trap Daniel using his faithful prayer life. What was their plan?

"O King Darius, live forever! . . . <u>A royal ban should be issued under sanction of an oath that whoever shall address a petition to any god or man, besides you, O king, during the next thirty days shall be thrown into a lions' den.</u>" Daniel 6:7, 8

This was another man-made law that contradicted God's law and which carried with it a death decree for disobedience. Although this is a historical account in the life of Daniel it is also prophetically pointing to the last great issues that will affect God's people at the end of time.

17. How did Daniel respond to this unfair law that restricted his freedom of religion?

When Daniel learned that it had been put in writing, <u>he went to his house . . . and three times a day he knelt down, prayed, and made confession to his God, as he had always done.</u> Daniel 6:11

Prayer was more important to Daniel than life on this earth. Daniel could have hid the fact that he was praying. He could have closed the windows or hid in a closet or just prayed silently as he walked through town. But like the situation with the statue, He did not want to even give the appearance that he was willing to obey man-made laws rather than be faithful to His God.

18. It was Daniel's custom to kneel down, praying and confessing to God, three times a day. How did King David express his similar experience?

As for me, I call to God; the LORD will deliver me. <u>Evening, morning, and noon.</u> Psalm 55:17, 18

It would be good for us to follow these godly men's examples. We should also pray, making our confessions to God, throughout each day. If we prayed more we would have more of an experience and life that these men of God had. Your prayers don't have to be ones that others have written down in a prayer book. Your prayers can come from your heart and be personal. God wants you to talk to Him like you would to a very close friend. He wants you to speak to Him of your feelings, your desires, your troubles, and your joys.

19. When the other politicians came running to the king, telling him that Daniel had broken the law, the king was very sad. He had not realized when he signed the law that it was designed to trap Daniel. How did the king react after Daniel was thrown into the lion's den?

> ***The king...said, "Your God, whom you serve so regularly, will deliver you... The king then went to his palace and spent the night fasting... Then, at the first light of dawn, the king arose and rushed to the lions' den... in a mournful voice; the king said to Daniel, "Daniel, servant of the living God, was the God whom you served so regularly able to deliver you from the lions?"*** Daniel 6:17, 19-21

King Darius never would have signed the law if he had known that the law would be used to restrict Daniel's religious liberty and freedom and be a cause of persecution against Daniel. Even good leaders who desire to do what is right can at times be tricked into passing bad laws that will cause the loss of religious freedoms. This, again, is an illustration of last day issues. It is very important for us as citizens to stand up for the religious liberty of everyone, even of religions that are different from ours. Unless everyone has equal freedom, no one has freedom.

20. Read the wonderful story as it happened that morning.

> ***Daniel then talked with the king... "My God sent His angel, who shut the mouths of the lions... inasmuch as I was found innocent by Him, nor have I, O king, done you any injury... Daniel was brought up out of the den, and no injury was found on him, for he had trusted in his God.*** Then... those men who had slandered Daniel were brought and... were thrown into the lions' den. They had hardly reached the bottom of the den when the lions overpowered them... Daniel* 6:22-25

There is power in prayer. If you have not yet developed a regular daily prayer time I strongly encourage you to do so now. David and Daniel's examples of praying morning, afternoon, and night are great examples. A tre-

16. DANIEL, THE GREATEST JEWISH STATESMAN

mendous way to start the day is to make prayer the first thing that is done in the morning. It prepares you for the day and sets your priorities. An afternoon prayer keeps you focused. And an evening prayer gives you a chance to reflect, with God, on what you are thankful for. The evening is also a good time to confess to the Lord any areas that you fell short of His will. An evening prayer prepares you for a good night's rest. It calms the mind and brings God's peace into your heart, especially after a hectic day. Other times in the day that make for good benchmarks for prayer include when reading the Bible, mealtime, before traveling, and before working on a project. As you pray before reading the Bible you are asking God to give you His divine wisdom to understand His divine Word. It would be good to pray before reading or watching anything and ask God to give you spiritual discernment. As you stop for a short prayer of praise and thanksgiving when you eat it will remind you of your dependency on God to provide for you. As you pause for a prayer for protection before you travel by car, bus, or plane you will be reminded of your need of God's protection. When you pray for Elohim's help before you undertake a project it will enforce your acknowledgement that all your talents are from God. Whether you are beginning to prepare a meal, start work, take a test at school, or change a light bulb it would be wise to invite God's presence to help you. True prayer will be communing with God Almighty. When you are intimately entering into a conversation with God in prayer it is impossible to feel alone. Prayer lifts us up above this world and seats us right at God's heavenly throne.

Daniel's prayer life did not keep him out of trouble, but it did give him the extraordinary spirit of peace and composure through the difficult times. Elohim does not always deliver us physically on this earth. But if the blood of the Messiah has covered our sins, just as the Passover blood of the lambs covered the Jewish homes in Egypt, we are assured a place in heaven. I like how Hananiah, Mishael, and Azariah put it when they said; *"Our God whom we serve is able to save us . . . and He will save us from your power, O king. But even if He does not, be it known to you, O king, that we will not . . . worship the statue of gold."* May God give you His Spirit, so you can live a faithful life as these men did.

It is not necessary to follow a certain pattern in prayer. Your prayers need to be unique and personal between you and God. You may find it helpful in focusing your prayers if you follow a pattern at least sometimes. One prayer pattern you might find helpful using is praying through the Sanctuary.

In lesson 5 we studied the first Jewish Temple, which God had Moses build. Later in history David financed and Solomon built a larger more permanent version of that Sanctuary. God's Temple included an entrance, an altar of sacrifice for forgiveness of sins, a large basin of water for washing and cleansing, a table of bread, a menorah, an altar for incense, and the ark containing the Ten Commandments covered by the mercy seat and angels. If we were to follow this temple pattern as a pattern of prayer it could go something like this: (we are not suggesting you physically have these items of the Temple. The Temple pattern of prayer is just to help you visualize and keep your prayers focused).

a. Entering the Sanctuary: Start with thanking God for something specific. *"Enter His gates with praise, His courts with acclamation. Praise Him! Bless His name!"* Psalm 100:4
b. Altar of burnt offering: Confess any specific sin you are struggling with and claim the Messiah's sacrifice for your forgiveness.
c. Water basin: Accept God's forgiveness and claim God's power to cleanse you from the guilt of the sin and to wash from you the habit of committing the sin.
d. Table of bread: Just as bread is a staple of life and gives us strength and energy, ask God to come into your life this day and give you the power you need to resist temptations and to fulfill the plans He has for you today.
e. Menorah: Ask for direction and guidance. Search the Bible for texts to help guide you. *Your word is a lamp unto my feet, and a light for my path.* Psalm 119:105
f. Altar of incense: Pray for other people—family, friends, colleagues, etc.
g. Ark of the covenant: Ask God to have mercy on you, to surround you with His angels, and to write His laws on your heart and mind. *The teaching of his God is in his heart; his feet do not slip.* Psalm 37:31. *I will put My Teaching into their inmost being, and inscribe it upon their hearts; then I will be their God, and they shall be my people.* Jere. 31:33

Regardless of whether you use a prayer pattern or not we strongly encourage you to spend time daily with God in prayer. Experience the power of God in your life by daily entering into communication with the Almighty. Spend time opening your heart to Him; spend time listening to Him. God is love and He wants to be intimately close with you. Daniel experienced this close connection with Adonai and so can you.

16. DANIEL, THE GREATEST JEWISH STATESMAN
REVIEW הזרה

1. What did Daniel, Hananiah, Mishael, and Azariah determine not to defile themselves with?

    a. Unhealthy foods and alcohol
    b. Hard work
    c. Talking to people who were not Jewish

2. When the king threatened to kill all the wise men what did Daniel, Hananiah, Mishael, and Azariah do?

    a. Tried to escape Babylon
    b. Prayed
    c. Called for a Jewish lawyer

3. According to the statue dream that Elohim gave to Nebuchadnezzar which time period are we living in now?

    a. Time of the Babylonian empire
    b. Time of the Persian empire
    c. Time of the Greek empire
    d. Time of divided Europe, the time of the end of days, shortly before the Messiah will come again to destroy the kingdoms of this world and set up a new heaven and new earth and a kingdom that will last forever.

4. Who was in the fiery furnace with Hananiah, Mishael, and Azariah?

    a. King Nebuchadnezzar
    b. Abraham
    c. A Divine Being, the Messiah

5. When Daniel was commanded, under penalty of death, not to pray, what did he do?

    a. Tried to run away
    b. Prayed
    c. Called for a Jewish lawyer

6. Would you like God to give you a prayer life like Daniel's, to help you through your problems now, and to help you be ready for life on God's new earth?

    a. Yes
    b. No

Tom Kapusta loved his father. Tom was proud of his career in the military. After learning about the seventh day Sabbath Tom's faith in God was challenged in both of these areas that were dear to him. His father disowned him for leaving the family faith and he was to be court marshaled for not attending military meetings on the Sabbath. Tom felt he had to prioritize his life; he had to decide what was most important to him - following God all the way or his relationship with his father and his career. His father's rejection was very hard to take. Tom found comfort in praying to God and in the hope that one day his father would understand and accept that following God came first in Tom's life. Tom was in the Air Force at the time and was released from active duty to serve in the active reserves. The reserves met on Saturdays and he was required to attend the meetings. He informed his commander that due to his newly found religious beliefs he would not be able to make any meetings between sunset Friday and sunset Saturday, but would be happy to pull extra duty at any other time. Tom tried to inform his commander of his constitutional right to religious freedom. The commander insisted that no other provision could be made and that if Tom did not report to the Saturday meetings he would be court marshaled or receive a dishonorable discharge.

In either case Tom's record would be marked for life and it could affect his career opportunities in the future. While his relationship with his father might one day heal, this type of a mark on his record would be permanent. Tom struggled in prayer with God for many days. His friends and the congregation he attended also prayed with and for Tom. The National Service Organization, the military support organization of his congregation, became very involved with his situation and after nearly ten months of prayer and deliberation between the military and the attorneys at the National Service Organization it was determined that Tom would be able to report back to active duty with Sabbaths off, not be court marshaled, and not be issued a dishonorable discharge. For ten months Tom was tried and tested. It wasn't easy. Many times he felt like giving in; the pressure was intense. But through prayer Tom was strengthened by God to stand for God's Word. Along with the commandment to remember God's Sabbath, God also gave Tom the power and the ability to follow the commandment.

And about Tom's relationship with his dad—his father refused to speak to

16. DANIEL, THE GREATEST JEWISH STATESMAN

him or let him in his home. After 6 months of earnest prayer by Tom and his friends, Tom's mother called and said, "Your father would like to meet with you." When Tom arrived at their home his father said, "I raised you to think for yourself and if you choose to believe the way that you do that is up to you but I don't want you to ever talk about your beliefs in my home." Tom told him that the experience he was having with God was so powerful that he could not keep it in and that it was such an important part of his life that he could not promise that the topic would never come up. His father replied, "Well, then, do the best that you can." And he reached over and gave Tom a big hug. It wasn't more than half a year after that before Tom's dad was asking Tom religious questions and reading books that Tom offered him.

As Babylon and Persia made man-made laws that contradicted God's laws and took away religious liberty, so it will happen again. In our next lesson we will look into the future and see how these issues have repeated themselves and will do so again.

TRADITIONS

Tallit

A tallit is a prayer shawl. Tallitot (plural of tallit) are rectangular in shape and have fringes called tzitzits at the four corners. Tallitot come in various sizes ranging from 24 inches by 72 inches to 60 inches by 72 inches. The most common colors are white with either black or blue stripes. Gold or silver stripes will usually accompany the black or blue stripes. While these colors are the most common there is no limit to the variety of colors on tallitot. In the past only men wore tallitot, but today it is common for women to wear them as well.

There is no Biblical injunction to wear a tallit, although there is a text that refers to the fringes on one's garments. Numbers 15:37-41 states; ***"The LORD said to Moses as follows: Speak to the Israelite people and instruct them to make for themselves fringes on the corners of their garments throughout the ages; let them attach a cord of blue to the fringe at each corner. That shall be your fringe; look at it and recall all the commandments of the LORD and observe them, so that you do not follow your heart and eyes in your lustful urge. Thus you shall be reminded to observe all My commandments and to be holy to your God. I the LORD am your God, who brought you out of the land of Egypt to be your God: I, the LORD your God."*** Most modern tallitot do not have the cord of blue that is mentioned in the text. The text does not say how long the fringes are to be or how they are to be tied. Typical tallitot have 8 fringes on each corner tied in a series of knots and coils in sequences of: double knot, 7 coils, double knot, 8 coils, double knot, 11 coils, double knot, 13 coils, double knot. Using numerological figuring the series of coils is equivalent to the sentence "God is one." Also adding the numerological equivalent for the word tzitzit, which is 600, to the 8 strands, plus the 5 double knots, equals 613, which is equal to the total number of commandments in the Torah. Typical tallitot have one of the eight strands longer than the others. It is referred to as the shamas and is the strand that is used to make the coils. Along the short edges of the tallit are shorter fringes.

The tallit is normally worn only for times of prayer. Some Jewish people wear an undergarment called a tallit katan or small tallit all the time. These are usually white, sometimes with colored stripes, and fit over the head like a poncho. They have fringes on the corners similar to the ones on the large tallit, but do not have the short fringes along the edges.

Psalm 104:1,2 says; *"O LORD, my God, You are very great; You are clothed in glory and majesty, wrapped in a robe of light."* Isaiah 61:10 says; *". . . My whole being exults in my God. For He has clothed me with garments of triumph, wrapped me in a robe of victory . . ."* Obviously these texts are not speaking about a physical tallit, but a beautiful symbolism is illustrated in God clothing us with His glory, righteousness, triumph, and victory.

TRADITIONS

Western Wall

The Western Wall is the western portion of the retaining wall of the Temple Mount where the Temple stood. The Hebrew for Western Wall is ha-Kotel ha-Ma'aravi, although it is usually called simply ha-Kotel, the Wall. Over the years, since the Temple was destroyed in 70 CE, we have had intermittent access to the Wall depending on who was controlling Jerusalem at the time.

In the 1530's Sultan Suleiman the Magnificent of the Ottoman Empire added on to the existing wall and gave the Jewish people freedom to worship.

From 1947 until 1967, during Jordanian rule over the Old City, no Jewish people were allowed at the Western Wall. On the third day of the Six-Day War, on June 7, 1967, the Israeli Defense Force liberated the Kotel. Since that time it has been open to the public.

Today the visible section of the Western Wall at the Western Wall Plaza is 57 meters (187 feet) long and about 18 meters (59 feet) high. But the full length of the Western Wall is actually 488 meters (1,600 feet) long! And the full height of the wall from its original foundation is 32 meters (105 feet) tall! Almost 90 percent of its length and 40 percent of its height is not seen from the Western Wall Plaza.

Millions of visitors come to the Western Wall in Jerusalem every year to pray, read from the Torahs, and insert pieces of paper with

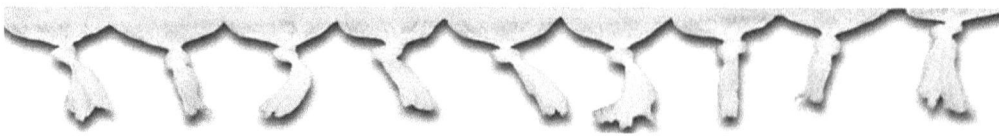

prayers written on them into the slots between stones. Many soldiers serving in the Israel Defense Forces pledge their loyalty to Israel at the Western Wall. Thousands of people come to celebrate their bar and bat mitzvah at the Wall.

On Friday evening hundreds of people come to the Western Wall to bring in the Shabbat with prayers, singing, and dancing. It is quite an event to experience.

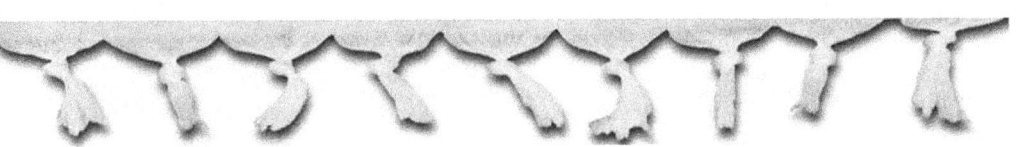

JEWISH HERITAGE
SCRIPTURE STUDIES

DANIEL
THE PROPHET

17. DANIEL—PROPHET OF GOD

In this lesson we are going to discover some fascinating and amazing predictions given by God hundreds of years before they came to pass. One of the reasons they are so important is that only God can write history in advance, and these prophecies help build our confidence in the Bible as the Word of God. These prophecies are going to bring us up to our day and on to the end of time as we know it. I have a hunch you will be surprised at some of the things you learn, and you may be startled to discover at least one of the reasons why there has been so much persecution of the Jewish people over the last 2,000 years. If you have not already done so, pause a moment now and pray that Elohim will prepare your heart for the awesome truths He will be revealing to you.

In our last lesson we learned about Daniel, a prayer warrior before God and a statesman in the governments of Babylon and Medo-Persia. We read about a time when the king of Babylon had a dream that none of his magicians, mediums, or astrologers could explain. After Daniel and his friends prayed, God explained the dream to Daniel. Daniel gave God the praise and credit for the wisdom given. The dream was of a statue made out of four different metals, each metal representing the different kingdoms that would come in succession over several centuries, from the time of Daniel until the end time.

This prophetic dream is very important because it lays the foundation for the rest of the prophecies in the biblical books of Daniel and Revelation. Each successive prophecy adds onto this foundation and stays within its framework. The Bible prophecies in the books of Daniel and Revelation work on a principle of repetition and expansion. It is similar to studying mathematics. Learning to count leads to learning to add. Multiplication builds on the principles of addition. All other forms of higher math expand on the foundations of addition and multiplication.

1. Let us start by reviewing the dream of Daniel chapter 2.

    ". . . there appeared a great statue. . . . The head . . . was of fine

gold; its breast ... were of silver; its belly and thighs, of bronze; its legs were of iron, and its feet part iron and part clay ... a stone was hewn out, not by hands, and struck the statue on its feet of iron and clay and crushed them ... a wind carried them off until no trace of them was left. But the stone that struck the statue became a great mountain and filled the whole earth ... You, O king ... are the head of gold. But another kingdom will arise after you, inferior to yours; then yet a third kingdom, of bronze ... But the fourth kingdom will be as strong as iron ... You saw the feet and the toes, part potter's clay and part iron ... it will be a divided kingdom ... part strong and in part brittle ... they shall intermingle ... but shall not hold together, just as iron does not mix with clay. And in the time of those kings, the God of Heaven will establish a kingdom that shall never be destroyed ... but shall ... last forever—just as you saw how a stone was hewn from the mountain, not by hands, and crushed the iron, bronze, clay, silver, and gold. Daniel 2:31-44

History shows us that these successive kingdoms were:
a. Babylon as the head of gold
b. Medo-Persia as the chest of silver
c. Greece as the belly and thighs of bronze
d. Rome as the legs of iron
e. Europe as the divided kingdoms represented by iron and clay which is part strong, part weak and has never joined together
f. Messiah's second coming as the stone that destroys all earthly kingdoms

Notice that the fourth metal, iron, is mentioned in the fourth and fifth time periods of the prophecy, both in the legs and in the feet and toes. Thus, Rome will have an influence in history from the time of replacing Greece in the year 168 BCE until the Messiah's second advent.

This time line is the basis of the rest of the prophecies upon which Daniel and Revelation will build. This is not to say that other countries are not important to God. The political powers that are listed in this prophecy, and the ones to follow, are listed because they are primarily the ones that directly affected people who were studying the Scriptures and following God. Even though more will be added to this prophetic outline, everything will be added to the original structure. To try to understand the other prophecies of Daniel and Revelation outside of this foundation prophecy would be like trying to learn algebra while ignoring the laws of multiplication. Each successive prophecy in

17. DANIEL—PROPHET OF GOD

Daniel and Revelation will build upon the foundation from Daniel 2.

2. The next great prophetic chapter in the biblical book of Daniel is chapter seven. In this vision God adds some flesh to the skeleton of the time line of Daniel 2. How are the four powers, Babylon, Medo-Persia, Greece, and Rome described in Daniel chapter seven?

> *"In my vision at night, I saw the four winds of heaven stirring up the great sea. Four mighty beasts different from each other emerged from the sea. The <u>first was like a lion but had eagles' wings</u>. As I looked on, its wings were plucked off, and it was lifted off the ground and set on its feet like a man and given the mind of a man. Then I saw a <u>second, different beast, which was like a bear but raised on one side</u>, and with three fangs in its mouth among its teeth; it was told, 'Arise, eat much meat!' After that, as I looked on, there was another one, like <u>a leopard, and it had on its back four wings like those of a bird; the beast had four heads</u>, and dominion was given to it. After that, as I looked on in the night vision, there was <u>a fourth beast—fearsome, dreadful, and very powerful, with great iron teeth—that devoured and crushed, and stamped the remains with its feet. It was different from all the other beasts which had gone before it; and it had ten horns</u>.*
> Daniel 7:2-7

Daniel saw four beasts coming up out of the sea. The first was like a lion with eagles' wings. Just as gold is chief among metals, the lion and the eagle are chief among the animals and birds. The first beast represented Babylon, just as the first metal of the statue represented Babylon. The second kingdom was represented as a second beast, a bear raised up on one side. The Persian part of the Medo-Persian kingdom was "raised up," or stronger, than the Median part of the kingdom. The third beast was a leopard with four wings and four heads. Leopards are fast enough without wings. Adding wings to the leopard indicated even more speed. By the time Alexander the Great was thirty-two years old, he and his Greek army had conquered the entire Persian Empire. One of the historical characteristics of Greece's conquest was its speed. (Remember, Daniel was shown this hundreds of years before it happened. Amazingly accurate, isn't it? Hold on, we have only just begun to see how accurate God's predictions are). The leopard was also pictured with four heads. After Alexander died the Greek kingdom was divided into four sections as depicted by the four heads of the leopard. Rome comes next in the time line of history. Notice some of the characteristics of this fourth beast. It had iron teeth like the iron of Rome mentioned in the legs and feet of the metal statue of Daniel chapter two. It also had ten horns like the ten toes mentioned on the metal statue. You can see the parallels of the two prophecies and how the second one built upon the first one. Now we're ready for some expansion within the time line.

Please note: Just because these kingdoms were represented as beasts does not mean that God was ascribing beastly characteristics to them. It is simply the Bible's method of painting a picture of world kingdoms. It certainly does not mean that the citizens of those kingdoms were beastly. The metals of the statue in Daniel chapter 2 represent the wealth and/or the metals that the various kingdoms used. Babylon was rich, Greece used brass weapons, Rome was as strong as iron, etc. Yet it does not mean that every Babylonian was rich or that every Roman was strong. Nebuchadnezzar's kingdom of Babylon was represented as a lion and eagle, two carnivorous animals, but he himself came to God in repentance and humility. Just because Medo-Persia was represented as a ferocious bear does not mean that all Medo-Persians were mean. Actually, Cyrus, a king of Persia, was very good to the Jewish people. God used him to allow the Jewish people to go back to Israel after years of captivity in Babylon. Cyrus was even prophesied by name by the Jewish prophet Isaiah as the one who would take over the Babylonian kingdom hundreds of years before Cyrus was even born. (It is an amazingly powerful prophecy describing how Cyrus would dry up the Euphrates River that ran through the city of Babylon and how his army would march through the gates that were left open. See Isaiah chapter 44:27-45:4.) Just because Greece was represented as a leopard does not mean all the Greeks were fast. The prophecies are not talking about individuals; they are talking about kingdoms and systems that control those kingdoms. Please do not mix up what the Bible says about the various kingdoms with how God feels about the people who are a part of those kingdoms. This is an important point to keep in mind to keep from condemning and judging people and individuals for the actions of a few leaders. (This type of condemning and judging of people has been done for centuries against the Jewish people because a few leaders 2,000 years ago falsely accused Y'shua and turned him over to the Roman authorities. We don't want to fall into that same trap of condemning individuals for the actions of a few leaders.) God is a God of love and He loves all His created people. Keep this in mind as you identify the prophesied powers.

17. DANIEL—PROPHET OF GOD

3. What else does Daniel see on the fourth beast that had iron teeth and 10 horns?

   While I was gazing upon these horns, a new little horn sprouted up among them; three of the older horns were uprooted to make room for it. There were eyes in this horn like those of a man, and a mouth that spoke arrogantly. Daniel 7:8

   Elohim built onto the Daniel 2 prophecy with this added insight regarding the fourth kingdom. Among the ten horns representing the ten nations of Europe that the Roman kingdom was divided into came a new little horn. We are going to look at the clues that God gives us in this prophecy about this little horn power and God is going to give you the wisdom to identify what "kingdom" this power represents. You may be surprised by what you discover so hold onto the LORD and prepare yourself with prayer for this amazing biblical revelation. Warning: do not try to interpret the prophecy until you have all the biblical clues. It is dangerous to jump to conclusions with only part of a biblical identification. As the evidence accumulates you will find that the conclusion is inescapable.

   From the Bible text we just read we are told:
   Clue #1: It is a power that came up from the Roman kingdom.
   Clue #2: It came to power after Rome was divided into ten European nations, which would be after the year 476.
   Clue #3: It uprooted, went to war with, and eliminated, three of the original ten nations of Europe.
   Clue #4: It is a man-made power with eyes and mouth of a man. It speaks its own words instead of the Word of God.

   There are seven more clues, so hold any conclusions just yet.

4. As Daniel was watching this little horn power the scene changed temporarily to heaven. What did Daniel see next?

   As I looked on, <u>thrones were set in place, and the Ancient of Days took His seat.</u> His garment was like white snow, and the hair of His head was like lamb's wool. His throne was tongues of flame; its wheels were blazing fire. A river of fire streamed forth before Him; <u>Thousands upon thousands served Him; myriads upon myriads attended Him; the court sat and the books were opened.</u> Daniel 7:9,10

   Adonai showed Daniel a heavenly court scene taking place between the time the little horn came to power and its final destruction. Notice that the court scene took place before this power was destroyed. It makes sense that a judgment decision would have to take place before the judgment can be enacted. We will come back to this thought at the end of this lesson, and find out even more about this heavenly judgment scene in our next lesson " The Ultimate Yom Kippur."

5. Even after being shown the heavenly judgment scene Daniel was still curious about the little horn power and asked God for some more clues. What else was revealed about this power?

... (It) was more conspicuous than its fellows. ... (It) made war with the holy ones and overcame them, (it) will be different from all the kingdoms; it will devour the whole earth, tread it down, and crush it. He will speak words against the Most High, and will harass the holy ones of the Most High. He will think of changing times and laws, and they will be delivered into his power for a time, times, and half a time. Daniel 7:20,21,23,25

Clue #5: It is more conspicuous or more prominent in history than any of the other European powers.

Clue #6: It made war against God's people, harassing and killing Jewish people as well as anyone who wanted to follow the Bible.

Clue #7: It is a different kind of power from the typical political powers. (Reading about this same power in Revelation 13:4,8 we see that this power has to do with worship. It is a political/religious power.)

Clue #8: It covers the whole earth. It has global influence; it is a worldwide power.

Clue #9: It speaks words against or in opposition to the Word of God, and thus against God.

Clue #10: It claims to have the authority to change God's laws and times. The only one of God's Ten Commandments that mentions time is God's Sabbath. This power thinks it can change the time of God's Sabbath.

Clue #11: It held power over people for 1,260 years.

The passage says the people of God will be under its power for a time, times, and half a time. "Time" in Bible prophecy represents a year. So this is speaking of three and a half years. But these three and a half years are prophetic years, not literal years. An example of prophetic time is seen when God told Moses that we would have to wander in the wilderness for 40 years. Jewish spies searched out the Promised Land for 40 days. When most of the spies

17. DANIEL—PROPHET OF GOD

came back, convincing the people it would be too dangerous for us to go into the promised land, God made this pronouncement: ***"You shall bear your punishment <u>for forty years, corresponding to the number of days—forty days—</u> that you scouted the land: <u>a year for each day</u>."*** Numbers 14:34 (This same principle is mentioned in Ezekiel 4:6 ***"<u>one day for each year.</u>"***) Hundreds of years ago Bible scholars discovered that in a scriptural time prophecy, a day of literal time is used to represent one year of prophetic time. If we take this three and a half year time period mentioned in Daniel chapter 7 and translate it into individual days, we find that in three and a half years there are 1,260 days (according to a 360 day biblical year). When the prophecy says the power will reign for 1,260 days it is really saying it will reign for 1,260 years because in prophecy one day equals a year. This 1,260 year period of time is mentioned seven times in the books of Daniel and Revelation: Daniel 7:25; 12:7; Rev 11:2,3; 12:6,14; 13:5. It is obviously a very significant time period. Sometimes it is mentioned as three and half years, which equals 1,260 days. Sometimes it is 42 months, which equals 1,260 days (according to a 30 day biblical month). And sometimes it is mentioned as 1,260 days. Each time it is telling us of different events that took place during this 1,260 year time period while this little horn power would be the most dominant power in the world, especially in those areas concerning God's Bible-believing people.

You may be wondering why Bible prophecy is not written in plainer words. Remember, much of it was written at a time when the writers were living under the authority of governments that were not favorable to their writings. So it is written in a type of secret code. But the keys to unlock the secret prophetic codes are within the Bible itself. Two examples of the Bible giving us its own keys to unlock its own prophetic code are: the Torah stating ***"a year for each day"*** and Daniel writing, ***"These great beasts, four in number [are] four kingdoms"*** Daniel 7:17. In Bible prophecy a year equals a day and a beast represents a kingdom.

Are you ready to identify the little horn power? Remember, the Bible is not talking about individuals here, but about powers or systems that will play the roles mentioned in the prophecy. There are many good people within each of the "beast" powers. Elohim is not condemning individuals with these prophecies. He is warning people about religious errors and revealing biblical truth.

With that important point in mind, you may wish to pause here and review the eleven clues to determine what power the little horn represents. When you think you have it figured out continue on to question six.

6. What power came out of Rome, held wide political control for 1,260 years starting sometime after 476, eliminated three other European nations as it came to power, is a political/religious power which has its own man-made doctrines which are in opposition to the Bible, has been the most prominent European power during the 1,260 years, persecuted Jewish people and anyone who disagreed with its man-made doctrines, claims to have the power to change God's times and laws, and is a world-wide power?

There is only one power that fits this description. The little horn power is the Papacy. The Papacy is headquartered in Rome. It received its unchallenged authority in the year 538 after it defeated and *"uprooted"* the three European nations, the Heruli, the Vandals, and the Ostrogoths. And it reigned more prominently than any other European power until the year 1798 when Napoleon took the Pope captive, exactly 1,260 years after it came to power. During those 1,260 years it killed and persecuted millions of Jewish people, and Protestants, and anyone who disagreed with its teachings. The Papacy claims it has the power to make its own doctrines in contrast to the Bible and to even change God's times and laws. Here is one of many incredulous statements made by the Papacy: "The Pope has the power to change times and abrogate laws and to dispense with all things even the precepts of Christ" (Decretal De Translat, Episcap, Cap.) Did you see the parallel between what God showed Daniel and what the Papal statement says? God showed Daniel that the little horn power would speak words against God's Word and *"think to change times and laws."* Then this statement says the Pope has power to change God's *times and laws.* Let's look at one more statement from their own writings: "Sunday is our mark of authority . . . The church is above the Bible, and this transference of Sabbath observance is proof of that fact." Catholic Record, Sept. 1, 1923. According to their own words changing God's time of His Sabbath law from Saturday to Sunday is the mark of their authority!

God's Word says: *"hallow My Sabbaths, that they may be <u>a sign</u> between Me and you, that you may know that I the Lord am your God."* Ezekiel 20:20. Elohim says that His Sabbaths are a sign between Him and us. It is His sign or mark that we are His. Yet the Papal power says their man-made Sunday rest and worship day is their mark of authority. This man-made "mark" is in direct opposition to God's "sign." God warned us this would happen hundreds of years before it took place!

Even though the Papacy professes to be uplifting the Messiah, in reality it is standing in place of the Messiah. It tries to replace the Messiah. In addition to the areas we have already looked at, the Papacy outlawed the reading of the Bible for much of the Dark Ages, it encourages the confession of sins to human priests instead of to the Messiah, and praying to dead people whom they call saints. It encourages prayers in front of stone statues, reciting words or performing penance to receive forgiveness instead of accepting the death of the Messiah for forgiveness, and referring of their leader as "holy father." These are just a few of the ways the Papacy stands in place of the role of the Messiah. By taking this stance it stands against the Messiah or is anti-Messiah. All of the early protestant reformers came to this same conclusion and began the move out of the Dark Ages and into the slow process of restoring those Bible truths that had been compromised.

As shockingly accurate as God's predictions are they are not a condemnation of individuals who are a part of the Roman Catholic Church, but rather a revealing of the dangerously erroneous doctrines which are in direct opposition to God's truth and which apply even broader than to just one church, but to all who teach these same errors. The real issue is truth versus error. It is vitally important that we stand and live on the side of God's truth while not being in a position of condemnation of other individuals. There are many sincere, loving individuals in all denominations and religions. Just as you have been learning truths from God as we have been studying these lessons together it is our responsibility to help others grow to learn more about God's truths. We should be just as patient and non-condemning of others as we want others to be of us as we have been learning about God's love and have been allowing God to work in our lives to bring us step by step, day by day, closer to Him.

This principle of non-condemning, loving, patient teaching applies to all of the areas we have been learning in Jewish Discoveries. It is not our role to condemn or judge someone who is not resting on God's holy Sabbath, or who is eating what God says should not be eaten, or who is involved with a group that the Bible describes as the little horn/beast power. It is our job, rather, to love freely, live godly, and teach biblically. Focus on Y'shua our Messiah, focus on His love, and invite Him into your life on a daily basis. Instead of condemning people because they are a member of the little horn/beast power allow Adonai to search your heart and see if you are allowing Him to give you faith like Abraham, repentance like Jacob, love so that you can forgive like Joseph, and His Spirit so you can have the power to live the godly way God's Word has been revealing to you.

Originally Christianity was a sect, or denomination, within Judaism. It was a long, slow descent that took Christianity to the point where it was persecuting Jewish people and anyone who wanted to follow the Bible, changing God's Sabbath, and making its own doctrines. Just as it was a long, slow process away from God's Word, it has been a slow, yet steady progress of more and more people being willing to learn God's truth and being willing to follow it. We trust that by the time you have come to this lesson your maturity in God has grown to the point that you can learn the biblical truth of this lesson and use the truths of this lesson to understand how Christianity has gotten so far away from God's word and not use it to condemn others. Notice that this is lesson number 17, not lesson number 1. It is not wise to switch the order. It would not be tactful to go to a person who is involved in the Catholic Church, or any church that is still following some of the papacy's teachings, and make this the first lesson you share with them. Until a person has accepted the Messiah as their Lord and Savior, and has allowed God to give them faith, repentance, forgiveness, love, obedience, etc. they are not ready for this lesson. Until a person is willing to allow Elohim to guide them in the right way it is not helpful to point out the wrong way. Better to be a truth revealer than an error exposer. Yes, there is a time to expose error, but let God's love pave the way first.

While the Papacy clearly is the only organization that fits the specific predictions in the Holy Scriptures there are individuals and groups that are not following God and who have, are, and/or will be following the Papal lead. Any individual or group that purposefully suppresses Bible truth or replaces it, and oppresses and persecutes others is manifesting the same spirit that the Bible accurately predicted the Papacy would do.

7. What will be the end result of this institution and all powers that work

17. DANIEL—PROPHET OF GOD

against God's truth?

Then the court will sit and his dominion will be taken away, to be destroyed and abolished for all time. Daniel 7:26

These facts may be shocking and even distressing to you. You may know sincere, wonderful people who are involved with these false systems of worship. Again, and we cannot over-stress this, God is not speaking about individual people that you and I know. He is talking about a worldwide system and its teachings and practices over a long period of time. People are not "bad" or "evil" just because they were born into or are a part of these false systems. God, in His love for these very people, gives an invitation for them to learn and come out of the false systems and to walk in His light. (See Revelation 18:1-4).

The prediction of this prophecy was so astonishing Daniel said: ***"I, Daniel, was very alarmed by my thoughts, and my face darkened; and I could not put the matter out of my mind."*** Daniel 7:28

Although God showed Daniel a thousand years in advance that our people and other Bible believers would be persecuted during the Dark Ages by this little horn/beast power, that is not the primary focus of the vision. God showed Daniel the succession of the kingdoms so that we could see the time frame concerning when God's judgment will take place. The successive kingdoms that would rule over the areas where the Bible and Bible-believing people would be is a time line, or land mark, so we can see when the major events of God's work would take place. The heart of Daniel chapter seven is not the little horn/beast power; it is the heavenly court scene.

As we learned earlier Daniel saw a heavenly court judgment scene taking place before the little horn power had its power and influence removed forever. In this vision God spent more time revealing to Daniel this judgment scene than He did concerning any of the political powers revealed in the vision. This could be because it is more important for us to have hope in the fact that God is judge and He sees and knows all of the suffering that our people have gone through and He will one day enact His final judgment. Knowing that Elohim is in control, that He sees and knows all things, and that final judgment is in His hands is more important than knowing who all the beast powers represent.

8. What happened in this heavenly court scene?

As I looked on, thrones were set in place, and <u>the Ancient of</u>

Days took His seat**. His garment was like white snow, and the hair of His head was like lamb's wool. His throne was tongues of flame; its wheels were blazing fire. A river of fire streamed forth before Him; **thousands upon thousands served Him; myriads upon myriads attended Him; the court sat and the books were opened. Daniel 7:9,10

On Rosh Hashanah we pronounce the blessing upon each other and say "L'Shanah Tovah Tikatevu" "May you be inscribed for a good year." We are asking God to write our name in His heavenly books for a good year. The statement from the book of Daniel that says: *"the court sat and the **books were opened**"* is very similar to a text in the book of Revelation that says; ***"I saw the dead, small and great, standing before God, and books were opened. And another book was opened, which is the Book of Life. And the dead were judged according to their works**, by the things which were written in the books."*** Revelation 20:12 NKJV. The books of Daniel and Revelation go hand in hand. One helps us understand the other. According to this text all of the dead will be judged together at the same time. As King Solomon wrote ***"God shall judge the righteous and the wicked**, for there is a time for every purpose and for every work."*** Ecclesiastes 3:17 NKJV. We might like to think that the judgment is only for those who reject God's offer of salvation. But that really doesn't make sense. When a teacher grades the final exams, she does not only grade the tests of the failing students; she grades all the tests. Her grading of the passing students proves that they deserve to pass. The judgment is not bad news for those who trust in God; it is a vindication of God's power in their lives. The judgment testifies to the myriads upon myriads who attend the judgment that God is able to forgive our sins, to clear our names of guilt, and to transform our hearts and lives. The Scriptures are very clear that we do not earn heaven by our good works, but rather by God's love, mercy, and forgiveness given us through the Messiah. Yet this text from Revelation and several others like it (Eccl. 12:14, Matt 16:17; 25:31-46, Rev. 22:12, etc.) make it clear that while we are saved by God's grace, whether or not we have received that grace will be demonstrated and judged by our actions.

9. What did Moses have to say about God's heavenly books?

*". . . Moses said to the people, "You have sinned a great sin. So now I will go up to the LORD; **perhaps I can make atonement for your sin**." Then Moses returned to the LORD and said, "Oh, these people have sinned a great sin, and have made for themselves a god of gold!*

17. DANIEL—PROPHET OF GOD

*Yet now, **if You will forgive their sin—but if not, I pray, blot me out of Your book which You have written**.*" *And the* LORD *said to Moses, "Whoever has sinned against Me, I will blot him out of My book."* Exodus 32:30-33. NKJV.

Moses used the term "make an atonement for your sins." Translation of "Yom Kippur" is "Day of Atonement" or "Day of Covering." It is the day when God covers the sins of those who repent. Elohim then makes atonement for us, an at-one-ment with Himself. Moses loved the people so unselfishly that he was willing to have his own name blotted out of the book of heaven for those who had sinned in making the golden calf while he was on Mt. Sinai. God did not accept Moses' offer, for only God Himself could become the atonement for our sins. We have all sinned. Even Moses sinned. We all deserve to be blotted out of God's book. Moses received atonement because of the sacrifice of the lambs representing the death of the Messiah as a substitute for him. You have atonement with God because you have accepted the Messiah's death as your substitute. (We are seeing how Rosh Hashanah and Yom Kippur are tied into the judgment. The next lesson, The Ultimate Yom Kippur, will dig deeper into this topic.)

10. Which books are opened during the judgment?

   a. *"Take this book of Teaching and place it beside the Ark of the Covenant of the* LORD *your God, and let it remain there as a witness against you."* Deuteronomy 31:26

   We will be judged by the standard of God's Torah.

   b. *"You number my wanderings; Put my tears into Your bottle; Are they not in Your book?"* Psalm 56:8 NKJV.

   God knows where we have been, what hardships and experiences we have been through. He records our tears. All of these are considerations brought into the judgment.

   c. *"may they be erased from the book of life, and not be inscribed with the righteous."* Psalm 69:29

   The book of life is the book that contains the names of all who profess to know and love God. But as this text says they can be blotted out if they do not choose to be covered by God's forgiveness and allow the Holy Spirit to transform their lives.

   d. *"At that time, the great prince, Michael, who stands beside the sons of your people, will appear. It will be a time of trouble, the like of* *which has never been since the nation came into being. At that time, your people will be rescued, <u>all who are found inscribed in the book</u>.*" Daniel 12:1.

Michael, the "one who is like God," the great prince, shall stand in behalf of those whose names are written in the book. We have an advocate, a lawyer, the defense attorney if you please, on our side. And not only is the defense attorney on our side in the judgment, the judge is on our side as well. He created us and loves us. He provided a way for us to be covered in the judgment. He wants us to be at-one-with Him. The judge Himself is pulling for us! We can't lose unless we refuse His love, power, forgiveness, and mercy and try to stand as our own defense attorney, presenting our own good deeds instead of allowing the Messiah to stand beside us presenting His righteousness.

e. *"The L<small>ORD</small> has heard and noted it, and a <u>scroll of remembrance</u> has been written at His behest concerning <u>those who revere the L<small>ORD</small> and esteem His name</u>."* Malachi 3:16

Elohim has a book of remembrance that records all the times we have spoken of Him, thought about Him, and allowed Him to work through us to bring glory to His name.

So how does this judgment work? Let me give you two scenarios, one negative and one positive. A person stands before God and his name comes up in the book of life as one who professes to love God. The Book of Tears is opened and all that this person has gone through is taken into consideration. The Book of Remembrance is opened and it is a large book with many good deeds in it. Then the Book of the Law is opened and it shows that there have been very few times this individual has broken God's laws. Most of the sins have been confessed; most have been covered by the sacrificial blood of the Messiah. But there is one known rebellious sin still left unrepented of. The man's advocate, the Messiah, speaks up sadly saying, "I tried everything I could to free this man of this sin. I offered my life and died for this sin for him. I sent My Spirit to him on many different occasions and convicted him of how wrong it was. I worked out opportunities for him to hear this topic spoken about. I placed literature at his disposal to wake him up to his need for help in this area. I sent humans to talk to him about this problem. I sent heavenly angels to work out circumstances to bring it to his attention. But for all of these many, many attempts he resisted each time. He chose rebelliously and consistently to hold onto the sin. This sin is more important to him than heaven. If we were to allow him into heaven he would take this sin with him and destroy all the peace and love that is there." With tears in His eyes He will say; "I am very sorry, but his name must be blotted out of the book." There will be weeping and wailing by everyone present.

Another name comes up before the Judge. The same process is repeated, looking at the Book of Tears and then the Book of Remembrance. In this case the Book of Remembrance of good deeds is very small. The Book of the Law reveals that this person has broken God's law many, many times. But it is also seen that each one of these sins is covered in blood with the words "Forgiven by the blood of the Messiah" written across them. The Messiah stands up and says, "This person has lived under very difficult circumstances and has endured many hard times. He has sinned time and time again. But when he heard about My love he was very open to receiving Me into his heart. He repented of all of his sins. Yes, he struggled time and time again, but he gained the victory through My love, forgiveness, and power. All of his sins are forgiven; blot those sins off of his record. Accept My sacrifice, My death, in place of his and accept My righteousness as his, and grant him eternal life in heaven with Me!" There will be shouting and singing by everyone present.

The choice is yours. Which one of these scenarios will apply to you? If there is any sin that you are still rebelliously holding onto, surrender it right now. Nothing is worth missing out on heaven. God has provided you with everything you need to receive forgiveness and power over the sin. Remember, it was only one sin that caused Adam and Eve to be removed from the Garden of Eden. It was only one sin that threw this planet into chaos, which was originally created "very good."

11. What is the end result of the judgment?

> ***One like a human being came with the clouds of heaven; He reached the Ancient of Days and was presented to Him. Dominion, glory, and kingship were given to him; all peoples and nations of every language must serve him. His dominion is an everlasting dominion that shall not pass away***, and his kingship, one that shall not be destroyed . . . then holy ones of the Most High will receive the kingdom, and will possess the kingdom forever—forever and ever. ***The kingship and dominion and grandeur belonging to all the kingdoms under Heaven will be given to the people of the holy ones of***

the Most High. Their kingdom shall be an everlasting kingdom, and all dominions shall serve and obey them. Daniel 7:13, 14, 18, 27.

The One like a human being who comes to the Ancient of Days, who receives full dominion, glory, and kingship, who every human will serve, and who has an everlasting dominion is none other than the Messiah, who became a human, died for our sins, and was raised back up to heaven. He will be our eternal King and we will inherit the new heavens and new earth forever and ever! Adonai will restore the Garden of Eden state and humans will once again be entrusted with dominion over all the new earth!

Alexander Bolotnokov grew up in the Soviet Union. His grandfather was a colonel with the KGB and Alexander joined the Communist Young Pioneers at the age of ten. But when he applied to the university to be a nuclear physicist he was turned down because he was Jewish. He decided if the communists did not want him because he was Jewish he would become the most religious Jew that he could. He joined an Orthodox group and became very religious and pious. At the university he was attending he enjoyed going to the Christian meetings and heckling the speaker and making fun of the other students. He was shocked to see how kind they were to him. Alexander had studied the prophecies of Daniel chapter 7 and reasoned that the little horn/beast power that would think to change times and laws had to be Jesus Christ since Christians went to church on Sunday. He stumped the Christians by telling them that Jesus Christ was the anti-Messiah because he was the one that tried to change the Sabbath to Sunday. Alexander was so smart and well studied that most of the other students could not answer him a word. That is until he met Tolik. Tolik told Alexander that not all Christians went to services on Sunday. He explained to Alexander that he belonged to a congregation that worshipped on the seventh day of the week, on the Shabbat. Alexander was shocked to find out that not only were there over 500 members in Tolik's congregation, but that there were over one hundred thousand congregations within the same denomination all over the world in more than 200 countries made up of Jewish people and Gentiles who rested on God's Holy Shabbat and who ate only what the Bible prescribed as fit to eat. When Alexander mentioned to Tolik's pastor his theory that Jesus was the little horn power that persecuted the Jews and abandoned the Torah, he was surprised that the pastor didn't oppose his theory entirely but said that it was not Jesus who tried to change the Sabbath but some professed Christians who tried to do so hundreds

17. DANIEL—PROPHET OF GOD

of years after Y'shua died and was resurrected. Alexander determined that if he could just prove to them that Y'shua was not the Messiah he could make them all Orthodox Jews. Rabbi Schneerson of New York City said that the Messiah was coming very soon. Alexander decided that when the Messiah came he would ask Him to explain the prophecies of Daniel so he could explain it to the congregation Tolik was attending, the Seventh-day Adventists. While Alexander was eagerly awaiting the arrival of the Messiah the followers of Rabbi Schneerson proclaimed him as the Messiah. Alexander knew from his studies of the prophecies regarding the Messiah that Rabbi Schneerson could not be the Messiah. Alexander realized that the only one who accurately fulfilled those prophecies regarding the Messiah was Y'shua. After many months of struggling over his decision and diligently searching the Scriptures, Alexander surrendered his life to Y'shua and accepted him as his LORD and Savior. (Alexander's full story is recorded in the book True Believer.)

REVIEW הזרה

For many this has been a very heavy study. You may want to review the lesson before answering the review questions.

1. The foundational sequence of predicted kingdoms outlined in Daniel chapter two that would dominate biblical affairs from the time of Daniel until the end of this world at the second coming of Messiah is:
   a. Babylon, Medo-Persia, Greece, Rome, divided Europe, second advent of Messiah
   b. Russia, China, Australia, Africa, United Nations, second advent of Messiah
   c. Edom, Moab, Amon, Egypt, and Assyria

2. The foundational sequence of predicted kingdoms outlined in Daniel chapter seven that would dominate biblical affairs from the time of Daniel until the end of this world at the second coming of Messiah is:
   a. Babylon, Medo-Persia, Greece, Rome, divided Europe, rise of papal power, heavenly judgment process, second advent of Messiah
   b. Russia, China, Australia, Africa, United Nations, second advent of Messiah
   c. Edom, Moab, Amon, Egypt, and Assyria

3. What institution is represented as the little horn power of Daniel chapter 7

that came out of Rome, held wide political powers for 1,260 years starting sometime after 476, eliminated three other European nations as it came to power, is a political/religious power which has its own man-made doctrines which are in opposition to the Bible, was the most prominent European power during the 1,260 years, persecuted Jewish people and anyone who disagreed with its man-made doctrines, claims to have the power to change God's times and laws, and is a world wide power?

   a. The Papal institution as a whole
   b. Individual Catholic people
   c. A strange unknown being possibly from Mars

4. As believers in the only true God, the Creator of heaven and earth, we should:
   a. Be loving, merciful, patient, and kind to everyone while asking God to reveal the truths in His Word to us.
   b. Condemn those who do not agree with us.
   c. Not try to understand the Bible.

5. In the heavenly judgment process which books will Elohim and His myriads of court attendants open?
   a. The Book of Life
   b. The Book of the Law (Torah)
   c. The Book of Tears
   d. The Book of Remembrance
   e. All of the above

6. You will pass the judgment because:
   a. You have accepted the Messiah's death as payment for your sins and are allowing Him to work in your life
   b. You are a nice person
   c. You try to be good

TRADITIONS

Tefillin

T'fillin, or phylacteries, are square black boxes traditionally worn on the head and arm. The t'fillin for the head is called t'fillin shel rosh and has four separate compartments. The t'fillin shel yod, for the arm and hand, has one compartment. Within the t'fillin are scrolls of paper that have quotes from the books of Deuteronomy and Exodus. One box is tied to the left arm and the other is tied to the forehead. This ritual of putting on t'fillin has been in existence for centuries. Usually they are worn during morning worship, but not on Sabbath or holidays. Usually only men over the age of thirteen put on t'fillin.

The Exodus portions are references to God redeeming the first-born sons at Passover. In Deuteronomy they are references to God's Law. Thus redemption and law are bound together. In Deuteronomy chapter 6, verse 6 the Torah states that "these words which I command you today shall be in your heart." The words that God commanded were the Ten Commandments, which are recorded in the previous chapter, chapter 5. Although the text is referring to the Ten Commandments, it is not the Ten Commandments of Deuteronomy chapter 5 that are in the t'fillin nor the references to the Passover redemption, but rather the instructions about t'fillin that are in the t'fillin.

The text in Deut. 6:6 says that these commandments need to be in our hearts. In other words, we should love them. They should become a part of our lifeblood. The text continues in verse 8 stating, "Bind them as a sign on your hand and let them serve as a symbol on your forehead." This needs to be understood in the same way as when it said "in your heart." God wants our hands to be active in doing His work and deeds. He wants our hands following His law. He does not want them stealing or cheating, He wants them helping and uplifting. In reference to God, Psalm 48:11 says, *"Your right hand is filled with beneficence."* And in reference to King David, Psalm 18:21 states, *"The Lord rewarded me according to my merit; He requited the cleanness of my hands."* Thus, it is not a physical manifestation of writing them on our hands that God is referring to, but rather, as with the heart, a figurative application.

The same would be true with the reference to having them as a symbol on our forehead. He wants His law to guide our thinking. It is interesting to note that the area of the brain at the forehead is the frontal lobe. This is the area of our brain where we make decisions. Adonai not only wants us to be doing good things, but He wants us to choose to do these things. There is a wonderful promise written by the Jewish prophet Jeremiah in chapter 31, verse 33 in the book in the Hebrew Scriptures named after him. It states, *"Says the Lord: I will put My law in their minds and write it on their hearts . . ."* NKJV. God Himself will write His laws into our minds! God will help us make the right choice if we allow Him to rule our lives.

Elohim is telling us to write the laws on our hearts—love them. Write them on our hands—do them. Write them on our forehead—think about them, decide to do them, want to do them. God wants our minds, our hearts, and our hands to be under His direction.

It is interesting that in the book of Revelation the Bible refers to the mark of the beast being placed on the hands and forehead. While the seal of God is having God's law figuratively written on our heart, hands, and foreheads, the mark of the beast will be the using of hands or foreheads to break God's law. The essence of the mark of the beast is choosing with the mind to disobey God's law and then breaking His law with actions or inactions. Just as the writing of God's commandments on our hearts, hands, and heads is figurative, so also the mark of the beast is not a literal marking on the outside of bodies but a figurative writing on the hands and foreheads by choosing to disobey God and to follow the little horn/beast institution's man-made laws.

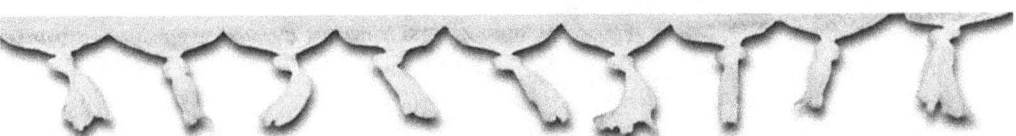

JEWISH HERITAGE SCRIPTURE STUDIES

18

THE ULTIMATE YOM KIPPUR

18. THE ULTIMATE YOM KIPPUR

The High Holy Days. Just the sound of those words brings vivid memories, a holy awe, and a religious respect and devotion to most of our people. Although Passover and Chanukah get the most media attention, to many Jewish people it is the High Holy Days that are the most important days of the year. The High Holy Days come in the fall of the year and include Rosh Hashanah, Yom Kippur, and Sukkot. In this lesson we are going to be looking at the High Holy Days from three different perspectives: 1) how they are observed today, 2) how they were observed in biblical times, and 3) their prophetic significance.

Before we go further it is important to point out that this is lesson 18 of Jewish Discoveries and is dependent on an understanding of the first seventeen lessons. Each lesson in this series is linked together as one unit; each lesson builds on those before it. All the lessons are interconnected forming one beautiful picture of the character of God. Like a jigsaw puzzle it is hard to see the picture when the pieces are apart. They look like a confusing jumble. In a jigsaw puzzle some pieces are easy to identify, like the corner pieces. From those distinctive pieces the rest of the puzzle can be put together. Without those foundational pieces it is much harder to put the puzzle together. If you have not read the first seventeen lessons and fully grasped their truths, the truths of this lesson will be harder to understand. Thus, we encourage you to stop and read the first seventeen lessons, especially lesson 17, before continuing to read this lesson. But if you feel you understand the truths studied in the first seventeen lessons, we urge you to pause and ask God to give you wisdom and understanding as we approach this very important subject.

Rosh Hashanah, literally "head of the year," is celebrated today as the Jewish New Year. It comes on the first day of the Jewish month of Tishri and is the first day on the modern Jewish calendar. On this day we wish each other "lashanah tovah tikatevu", (לשנה טובה תכתבו) "may you be inscribed in God's book for a good year." To emphasize this wish for a blessed year we eat challah bread with raisins in it to make it sweeter, and then we dip the bread in honey to give it an extra sweetness. In contrast to secular New Year's celebrations, Rosh Hashanah is not all rejoicing. There is a solemnity mixed with the rejoicing because Rosh Hashanah announces that Yom Kippur is only ten days away. On Rosh Hashanah people will bring bread to a body of water and cast the bread into the water symbolizing the ridding of the sins we have committed. This is referred to as "tashlich" (תשליך) and literally means "you will cast." Although the casting of bread into water cannot remove the guilt of our sins the Jewish prophet Micah wrote, *"Who is a God like You, forgiving iniquity . . . He will take us back in love; He will cover up our iniquities, <u>You will hurl all our sins into the depths of the sea</u>."* Micah 7:18,19 Notice, we do not rid ourselves of sin, but it is God who symbolically hurls our sins into the depths of the sea. As Moses told us in the Torah, *"<u>it is the blood, as life, that effects expiation</u>"* (forgiveness). Lev. 17:11. It is Messiah Y'shua's death that grants us forgiveness.

In the synagogue on Rosh Hashanah the shofar will be sounded close to 100 times using a series of shofar blasts. The account of Abraham being willing to sacrifice Isaac is usually recounted because of the connection of the ram being caught in the bush by his horn or shofar (see lesson 1) and because Abraham was being judged or tested. The term Rosh Hashanah, New Year, is never used in the Bible for this holy day. The Torah refers to the month Nissan, the one that Passover is in, which comes in the spring, as the first month of the year. The Torah does not have much to say about this holy day. What it does say is, *"The Lord spoke to Moses, saying: . . . In the seventh month, on the first day of the month, you shall observe complete rest, <u>a sacred occasion commemorated with loud blasts</u>. You shall not work at your occupations; and you shall bring an offering by fire to the Lord."* Leviticus 23:23-25. The loud blasts referred to the blowing of the shofar, thus the day has also become known as the Feast of Trumpets or Yom Turah, the day of blasts. There are ten days between Rosh Hashanah's warning blast and Yom Kippur. These ten days are called the Days of Awe and are spent in soul searching and repentance. The blowing of the shofars on Rosh Hashanah serves as a warning message that there are only ten days left to make sure our record is cleansed as we approach the Day of Judgment, Yom Kippur. The Sabbath that comes during these ten

18. THE ULTIMATE YOM KIPPUR

days of awe is referred to as Shabbat Shoo-vah, Sabbath of repentance.

Yom Kippur is the highest holy day of the year today, and was during biblical times as well. It is known as the Day of Judgment. God's judgment separates those who have received God's mercy, forgiveness, and had their sins removed from those who choose not to. Another name for this solemn day is Day of Atonement, again giving the impression that God wants to use the judgment day to bring about an at-one-ment with His people. As we saw in lesson 17, judgment time is a very real and serious time. It is when God separates those who have accepted His forgiveness granted through the sacrifice of the Messiah and those who have not. King David reminds us, "<u>**All have turned bad**</u>..." Psalm 14:3. Thus, the judgment is not about who is "good" or "bad," but about who has or has not received God's forgiveness and transformation through the Messiah.

Today Yom Kippur is usually observed by fasting and by attending synagogue. It is customary to wear white to services on Yom Kippur. Some people will choose to immerse themselves in a mikvah (immersion tank). On the eve of Yom Kippur the Kol Nidre prayer is chanted renouncing wrong decisions. The day of Yom Kippur is seen as the last opportunity in the year to repent of any sins. A prayer of confession called Ahl Chait (על חטא), meaning "for the sin," is usually recited. Yom Kippur is concluded with a blowing of the shofar. This is the last trump, or last shofar sound of the High Holy Days.

Sukkot comes after Yom Kippur. In direct contrast to Rosh Hashanah and Yom Kippur, Sukkot is a festive, joyful occasion. Sukkot means booths or tabernacles. The Torah tells us: *"on the fifteenth day of the seventh month, when you have gathered in the yield of your land, you shall observe the festival of the* LORD *[to last] seven days: a complete rest on the first day, and a complete rest on the eighth day. On the first day you shall take the product of hadar trees, branches of palm trees, boughs of leafy trees, and willows of the brook, and <u>you shall rejoice before the* LORD *your God seven days</u>."* Leviticus 23:39,40. Today people build booths covered with palm branches and various fruit. Generally, meals are eaten in the sukkah. Also, the items indicated in the Scripture, a citron fruit, a willow branch, a myrtle branch, and a palm branch, referred to as a luluv,(לולב) are held together and waved in the air to the LORD while saying Baruch ata Adonai Elohanu melech ha-olam asher kedshanu b'mitsvotav vetsevanu al netilat lulav. Blessed are you LORD our GOD, King of the universe who has sanctified us with your commandments and commanded us to take hold of the lulav.

This seven-day time of rejoicing is followed by an eighth day currently referred to as Simcha Torah, Celebrating the Torah. These days spent in booths are both a remembrance of the time we spent in the wilderness when we came out of Egypt and a foreshadowing of the new heaven and new earth God has promised us when we **"shall build houses and dwell in them and shall plant vineyards and enjoy their fruit."** Isaiah 65:21 We will elaborate more on Sukkot in the next lesson.

Let's go back a step and take an in-depth look at Yom Kippur. We have looked briefly at how it is observed today. Now we will look at how it was observed in biblical times. The entire sixteenth chapter of the fifth book of the Torah, Leviticus, gives us a detailed description of what took place on Yom Kippur. (We are going to touch the highlights of the chapter here. You will want to read the entire chapter yourself). Leviticus 16 contains the instructions for Moses' brother Aaron as the Temple's cohen gadol (high cohen, or priest). We recommend that you go back and review lesson 5 "Moses the Temple Builder" before you continue this lesson to reacquaint yourself with the furniture and purpose of the first Jewish Temple.

1. How often was Aaron allowed to go into the Temple's Most Holy Place, or the Shrine, to cleanse the Temple of the sins of the people and to make atonement for the people?

    "He shall purge the innermost Shrine; he shall purge the Tent of Meeting and the altar; and he shall make expiation (forgiveness) *... for all the people of the congregation. ... to make atonement for the Israelites for all their sins <u>once a year</u>."* Lev. 16:33,34

    Once a year, on Yom Kippur, and only on Yom Kippur, the cohen gadol (the high priest), and only the high priest, was allowed to enter the innermost Shrine (the Most Holy Place) of the Temple. This was to purge, or cleanse, the Temple of the sins of the people.

2. What did the high priest wear on Yom Kippur and what animals did he have with him?

    He shall be dressed in a sacral <u>linen</u> tunic, with linen breeches next to his flesh, and be girt with a linen sash, and he shall wear a

18. THE ULTIMATE YOM KIPPUR

linen turban. They are sacral vestments; he shall bathe his body in water and then put them on. And from the Israelite community he shall take <u>two he-goats</u> for a sin offering and <u>a ram</u> for a burnt offering. Lev. 16:4,5

The everyday garments of the high priest included a gold band on his head covering which said "Holiness to the Lord," a gold breast plate with precious jewels on it, as well as garments of red, blue, and purple. But since it was Yom Kippur, the time of judgment, the jewelry and decorations were removed and he wore a simple white linen garment. He washed in the laver and brought two he-goats and a ram. The goats and ram will take on more significance in just a minute.

3. What was done with the two goats?

> *Aaron shall take the two he-goats . . . <u>one marked for the Lord and the other marked for Azazel</u>. Aaron shall bring forward the goat designated by lot for the Lord, which he is to offer as a sin offering; while the goat designated by lot for Azazel shall be left standing alive before the Lord, to make expiation with it and to send it off to the wilderness for Azazel . . .* Lev. 16:7-10

One goat was marked for the Lord; the other goat was marked for Azazel, or not for the Lord. The goat marked for the Lord was sacrificed as a sin offering, representing the death of the Messiah for the forgiveness of our sins. The other goat, the goat for Azazel, was not sacrificed as a sin offering, but was sent off alive into the wilderness to die, never more to be in the presence of the people.

4. What did the high priest do with the Lord's goat and what did his actions accomplish?

> *He shall then <u>slaughter the people's goat of sin offering</u>, bring its blood behind the curtain, and . . . sprinkle it over the cover and in front of the cover. Thus he shall purge the Shrine of the uncleanness and transgression of the Israelites, whatever their sins; and he shall do the same for the Tent of Meeting, which abides with them in the midst of their uncleanness. . . . he has made expiation for himself and his household, and for the whole congregation of Israel, he shall go out to the altar that is before the Lord and purge it: he shall take some of the blood of the bull and of the goat and apply it to each of the horns of the altar; and the rest of the blood he shall sprinkle on it with his finger seven times. <u>Thus he shall cleanse it of the unclean-</u>*

<u>ness of the Israelites and consecrate it.</u> Lev. 16:15-19

The blood of the LORD's goat, also called the people's goat, was brought into the Most Holy Place and sprinkled seven times on the cover of the Ark of the Covenant containing the Ten Commandments. It was also applied to the altar of burnt offerings. The sprinkling of the blood on the pieces of furniture cleansed the Sanctuary of the sins of the people. How did God's holy Sanctuary become defiled with the sins of the people? Each day throughout the year individuals would bring their lambs to the Temple, lay their hands on the lamb and confess their sins, symbolically transferring their sins from them to the lamb. The sinner then cut the lamb's jugular vein, killing it as quickly and painlessly as possible. The lamb's blood was sprinkled at the base of the altar of burnt offering and its body was burned on the altar. These transferred sins defiled the Temple until the Day of Judgment, the Day of Atonement, Yom Kippur, when the sins were totally purged, removing the record of sins from before God's presence. This demonstrated God's process of freeing us from sin. First, He granted us expiation, forgiveness, through the death of the lambs and sacrifices on a daily basis. This foreshadowed the death of the Messiah on Passover who gives us forgiveness for our sins and gives us salvation. As we confess our sins and accept the Messiah's death as our substitute, our sins are transferred to God's heavenly Sanctuary, which the earthly is patterned after. Then, on Yom Kippur, at the end of the year, the Sanctuary itself was purged, representing judgment day at the end of time, when the "record" of the sins is purged, cleansed, from the books of heaven.

5. After the Sanctuary was cleansed, what was done with the live goat, the goat for Azazel, the goat that was not for the people?

   When he has finished purging the (Sanctuary), the live goat shall be brought forward. Aaron shall lay both his hands upon the head of the live goat and confess over it all the iniquities and transgressions of the Israelites, . . . and it shall be sent off to the wilderness through a designated man. Thus the goat shall carry on it all their iniquities to an inaccessible region . . . Lev. 16:20-22

Notice that this Azazel goat was only brought forward after the Sanctuary and people had been purged and cleansed. He did not have any part in the forgiveness aspect. This Azazel goat was not sacrificed, was not for the LORD, and was not for the people. It was led into the wilderness, an inaccessible region, never to be seen again. This Azazel goat represented Satan the originator of

18. THE ULTIMATE YOM KIPPUR

sin. He will be separated from us forever. The pronouncing of the sins over him represents God holding him responsible for the sins he has tempted us to commit. In Israel today there is a phrase that corresponds to the English "go to hell." It is "go to Azazel."

6. What were the people doing while the high priest was cleansing the Temple and what did the high priest's work in the Temple do for the people?

*<u>**You shall practice self-denial; and you shall do no manner of work**</u> . . . **For on this day <u>atonement shall be made for you to cleanse you of all your sins; you shall be clean before the** L<small>ORD</small>.</u>* Lev. 16:29,30

The people practiced self-denial. They fasted and prayed. Like Aaron, they put away the outward adorning and focused on their hearts in soul searching. They went to their family and associates and asked forgiveness for wrongs committed. They paid any debts and forgave any wrong done to them. They trusted in the substitutionary atonement of the L<small>ORD</small>'s goat in their behalf to grant them forgiveness and cleansing.

There was an intimate relationship between the cleansing of the people and the cleansing of the Temple. There is an intimate relationship between the cleansing of our hearts and minds and the cleansing of the heavenly temple. As we allow the Messiah to work in us, forgiving us of our sins and transforming our lives, the record books in heaven are also adjusted accordingly.

The text says that atonement would be made that would cleanse you of all your sins and that you shall be clean before the L<small>ORD</small>. That is powerful! Elohim will totally cleanse us. He will cleanse us of the guilt of sin, the record of our sins, and also from the power of sin. Our conscience as well as our character will be cleansed of sin. As we enter into this cleansing experience with God we will no longer desire to sin and God will give us victory over all known rebellious sinning!

We have looked briefly at how the High Holy Days are commonly observed today and have also learned a little about their observance during biblical times. Now we are going to look at the Ultimate Yom Kippur. Just as Passover is both a celebration of our deliverance from the bondage in Egypt and a prophetic picture of the work of Messiah delivering us from the bondage of sin (see lesson 6 the Ultimate Passover), so also the High Holy Days are both historic and prophetic of the Messiah's completing His work in our behalf. In order to more fully understand the Ultimate Yom Kippur we need to continue our study of the prophetic chapters of the book of Daniel. In lesson 17 we learned about the visions recorded in Daniel 2 and 7 that outlined the political powers that would rule the parts of the earth that would dramatically affect God's people from the time of Daniel until the end of this world as we know it. In those chapters God laid out the reign of Babylon, Medo-Persia, Greece, Rome, Papal Rome, the heavenly judgment decision, God's judgment enacted, followed by God's eternal rule. Chapters 8 and 9 of the book of Daniel will give us additional insight into these prophecies, including how the High Holy Days are fulfilled in last day events and of the Ultimate Passover and the Ultimate Yom Kippur!

7. What animals are shown to Daniel in chapter 8?

. . . a vision appeared to me . . . Daniel, after the one that had appeared to me earlier (a reference to the vision of chapter 7) *. . . I looked and saw <u>a ram</u> . . . he had <u>two horns</u> . . . with <u>one higher than the other, and the higher sprouting last.</u> . . . He did as he pleased and grew <u>great</u>. . . . <u>a he-goat came from the west, passing over the entire earth without touching the ground.</u> The goat had <u>a conspicuous horn</u> on its forehead. He came up to the two-horned ram . . . and charged at him with furious force. . . . he struck the ram and broke its two horns, and . . . trampled him . . . the he-goat grew <u>very great</u>, but <u>at the peak of his power his big horn was broken. In its place, four conspicuous horns sprouted toward the four winds of heaven.</u>*
Daniel 8:1-8

Immediately some very interesting points come to light. In contrast to the ferocious beasts of Daniel 7 these two animals are domestic animals that were specifically used on Yom Kippur. This is a very significant point; it clearly links this prophecy to Yom Kippur. The ram had one horn higher than the other, just as the bear of chapter 7 was lifted up on one side. The ram represented Medo-Persia. The higher horn that sprouted last very accurately predicted the Persian part of the kingdom that was stronger than the Median part. The he-goat, which flew across the earth without touching the ground, reminds us of the four-winged leopard of chapter 7. The goat unmistakably represented Greece's rapid conquests and the conspicuous horn represented none other than Alexander the Great. Hundreds of years before Alexander took on the title "the great" Daniel referred to this power as "very great." Daniel saw this horn

18. THE ULTIMATE YOM KIPPUR

broken at the peak of its power with four horns taking its place, a prediction, no doubt, of Alexander's early death and Greece's division into four sections.

8. The *"four conspicuous horns sprouted toward the four winds of heaven."* What emerged from one of these four winds?

   From one of them (one of the winds) ***emerged a small horn, which extended itself greatly toward the south, toward the east, and toward the beautiful land. It grew as high as the host of heaven and it hurled some stars of the [heavenly] host to the ground and trampled them. It vaunted itself against the very chief of the host; on its account the regular offering was suspended, and His holy place was abandoned. An army was arrayed iniquitously against the regular offering; it hurled truth to the ground and prospered in what it did. . . . He will have great strength, but not through his own strength. He will be extraordinarily destructive; he will prosper in what he does, and destroy the mighty and the people of holy ones. By his cunning, he will use deceit successfully. He will make great plans, will destroy many, taking them unawares, and will rise up against the chief of chiefs, but will be broken, not by [human] hands.*** Daniel 8:9-12, 24,25

This small horn is a parallel to the small horn of chapter 7 representing the Roman Empire in both its pagan form and its papal form. Some mistakenly think this little horn refers to Antiochus Epiphanes of Chanukah fame, but for several reasons he does not fit the description. Antiochus did not *"extend himself greatly."* When he was fighting with Egypt to the south, Rome commanded him to withdraw his forces. He sheepishly obeyed and turned his wrath on Israel, which, under the leadership of Judah Maccabee defeated his armies. He did not *"prosper."* He was not *"extraordinarily destructive"* especially compared to Rome, which brought the Temple down to the ground so fully that not one stone was left upon another. There is a clear overlapping of what is written in Daniel chapter 8 about the small horn and what Daniel 7 says about the fourth beast and its little horn, thus keeping with the pattern of chapter 2 and 7 of Rome coming after Greece. Also Daniel was told *"that the vision refers to the time of the end* (Verse 17)." Just as in chapters 2 and 7, Rome, not Antiochus, plays a role in events affecting God's people until the end. It is Rome in both its pagan and papal forms that *vaunted itself against the very chief of the host,* the Messiah.

9. Daniel heard a holy being ask a question that must have been on his mind—*"How long will* [what was seen in] *the vision last . . . ?"* verse 13. What answer was given?

"For twenty-three hundred evenings and mornings; then the Sanctuary shall be cleansed." Daniel 8:14

Daniel was told that the vision would last 2,300 years from some time during the Medo-Persian Empire until the heavenly Yom Kippur cleansing of the heavenly Sanctuary would begin. ("Evenings and mornings" refers to days just as they were referred to during the creation week in Genesis chapter 1. 2,300 days equals 2,300 years using the year for each day principle we learned in lesson 17).

Daniel was sickened by the thought that the Sanctuary was not going to be cleansed for another 2,300 years. When he received this vision the Sanctuary had been in ruins for many years as a result of Babylon's attack on Jerusalem. The angel Gabriel clearly explained most of the vision, but was not able to explain the time portion to Daniel because Daniel became so sick.

God wanted Daniel and us to understand when the heavenly Sanctuary would be cleansed and we will find that out shortly, but first it is important to point out that this time period will take us from the time of Medo-Persia to the time of the beginning of the judgment, not the end of the judgment. There are several stages to God's judgment just as there are several stages to the judicial system in the United States. In the U.S. when a murder is committed and a suspect is picked up the judgment process has begun. He may eventually be judged innocent or he may be judged guilty, but as soon as he becomes a suspect he is involved in the judgment process. His motives, his actions, his testimony all begin to be judged when he is suspected. When the trial date arrives it can last for months. Even after the trial is completed judgment is not completed; the jury of his peers has to deliberate. Even after the deliberation is done and a judgment has been made, judgment is not yet completed. The defendant can then appeal. In the case of a death sentence, when all appeals are exhausted a date for execution is set and only when the execution takes place, in this example, is the judgment process fully completed. Certainly man is not more just than God. If humans will be this thorough in a judgment, how much more will God be regarding His judgment, the effect of which will last for eternity.

18. THE ULTIMATE YOM KIPPUR

You may ask, "Doesn't God already know who deserves heaven and who does not?" Certainly God knows, but trials are not necessarily for the judge's benefit. In earthly judgments society wants evidence that the suspect is really innocent before he is allowed to live freely among them. In a guilty case the family members will want to know that there is evidence proving that their loved one is guilty. As the "Ultimate Judgment" takes place heavenly beings want to see the evidence that we fallen, sinful human beings should be allowed and trusted in their perfect sinless environment. If one of your loved ones does not make it into heaven wouldn't you want to know why? Thus the judgment process is for the sake of the heavenly beings and for us. Really, God is allowing us to judge His decision. Of course we will all agree with His decision because He does not make mistakes, but it is a loving, open, transparent God who would want us to know why He judged the way He did.

In chapter 8 Gabriel did not give Daniel a starting date for the 2,300 years, but chapter 9 does. Daniel chapter 9 starts with Daniel fasting and praying. His prayer is one of the longest and most beautiful prayers of repentance in the Scriptures. In lesson 16 we learned what a prayer warrior Daniel was, and chapter 9 gives us one of his prayers. We encourage you to read it for yourself in your Bible. It is a great pattern of a corporate repentance prayer.

This lesson has already made reference to several previous lessons, an indication of how intricately connected God's word is.

10. Who visited Daniel while he was praying and what did he tell him?

> *... while I was uttering my prayer, the man <u>Gabriel</u>, whom I had previously seen in the vision, was sent forth in flight and reached me about the time of the evening offering... "Daniel, I have just come forth to give you understanding... mark the word and <u>understand the vision</u>."* Daniel 9:21-23.

In Daniel chapter 9 the same angel, Gabriel, of chapter 8 came back to give Daniel understanding of the vision. Which vision? The part of the vision in chapter 8 that Daniel did not understand, the part concerning the time period of the 2,300 years until the Sanctuary would be cleansed. It is interesting that Gabriel came at about the time of the evening offering. This is another Sanctuary reference. Even though the Sanctuary had not been in existence for close to 70 years Daniel still marked time by the timing of the sacrificial offerings that used to take place every day in the Temple.

Before Gabriel gave Daniel a starting time he divided the time period into smaller sections. (The time portion might seem a little confusing but you will understand it if you take each week and turn it into 7 days and remember that in Bible prophecy, each day equals a year.) Gabriel said: *"Seventy weeks have been decreed for your people and your holy city until the measure of transgression is filled and that of sin complete, until iniquity is expiated, and eternal righteousness ushered in; and prophetic vision ratified, and the Holy of Holies anointed."* Daniel 9:24. 70 weeks is equal to 490 days. Using the day for a year principle, 490 days means 490 years. God divided the 2,300 year prophecy into two sections, the first section being 490 years leaving 1810 years in the second section.

In the next verse Gabriel gave the starting event and then divided the 490 years into smaller sections, giving us some landmarks along the way. As Gabriel laid out the various landmarks he went back and forth between what events God will do and what events Satan will cause. Verses 25-27 follow a poetic pattern where the first part of the verse describes events that transpire in harmony with God's will while the second part deals with the work against God's will. In verse 25 the first part describes the work in relation to the rebuilding of the Temple, the second part describes the work against the Temple.

11. What is the starting event for the time line and what are some of the landmarks?

> *". . . From the issuance of the word to restore and rebuild Jerusalem until the [time of the] anointed leader is seven weeks; and for sixty-two weeks it will be rebuilt, square and moat, but in a time of distress."* Daniel 9:25

The time prophecy now has a starting point! It was revealed to Daniel that there would be an official decree to restore and rebuild Jerusalem! This decree to fully **restore and rebuild Jerusalem** came as a result of a culmination of three decrees from three Medo-Persian rulers and is recorded in the Holy Scriptures in Ezra 6:14; 7:12—26. The last decree, fulfilling the prophecy, came in the year 457 BCE. God had given Daniel the starting date of the 2,300 year prophecy; it would start in 457 BCE. The 70 weeks or 490-year portion of the 2,300 year prophecy was divided into three smaller units, 7 weeks, 62 weeks, and 1 week. 7 weeks equals 49 days, and when using the year day principle equals 49 years. It is believed it took 49 years to restore and rebuild

18. THE ULTIMATE YOM KIPPUR

Jerusalem from the time of the decree until it was completed. As mentioned in the prophecy it would be done *in a time of distress*. There was strong resistance to this rebuilding process and it can be read in the Bible books Nehemiah & Ezra. After the 7 weeks, or 49 years, there would be 62 weeks, or 434 years until the Anointed leader. Anointed in Hebrew is Mashiach (משיח) or Messiah. God was showing Daniel that it would be 49 years plus 434 years equaling 483 years, from the decree to restore & rebuild Jerusalem until the Messiah! God has given us the exact time of the first advent of the Messiah! If we travel 483 years from 457 BCE we come to 27 CE—the exact year that Y'shua was immersed and anointed with the Holy Spirit! (See Matthew 3:13-17)

12. The last two verses of Daniel chapter 9 continue the same poetic structure. The first part of each verse speaks about God's work through the Messiah; the second part speaks about Satan's work against God's Sanctuary. What do the last two verses tell us about the Messiah and the Sanctuary?

After those sixty-two weeks, <u>the anointed one will (be cut off) disappear and vanish</u>. The army of a leader who is to come will destroy the city and the Sanctuary, but its end will come through a flood. Desolation is decreed until the end of war.

<u>And he shall confirm a covenant with many for one week. And in the middle of the week he shall cause the sacrifice and offering to cease</u>; and on a corner of the altar desolating abominations even until the end. And that which was decreed shall pour out on the desolator." Daniel 9:26, 27 ("be cut off" in verse 26 and all of verse 27 are quoted from The Interlinear Bible, Hebrew English Volume 3, by Jay P. Green, Sr. Hendrickson Publishers 1984).

The first part of verse 26 tells us that some time after the end of the 7 weeks and 62 weeks (483 years) the Messiah would be cut off and then disappear and vanish from this earth—He would die and be resurrected back to heaven. The second part says that some time after the 69 weeks (483 years) the city of Jerusalem and the Sanctuary would be destroyed.

Verse 27 gets more specific and tells us that in that last 7 years (one week) of the 490 years (70 weeks) the Messiah would confirm the covenant and then at the end of 3½ years (first half of the week) the Messiah would put an end to the need for sacrificing lambs because He would die as the Ultimate Passover Lamb in the year 31 CE on the day of Passover! It is not a coincidence that the period of Y'shua's ministry from His immersion and anointing to His death was exactly three and a half years! The Messiah would continue to confirm the covenant in Jerusalem through His disciples for an additional 3½ years completing the last 7 years of the 490-year portion of the prophecy. Then in 34 CE the message would be taken to the ends of the earth. Rabbi Saul became a believer that very year. His name was changed to Paul and he took the message of the Messiah throughout the Roman Empire and wrote letters that later became a portion of the second part of the Bible. Then the Romans destroyed the city of Jerusalem and the Sanctuary in 70 CE causing **desolating abominations,** or "abominations of desolations," as some translations quote it.

Amazingly, some people try to take these last 7 years (week) and separate it from the rest of the 490 years (70 weeks) and put it at the end of time. They place a gap of unkown duration right in the middle of the time line. How can you have a gap of unknown duration in the middle of a time prophecy and still have it as a "time" prophecy? Could you imagine a furniture company saying they will deliver your furniture in 7 days and after 6 days they call and say they were going to take a very long, indefinite break of many years, but when they start working again they will begin counting again and you will still receive your furniture on time as promised? As ridiculous as that example is so also is the thought that we can arbitrarily break up God's timeline. Even worse than breaking apart God's timeline, some take the portion that applies to Y'shua's death and resurrection and apply it to the anti-Messiah.

Y'shua is the One who is the Anointed One. He is the One who confirms His covenant with us. He was cut off exactly 3½ years after His anointing, and He was taken back to heaven to intercede for us!

Elohim has given us the date for the Ultimate Passover, Y'shua's death as the Passover lamb, and the date for the Ultimate Yom Kippur, the beginning of the judgment process in heaven. Let us review the timeline of Daniel chapters 8 and 9. Think of it as traveling through time with several landmarks along the way. We are going to travel 2,300 years from the time of the Medo-Persian Empire starting with the decree to restore and rebuild Jerusalem in 457 BCE. We travel 49 years to the finishing of the restoration, and then another 434 years to the anointing of the Messiah and the beginning of His ministry on earth in 27 CE. We go another 3½ years to His death being cut off and resur-

18. THE ULTIMATE YOM KIPPUR

rection on Passover in 31 CE. 3 ½ more years takes us to the time the gospel goes out from Jerusalem to the rest of the then known world. We have now traveled 490 years down the timeline with several landmarks confirming we are on the right course. The last leg of our journey is the 1,810 years left in the second division of the 2,300 years, taking us to 1844, the time the Ultimate Yom Kippur judgment process began in heaven.

Just as Rosh Hashanah comes just before Yom Kippur and announces its coming with shofar blasts, there were several events that took place just prior to the Ultimate Yom Kippur, events that parallel what was predicted in Matthew 24:29 and Revelation 6:12, 13. *"There was a great earthquake; and the sun became black as sackcloth of hair, and the moon became like blood. And the stars of heaven fell to the earth, as a fig tree drops its figs when it is shaken by a mighty wind."* The Lisbon earthquake of November 1, 1755 rocked much of Europe, parts of Africa, and as far away as Barbados. In 1776 the U.S. declared independence and became a lamb-like land of freedom from the flood of persecution in Europe against those who preached the Bible. On May 19, 1780, known as The Dark Day, the sun was darkened throughout New England and that night the moon was blood red. In 1798 the Pope and Papacy were taken captive and their power was removed just as prophesied in Daniel chapter 7 (see lesson 17). In 1804 the British and Foreign Bible Society began dispersing the Bible in various languages around the world, followed in 1816 by the American Bible Society. The Leonid meteor storm of November 13, 1833 was so intense that for several hours there was a continual blaze of thousands and thousands of meteors at a time over the United States. It gave the impression that all the stars were falling from heaven. July 15, 1840 marked the beginning of the end of the Islamic Ottoman Empire. Throughout the 1830's and 40's revivals took place as the warning of God's judgment was proclaimed by William Miller in the US, by Lacunza, under the pen name of Ben-Ezra, in South America, and by Joseph Wolff, a Jewish believer, throughout Africa and the Middle East, as well as by many other people. In an 80-year time period one major event after another took place, drawing people's attention to the Bible. All of these were like Rosh Hashanah shofar announcements that the heavenly judgment was about to begin. Then in 1844, at the end of the 2,300-year prophecy, the heavenly Ultimate Yom Kippur began. The cleansing of the Sanctuary had begun. Since then a great work has continued that is cleansing people's hearts of sin and bringing their lives into harmony with the Scriptures. . . . ***Having the everlasting gospel to preach to those who dwell on the earth to every nation, tribe, tongue, and people saying with a loud voice, "Fear God and give glory to Him, for the hour of His judgment has come; and worship Him who made heaven and earth, the sea and springs of water."*** Rev. 14:6,7 NKJV.

The next great event to take place will be the return of the Messiah to take us to heaven. The wicked will be destroyed with the brightness of the Messiah's coming. The earth will experience a 1,000-year sabbatical rest as a wilderness. Satan will be bound to this empty abyss of an earth, while we are reigning with the Messiah in heaven. God will allow us to be the appeals court and look over His shoulder as it were, to discover why He made the judgment decisions that He did. At the end of the sabbatical rest the heavenly Jerusalem, with us in it, will come down to this earth. The wicked will be raised to receive their final judgment, their final destruction, their second death. Fire will come down from heaven and turn this earth and all the garbage and pollution on it into a lake of fire purifying it. After the wicked and Satan are turned to ashes on the face of the earth God will create a new heavens and a new earth out of the ashes. This will begin the Ultimate Sukkot, where we will dwell in perfect tabernacles forever and ever—amen!

Our next lesson will look at these last day events a little closer as we focus on the Ultimate Promised Land, the Ultimate Sukkot.

Outwardly Alan Reinach appeared to be an unlikely candidate for God's kingdom, but in his heart he was searching for truth. But a phone call from an old friend, inviting him to Hawaii to hear the truth of the universe, dramatically changed Alan's life. Alan had to go see his friend in Hawaii. He didn't really understand why, but he knew he had to go. Sitting on a mountaintop overlooking the rain forest, he learned about how God created such beauty out of love for humanity. Back in his friend's home Alan studied the time prophecies of Daniel 9, the seventy weeks. Alan was Jewish, raised in a secular New York City home. The Scriptures told of a Messiah to come. When would He come? Alan's friend David provided a crucial link—Daniel 9 and the Passover. The Passover was a prophecy of the Lamb of God, whose death would cover

18. THE ULTIMATE YOM KIPPUR

the sins of the world, providing atonement. Daniel told when the Lamb of God would die—in seventy prophetic weeks. Daniel nailed the year of Messiah's death; the Passover provided the day, and even the time of day. It was precise clockwork. No guess work about it. We could know that Messiah had truly come, and had fulfilled the plan to the minutest detail! The year, month, day, and hour. Alan was totally convinced. He knew in his heart that God was real, and that the Messiah had come, just as predicted. Daniel 9 held the key to Alan's newfound faith.

Alan met with a rabbi who tried to convince him that the 70 weeks did not point to the time of the Messiah. Alan pointed out that this was not just any anointed person, but the Anointed Prince. The rabbi had to concede that this was THE Messiah. Then the rabbi tried to finagle with the dates. The 70 weeks extended from the destruction of the first Temple to the destruction of the second Temple, he insisted. Alan was not fooled. He knew his history. What date do you want to use for the destruction of the first Temple, he asked? 605, when Nebachadnezzar first invaded, 597 or 586, the dates of his second and third invasions? Either way, since the second Temple was destroyed in 70 C.E., adding 70 to either date makes more than 600 years, not 490. The rabbi was in retreat. He had developed many explanations to prove that the Messiah had not yet come, but he could not refute the obvious logic of Daniel 9. Alan's faith had been shaken during their discussion, but his faith emerged triumphant after the discussion of Daniel 9. You can try to explain away as many Messianic prophecies as you like, but there is no wiggle room in Daniel 9. It leads to only one possible conclusion, a faith-confirming conclusion for Alan.

JEWISH DISCOVERIES

REVIEW הזרה

1. The sequence of the High Holy Days is:

    a. Rosh Hashanah (Feast of Trumpets), Yom Kippur (Day of Atonement), Sukkot (Feast of Booths)
    b. Purim, Passover, Chanukah
    c. Bris, bar mitzvah, wedding, funeral

2. This sequence represents:

    a. The warning to get ready for the day of judgment, the judgment in all of its phases, heaven
    b. The exodus from Egypt, deliverance by Maccabees, the faithfulness of Queen Esther

3. The time prophecies of Daniel 8 and 9 predicted:

    a. The decree to rebuild Jerusalem and the Temple
    b. The completion of the rebuilding of the Temple
    c. The anointing of the Messiah
    d. The cutting off of the Messiah
    e. The time when the heavenly judgment process began
    f. All of the above

4. The Sanctuary became defiled by:

    a. Rodents
    b. Flies
    c. The sins of the people

5. The Sanctuary was cleansed:

    a. By the blood of the LORD's goat only on Yom Kippur
    b. With bleach every Friday
    c. Soap and water whenever needed

6. The cleansing of the Sanctuary represented:

    a. The Messiah's cleansing our heavenly records during the time of the judgment
    b. That we should keep our rooms clean
    c. That cleanliness is next to godliness

TRADITIONS

Kippah

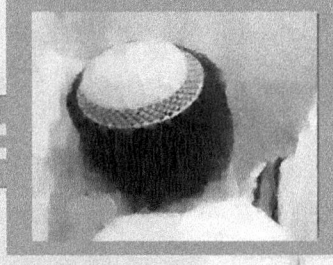

A yarmulke in Yiddish, or a kippah in Hebrew, is a small head covering. Kippah literally means covering. Professor Jacob Lauterbach has been quoted as saying that the question of praying bareheaded or with covered head is not at all a question of law. It is merely a matter of social propriety and decorum.

In trying to find a reason for the head covering some have speculated that since the prayer shawl covers the head during prayer the reasoning developed that it would be good to cover the head all the time. Another suggested explanation is that the tradition of wearing a head covering could have come from the fact that the sun is so strong in the Middle East that a head covering was needed. In some countries hats have been a fashionable symbol of respect and reverence, so it could have been a status symbol established during the time Jewish people were dispersed among the nations. It could also be a carry over from when the Levites and Cohanim were commanded to wear a head covering when ministering in the Temple (Exodus 29:6). Or it could have stemmed from a desire to demonstrate humility before God. Other than for the Levites ministering in the Temple, nowhere in the Bible are we told that all people or even all males need to have their heads covered at all times.

JEWISH HERITAGE
SCRIPTURE STUDIES
19

THE ULTIMATE PROMISED LAND

19. THE ULTIMATE PROMISED LAND

Jewish funerals have interesting traditions. Loved ones put soil on the casket after it is lowered into the ground, putting closure on the reality before us. During the seven days after the funeral we sit shiva as friends visit with us to help us remember what our loved one meant to us. We light the yahrtzrit candle. We say the mourner's kaddish, although it is not mournful; in reality it is a praise to the giver of life. We place rocks on the grave stone when we visit the grave.

With all our ceremonies it is still often wondered, what happens to our loved ones after they have died? Is there life after death? Can our deceased loved ones see us? Can we communicate with them? Is there a real place called heaven? If heaven does exist, where is it located and what is it like? Does everyone get to go there? How do you get there? Will it be boring? Will my friends be there? People throughout the world are asking these questions. You may have asked them, too. We can find the answers in God's Word.

In the beginning when Adonai created Adam and Eve he placed them in the most beautiful place that ever existed. It was called Gan Eden in Hebrew or Garden of Eden in English. They had every joy they could possibly imagine. Every animal was their friend. It was a perfect environment with nothing to mar their happiness. There was no death; there was no pain. And according to the Scripture record, they had face-to-face conversation with God every day. What could be better than that?

God wanted them to enjoy it forever, but God's original plan has been interrupted. Not destroyed, mind you, just interrupted. Abraham, Isaac, and Jacob were promised a land flowing with milk and honey, but they never actually possessed it in their lifetimes. Moses never stepped into the land of Israel. Even at the peak of Israel's glory, during the reign of King Solomon, Israel's beauty did not compare with the beauty of Eden. God desires much more for us than this present world could ever offer to us. God will restore to us the beauties of the Garden of Eden and the interruption that sin has caused will be forever in the past.

JEWISH DISCOVERIES

1. How did the Jewish prophet Isaiah describe God's future home for us?

   And none who lives there shall say, "I am sick"; it shall be inhabited by folk whose sin has been forgiven . . . For the nation or the kingdom that does not serve you shall perish; such nations shall be destroyed . . . And you shall know that I the LORD am your Savior, I, The Mighty One of Jacob, am your Redeemer.

   I will appoint Well-being as your government, Prosperity as your officials. The cry "Violence!" shall no more be heard . . .

   For the LORD shall be a light to you forever, and your days of mourning shall be ended. And your people, all of them righteous, shall possess the land for all time. Isaiah 33:24, 60:12, 16-21

   No sickness, no violence. The only neighbors we will have will be people who have been forgiven. They will be righteous people who know the LORD as their Savior and Redeemer. God promises us prosperity and well being. It sounds like a great place to me. How about you?

2. When will we get to experience this magnificent place?

   Strengthen the hands that are slack; Make firm the tottering knees! Say to the anxious of heart, "Be strong, fear not; behold your God! <u>Requital is coming, the recompense of God—He Himself is coming to give you triumph</u>." Then the eyes of the blind shall be opened, and the ears of the deaf shall be unstopped. Then the lame shall leap like a deer, and the tongue of the dumb shall shout aloud . . . And a highway shall appear there, which shall be called the Sacred Way. No one unclean shall pass along it . . . But the redeemed shall walk it; and the ransomed of the Lord shall return, and come with shouting to Zion, crowned with joy everlasting. They shall attain joy and gladness, while sorrow and sighing flee. Isaiah 35:3-10

   Our requital or redemption is coming; it is coming when Messiah Himself comes again. He came the first time to be Immanuel—God with us—and to die for us as the sacrificial lamb of Passover and of the Sanctuary. The next time He comes He will take us to heaven with Him.

3. If heaven is not until the Messiah comes again, then what has happened to all those who have died already, such as Moses, King David and King Solomon, and our relatives?

   . . . <u>the LORD said unto Moses, Behold, thou shalt sleep with thy fathers. David slept</u> with his fathers, and he was buried in the City of David . . . <u>Solomon slept</u> with his fathers and was buried in the city of

19. THE ULTIMATE PROMISED LAND

David his father. Deut. 31:16; 1 King 2:10; 11:43 KJV

The Jewish Bible, the Tanach, describes death as being similar to a state of sleep and is mentioned over 50 times in the Bible.

Even though the Bible uses the terms sleep or rest well over 50 times to describe the state we are in before the Messiah returns, it is one of the most difficult truths for people to comprehend or accept. This might be because our emotional nature strongly resists the thought of death in any form. This is one reason why Satan's first and most successful lie, "you shall not surely die," worked so well against Eve. If we can set aside our emotional dreams for a few minutes and allow our logical brains to listen to God's Word, we will find ourselves enlightened and protected against Satan's strongest deception. While Satan's lies usually sound better at first, God's truths are always better in the long run.

4. How did King David himself describe the state he would be in at death?

> ***Look at me, answer me, O L*ORD*, my God! Restore the luster to my eyes, lest I sleep the sleep of death;*** Psalm 13:4

In society we use this analogy in many different ways. We say, "may he rest in peace," or "he is at rest," or "we had to put our pet to sleep." Where do you think these terms originated? That's right, the Bible. Nearly every Bible author, as well as Y'shua, used the term sleep or rest to describe death.

5. According to King Solomon, the author of the book of Ecclesiastes, how much do the deceased know or do, and until when do the deceased remain in this condition of sleep?

> ***Whatever it is in your power to do, do with all your might. For there is no action, no reasoning, no learning, no wisdom in Sheol, where you are going. . . . since the living know they will die. But the dead know nothing . . . Their loves, their hates, their jealousies have long since perished; and they have no more share till the end of time in all that goes on under the sun.*** Ecclesiastes 9:10, 5, 6

King Solomon is very clear; there is a time when they will wake up, but until then he says, ***"The dead know nothing."*** When we are sleeping we don't know if it is raining outside or if our cat came into the room. The Bible is very clear. The deceased are not doing any actions, they are not learning, they are not reasoning. They are sleeping. They are not watching us or suffering with us as we go through our trials and heartaches. They are resting in peace. Imagine how hard it would be for Adam and Eve if they had to see all the suffering their rebellion has caused. They, too, are resting in peace until the end of time for this earth. They are taking a nap, but God will awaken them.

The Scriptures mention more than ten people who died and were raised back to life. Not one of them wrote a book, or a chapter, or even one line about what their experience was like. Why didn't they tell us what it was like to be dead? It is because, as King Solomon wrote, *"the dead know nothing."* There was nothing to write about. The modern books about near death experiences (NDEs) are just that, NEAR death experiences, not death experiences. When do most people experience near death experiences? When they are near death, of course. What condition are most people in when they are near death? Often they are on pain medication or under anesthesia, or are not getting enough oxygen to the brain because of blockages or loss of blood, or their bodies are in extreme pain because of a surgical procedure or accident that has caused them to be near death. Medications, lack of oxygen to the brain, or extreme pain can cause the mind to hallucinate. This explanation covers the physical reason of how an NDE can take place and does not even take into consideration the fact that Satan is a deceiver and can put his lies into our minds. Studying, understanding, and believing God's Word are important to keep us from falling for Satan's lies.

6. At the end of that time what is it that will awaken the dead from their sleep?

Mortals languish and die; man expires; where is he? . . . <u>*he will awake only when the heavens are no more. Only then be aroused from his sleep*</u> *. . .*

"At that time, the great prince . . . will appear. It will be a time of trouble, the like of which has never been since the nation came into being. At that time, your people will be rescued, all who are found inscribed in the book. Many of those that sleep in the dust of the earth will awake, some to eternal life, others to reproaches, to everlasting abhorrence. And the knowledgeable will be radiant like the bright expanse of sky, and those who lead the many to righteousness will be like the stars forever and ever. Job 14:10,12; Daniel 12:1-3

The Scriptures teach us that there is an awakening day, a day when our loved ones will be aroused from their peaceful nap and raised to eternal life! It is when Messiah, our Great Prince, the Prince of Peace, appears a second time. He will rescue us, all of us whose names have been inscribed in God's book of life, and He will take us to heaven with Him. Just before the Messiah returns there will be a time of trouble such as has never been seen before, but God will rescue us.

19. THE ULTIMATE PROMISED LAND

Psalm 104:29,30 beautifully describes the dieing and awakening experience by stating, ***take away their breath, they perish and turn again into dust; send back Your breath, they are created, and You renew the face of the earth.***

Moses received a special, early resurrection from his sleep (see Jude 1:9). The Jewish prophet Elijah was taken to heaven without seeing death (see 2 Kings 2:11). These two men represent all those who will be taken to heaven when the Messiah returns. Moses represents those who died and who will be resurrected. Elijah represents those who will still be alive when the Messiah returns at the second advent and who will be taken straight to heaven without seeing death.

7. Until that awakening day Elohim strictly warns us not to try to communicate with the dead.

> ***Let no one be found among you . . . who consults ghosts or familiar spirits, or one who inquires of the dead. For anyone who does such things is abhorrent to the LORD . . . Now, should people say to you, "Inquire of the ghosts and familiar spirits that chirp and moan; . . . of the dead on behalf of the living—for instruction and message," surely, for one who speaks thus there shall be no dawn . . . Distress and darkness, with no daybreak; Straitness and gloom, with no dawn.*** Deuteronomy 18:10-12; Isaiah 8:19-22

The Bible strongly warns us not to try to communicate with the dead. Why? The Bible is plain; our deceased loved ones are sleeping and do not know anything. Satan uses communication with the dead as a way to deceive people. He took the form of a serpent when deceiving Eve. He can take different forms now, even that of someone who has died, even someone who is familiar to us. These "familiar spirits," impersonations of people we are familiar with, can come and tell us secrets that only the person they are impersonating knew. But Satan has heard and seen our secrets and he uses familiar spirits to deceive people.

The teaching that we go straight to heaven at death directly contradicts the vast majority of clear texts on this subject just as directly as when Satan came in the form of a serpent and contradicted God and deceived Eve. If Satan can get us to believe that our deceased loved ones are already in heaven he makes God a liar, he makes the future judgment a non-necessity, and the need for the Messiah to return again to *"awake" "those that sleep"* purposeless. Worst of all, he can impersonate one of our deceased loved ones and deceive us and cause us to fall like he did to Eve.

8. Who has the privilege of living forever, and who does not?

> ***For <u>evil men will be cut off</u>, but <u>those who look to the Lord—they shall inherit the land</u> . . . The <u>righteous shall inherit the land, and abide forever in it</u>.*** Psalm 37:9,29

Heaven is only for those who choose God and choose to follow God's ways. Those whom the Holy Scriptures refer to as righteous are those who lived up to all the knowledge of God that they had the opportunity to know. God winks at the ignorance of those who died before having the opportunity of knowing the truth about the Messiah's dying for their sins. Thus we might have deceased loved ones who did not know about the Messiah, yet there is a place reserved for them in heaven because they lived up to the truth that they had revealed to them. You and I are very privileged to have this wonderful opportunity of knowing more about our loving God, His empowering Spirit, and our forgiving Messiah.

The people whom God refers to as evil are those who constantly resisted and continually rejected the truths that God had presented to them. They will be *"cut off."* In many ways it is a mercy to them. If they did not want to love God here how would they enjoy heaven that is full of love for God? If they did not want to live righteous lives here they would be miserable in a place that is filled with righteousness.

9. How will God cut off those who continually refuse to accept the Messiah's death for the forgiveness of their sins and refuse to allow God's Spirit to give them power to follow God?

> *. . . <u>the Lord is coming with fire</u> . . . For <u>with fire</u> will the Lord contend . . . <u>many shall be the slain of the Lord</u>. Those . . . eating the flesh of the swine, the reptile, and the mouse, shall one and all come to an end—declares the Lord.* Isaiah 66:15-17
>
> *<u>Our God shall come, and shall not keep silent; a fire shall devour before Him</u> . . . He shall call to the heavens from above, and to the earth, that He might judge His people: "Gather My saints together to Me, those who have made a covenant with Me by sacrifice." Let the heavens declare His righteousness, <u>For God Himself is Judge</u>.* Psalm 50:3-6 NKJV.

When the Messiah comes again to awaken those who have died trusting in God, He will take us with them to heaven. At that same time He will come with fire to destroy those who have chosen to follow Satan's ways. This is how He rescues us from the time of trouble mentioned in question 6.

19. THE ULTIMATE PROMISED LAND

In the text just quoted God is referred to as *"**Judge**"* when He comes the second time with a devouring fire before Him. His coming as Judge is in harmony with what we learned about His role as our Cohen Gadol (high priest) in the heavenly Sanctuary during the Ultimate Yom Kippur. This text also says that when He comes He *"**shall not keep silent.**"* At the end of Yom Kippur the shofar is sounded one last time; this is the last trump that awakens those resting in the graves.

The Messiah comes in three ways at three different times. He comes as Suffering Servant/Prophet, as Priest/Judge, and as King. At the first advent He came as a Suffering Servant—Prophet. At the second advent He will come as a Priest/Judge. At the third advent He will come as King. Some people did not receive Him at His first coming because they were looking for Him to come as a King that would destroy their enemies, the Romans. We don't want to make a similar mistake of applying the prophecies of His third coming with His second coming. Satan will try to impersonate Y'shua's coming, but we do not need to be deceived. Satan will come pronouncing peace on earth. He will do wonders and miracles. The majority of the world will follow Him and be deceived. But when Y'shua comes the next time He will not come as a miracle working King, He will come as a Judge. When He returns He will come in the sky with all of His angels; every eye shall see Him; there will be the loud shofar sound; the righteous dead will be resurrected in one huge awakening, and together with the righteous that are alive they will be taken to heaven to meet the LORD in the air. The wicked will be destroyed with the brightness of His coming. Rabbi Paul describes these events in this fashion: ***I do not want you to be ignorant, brethren, concerning those who have fallen asleep, lest you sorrow as others who have no hope . . . For this we say to you by the word of the LORD, that we who are alive and remain until the coming of the LORD will by no means precede those who are asleep. For the LORD Himself will descend from heaven with a shout, with the voice of an archangel, and with the trumpet of God. And the dead in*** (Messiah) ***will rise first. Then we who are alive and remain shall be caught up together with them in the clouds to meet the LORD in the air. And thus we shall always be with the LORD. Therefore comfort one another with these words.*** 1 Thess 4:13,15-18 NKJV.

10. Since we are taken to heaven and the wicked are cut off with fire when

Messiah comes as Judge, what happens to the earth?

> *I look at <u>the earth, it is unformed and void</u>, at the skies, and their light is gone . . . <u>I look: no man is left</u> . . . <u>all the towns are in ruin—</u> because of the L<small>ORD</small>, because of His blazing anger. <u>In that day, the earth shall be strewn with the slain of the L<small>ORD</small> from one end of the earth to the other. They shall not be mourned, or gathered and buried;</u> they shall be dung upon the face of the earth.* Jeremiah 4:23-26; 25:33

When the L<small>ORD</small> comes to rescue us out of the time of trouble He will come in His blazing anger and destroy the wicked. They will not be buried or gathered because there will be no one left to bury them. The wicked will all be dead and the righteous will have been taken to heaven at that same time. There will be no one left, as the prophet wrote *"I look: no man is left."* The earth will then experience a thousand year sabbatical rest while we reign with God in heaven. What will we be doing as we reign with God in heaven for the thousand years? ***Do you not know that the saints will judge the world? I saw thrones, and they sat on them, and judgment was committed to them. . . . They lived and reigned with*** (Messiah) ***for a thousand years.*** 1 Cor. 6:2; Rev. 20:4 N<small>KJV</small>. We will be the appeal judges for our fellow humanity. We will look over the record books and completely agree with God that those who truly did not want to be in heaven, those who did not want to allow their lives to come into harmony with heaven's ways, should be kept out. This is a very open, loving, and merciful act on God's part. By allowing us to judge the record books with Him there will never be a question or a doubt as to why a loved one is not in heaven with us. Thus doubt and rebellion against God will never happen again. It is during this time that God will answer all our questions of why He allowed suffering and all the other why questions we have. Why did He allow the cancer? The early death? The divorce? The abuse? The violence? The rape? The war? The pain? It will all be answered. In many ways by allowing us to sit on thrones and allowing us to judge, we are judging God's judgment. And when all the evidence is in we will say; "***true and righteous are His judgments.***" Rev 19:2 N<small>KJV</small>. By the time the whole process is completed there will be no more tears and no more sorrow.

11. At the end of the thousand years, at the third advent of the Messiah, the wicked will be resurrected to stand before the L<small>ORD</small> to receive their final sentencing. What happens?

> ***Then the L<small>ORD</small> <u>will come</u> forth and make war on those nations***

19. THE ULTIMATE PROMISED LAND

as He is wont <u>to make war</u> on a day of battle. On that day, <u>He will set His feet on the Mount of Olives</u>, near Jerusalem on the east; and <u>the Mount of Olives shall split across from east to west</u>, and one part of the Mount shall shift to the north and the other to the south, <u>a huge gorge</u> . . . As for <u>those peoples that warred against Jerusalem, the L<small>ORD</small> will smite them with this plague: Their flesh shall rot away while they stand on their feet; their eyes shall rot away in their sockets; and their tongues shall rot away in their mouths</u>. Zechariah 14:3,4,12

At the third advent Y'shua will come down and land on the Mount of Olives and split it in two, making a huge gorge, a huge landing plain for the New Jerusalem to come down out of heaven with us in it. The landmass that was promised to Abraham, from the Nile River to the River Euphrates, will now be covered with the New Jerusalem, fulfilling God's promise to him and his descendants. The wicked will be resurrected. They will awaken with the same selfishness that they went into the grave with. *When the thousand years have expired, Satan will be released from his prison and will go out to deceive the nations . . . to gather them together to battle . . . They went up on the breadth of the earth and surrounded the camp of the saints and the beloved city. And fire came down from God out of heaven and devoured them.* Revelation 20:7-9 NKJV. This is the great last battle, the battle of Armageddon.

12. What will be the end result to those who refused Adonai's love and mercy?

> *And you shall come to see the difference between the righteous and the wicked, between him who has served the L<small>ORD</small> and him who has not served Him. For lo! <u>That day is at hand, burning like an oven</u>. All the arrogant and all the doers of evil shall be straw, and <u>the day that is coming—said the L<small>ORD</small> of Hosts—shall burn them to ashes</u> . . .*
>
> *"But for you who revere My name a sun of victory shall rise to bring healing.*
>
> *. . . <u>the wicked . . . shall be dust beneath your feet on the day that I am preparing</u>—said the L<small>ORD</small> of Hosts . . . <u>they shall sleep an endless sleep, never to awaken</u>—declares the King whose name is L<small>ORD</small> of Host . . ."*
>
> *"You may seek, but shall not find those who struggle with you; <u>less than nothing</u> shall be the men who battle against you."* Malachi 3:18-21; Jeremiah 51:57; Isaiah 41:12

Very descriptive words. A day is coming when the wicked shall be burned to ashes on the ground. They shall sleep an endless sleep. They shall be less than nothing.

Elohim is very merciful even to those who reject His love. He does not torment them forever and ever because of the sins that they committed in their relatively short lives here on earth. God has no desire to keep alive and in pain those who have chosen not to follow Him. God told Adam that disobedience would cause death, not life in a fire. It was Satan who lied and said they would not die. Satan is still using that lie today, insinuating that there is no end to the wicked. That lie paints a very distorted picture of God. That lie makes God out to be a monster, tormenting His created beings for millions of years because of 80 or so years of refusing His love. The Bible does not support that lie. The Scriptures say those who refuse God's love will ***sleep an endless sleep***. They will die an endless death. They would not be happy in heaven where there is love, forgiveness, and righteousness since they have chosen to hold onto sin and have refused love, forgiveness, and righteousness. Thus, in mercy to them God will destroy them, just as we would do to our beloved pet if it came down with rabies. The fire God will use is hotter than many people think. Some think it is hot enough to torment but not hot enough to destroy. But the Scriptures say that the fire of God is so hot it will burn them to ashes; it is so hot it cannot be quenched until there is nothing left to burn. That fire will cleans this earth of sin and sinners. Y'shua repeated this thought when He said ***"fear Him who is able to destroy both soul and body in hell."*** Matt. 10:28 NKJV. Satan may be able to destroy our bodies but he cannot touch our soul. Only God can and will, quickly and completely, destroy both the souls and bodies of those who refuse His love.

13. What are God's feelings toward those who are rejecting Him?

> ***For it is not My desire that anyone shall die—declares the Lord God. Repent, therefore, and live!*** Ezekiel 18:32

God's love for His creatures is an everlasting love. He does not desire that any of us should die. That is why He sent His Messiah to die for us, so that we could repent and live forever.

14. What about Satan? What will happen to him?

> ***By the greatness of your guilt, through the dishonesty of your trading, you desecrated your sanctuaries. So I made a fire issue from you, and it has devoured you; <u>I have reduced you to ashes on the ground, in the sight of all who behold you</u>. All who knew you among***

19. THE ULTIMATE PROMISED LAND

the peoples are appalled at your doom. You have become a horror <u>and have ceased to be forever.</u> . . . Ezekiel 28:18,19

Like the rest of the wicked, the Scriptures here say Satan will be *reduced to ashes* on this earth and then *cease to be*. Both Peter and Jude (2 Peter 2:6; Jude 1:7) state that Sodom and Gomorrah are examples of hell. They were quickly and completely destroyed with fire and turned to ashes. *"The day of the LORD will come . . . the elements will melt with fervent heat both the earth and the works that are in it will be burned up."* 2 Peter 3:10. *"He will rain down upon the wicked blazing coals and sulfur."* Psalm 11: 6. God will burn up and melt all the junk that we have destroyed this earth with. All the rusted metal, the styrofoam garbage, the non-biodegradable plastics and rubber, the asphalt and concrete, all will be dissolved, including Satan and the wicked. This earth will become one big lake of fire and burn down to ashes. Satan is not in charge of hell. Hell is where he will be destroyed, reduced to ashes. He will never more cause problems to God or His people. Praise the LORD, Hallelujah!

15. What does Elohim do with this earth after all the wicked have been reduced to ashes upon it?

> *For behold! I am creating <u>a new heaven and a new earth</u>; the former things shall not be remembered, they shall never come to mind.* Isaiah 65:17

After the earth has received its Sabbatical rest during the millenium and has been cleansed by fire God will create a new heaven and a new earth out of the ashes. It will be the Garden of Eden all over again. From our vantage point in the New Jerusalem we will get to see God recreate this earth. It is in this new earth that the Messiah will reign as King. *And the LORD shall be king over all the earth . . . All who survive . . . bow low to the King LORD of Hosts and to observe the Feast of Booths* (Sukkot). Zechariah 14:9, 16

16. What are some of the things we will delight in doing in this beautiful new earth?

> *For as the new heaven and the new earth which I will make shall endure by My will—declares the LORD—so shall your seed and your name endure . . . and Sabbath after Sabbath, all flesh shall come to worship Me said the LORD . . .*
>
> *Never again shall be heard there the sounds of weeping and wailing . . .*

They shall build houses and dwell in them, they shall plant vineyards and enjoy their fruit. They shall not build for others to dwell in, or plant for others to enjoy . . .

The wolf and the lamb shall graze together, and the lion shall eat straw like the ox . . .

In all of My sacred mount nothing evil or vile shall be done; for the land shall be filled with devotion to the Lord *as water covers the sea.* Isaiah 66:22-23; 65:19-25; 11:9

We will be active in the new earth. We will go up to worship God Sabbath by Sabbath. He will reign as our King forever and ever. We will build houses and plant gardens. It will be beautiful. We will get to travel anywhere we want and we will not need a passport or a plane ticket. The animals will not be afraid of us and we will not have to fear them. We will get to enjoy all of God's creation. We will be continually learning more about God's creation and His love for us. It will be absolutely wonderful. There is no sin worth holding onto, to cause you to miss out on the glorious place God has in store.

Just as the High Holy Days of Rosh Hashanah, Yom Kippur, and Sukkot come in order, so do the final events for earth. Rosh Hashanah's shofar blasts represent the warnings regarding the coming judgment. Yom Kippur represents God's judgment in all its forms, including investigation, books and evidence being opened and examined, a decision, an appeal, a sentencing, and an enactment of judgment. Sukkah represents our living for eternity in the new heavens and the new earth after the entire judgment process has been completed. We will build our own sukkot/house. We will have all the fresh fruit we could desire. We will rejoice with the Lord forever as is written regarding Sukkah; *you shall rejoice before the Lord your God.* Lev. 23:40

17. Will you and I be happy living there?

Better one day in Your courts than a thousand [anywhere else] *. . . In Your presence is perfect joy; delights are ever in Your right hand.* Psalm 84:11; 16:11

Perfect joy in God's presence, that is what it is all about. The beautiful homes, the wonderful foods, the enjoyment of animals, the freedom from all fear, and the absence of tears, death, distrust, jealousy, and sickness are all wonderful things that we should look forward to, but the best part of Heaven will be living in God's presence. God will call your name with His beautiful voice. He

19. THE ULTIMATE PROMISED LAND

will take hold of your hand and walk you through His gardens. You will smell the fragrant flowers all in bloom. He will walk you to the Tree of Life and pull off one of its delicious fruit and hand it to you. It will taste better than anything you have ever eaten. He will look you in the eye and tell you how much He loves you. It will be perfect joy. Do you want to experience this gift God has in store for you?

There is nothing more important than living for Elohim now. No matter what problems we go through in our daily lives on this old earth, there will be no difficulty or temptation that, in His strength and power, we cannot overcome. When we get to heaven we will say, "It was worth it all."

You can start enjoying the peace and joy of heaven right now by inviting God to remove from your heart all desires and attitudes that are contrary to His character. Just ask Him to fill you with His love each day. Is there anything on this earth worth trading for the happiness of heaven? Why not tell God right now how much you love and appreciate Him. Surrender to Him any thoughts, attitudes, desires that are not heavenly. Accept the Messiah as your Savior right now. Invite Him into your heart and life. The joys of heaven are awaiting you and I know you are eager to receive them.

It was 2:00 a.m. when Bob Quillen's phone rang. To his surprise, it was Ray Seigal. Bob had conducted the funeral of Ray's wife, Evie, a few days earlier. Ray said, "I'm sorry to call you at this hour, but you have to come over right away!" Bob anxiously responded, "Why Ray? Has something happened?" With a shaking voice Ray said, "Yes, I'll tell you about it when you arrive."

When Bob arrived at Ray's house Ray seemed more angry than afraid as he told Bob the events. "I had been lying in bed, reading. I had music playing. The bedroom lamp was on. I was lonely, thinking about Evie. I closed my eyes and listened to the music, when I felt an eerie sensation that someone was looking at me. I was NOT asleep!!! I opened my eyes and there (he pointed) at the foot of my bed stood my wife! Without thinking, I got out of my bed and started toward her, to put my arms around her, when she began to speak. The voice was just like Evie's. "Suddenly, I stopped in my tracks! Into my mind flashed Ecclesiastes 9:5 and 6, 'For the living know that they shall die: but the dead know not any thing, neither have they any more a reward; for the memory of them is forgotten. Also, their love, and their hatred, and their envy, is now perished; neither have they any more a portion for ever in any thing that is done under the sun.' I shouted to the apparition, 'I know who you are, Old Clove Foot!' My Evie sleeps in her grave until the Messiah calls her to live again! In the name of Yeshua, the Messiah, I command you to be gone from me!'

"The apparition gave a fiendish laugh and suddenly disappeared! I was angry that the Devil took advantage of my vulnerability and sorrow to try to deceive me! I built this house. I was here before he was, and I'm staying. My God is stronger than he is! He will protect me with His angels!" Ray continued to live in that house for several more years, until his death from old age. Bob didn't worry about him, because he knew that Ray was in very capable and safe hands!

REVIEW הזרה

1. When will people be able to start living in the new earth?
   a. At death.
   b. After the Messiah returns and after the entire judgment period is completed.
   c. We are experiencing it now.

2. What is it like when we die?
   a. We become angels.
   b. Like sleep, until Messiah comes again.
   c. The Scriptures do not tell us.

3. What will happen to those who refuse to accept God's love?
   a. They become good all of a sudden.
   b. They burn up quickly into ashes and become as nothing.
   c. God torments them forever and ever.

4. Do you want to accept the Messiah's death for the forgiveness of your sins, to allow God's Spirit to give you the power to follow His ways, and to receive the promise of Heaven?
   a. Yes.
   b. No.

TRADITIONS

Kaddish

There are several Jewish traditions surrounding the death of loved ones. We say the mourner's kaddish. It is not a mournful dirge, but rather praise to the Giver of Life. Mourners tear their garments, expressing their grief, and put soil on the casket after it is lowered into the ground, putting closure on the reality before us. For seven days we sit shiva (seven) mourning and remembering those who died. During the seven days that we sit shiva friends visit with us to console us and help us remember what our loved one meant to us. On the anniversary of the death of our loved one we light the Yahrzeit (year time) candle to remember the person who died. The Yizkor (remembrance) service is the time when we remember our loved one.

Some other traditions associated with death include the using of a plain wood casket to help the body return to dust as quickly and as naturally as possible. The gravestone is normally unveiled a year after the death, but in Israel it is done a month after death. Those visiting the gravesite place pebbles there instead of flowers, possibly because pebbles are more abundant than flowers or possibly because they are more enduring.

None of these traditions are in the Bible, but all of them are helpful as we go through the grieving process. They can give us the ability to physically, visually, and audibly walk through our loss. These traditions are intended to give us time to mourn our loss before getting back into the necessary routine of life.

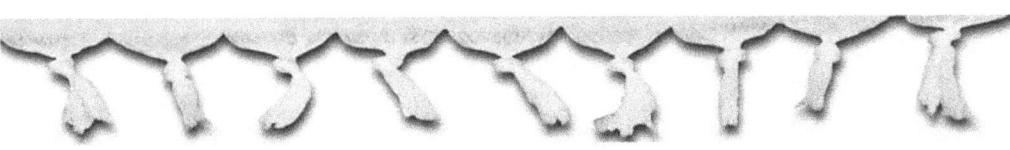

TRADITIONS

Israel's Independence

Out of the tears of the Shoah (holocaust) God birthed the modern nation of Israel. On May 14, 1948 David Ben-Gurion proclaimed Israel an independent nation. Israel's Independence Day, Yom Ha-Atzmaut, is celebrated each year on the fifth day of the Hebrew month of Iyar. In 1897 Theodor Herzl called together the first Zionist Congress in Basle, Switzerland to promote the idea of the Jewish people having their own country in the land of Israel.

As soon as independence was declared, seven Arab nations attacked Israel, bent on its destruction and annihilation. Miraculously Israel won the war. Two other major, miraculous victories when several countries attacked Israel are the Six-Day war of 1967 and the Yom Kippur war of 1973. During the Six-Day war Jerusalem was liberated and Jewish people are now allowed to pray at the Western Wall.

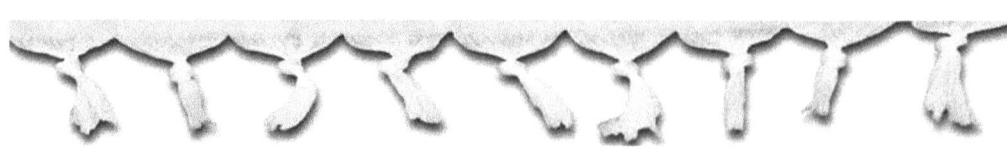

TRADITIONS

Sukkot

Sukkot is the last holy convocation of the biblical calendar year. It is also called the Feast of Tabernacles, or the Feast of Booths. Sukkot is the Hebrew word for booths. Since this feast comes during the fall harvest it has also been called the Feast of Ingathering, or of Harvest. The biblical roots for this feast are in the Torah in Leviticus 23:33-43 and Deuteronomy 16:12-15. *On the fifteenth day of this seventh month there shall be the Feast of Booths to the Lord . . . When you have gathered in the yield of your land, you shall observe the festival of the Lord . . . On the first day you shall take the product of hadar trees, branches of palm trees, boughs of leafy trees, and willows of the brook, and you shall rejoice before the Lord your God seven days. . . . You shall live in booths seven days; all citizens in Israel shall live in booths, in order that future generations may know that I made the Israelite people live in booths when I brought them out of the land of Egypt, I the Lord your God. Lev. 23:33,39,40,42,43* Gathering branches and building booths reminds us of living in the wilderness under God's protection and care when God delivered us out of Egypt and bondage. Sukkot is a time for rejoicing. The feast begins on the 15th day of Tishrei, the seventh month of the Jewish calendar, and continues for seven days. It is the culmination of all the feasts and comes five days after Yom Kippur.

Rosh Hashanah and Yom Kippur represent the events that take place during the time of the judgment. Sukkot represents life in heaven and on the new earth, after the judgment is completed, where we will rejoice before the Lord forever.

Today during Sukkot it is traditional to build a booth decorated with branches and various fruit. Some people sleep in their sukkah (booth); others just have their meals in it. A collection of branches from a willow, a myrtle, and a palm are tied together and called a luluv. The luluv, together with a piece of fruit called an etrog, or citron, is held while facing east and shaken three times in each direction, east, south, west, north, up and then down. A traditional blessing is recited at that time. The luluv and etrog are also marched around the synagogue and waved before the Lord as the hoshanot from Psalm 118:25 is said, *"Save, we beseech You, for Your sake, our God, save, we beseech You."* On the seventh day of the feast, called the Hosanna Rabba, the Great Hosanna, the luluv and etrog are marched around the synagogue seven times.

At the Temple in Jerusalem 2,000 years ago there was a water drawing ceremony. In the desert wilderness God miraculously provided water to drink out of a rock, thus the water drawing ceremony was reminiscent of that miracle. It also preceded the rainy season and was a plea for God to send rain for a prosperous year. Zechariah prophesied that water was going to flow from Jerusalem. This ceremony pointed forward to that time. In the morning Levites drew water from the Pool of Siloam and carried it up to the Temple with trumpets sounding. As the morning burnt offering was being offered on the altar they entered the Temple through the Water Gate, named for this ceremony. The basin of water and another basin with the drink offering of the juice from grapes were poured together into silver basins with openings at the bottom which allowed the red liquid and the clear water to mix together and run out at the base of the altar. The people shouted, *"With joy you will draw water from the wells of salva-*

tion" Isaiah 12:3. The harvest had just finished. People had worked hard for several months and were now rejoicing and celebrating with the fruit of their labors. It was still hot in Israel at this time of year and seeing the water and wine pouring forth must have brought thirst to the people's mouths. It was the last day of the feast, the day of the Great Hosanna, and the people desired more; they longed for a time of continual joy and satisfaction. At this time, during this ceremony, Y'shua stood up and called out, *"If anyone thirsts, let him come to Me and drink. He who believes in Me, as the Scripture has said, out of his heart will flow rivers of living water."* John 7:37 NKJV. Y'shua proclaimed Himself to be the true source of satisfaction and life. As we feast on Him out of our hearts will flow living waters of love and goodness. As we drink in His Word and love we will never thirst again.

Another tradition that was done at that time was the lighting of four huge golden menorahs in the courtyard of the Temple. This ceremony reminds us of how God led us with a pillar of fire to light our way when we wandered in the wilderness. The cups on the menorahs were so large they each held 120 logs of oil. The old garments of the Levites were used as the wicks. There wasn't a courtyard in Jerusalem that wasn't lit by their light. In addition to the light of the giant menorahs, Sukkot always began at the time of the full moon. With all of this light the people rejoiced throughout the night. As the sun rose, shedding even more light upon Jerusalem, the Levites marched into the Temple blowing the trumpets. The Messiah said, *"I am the light of the world. He that follows me shall not walk in darkness."* John 8:12 NKJV.

Y'shua is the true light that gives light, hope, and guidance to everyone who believes. Let Him light up your life!

JEWISH HERITAGE
SCRIPTURE STUDIES  20

THE MOST FAMOUS JEWISH PERSON

20. THE MOST FAMOUS JEW

There are many famous Jewish people in history, both biblical and post biblical. Some of the influential Jewish people down through the ages include Moses, Abraham, David, Deborah, Esther, Albert Einstein, Theodore Hertzel, David Ben Gurion, Yitzhak Pearlman, the Rothschild family, Maimonides, Josephus, and Sam Jacobson. Each one has had his or her impact on this world, but the most famous Jewish person is not any of these. Before we look at the most famous, the most influential, Jewish person let's do a little research about the terms Hebrew, Jew, Israel, and what it means to be a child of God.

1. Who was the first person in the Bible referred to as a Hebrew?

[The invaders] seized all the wealth of Sodom and Gomorrah . . . They also took Lot, the son of Abram's brother . . . A fugitive brought the news to <u>Abram the Hebrew</u> . . . Genesis 14:11-13

Hebrew means to cross over. Abraham crossed over from one country to another. He also crossed over from his father's idol worshipping custom to worshipping the LORD God, the Creator of heaven and earth. The term Hebrew is used only thirty-four times in the Hebrew Scriptures. Godly people such as Adam, Eve, Abel, Enoch, Noah, and Methuselah lived before the term Hebrew was used. Certainly they were children of God; they just were not designated by a single nationality, or race, or religious term. The term is rarely used to describe a people group any longer. Today the word Hebrew is used to describe a language and is the official language of the modern nation of Israel.

2. Where does the term Jew come from?

After the death of King Solomon the 12 tribes of Israel split and became two separate nations, one known as Israel and the other one called Judah. At times they warred against each other. The northern ten tribes split off from the kings of David's line. These northern tribes, then known as Israel, set up their own kings. They continued to rebel more and more and eventually were taken over by foreign nations. They were dispersed and have become known as the ten lost tribes of Israel. The southern kingdom, which maintained its allegiance to the kings of the linage of David, was made up of the tribes of Judah, Benjamin, and Levi. (There were many people from the other ten tribes who did move to the south and lived with these tribes. Even as late as 4 BCE we read of Anna, of the tribe of Asher, and of Simeon, probably from the tribe of Simeon, prophesying in the Temple in Jerusalem.) The landmass and population of the tribe of Judah was the largest of these southern tribes and so all the tribes of the southern kingdom simply became known as Judah. Jerusalem remained the capital of the nation of Judah. The descendants of David reigned as the kings of Judah. The people of this southern kingdom, the nation of Judah, became known as the people of Judah. Jew is short for Ju-dah. After the dispersion of the northern tribes of Israel all of the surviving descendants of Abraham, Isaac, and Jacob became known as Jews. (To learn more about the history of how the 12 tribes of Israel split as well as the history of the kings of Israel and the kings of Judah read 1 Kings chapter 12, as well as the rest of 1 Kings, 2 Kings, 2 Chronicles and most of the books of the prophets recorded in the Hebrew Scriptures.)

With this knowledge we see that Adam, Eve, Noah, Abraham, Isaac and Jacob, etc. were not known as either Hebrews or as Jews, as neither term was was used at that time. The term Jew is not used in the Scriptures until the time of the Babylonian takeover, which did not happen until close to one thousand years after Abraham, Isaac, and Jacob lived. Not even Moses, Joshua, David, or Solomon was ever referred to as a Jew, even though David and Solomon were of the tribe of Judah.

Today those who are physical descendants of Abraham, Isaac, and Jacob are referred to as Jewish. Those born in the nation of Israel and those who make aliyah (become citizens of Israel) are known as Israelis. Citizens of the nation of Israel who are descendants of Abraham, Isaac, and Jacob are both Jewish and Israeli.

Jewishness is not merely a religion, nor merely a culture. It is not merely a nationality, nor a race. It is any of the four, all four, or any combination of the four.

The term Israelite is used very infrequently in the Bible. "The children of Israel" is the term that is most often used in the Scriptures to describe the descendants of Abraham, Isaac, and Jacob. It is used hundres of times.

3. When was the first time the name Israel was mentioned?

Jacob was left alone. And a man wrestled with him until the break of dawn . . . Said the other, "What is your name?" He replied, "Jacob." Said he, "<u>Your name shall no longer be Jacob, but Israel, for as a prince you have striven with God and man and have prevailed</u>."
Genesis 32:25, 28, 29 (margin)

Israel means "Prince with God," "prevailer," or "over-comer with God." Jacob had prevailed in obtaining forgiveness for his deceit from both God and his brother Esau. Jacob was the first person in the Scriptures called Israel. His twelve sons became the fathers of the twelve tribes of Israel. It is from Jacob/Israel and his twelve sons that God birthed every Jewish person from that time until today. God has miraculously sustained us as a people for 4,000 years. He has kept us alive and intact as a testimony to all the world of His power and promises.

God did not change Jacob's name because He got tired of the name Jacob. There was a reason for it. At times names in the Bible have meaning. Originally, Jacob got his name because he was holding onto Esau's heal when he came out of the womb behind his fraternal twin brother. Isaac might have thought it was cute to call him "supplanter," heel grabber—one who trips others up to displace them. It turned out that this is what Jacob ended up doing in life. Jacob pressured Esau to give up his birthright for a bowl of soup (not that Esau was innocent for giving it up so easily) and he deceived his father into giving him the blessing. When God changed Jacob's name He was saying to Jacob, "You will no longer be known as Jacob, the supplanter, but Israel, the prince who prevails and overcomes with God."

Even after God changed his name, Jacob was sometimes referred to as Jacob and sometimes he was referred to as Israel. Jacob was still his name. In some ways the name Israel could be thought of as an extra name, a nickname, or as a title. It was God's way of assuring Jacob that a change had taken place in his character. He was now a prince with God, an over-comer.

The Jewish prophet Daniel referred to the Messiah as "***the Prince***" (Daniel 9:25) and the Jewish prophet Isaiah referred to Him as "***Prince of Peace***" (Isaiah 9:6,7). The Messiah is the ultimate Israel in the truest sense of the word. He is the complete Over-comer, the supreme Prevailer with God, the real Prince with God. Thus all who unite themselves with the Messiah also become over-comers, prevailers, princes with God, children of the ultimate Israel.

The Jewish prophet Hosea made an interesting statement when he said, ***"When Israel was a child, then I loved him, and called my son out of Egypt."*** Hosea 11:1 (the Holy Scriptures, Hebrew Publishing Company 1939). At face value it might seem that Hosea was referring to God using Moses to bring the children of Israel out of Egypt when we were only a young nation. Certainly the text does fit that description, but remember Hosea was a prophet not a historian. Let's look at how another Jewish writer applied Hosea's text. Right after Y'shua was born Herod, the Roman puppet king of Israel, heard that the next ruler of Israel had been born. Herod was so insecure and jealous that he sent soldiers to Bethlehem to kill all the children less than 2 years of age. Y'shua's mother and stepfather fled to Egypt. Matthew applied Hosea's prophecy by saying "***And*** (Y'shua) ***was there*** (in Egypt) ***until the death of Herod: that it might be fulfilled which was spoken of the Lord by the prophet, saying, "Out of Egypt have I called my son."*** Matthew 2:15 KJV. Did you catch the words that Matthew saw as interchangeable? Hosea said "***Israel***" "***My son***" came "***out of Egypt,***" Matthew said that "***Y'shua***," "***My Son***" came "***out of Egypt.***" Matthew understood that Y'shua is the supreme Prince with God, the true over-comer, the ultimate fulfillment of the name Israel. Thus Matthew felt justified in interchanging the name Israel with Y'shua.

Y'shua did not replace the Jewish people as Israel. Y'shua is the original Prince with God. Through His power Y'shua made Jacob a prince with God. Jacob could only be Israel, an overcomer with God, because Y'shua empowered him to do so, and because Y'shua is first and foremost the ultimate Over-comer. Remember, Y'shua is the "man" that Jacob wrestled with, whom Jacob then referred to as God when Jacob called the place Peniel, meaning face of God, because he said he wrestled with God face to face and was spared. Even though Adam, Noah, Abraham and others lived before the name Israel was given to Jacob they also were over-comers, princes with God, because Y'shua made them over-comers with Him. The same would then apply to everyone who has ever overcome since the beginning of time.

This important understanding of the original use and nature of the name Israel is important as it is applied to Bible prophecy.

4. Does the Bible give us any examples of non-Jewish people, Gentiles,

20. THE MOST FAMOUS JEW

becoming children of Israel in an adopted sense? Let's look at what the Bible says about King David's great grandmother, Ruth.

... a man of Bethlehem in Judah, with his wife and two sons, went to reside in the country of Moab. The man's ... wife's name was Naomi, and his two sons ... married Moabite women ... one named Orpah and the other Ruth ... (Naomi's husband and two sons died, so she decided to go back to Israel; she encouraged her daughters-in-law to stay in Moab and find new husbands). ***<u>But Ruth replied, "Do not urge me to leave you, to turn back and not follow you. For wherever you go, I will go; wherever you lodge, I will lodge; your people shall be my people, and your God my God</u>****... Now Naomi had a kinsman ... whose name was Boaz. So Boaz married Ruth ... All the people ... answered, "... May the* LORD *make the woman who is coming into your house like Rachel and Leah, both of whom built up the House of Israel!* ***<u>The</u>*** <u>LORD</u> ***<u>let her conceive, and she bore a son. They named him Obed; he was the father of Jesse, father of David</u>****.* Ruth 1:1, 2, 4, 16; 2:1; 4:13, 11, 13, 17

Ruth did not have to be born Jewish to be a child of God and receive the promises of God. Ruth became a princess with God as she, by God's power, overcame her natural tendencies and chose to follow God.

5. According to the Torah, is it possible for someone who was born as a citizen of ancient Israel to be cut off from the people and miss out on the promises because they refused to allow God to give them forgiveness and victory over sin? (Note: This is a reference to what the Bible says about biblical times, and has nothing to do with the modern political state of Israel.)

<u>The person, be he citizen or stranger, who acts defiantly reviles the</u> <u>LORD</u>***<u>; that person shall be cut off from among his people</u>****. Because **<u>he has spurned the word of the</u>*** <u>LORD</u> ***<u>and violated His commandment, that person shall be cut off—he bears his guilt</u>****.* Numbers 15:30, 31

6. How did David describe the eternal results of being cut off?

*Mark the blameless, note the upright, for there is a future for the man of integrity. But **<u>transgressors shall be utterly destroyed, the future of the wicked shall be cut off</u>***. Psalm 37:37, 38

God makes it clear that regardless of whether we are born Jewish or Gentile if we spurn the work of the LORD and violate His commandments we will be cut off and utterly destroyed. We can see from these texts that being a child of God, a prince with God, an over-comer with God, is not something we are born into, but it is something we choose. Esau, although Isaac's first born child, chose to spurn the birthright, while Jacob accepted God's call to follow Him. (Again, do not confuse the terms with the modern day Israeli citizens in the modern nation of Israel. We are looking at biblical terms to understand biblical concepts, and prophetic applications, not to set political agendas for nations.)

Let's look at the lives of three people who lived at the same exact time. Two of them were children of Israel because of their birth lineage and two of them were over-comers with God because they chose to follow God and be His children. The three people were Joshua, Achan, and Rahab. They lived at the end of our forty years of wandering in the wilderness. Moses had just died and the leadership of the nation was given to Joshua. Joshua sent two spies into the Canaanite city of Jericho. There they met a Gentile lady named Rahab who had been living a life of sin. But she had heard about the God of Israel and she chose to believe in Him. She helped the Jewish spies and they promised her that when God destroyed the city she and her household would be saved. God had the army of Israel march around the city of Jericho for seven days. On the seventh day of marching God had the army shout and blow shofars. When they did so the walls of Jericho came down and Israel took the city but saved Rahab and her family. Rahab became part of Israel. One of the soldiers in Joshua's army was a Jewish man named Achan. He stole some of the spoils from Jericho and hid it under his tent. God revealed Achan's sin to Joshua and Achan was cut off from the people of Israel.

In this biblical historical snapshot, who among these three, Joshua, Rahab, and Achan, were a part of Israel? It depends on if we are asking about the Israel who are bloodline descendants of Abraham, Isaac, and Israel or the Israel that is referred to as over-comers with God. If we limit the question to the Israel defined as bloodline descendants of Abraham, Isaac, and Jacob, then the answer is Joshua and Achan were a part of Israel. If we limit the question to those who have faith in God and are united with Him in heart, mind, and action and are thus over-comers with God, then the answer is Joshua and Rahab.

    a. Joshua was physically born Jewish as a child of Israel and he was also born in heart as a child of God, an over-comer with God, a prince with God, Israel in the original sense of the word.

b. Rahab was physically born as a Gentile, but she was born in heart as a child of God, an over-comer with God, a princess with God, Israel in the original sense of the word.
c. Achan was physically born Jewish, as a child of Israel, but in heart he did not love God and did not want to follow God. He did not overcome the sinful tendencies in his heart by God's power. He was not a part of Israel in the original sense of the word.

These three people all lived over a thousand years before Y'shua the Messiah came to this earth. <u>Thus we see that there has always been these two definitions of Israel. One definition being the physical definition of being born in the bloodline of Abraham, Isaac, and Israel. And one being the definition of choosing to invite God to come into your heart and transform you into a prince with Him, an over-comer with Him, a child of the ultimate Israel, the Messiah. One definition does not replace the other. The two definitions have always run parallel throughout history and have often run together, like in the life of Joshua.. Both Israels are important to God. One cannot replace the other. They both stand as testimonies for God. It is God's ideal that they overlap and blend together as one.</u>

While we should not forget the importance of Israel through the bloodline (descendants of Jacob), we should also not neglect the importance of being an Israelite through faith, an overcomer through the Messiah. <u>There are two ditches on either side of the truth. One is to make being physically born from the bloodline of Abraham, Isaac, and Israel the only thing that is important while ignoring the importance of a heart commitment. The other ditch is to only be concerned with the heart commitment and ignore the importance that God has sustained a bloodline of Children of Abraham, Isaac, and Israel.</u>

Both Jewish people and Gentiles need to become over-comers with God in order to have a place reserved for them in heaven. That is how it has been from the beginning, thousands of years before the term Israel was created, even as far back as Cain and Abel, two of Adam and Eve's children. Abel chose God and Cain did not. And that is how it is today. Where we will go in the end comes down to the choices we make now. That is how it has always been and how it always will be. There is no replacing or changing of God's plan or his requirements. He is the same yesterday, today, and forever. As King David wrote and Y'shua quoted, ***"The meek shall inherit the earth."*** Psalm

37:11 (The Holy Scriptures, Hebrew Publishing Society 1939). God will give the land, the whole land, the entire earth, to those who realize their total dependence upon God.

7. Can a wicked person change and become an over-comer with God and avoid being eternally cut off and destroyed when the judgment comes?

> *... **When a righteous person turns away from his righteousness and does wrong, he shall die for it**; he shall die for the wrong he has done. And **if a wicked person turns back from the wickedness that he practiced and does what is just and right, such a person shall save his life**. Because he took heed and turned back from all the transgressions that he committed, he shall live; he shall not die.... **I will judge each one of you according to his ways**—declares the LORD God. **Repent and turn back from your transgressions**; let them not be a stumbling block of guilt for you. **Cast away all the transgressions** by which you have offended, and **get yourselves a new heart and a new spirit, that you may not die, O House of Israel. For it is not My desire that anyone shall die**—declares the LORD God. **Repent, therefore, and live!*** Ezekiel 18:26-32

God give us the freedom to choose which direction we want to go. God allows U-turns! Freedom to choose is a freedom He never removes from us. You can have this new heart and new spirit every day by accepting and reaccepting the Messiah's death as your substitute for the wrongs you have done and by asking God to come into your heart and give you new thoughts and pure desires.

8. As you confess your sin and accept the Messiah's death for the forgiveness of the sin, God graciously grants you forgiveness and removes your guilt. What does God give us to keep us from sinning in the future?

> ***Fashion a pure heart for me, O God; create in me a steadfast spirit. Do not** cast me out of Your presence, or take Your holy spirit away from me. Let me again rejoice in Your help; let a vigorous spirit sustain me ...*
>
> *I will give you a new heart and put a new spirit into you; I will remove the heart of stone from your body and give you a heart of flesh; and I will put My spirit into you. Thus I will cause you to follow My laws and faithfully to observe My rules.* Ps 51:12-14; Ezekiel 36:26, 27

God does more than just forgive us; He transforms us, just as He trans-

20. THE MOST FAMOUS JEW

formed Jacob from being a deceiver to being Israel, an over-comer, a prince with God. He is able to remove the spots from our character. He puts His Spirit in you and starts living His life, His thoughts, His desires, and His obedience in and through you. If you have not yet given yourself to God, if you have not yet asked Him to forgive you for your mistakes and sins, do not wait any longer. Or if you have and need to renew that decision, right now ask God to forgive you and accept Y'shua the Messiah as your substitute. Ask God to give you His Holy Spirit to sustain you and cause you to follow His laws.

9. How is God's house of prayer described by the prophet Isaiah?

> ***Thus said the LORD: "Observe what is right and do what is just; for soon <u>My salvation shall come</u>, And my deliverance be revealed. <u>Happy is the man who does this</u>, The man who holds fast to it: <u>Who keeps the sabbath</u> and does not profane it, And stays his hand from doing any evil. Let not <u>the foreigner</u> say, who has attached himself to the LORD, "The LORD will keep me apart from His people . . . For thus said the LORD: <u>I will give them an everlasting name which shall not perish</u>. As for <u>the foreigners who attach themselves to the Lord, to minister to Him, and to love the name of the Lord, to be His servants—All who keep the sabbath</u> and do not profane it, and <u>who hold fast to My covenant—I will bring them to My sacred mount and let them rejoice in My house of prayer. Their burnt offerings and sacrifices shall be welcome on My altar; for My House shall be called A house of prayer for all peoples.</u>"*** Isaiah 56:1-7

While the physical nation of Israel today is precious in God's sight and is very important in God's heart, God's house of prayer is broader than a physical land mass with a democratically elected government. God's house of prayer is for all people, Jewish people and Gentile people, who have received God's salvation. It is described as a happy people who keep God's Sabbath, who are saved, have an everlasting name, who minister to the LORD, love His name, are His servants, and rejoice in His house together. This is a beautiful description of princes and princesses of God with the Prince of Peace as their LORD and Savior. This house of prayer is made up of all people who fully give themselves to the LORD God, Creator of the heaven and earth.

God's house of prayer is described in Isaiah 56 as:
a. Made of Jewish people and foreigners or Gentiles.
b. Those keeping God's Seventh-day Sabbath.

10. Read how these people are also described in the biblical book of Revelation:

   "Here is the patience of the saints: here are they that keep the commandments of God, and the faith of"~Y'shua. Rev. 14:12 KJV.
   c. Keep the commandments of God.
   d. Have faith in Y'shua. They have faith in His atonement for their sins, they have faith that He came in His first advent and that He is coming again in a second advent.

11. In addition to these four identifications that are listed thus far, what are some additional descriptions?

   ". . . having the everlasting gospel to preach unto them that dwell on the earth, and to every nation, and kindred, and tongue, and people, Saying with a loud voice, Fear God, and give glory to him; for the hour of his judgment is come: and worship him that made heaven, and earth, and the sea, and the fountains of waters." Revelation 14:6,7 KJV.
   e. Bring the Good News of God's salvation to every nation, ethnic group, language group, and people group in the world.
   f. Call people to respect God and give glory to Him.
   g. Announce God's judgment.
   h. Bring people back to worshipping God as Creator of the heaven, earth, and sea.

12. In addition to taking the Good News of God to the world what will they be doing?

   Then the King will say to those on His right hand, 'Come, you blessed of My Father, inherit the kingdom prepared for you from the foundation of the world: for <u>I was hungry and you gave Me food</u>; <u>I was thirsty and you gave Me drink</u>; <u>I was a stranger and you took Me in</u>; <u>I was naked and you clothed Me</u>; <u>I was sick and you visited Me</u>; <u>I was in prison and you came to Me</u>.' "Then the righteous will answer Him, saying, 'Lord, when did we see You hungry and feed You, or thirsty and give You drink? When did we see You a stranger and take You in, or naked and clothe You? Or when did we see You sick, or in prison, and come to You?' And the King will answer and say to them, 'Assuredly, I say to you, inasmuch as you did it to one of the least of these My brethren, you did it to Me.' Mathew 25:34-40 NKJV.
   i. Bring food and drink to those that are hungry.
   j. Minister to those who have no place to stay.
   k. Give clothing to those who don't have it.

20. THE MOST FAMOUS JEW

l. Have hospitals and clinics to minister to those who are sick.

m. Have ministries that help people in prison.

13. What does Satan think of these people who keep the commandments of God and have the testimony of Y'shua?

The dragon was enraged with the woman, and he went to make war with the rest of her offspring, who keep the commandments of God and have the testimony of" ~Y'shua the Messiah. Revelation 12:17 NKJV.

Satan, the dragon, is furious with those who are princes and princesses under the Prince of Peace. Satan does everything he can to harass God's children. Notice that Satan is furious with those who keep the commandments AND have the testimony of Y'shua. It is the combination of keeping the commandments and having the testimony of Y'shua that makes him the maddest. Satan is not nearly as threatened if we try to keep God's commandments but don't have salvation in Y'shua. Nor is he as threatened if we profess to believe in Y'shua but don't keep the ten commandments.

n. They will be hated by Satan and he will be at war with them.

Let's review all 14 (a-n) of the identifications listed in these verses:

a. Made of Jewish people and Gentiles.
b. Keep God's Seventh-day Sabbath.
c. Keep the commandments of God.
d. Have faith in Y'shua. They have faith that He came in His first advent and that He is coming again in a second advent.
e. Bring the Good News of God's salvation to every nation, ethnic group, language group, and people group in the world.
f. Call people to respect God and give glory to Him.
g. Announce God's judgment.
h. Bring people back to worshipping God as Creator of the heaven, earth, and sea.
i. Bring food and drink to those that are hungry.
j. Minister to those who have no place to stay.
k. Give clothing to those who don't have it.
l. Have hospitals and clinics to minister to those that are sick.
m. Have ministries that help people in prison.
n. They will be hated by Satan and he will be at war with them.

Obviously no one single congregation could fulfill all of these requirements, yet it can and is being done through a network of congregations, a denomination, that is united together, is situated throughout the world, and has a common faith and goal. There is a denomination that fulfills all of these requirements and that has a common faith in the truths that have been brought out in this series of lessons. I encourage you to join such a united network of congregations and be a part of bringing God's message to every nation, ethnic group, language group, and people group.

God has faithful people in the world who are doing His will and following Him who are not a part of this group. There is no attempt here to say that this group is the only "good" group or that it is the only group being used by God. The point is that thousands of years ago God's Word prophesied that there would be a group that would be doing and believing all of the things quoted above and that prophecy is being fulfilled today. Why not be a part of the denomination that the Bible predicted would do all of these things? Y'shua said, *"other sheep I have which are not of this fold,"* but He desires to be the *"**One Shepherd***" of *"**one fold.**"* John 10:16 KJV

14. Now that we have covered the meaning of the terms Hebrew, Jew, and Israel, and looked at what it means to be a part of God's house of prayer, let's find out who the most famous Jewish person in history is.

    Here are some hints:
    - He was Jewish.
    - He was of the tribe of Judah, from the line of King David.
    - He was born to a very poor family, inside a cow stable.
    - He worked as a laborer until about the age of 30.
    - He never received any kind of formal education, yet His words are among the most quoted.
    - He never had much money, yet He provided food to thousands.
    - He never held a political office, yet thousands listened to him.
    - He did not have a medical degree, but he brought relief to many suffering from sickness and disease.
    - He never wrote a book even though more has been printed about Him than any other man.
    - He never traveled very far from his birthplace, yet He is known in every country of the world.
    - He died at about the age of 33, sentenced to death by the court system and killed as a criminal.
    - Almost no one attended His funeral, yet today his name is mentioned at billions of funerals.
    - Many nations base their calendars and events in their history books as being either before or after his birth.

20. THE MOST FAMOUS JEW

- Even though He died many years ago, He still brings comfort to the lonely, joy to the sad, strength to the weak, hope to the fearful, relief to the suffering, peace to the troubled, and victory to the struggling.
- The most famous Jewish person of all time, who has had the greatest impact on the world, is Y'shua the Messiah.

Rabbi Joe Kagan had a beautiful tenor voice. At age 13 he sang at Carnegie Hall. He was very educated and became a rabbi. In addition to his career as a rabbi he was a researcher for Ronald Reagan when Reagan was governor of California.

Artist Elfred Lee met Rabbi Kagan at Weimar Lifestyle Center in Weimar California. At that time Rabbi Kagan would never touch the New Testament. One of the horrid memories he had was hearing about his aunt being raped while a priest stood over her with a crucifix saying, "This is what you get for killing Christ." As a result he had a very negative attitude toward Christianity. Rabbi Kagan came across a book called Patriarchs and Prophets by Ellen G. White. He read it with astonishment and asked Elfred which university the author attended and if he could meet her. Elfred replied that she only had a third grade education and that she had passed away in 1915. "Then where did she learn Hebrew?" the rabbi asked. Elfred told him that she never knew Hebrew, but was one of the most prolific female writers in history and that this was only one of her many books. Rabbi Kagan was amazed at her knowledge, saying that the information in Patriarchs and Prophets is Mishnaic. The Mishnah is part of Hebrew scholarship. He said that since she died before the Mishnah was translated into English, she would either have had to know Hebrew extremely well or was inspired by the same source that inspired the prophets and sages. He said you had to know Hebrew to be able to write like this because the rhythm, the meter, the arrangement of words and expressions are more like Hebrew than English. He said it was as if she wrote in Hebrew and it was translated into English.

In time Rabbi Kagan accepted Y'shua as his Messiah and was immersed in the Bear River above Sacramento on Saturday night Dec 22, by Pr. Bill Jamerson. As he came up out of the cold water with a shout praising God and singing to his new Messiah, he said, "I am now a completed Jew. I have now accepted the entire Bible and the Messiah that all Jewish prophets told us about!" He was happy to be a member of a worldwide organization that is unified in its beliefs and is working to share the love of God around the world. In 2007 the denomination consisted of one hundred and twenty six thousand congregations meeting in over two hundred countries around the world with over sixteen million members and growing at a rate of over one million a year. In addition to the congregations there are more than seven thousand four hundred religious schools and more than eight hundred and fifty hospitals, nursing homes, clinics and orphanages that are operated by this denomination throughout the world. While it might just sound like numbers, Rabbi Kagan realized that no one other organized Sabbath keeping group was making such a huge impact around the world. One of the things that Rabbi Kagan appreciated about being a part of a worldwide organization is that he sensed a family bond with people of all different backgrounds, cultures, languages, and races who all share the same common bond of the basic beliefs brought out in the Scriptures.

Many times Elfred saw Rabbi Kagan cry. One time Rabbi Kagan assisted Elfred with a painting, which among many other aspects depicted Y'shua eating Passover with His disciples. Rabbi Kagan helped Elfred make sure that the head coverings were correct and that the cups, the unleavened bread, and the bitter herbs were exactly as they would have been. Rabbi Kagan approved of the whole painting and sang at the unveiling ceremony at the denomination's headquarters in Silver Springs, MD. He wept as he sang in Hebrew the words of Psalm 22 by King David prophesying the death of Y'shua. Rabbi Kagan sang and sang and wept and wept; his whole body was shaking. His voice was so beautiful. It was such an emotional experience that there was not a dry eye in the whole congregation.

Rabbi Kagan has since passed on, but you too can know the most famous Jew as your personal Savior, Friend, and Lord. You too can unite with and be an important part of the work that God is doing through His followers. You too can join God's family of believers who keep the commandments of God, who have faith in Y'shua, and are sharing His love around the world.

We know that the Holy Spirit has been speaking to your heart as you have read these pages. We want to encourage you, while all this is fresh in your mind, to take the next steps in your journey toward the congregational home God has for you. We are eager to be helpful in any way we can.

20. THE MOST FAMOUS JEW

REVIEW הזרה

1. God changed Jacob's name to Israel because:
   a. Jacob didn't like the name Jacob.
   b. Jacob was hiding from Esau.
   c. Jacob became a prince with God, an over-comer with God.

2. The One who is the original over-comer with God, the Prince with God, the ultimate Israel, and who gave Jacob the power to be an over-comer is:
   a. Isaac.
   b. Esau.
   c. Y'shua the Messiah.

3. Which two of these people were natural citizens of the ancient nation of Israel?
   a. Joshua.
   b. Achan.
   c. Rahab.

4. Which two of these people were over-comers with God, princes with God?
   a. Joshua
   b. Achan
   c. Rahab

5. In the judgment God will determine who are truly His by:
   a. What nation we are born in.
   b. What our race is.
   c. Whether or not we choose to follow the Lord God.

6. If a person, whether Jewish or Gentile, is not following the Lord God, that person should:
   a. Repent of his sins, accept the Messiah's death as the forgiveness for those mistakes, and allow God to give him a new heart and a new spirit, making him an over-comer with God, a prince with God.
   b. Move to Israel.
   c. Give up; it is too late.

7. God's Word prophesied that at the end of time there would be a group of Jewish people and non-Jewish people who would:
   a. Keep the commandments of God (which would include keeping God's seventh-day Sabbath), have faith in Y'shua, that He came in His first

advent and that He is coming again in a second advent.
   b. Bring the Good News of God's salvation to every nation, ethnic group, language group, and people group in the world. Call people to respect God and give glory to Him. Announce God's judgment. Bring people back to worshipping God as Creator of the heaven, earth, and sea.
   c. Have ministries for those who are poor, those who need clothes, are hungry, are sick, and those who are in prison.
   d. Be hated by Satan.
   e. All of the above and I would like more information about this group.
   f. All of the above and I would like to join this group

8. The most influential Jewish individual in history is:
   a. Samuel Jacobson.
   b. Queen Esther.
   c. Y'shua the Messiah.

TRADITIONS

Mikvah

A mikvah, מקווה, is an immersion pool that is used for ceremonial cleansing. Mikvahs that date back 2,000 years can be found in various parts of Israel, such as just opposite the southern portion of the Western Wall in Jerusalem, and in Qumran near where the Dead Sea Scrolls were written.

According to the Torah the Levites were to wash their bodies before ministering in the Sanctuary (Ex. 29:4, Lev. 14:8,9; 16:4). Likewise, lepers, those who had a bodily discharge of any kind (Lev. 15:5-13), and those who touched dead bodies or unclean animals (Lev. 22:6) were commanded to wash their bodies. The Torah also mentions that any metals that were taken after a war should pass through water (Numbers 31:21,22). Many, if not all, of these admonitions can be fulfilled by the daily washing that is commonly practiced in many societies today.

Today it is a tradition in some Jewish groups for members to immerse themselves in a mikvah at certain times, such as after a monthly menstrual cycle, after marital relations, after bearing a child, before certain holy days such as Yom Kippur, before conversion, and for a bride and groom, before their wedding.

Two thousand years ago a Jewish man from the tribe of Levi named Yochanan began to immerse people as a demonstration of their desire to be cleansed from sin. This concept could very well have come from David's prayer in Psalm 51 that we have looked at several times in these studies. In Psalm 51:4 & 9 King David wrote, *"__Wash__ me thoroughly of my iniquity, and __purify__ me of my sin . . . purge me with hyssop till I* *am pure; <u>wash</u> me till I am whiter than snow."* In addition, two Jewish prophets, Isaiah and Jeremiah, made this same spiritual analogy between cleansing from sin and being washed. The prophet Isaiah wrote, *"<u>Wash</u> yourselves <u>clean</u>; put your evil doings away from My sight. Cease to do evil, Learn to do good... Be your sins like crimson they can turn snow-white"* (Isaiah 1:16-18). And the prophet Jeremiah wrote, *"<u>Wash</u> your heart <u>clean</u> of wickedness..."* Jeremiah 4:14.

Tevilah, טבילה, is the Hebrew word for immersion. The Greek word for immersion is baptismo, and is the origin of the word baptism. The Levite Yochanan, who was immersing people for the forgiveness of sins, became known as Yochanan ha-matvil (המטביל) or Yochanan the immerser, or John the baptist.

One day Y'shua the Messiah came to Yochanan the immerser to be immersed. Yochanan was surprised and said that Y'shua did not need to be immersed because He was already pure, but Y'shua insisted on being immersed to fulfill all righteousness and to be an example. Y'shua was immersed for all those who, for whatever reason, never had the opportunity to be immersed.

After Y'shua was killed and resurrected back to heaven during the feast of Passover and Unleavened Bread His followers continued to tell others about Him. Fifty days later, during the feast of Shavuot, 3,000 Jewish people in Jerusalem wanted to accept Y'shua into their hearts as Messiah. Y'shua's followers told the people to *"turn from your sin, return to God, and each of you be immersed on the authority of Yeshua the Messiah into forgiveness of your sins, and you will receive the gift of the Ruach HaKodesh* (Holy Spirit)!" Acts 2:38 Complete Jewish Bible. The text continues by saying that *"those who accepted what he said were immersed, and there were added to the group that day about three thousand people. They continued faithfully in the teaching of the emissaries, in fellowship, in breaking bread and in the prayers."* Acts 2:41,42 CJB. We notice from this example that when the people were immersed they were "*added to the group,*" and continued following the teachings, in fellowship, and in worship together. The people were not just immersed and sent on their way. They became part of the congregation, part of the mispacha (family) of God.

Immersion is in many ways like a wedding. The couple doesn't fall in love at the wedding; it is the time when they publicly demonstrate that they are in love and that they are committed to each other for life. The same is true with immersion. The immersion is not when we choose to follow the LORD. But it is the public demonstration that we love Y'shua, and have chosen to follow Him, and of our desire to have Him forgive and wash away our sins, and that we want to be filled with His Spirit so we can have the power to walk in the ways of the Word of God.

Just as the wedding ceremony does not create love in the hearts of the couple, the immersion ceremony itself does not cleanse away the sin. It is a ceremony demonstrating that God has cleansed us from sin through the sacrifice of the Messiah. In immersion a person goes down under the water and then comes back up. Just as Y'shua died, was buried in the grave, and was raised back to heaven, immersion symbolizes that our old life of sin has died and that a new life, empowered by God, is coming alive in us.

During a wedding the individuals getting married not only get a spouse, they get a mother-in-law, a father-in-law, brothers-in-law, and sisters-in-law, etc. We don't marry just an individual; we marry into a family. The same is true with immersion. It is a time when we publicly unite our hearts with Y'shua and become brothers and sisters with fellow believers in the congregation. We are then, by God's power, to continue in the teachings of the Word of God, in fellowship with the congregation, and in worshiping together with the congregation to which we have been added.

Continuing in the teachings is an important part of being a follower of Y'shua. Since you have prayerfully read this far I am sure your heart is in harmony with the biblical teachings we have studied together. If you have not been immersed and added to a congregation that teaches the biblical teachings taught here I encourage you to do so right away. If you do not know of a congregation that teaches these truths, contact those from whom you received this book and they will assist you. If you are not able to reach someone locally please go to www.Jewishheritage.net and contact us and we will be in touch with you right away.

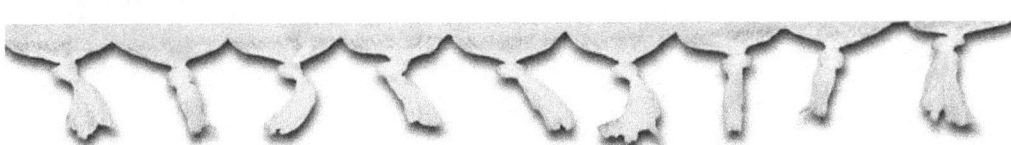

JEWISH HERITAGE SCRIPTURE STUDIES

ESTHER THE QUEEN

21. QUEEN ESTHER (ESTER)

One of the most famous heroines in Jewish history is Queen Esther. The Megillah or scroll of Esther is a story of rags to riches, of weakness to power, of sorrow to joy. While the account of Esther is a true story it has within it all of the elements of an interesting novel, including romance, murder plots, greed, power, villains, heroes, suspense, and even a little humor. The events seem to take place in rapid succession, yet in reality they happened over a ten-year time period.

God's name, in any of its forms, is never mentioned in the book of Esther. That is not to say that God is not there. He plays a significant role throughout the life of Esther. The account of Esther becomes very important as we see how the events that took place during the time of Esther closely parallel the final events of this earth's history. This lesson, like all the lessons in this book, is linked together with the previous lessons. Thus it is important to have first read and understood the previous lessons to fully appreciate and grasp the message found in this lesson.

The story of Esther takes place around 480 BCE, after the Medo-Persians took over the kingdom of Babylon, after Daniel died, and after the first two of three decrees that allowed the Jewish people to return to Israel. Unfortunately, relatively few people returned to Israel during those first two decrees. We had a lot of freedom and opportunities in Medo-Persia, so the people did not want to leave the comforts available to them.

1. Who raised Esther and why?

   "In the fortress Shushan lived a Jew by the name of <u>Mordecai</u>, ... a Benjaminite. ... He was foster father to Hadassah—that is, Esther—his uncle's daughter, for she had neither father nor mother. The maiden was shapely and beautiful; and when <u>her father and mother died</u>, Mordecai adopted her as his own daughter." Esther 2:5-7

   The Bible does not say how Esther's parents died, but she became an orphan and was adopted by her cousin Mordecai. Esther's parents named her Hadassah, after a flower. Hadassah's name was changed to Esther, possibly to hide the fact that she was Jewish.

2. What was taking place in the Medo-Persian political world when Esther was young?

In the days of Ahasuerus . . . in the third year of his reign, he gave a banquet for all the officials . . . when the king was merry with wine, he ordered . . . Queen Vashti before the king wearing a royal diadem, to display her beauty . . . But Queen Vashti refused . . . The king was greatly incensed . . . Memucan declared . . . "Queen Vashti has committed an offense . . . the queen's behavior will make all wives despise their husbands . . . let a royal edict be issued . . . that Vashti shall never enter the presence of King Ahasuerus. And let Your Majesty bestow her royal state upon another who is more worthy than she . . . " The king did as Memucan proposed . . ." Esther 1:1,3,10-12,16-19,21

3. What method was devised to find a new queen?

Assemble all the beautiful young virgins at the fortress Shushan, in the harem . . . And let the maiden who pleases Your Majesty be queen instead of Vashti. Esther 2:3,4

4. Who ended up in the harem?

<u>Esther</u> too was taken into the king's palace . . . Esther did not reveal her people or her kindred, for Mordecai had told her not to reveal it. Every single day Mordecai would walk about in front of the court of the harem, to learn how Esther was faring . . . Esther 2:8,10,11

At first this might seem like an exciting opportunity for Esther, especially if we know the end of the story. But for Esther this must have been a terribly frightening ordeal. She was removed from her home, her friends, her congregation, and the freedom she knew. She was confined to a women's chamber for at least twelve months before she went in for a one-night stand with the king. If he liked her she would become a state figure for the pagan king to call on when he felt like it. If she was rejected she would spend the rest of her life locked up with the other girls in the harem. All her dreams of a loving husband, freedom of movement, and choices were gone.

5. How did the harem's supervisor, Hegai, treat Esther?

<u>The girl pleased (Hegai) and won his favor . . . and he treated her . . . with special kindness</u> . . . When the turn came for Esther . . . to go to the king, she did not ask for anything but what Hegai, the king's eunuch, guardian of the women, advised. Esther won the admiration

21. QUEEN ESTHER (ESTER)

of all who saw her. Esther 2:9,15

This account is reminiscent of Joseph's when he was sold to the Egyptians and found favor in their sight. Esther was not only beautiful but she was humble and wise. When offered anything she wanted from the women's wardrobe she only took what Hegai recommended. She could have kept anything she took and could have selfishly taken the most expensive items, yet she allowed Hegai to choose for her. Hegai knew the king and was able to choose what would please him most.

6. What happened when Esther went in to the king?

Esther was taken to King Ahasuerus . . . in the seventh year of his reign. <u>The king loved Esther more than all the other women, and she won his grace and favor more than all the virgins. So he set a royal diadem on her head and made her queen instead of Vashti.</u> The king gave a great banquet for all his officials and courtiers, "the banquet of Esther." Esther 2:16-18

The king had been looking for his queen for four years, but when Esther came into his life the search was over. We can only imagine how many other women he rejected in four years and how anxious Esther must have been as she waited for her turn. The godly character that she developed by trusting in God, being obedient to her cousin Mordecai's advise, humbly trusting Hegai's opinion, and her God-given beauty paid off. Unfortunately, the story does not end there with a "happily ever after."

7. What event nearly brought a crisis to the empire?

<u>Bigthan and Teresh, two of the king's eunuchs who guarded the threshold, became angry, and plotted to do away with King Ahasuerus.</u> Mordecai learned of it and told it to Queen Esther, and Esther reported it to the king in Mordecai's name. The matter was investigated and found to be so, and the two were impaled on stakes. Esther 2:21-23

We see God's hand protecting the king. Mordecai was in the right place at the right time and he did the right thing. In a sense we see Mordecai representing godly people of all ages who have worked with and been loyal to the nations where we have been scattered.

While this crisis was averted by Mordecai's willingness to speak up and do what was right, the big crisis for Mordecai and Esther had not even begun.

8. What series of events set the stage for the crisis Mordecai and Esther were now called to face?

> *Some time afterward, <u>King Ahasuerus promoted Haman . . . the Agagite; he advanced him and seated him higher than any of his fellow officials. All the king's courtiers in the palace gate knelt and bowed low to Haman, for such was the king's order concerning him; but Mordecai would not kneel or bow low.</u> When Haman saw that Mordecai would not kneel or bow low to him, Haman was filled with rage. But he disdained to lay hands on Mordecai alone; having been told who Mordecai's people were, <u>Haman plotted to do away with all the Jews</u> . . .* Esther 3:1-6

Haman was an Agagite of the Amalekites who had been enemies of the Jewish people since the time of Moses. During the reign of King Saul, Samuel the prophet had the king of the Amalekites, King Agag, executed for his war crimes. Now hundreds of years later the clash began again. Mordecai refused to bow, in a form of worship, to a human. Haman was not satisfied with removing only Mordecai; he wanted to annihilate all the Jewish people. While the Egyptians wanted to enslave us, and the Babylonians wanted to control us, this was the first time anyone wanted to totally annihilate us. Haman, and Adolph Hitler later, both took their cue from Satan himself, the real enemy of God's people.

While Haman is a representation of all those who have been filled with jealousy, anger, bitterness, and hatred, we see the king, at this point, representing national leaders who through the ages have allowed religious intolerance to be permitted within their realm.

9. When did Haman plan on killing all the Jewish people?

> *In the first month, that is, the month of Nisan, in the twelfth year of King Ahasuerus, pur —which means "the lot"—was cast before Haman concerning every day and every month, [until it fell on] <u>the twelfth month, that is, the month of Adar.</u>* Esther 3:7

In the twelfth year of the reign of King Ahasuerus, five years after he made Esther queen, Haman went to the religious leaders to cast the pur, or lot, to determine when he should put his plan into action. The lot fell on a date eleven months later.

10. How did Haman convince the king to kill the Jewish people?

> *Haman then said to King Ahasuerus, "<u>There is a certain people, scattered and dispersed among the other peoples in all the provinces</u>*

21. QUEEN ESTHER (ESTER)

of your realm, whose laws are different from those of any other people and who do not obey the king's laws; and it is not in Your Majesty's interest to tolerate them. If it please Your Majesty, let an edict be drawn for their destruction, and I will pay ten thousand talents of silver to the stewards for deposit in the royal treasury." Thereupon the king removed his signet ring from his hand and gave it to Haman, . . . the foe of the Jews. And the king said, "The money and the people are yours to do with as you see fit." . . . The king's scribes were summoned and a decree was issued, as Haman directed . . . written instructions were dispatched by couriers to all the king's provinces to destroy, massacre, and exterminate all the Jews, young and old, children and women, on a single day, on the thirteenth day of the twelfth month—that is, the month of Adar—and to plunder their possessions. . . . The king and Haman sat down to feast, but the city of Shushan was dumfounded. Esther 3:8-13,15

Haman didn't come out and tell the king that his plot was against the Jewish people. He merely mentioned that there was a scattered group who were different from everyone else. They were a minority and they had their own laws that were not in harmony with the laws of the land. These were the same accusations used against Daniel's friends when they would not bow down in worship to the king's statue like everyone else did.

While Mordecai was a threat to Haman's desire to be worshipped like a god, Mordecai was not a threat to the king or the kingdom. Haman tricked the king by not giving all the facts and by putting his own spin on the situation. The king gave Haman his signature ring and Haman wrote out a decree to kill all the Jewish people.

This story becomes especially of interest to us when we realize that the book of Revelation prophesies that a similar situation will happen again. The religious power described in Daniel chapter 7 and Revelation 13 will unite with the kings (nations) of the earth (see Revelation 17 and 18) and will use the nations' political power to persecute God's faithful people. . . . *He deceives those who dwell on the earth . . . he was granted power to . . . cause as many as would not worship the image of the beast to be killed. Satan was enraged . . . and went to make war with the rest . . . who keep the commandments of God and have the testimony of~* Y'shua the Messiah. Revelation 13:14,15; 12:17 NKJV.

Haman wanted to be worshipped. He commanded that anyone who would not worship according to his religious law would be killed. Again we see the parallel to Daniel's situation when the king was tricked into making a law that said that anyone who prayed, or worshipped, except the way the Persian law said to pray and worship, would be thrown into the lions' den.

11. How did the Jewish people respond to this death decree?

> *... Mordecai tore his clothes and put on sackcloth and ashes. He went through the city, crying out loudly and bitterly, until he came in front of the palace gate ... there was great mourning among the Jews, with fasting, weeping, and wailing, and everybody lay in sackcloth and ashes.* Esther 4:1-3

The people faithfully turned to Elohim in their great distress.

12. What scene transpired between Esther and Mordecai when she heard that he was in sackcloth?

> *... the queen was greatly agitated. She sent clothing for Mordecai to wear ... but he refused. Esther summoned Hathach ... and sent him to Mordecai to learn the why ... Mordecai told him ... about the money that Haman had offered to pay into the royal treasury for the destruction of the Jews. He also gave him the written text of the law ... [He bade him] show it to Esther and ... charge her to go to the king and to appeal to him and to plead with him for her people. When Hathach delivered Mordecai's message to Esther, Esther told Hathach to take back to Mordecai the following reply: "All the king's courtiers and the people of the king's provinces know that if any person, man or woman, enters the king's presence in the inner court without having been summoned, there is but one law for him—that he be put to death. Only if the king extends the golden scepter to him may he live. Now I have not been summoned to visit the king for the last thirty days."* Esther 4:4,5,7-11

What drama! Esther didn't know of the decree or why Mordecai was mourning. When he informed her he told her to go to the King and plead their case, but Esther was concerned because no one could come before the king uninvited on penalty of death! If she went, she might die. If she didn't go, her people would die!

Esther was a common citizen like the rest of the Jewish people, but was exalted to the right hand of the king and now needed to come before the king and intercede for her people at the risk of her life. Esther represents our mediator, our Messiah, who dwelt among us. The Jewish prophet Isaiah prophesied He would be called Immanuel—God with us. And yet He would also come before

21. QUEEN ESTHER (ESTER)

the Ancient of Days, as Daniel prophesied: *"One like a human being came with the clouds of heaven; He reached the Ancient of Days and was presented to Him."* Daniel 7:13

13. What happened next?

> *Mordecai had this message delivered to Esther: "Do not imagine that you, of all the Jews, will escape with your life by being in the king's palace. On the contrary, <u>if you keep silent in this crisis, relief and deliverance will come to the Jews from another quarter</u>, while you and your father's house will perish. And who knows, <u>perhaps you have attained to royal position for just such a crisis.</u>" Then Esther sent back this answer to Mordecai: "Go, assemble all the Jews who live in Shushan, and fast in my behalf; do not eat or drink for three days, night or day. I and my maidens will observe the same fast. Then <u>I shall go to the king, though it is contrary to the law; and if I am to perish, I shall perish</u>!"* Esther 4:13-16

Mordecai didn't give up. He continued to petition Esther to go before the King in the people's behalf. Esther finally surrendered and said those brave words, *"If I am to perish, I shall perish!"*

In a striking parallel, when Y'shua our Messiah knew it was time for Him to die as our sacrifice, His humanity shrank from the thought of death. He cried out to the Father, *"My soul is exceedingly sorrowful even to death ... O My Father, if it is possible, let this cup pass from Me; nevertheless, not as I will, but as You will."* Matthew 26:38,39 NKJV.

14. What happened when Esther went in before the king?

> *On the third day, Esther put on royal apparel and stood in the inner court of the king's palace ... As soon as the king saw Queen Esther standing in the court, she won his favor. <u>The king extended to Esther the golden scepter</u> which he had in his hand, and Esther approached and touched the tip of the scepter. "<u>What troubles you, Queen Esther?" the king asked her.</u> "And what is your request? Even to half the kingdom, it shall be granted you." "If it please Your Majesty," <u>Esther replied, "let Your Majesty and Haman come today to the feast that I have prepared</u> for him." The king commanded, "Tell Haman to hurry and do Esther's bidding."* Esther 5:1-5

The king accepted Esther's intrusion and held out his scepter to her. The three days of fasting and praying paid off. So far so good, but it was not over yet. She still had to convince the king not to listen to his chief advisor, Haman, and to save the Jewish people.

The king must have spent the day wondering, "What could be so important to the queen that she would risk her life for it? Why doesn't she ask me now? Why does she want Haman at the feast?"

15. During the feast what did Esther ask for?

> *... The king asked Esther, "What is your wish? ... " "My wish," replied Esther, " ... <u>let Your Majesty and Haman come to the feast which I will prepare for them; and tomorrow I will do Your Majesty's bidding.</u>"* Esther 5:6-8

It must have dramatically raised the king's anxiety to have to wait another twenty-four hours to find out what could be so important to Esther that she would risk her life over it. Perhaps that was Esther's strategy.

16. How did Haman feel after he left Esther's feast?

> *That day <u>Haman went out happy and lighthearted. But when Haman saw Mordecai in the palace gate, and Mordecai did not rise ... Haman was filled with rage</u> at him. ... He sent for his friends and his wife Zeresh, and Haman told them about his great wealth and his many sons, and all about how the king had promoted him and advanced him above the officials and the king's courtiers. "What is more," said Haman, "Queen Esther gave a feast, and besides the king she did not have anyone but me. And tomorrow too I am invited by her along with the king. Yet all this means nothing to me every time I see that Jew Mordecai sitting in the palace gate."* Esther 5:9-13

Haman is a perfect example of how hatred can destroy all the joy in our lives. Haman had everything to be thankful for: wife, children, friends, riches, possessions, honor, position, influence, power. Yet all that meant nothing as long as he held onto his hate.

Even if Haman got rid of Mordecai and all the Jewish people, the spirit of hatred would have cropped up again against someone else and would have destroyed his peace. The solution to our hatred of others is not getting rid of them; it is getting rid of the spirit of hatred. This can only be accomplished through the power of God transforming us. As we accept the Messiah's sacrificial death for our sins God's character takes over our lives. Then the hatred is replaced with love and forgiveness. (This process is reviewed several times earlier in this book. If you are still struggling with anger we encourage you to reread those chapters,

21. QUEEN ESTHER (ESTER)

especially lesson 3 and allow God to give you His victory.)

17. What plan did Haman's wife come up with?

> ... *Zeresh and all his friends said to him,* <u>*"Let a stake be put up, fifty cubits high, and in the morning ask the king to have Mordecai impaled on it.*</u> *Then you can go gaily with the king to the feast."* Esther 5:14

Their hatred and lust for power was so great that they could not wait until the end of the year to kill Mordecai. They planned to kill him that very day by hanging him seventy-five feet in the air!

18. How did Adonai intervene to save Mordecai?

> *That night, sleep deserted the king, and he ordered the book of records, the annals, to be brought; and it was read to the king. There it was found written that Mordecai had denounced Bigthana and Teresh ... who had plotted to do away with King Ahasuerus. "What honor or advancement has been conferred on Mordecai for this?" the king inquired. "Nothing at all has been done for him," replied the king's servants ... Haman had just entered the outer court of the royal palace, to speak to the king about having Mordecai impaled on the stake he had prepared for him. Haman entered, and the king asked him, "What should be done for a man whom the king desires to honor?" Haman said to himself, "Whom would the king desire to honor more than me?" So Haman said to the king, "For the man whom the king desires to honor, let royal garb which the king has worn be brought, and a horse on which the king has ridden and on whose head a royal diadem has been set; and let the attire and the horse be put in the charge of one of the king's noble courtiers. And let the man whom the king desires to honor be attired and paraded on the horse through the city square, while they proclaim before him: This is what is done for the man whom the king desires to honor!" "Quick, then!" said the king to Haman. "Get the garb and the horse, as you have said, and do this to Mordecai the Jew ..." So Haman took the garb and the horse and arrayed Mordecai and paraded him through the city square ... Then Mordecai returned to the king's gate, while Haman hurried home, his head covered in mourning.* Esther 6:1-4,6-12

The king could not sleep that night, no doubt wondering what Esther was willing to risk her life for. Since he could not sleep he decided to have his servant read to him from the court record. Providentially his servant read about the time that Mordecai saved the king's life. And just as Haman walked in the door of the palace to ask that Mordecai be killed, the king learned that nothing had been done to reward Mordecai. Before Haman could open his mouth the king asked him what should be done for the man whom he wished to honor. This is where the story gets funny. Haman was so caught up in himself that he couldn't think that it would be possible for the king to want to honor anyone except himself. So he suggested that the man to be honored be treated like a king wearing a royal robe and riding on a royal horse. It would have been great to see Haman's face when the King told him to go and lead Mordecai around the city announcing loudly, "This is what is done for the man whom the king desires to honor!"

Although God's name is not mentioned in the book of Esther, we see His powerful providential hand moving behind the scenes. There are too many coincidences for it to be accidental. For some reason Esther did not tell the king her request at the first feast. The King couldn't sleep. The portion about Mordecai was read to the King. He noticed that nothing was done for Mordecai. And then Haman came in, just at that moment. God's timing is perfect.

19. What happened during Esther's second feast?

> *... The king again asked Esther ... "What is your wish, Queen Esther? It shall be granted you ..." Queen Esther replied: "If Your Majesty will do me the favor, and if it pleases Your Majesty, let my life be granted me as my wish, and my people as my request. For we have been sold, my people and I, to be destroyed, massacred, and exterminated. Had we only been sold as bondmen and bondwomen, I would have kept silent; for the adversary is not worthy of the king's trouble." Thereupon King Ahasuerus demanded of Queen Esther, "Who is he and where is he who dared to do this?" "The adversary and enemy," replied Esther, "is this evil Haman!" And Haman cringed in terror before the king and the queen. The king, in his fury, left the wine feast for the palace garden, while Haman remained to plead with Queen Esther for his life; for he saw that the king had resolved to destroy him. When the king returned from the palace garden to the banquet room, Haman was lying prostrate on the couch on which Esther reclined. "Does he mean," cried the king, "to ravish the queen in my own palace?" No sooner did these words leave the king's lips than Haman's face was covered. ... One of the eunuchs in attendance on the king, said, "What is more, a stake is standing at Haman's house, fifty cubits high, which Haman made for Mordecai—the man whose*

21. QUEEN ESTHER (ESTER)

words saved the king." "Impale him on it!" the king ordered. So they impaled Haman on the stake which he had put up for Mordecai . . . Esther 7:2-10

Haman's suggestion to have himself wear the king's garments and ride on the king's horse could indicate that Haman's greed for power would not have stopped with the destruction of the Jewish people. He was really coveting the throne itself. This is what Satan desires, as the Scriptures say regarding him; *"How are you fallen from heaven, O Shining One, son of Dawn! How are you felled to earth, O vanquisher of nations! Once you thought in your heart, "I will climb to the sky; higher than the stars of God I will set my throne . . . I will match the Most High." Instead, you are brought down . . . to the bottom of the Pit.* Isaiah 14:12-15

Satan is not done yet; he will once more try to use human instruments to destroy all of God's faithful people. But God will bring him down! God will exalt His people. *"Humble yourselves in the sight of the LORD and He will lift you up."* James 4:10 KJV. Esther, as the advocate for the Jewish people, pled before the king just as our Messiah is interceding in our behalf right now.

20. What did the king do for Mordecai and Esther?

> *King Ahasuerus gave the property of Haman, the enemy of the Jews, to Queen Esther. Mordecai presented himself to the king, for Esther had revealed how he was related to her. The king slipped off his ring, which he had taken back from Haman, and gave it to Mordecai . . . The king said; "you may further write with regard to the Jews as you see fit . . ."* Esther 8:1,2,8

21. After the deliverance of the Jewish people what did Mordecai tell the people to do?

> *Mordecai . . . sent dispatches to all the Jews . . . charging them to observe the fourteenth and fifteenth days of Adar . . . as days of feasting and merrymaking, and as an occasion for sending gifts to one another and presents to the poor. . . . Haman had cast pur—that is, the lot . . . for that reason these days were named Purim, after pur.* Esther 9:20-22,24-26

It is very interesting to note that there are several remarkable parallels between the account of Esther and last day events. Let's look at them in detail.

You will remember in lesson 18 we learned that the prophet Daniel was given a vision in which Medo-Persia is depicted as a ram with two horns. A ram is an adult male lamb. Revelation 13:11 describes a lamb-like beast with two horns. ***Then I saw another beast coming up out of the earth, he had <u>two horns like a lamb</u> and <u>spoke like a dragon</u> and he exercises all the authority of the first beast in his presence, and <u>causes the earth and those who dwell in it to worship the first beast</u>, whose deadly wound was healed. <u>He performs great signs</u>, so that he even <u>makes fire come down from heaven</u> on the earth in the sight of men. And <u>he deceives those who dwell on the earth</u>— by those signs which he was granted to do in the sight of the beast, <u>telling those who dwell on the earth to make an image to the beast</u> who was wounded by the sword and lived. He was granted power to give breath to the image of the beast, that the image of the beast should both speak and cause as many as would not worship the image of the beast to be killed. He causes all, both small and great, rich and poor, free and slave, to receive a mark on their right hand or on their foreheads, and that <u>no one may buy or sell except one who has the mark</u> or the name of the beast, or the number of his name.*** Revelation 13:11-17

For many years Medo-Persia was very good for the Jewish people, granting us religious liberty; but overnight it quickly turned and began to act like a dragon. The two-horned lamb in Revelation 13 also changes from being lamb-like to acting like a dragon. Lamb-like represents a nation that is "Messiah-like" with good godly attributes such as being fair, just, and giving freedoms. Dragon-like is being "Satan-like" with such attributes as force and oppression. *(. . . he had two horns like a lamb and spoke like a dragon.* Revelation 13:11 NKJV.)

Another parallel between the Medo-Persian kingdom and the end time lamb-like nation is that they both dominate world events of their time. We see the end time lamb-like nation coming up out of the earth (verse 11), an unpopulated, previously barren area. We read that it comes up around the time the first beast received its deadly wound (verse 12). The first beast is described in the first part of Revelation chapter 13 and is the beast you identified from Daniel 7 in lesson 17 of this book. Thus, this lamb-like nation comes up after the papal power received its deadly wound of 1798 (see lesson 17). It eventually works closely with the first beast in influencing world affairs. And it uses economic sanctions (not being able to buy or sell—verse 17) against those who do not cooperate with its goals.

Just as Haman demanded Mordecai to bow down in worship and reverence

21. QUEEN ESTHER (ESTER)

him the way the other Medo-Persians did, this peaceful end-time internationally powerful nation will surprisingly turn from being peaceful and allowing people to worship according to the dictates of their conscience to commanding everyone to worship the same way. Just as Mordecai did not follow the man-made commandment regarding worship, which would have caused him to break God's commandments, God's faithful people in the last days will not obey a man-made form of worship if it means breaking one of God's commandments.

It is interesting to note that the political worship decree that affected Esther and the political worship decree that affected Daniel were signed into law by their respective kings without either king fully realizing the end results of what they signed. In the same way, it is possible that this lamb-like, religious liberty and freedom loving nation can turn overnight and make laws like a dragon forcing everyone to worship a certain way without those who signed the law fully realizing how it will affect those who, like Mordecai and Daniel, keep God's commandments.

For example, some have reasoned that acts of terrorism, or natural disasters, or a cataclysmic financial depression could cause people and legislators alike to feel that this nation is being punished for rejecting God. In an attempt to please God and bring about national unity, some could feel compelled to enact a law that would force everyone to worship God on Sunday. If that sounds like an outrageous example, recall how history demonstrates that that very situation has taken place time and time again. Roman Emperor Constantine enacted a law in 321 that stated, "On the venerable day of the Sun let the magistrates and people residing in cities rest."[1] The day was called "the venerable day of the Sun" because it was on this day that those of pagan beliefs worshipped the sun. This is where we get the term Sun-day. In Emperor Constantine's law there was no restriction against people resting on the Sabbath. It only stated that people were to rest on the venerable day of the sun. Those who kept God's Sabbath holy by resting on Saturday found it a financial hardship to have to rest on another day as well. Just a few years after Emperor Constantine's law was signed the Council of Laodicea decreed, "Christians shall not Judaize and be idle on Saturday (the Sabbath), but shall work on that day; but the Lord's Day *(Which they incor-*

---

1 (Codex Justininus, lib. 3 tit. 12, 3; translated in History of the Christian Church, by Philip Schaff (Scribners, 1902 ed.) vol.3, p 380. Quoted in Bible Readings for the Home p.326 1980 Ed.)

rectly identified as Sunday. Ed.) they shall especially honour . . . if however they are found Judaizing, they shall be shut out . . . "² It did not take long to go from enforcing a man-made day of worship to the next step of restricting the free exercise of religion. Originally Christians rested on the seventh-day biblical Sabbath. Originally all Christians were Jewish and for the first several decades Jewish people were the majority of believers in Y'shua so seventh-day Sabbath observance was natural. Besides the Jewish heritage of Christianity early Christians used the Bible as their source of instruction. It was not until around 100 CE that some Christians began to rest on Sunday. The Bar Kokhba revolt of 132-135 CE resulted in the Romans oppressing and suppressing Judaism even more. At that time Christianity was still considered a sect of Judaism and some Christians thought it pragmatic to distance themselves from Judaism. One demonstrative way was to cease resting on Sabbath and to start resting on Sunday with the other people of the Roman Empire.

Throughout the dark ages "the medieval decrees and canons of popes and councils concerning Sunday observance were enforced by the civil power."³ Notice that the popes and councils for over one thousand years used the civil powers to enforce their decrees. That is exactly how religious laws were enforced in the books of Daniel and Esther. Since the religious leaders admittedly did not have a "thus saith the LORD" they used man-made laws and the civil police and military forces to give weight to their Sunday laws. A quote from the American Catholic Quarterly Review will demonstrate this fact.

"For ages all Christian nations looked to the Catholic Church, and, as we have seen, the various states enforced by law her ordinances as to worship and cessation of Labor on Sunday. Protestantism, in discarding the authority of the church, has no good reason for its Sunday theory, and ought logically, to keep Saturday as the Sabbath."

"The State, in passing laws for the due Sanctification of Sunday, is unwittingly acknowledging the authority of the Catholic Church, and carrying out more or less faithfully its prescriptions."

"The Sunday, as a day of the week set apart for the obligatory public worship of Almighty God to be sanctified by a suspension of all servile labor, trade,

2 (Charles Joseph Hefele, A History of the Councils of the Church. vol. 2 (1896 English Ed.) Quoted in ibid p. 328).
3 (See The New Schaff-Herzog Encyclopedia of Religious Knowledge. Vol. 11. p 147. Quoted in ibid p. 359).

and worldly avocations and by exercises of devotion, is purely a creation of the Catholic church."[4]

History demonstrates over and over again that it is not long after a government begins to establish religion that it takes the next step of restricting the free exercise of religious minorities. And in one way or another we are all minorities. One thing that has made America great is the concept of equal freedom and equal rights for everyone. The Untied States votes its legislators into office by a democratically voted majority, but it functions as a republic with those legislators enacting laws based on their representation of the freedom and rights of all the people. U.S. laws are not supposed to be made for the benefit of the majority while suppressing the rights of the minorities. U.S. laws are supposed to represent the rights of all the citizens. This concept of fundamental rights to all people is an important distinction that made the United States different from old Europe.

It is clear that not everyone agrees with the concept of equal rights for all people. Another Catholic source stated, "The Roman Catholic Church, convinced, through its divine prerogatives, of being the only true church, must demand the right to freedom for herself alone, because such a right can only be possessed by truth, never by error. As to other religions, . . . she will require that by legitimate means they shall not be allowed to propagate false doctrine. Consequently, in a state where the majority of the people are Catholic, the church will require that legal existence be denied to error, and that if religious minorities actually exist, they shall have only a de facto existence without opportunity to spread their beliefs."[5] This is a shocking and an alarming statement, to say the least. What does this mean for Jewish and non-Jewish people who choose to keep God's Sabbath holy? What does this mean for literally every religious group? The quote speaks for itself; we would be considered heretics at worst, second class citizens at best.

The Pilgrims fled from Europe to America to get away from a compromised form of Christianity that was managed by the government and a government that was controlled by the church. They fled not only from Catholic countries. Protestant countries, such as England, also persecuted minorities and were just as

---

4 (TheAmerican Catholic Quarterly Review, January, 1883, pp.152, 139. Quoted in ibid p. 328)
5 (F. Cavalli, S. J., in La Civilta Cattolica (a Jesuit organ published at Rome), April, 1948, quoted in an editorial in The Christian Century, June 23, 1948, p. 623. Quoted in ibid p. 362)

intolerant. Yet even after fleeing such intolerance early Americans began copying what they had learned in Europe. They passed laws enforcing the observance of Sunday. In 1610 a law was enacted in Virginia which stated, "Every man and woman shall repair in the morning to the divine service, and sermons preached upon the Sabbath day, and in the afternoon to divine service and catechizing, upon pain for the first fault to lose their provisions and the allowance for the whole week following, for the second to lose the said allowance and also be whipped, and for the third to suffer death."[6] (The Sabbath day mentioned here was a reference to Sunday). It is shocking that the third offense was punished with death! And that was in America! Notice that this law was not just for Christians. It stated, "Every man and woman shall . . ." We might think that that could never happen here again. We now have a Constitution and the First Amendment says, "Congress shall make no law respecting an establishment of religion, or prohibiting the free exercise thereof." But remember, even the kings of Medo-Persia were shocked to find out that the laws they signed almost caused the death of their nobleman Daniel and their Queen Esther. Note, the Bible says it is a peaceful, lamb-like nation that surprisingly turns and speaks like a dragon, forcing all to worship the decrees of the papal power.

We should remember that Satan was behind all of these man-made religious/political laws that caused the deaths of millions of people over the last 2,000 years, not the humans who wrote, signed, and enforced these laws. They were deceived into thinking they were doing the right thing by doing it. Y'shua Himself said, *". . . The time is coming that whoever kills you will think that he offers God service."* John 16:2 NKJV. Satan *"was enraged . . . and went to make war with the rest . . . who keep the commandments of God and have the testimony of"*~ Y'shua the Messiah. Revelation 12:17 NKJV.

In the Constitutional amendment quoted above we notice that the first part states that Congress cannot establish a religion and the second part states that Congress cannot stop the free exercise of religion. It is interesting that in the book of Daniel we see both of these foundational principles were trampled. In chapter 3, before the golden statue, everyone was commanded to worship in exactly the same way. The government of Babylon established and enforced its form of worship. In chapter 6 the Medo-Persian government restricted the

---

6 (For the Colony in Virginea Britannia, Lavves. Morall and Martiall & c. in Peter Force. Tracts Relating to the Colonies in North America (Washington 1844), Vol. 3 No. 2, p. 10. Quoted in ibid)

21. QUEEN ESTHER (ESTER)

free exercise of religion by telling Daniel he could not worship the way he was accustomed to, but had to worship the way their man-made law dictated. (See lesson 16 and/or Daniel chapters 3 & 6). Could it be that the last day "Babylon-like" power, mentioned in Daniel 7 and in the first part of Revelation 13, will unite with the last day "lamb-like" nation to force its form of worship and restrict those who choose to follow God's commandments from doing so? The books of Daniel, Revelation, and Esther seem to indicate they will. Political leaders will unite with religious leaders to enforce worship on a man-made sabbath and will restrict people from obeying God and worshipping Him on His seventh-day Sabbath.

But we have nothing to fear for the future except if we forget how Elohim has led in the past. God sustained Daniel, Esther, the Jewish people, and His truth until this time and He will sustain us until the end. Mordecai was not rewarded when he first demonstrated his loyalty to the king, but later. Just when the enemy was poised to take Mordecai's life the king opened the books and determined to reward Mordecai. As we read in lesson 18, the King of the Universe has opened the books of heaven and the time of our reward is at hand! As Esther came before the king just in time to save the people, one like the Son of Man has come before the Ancient of Days to stand in our behalf! While God is never late, he is rarely early. He is always right on time.

The Messiah will return right on time to deliver us from the coming trial. He will raise our loved ones from the grave and together with them we will meet the Messiah in the air. From there He will bring us to the heavenly Jerusalem to be with Him where we will reign with Him. The wicked, like Haman, will be destroyed by the brightness of His coming and the earth will experience its sabbatical rest. At the end of the thousand year Sabbath the heavenly Jerusalem will descend to this earth with us—God's people—inside. Our Messiah will descend before us, splitting the Mount of Olives in two and flattening a place for the Holy City. The wicked will be resurrected to receive the execution of their judgment. They will awake with the same selfishness, anger, and hatred with which they went down into the grave. They, with Satan's help, will attack the city to take it over, but God will bring fire down from heaven, turning this old sin stained, polluted earth into a lake of fire. The fire will purify everything and destroy all the remnants of sin and sinners. God will recreate the new heavens and the new earth out of the ashes. It will be as beautiful as the original Garden of Eden. God will then open the gates of the New Jerusalem and we will enjoy the earth made new for all eternity. (See 1 Thessalonians 4:16,17; 2 Thessalonians 1:8; 2:8; Jeremiah 25:33; 4:23-26; Rev. 20:4-9; 21:2; 2 Peter 3:7-13; Malachi 4:3)

Why have all faces turned pale? Ah, that day is awesome; there is none like it! It is a time of trouble for Jacob, but he shall be delivered from it. In that day—declares the L<small>ORD</small> of Hosts—I will break the yoke from off your neck and I will rip off your bonds. . . . they shall serve the L<small>ORD</small> their God and David, the king whom I will raise up for them. Jeremiah 30:6-9

At that time, the great prince Michael who stands beside the sons of your people, will appear. It will be a time of trouble, the like of which has never been since the nation came into being. At that time, your people will be rescued, all who are found inscribed in the book. Many of those that sleep in the dust of the earth will awake, some to eternal life, others to reproaches, to everlasting abhorrence. And the knowledgeable will be radiant like the bright expanse of sky, and <u>those who lead the many to righteousness will be like the stars forever and ever.</u> Dan. 12:1-3

By the way, Esther means star! Be a star today. Now is the time to be leading many to righteousness before the final events of this world's history come upon us and we experience *the time of trouble, the like of which has never been since the nation came into being.* Let us awake to the time that is at hand. Right now consecrate your life to the King of the Universe. In light of what lays before us, is your faith in God strong enough to believe in God's promises to the point, like Abraham, where you are willing to surrender all for Him? Is your faith in God strong enough to withstand rejection, trials, and hardships like Jacob, Joseph, and Moses did? Is your faith in God strong enough to step out in faith and live a lifestyle in harmony with God's word? Is your faith in God strong enough to stand against temptation, peer pressure, and intolerance like Daniel, Esther, and Mordecai did? Is your faith in God strong enough to love God with all your heart, soul, mind, and strength and to love your neighbor, even your enemy, as yourself? Right now stop and ask Adonai Elohim, L<small>ORD</small> God, to fill you with faith. Ask Him to remove from you, through the sacrifice of the Messiah, all weaknesses in your character. Ask Him to fill you with the Ruach Hakadosh, the Holy Spirit, to empower you to stand strong in the L<small>ORD</small>.

21. QUEEN ESTHER (ESTER)
REVIEW הזרה

1. When there was a plot to kill the king, Mordecai:
   a. Decided it was none of his business.
   b. Helped the murderers so he could get his niece back.
   c. Sent a message to Queen Esther reporting the plot

2. Mordecai would not bow down to Haman because:
   a. Haman did not ask nicely.
   b. He did not want to break one of the Ten Commandments.
   c. Mordecai did not like Haman

3. The king agreed to allow Haman to write a law to kill the Jewish people because:
   a. It was easier than trying to divorce Esther.
   b. He did not like Mordecai.
   c. He didn't know who the law would affect. He was only told it was a scattered people whose laws were different.

4. When Mordecai told Esther she must go before the king and plead for her people she:
   a. Did not want to go at first because she could be killed for going before the king without being called.
   b. Got to the point were she determined she would go and if she perished she perished.
   c. Prayed and fasted with her maids and told Mordecai and the Jewish people to pray and fast as well.
   d. All of the above.

5. After the first feast with Esther, Haman:
   a. Was happy and lighthearted.
   b. Became angry when he saw Mordecai.
   c. Determined to kill Mordecai as soon as possible.
   d. All of the above.

6. Prophetically, Mordecai might be likened to:
   a. Jewish people, and all people down through the ages, who have followed God with all their hearts, souls, and minds.
   b. Stubborn employees.
   c. Disobedient servants.

7. Prophetically, Queen Esther might be likened to:
   a. The Messiah who intercedes for us.
   b. Orphan girls who make it big in life.
   c. All the queens of the earth.

8. Prophetically, Haman might be likened to:
   a. Satan and all groups that demand and force worship.
   b. Mean bosses.
   c. People with ego trips.

9. Prophetically, the king might be likened to:
   a. Political leaders who are willing to use their military and police powers to enforce man-made laws of worship.
   b. Drunken husbands who divorce their wives.
   c. Polygamists.

10. In the last days of earth's history:
    a. Satan will try to destroy God's people.
    b. Intolerant religious majorities will unite with political powers and persecute religious minorities who want to keep God's commandments and have faith in Y'shua.
    c. God will intervene and deliver His people.
    d. All of the above.

21. QUEEN ESTHER (ESTER)

The story of Esther is just one episode in the continual battle that Satan wages against all who desire to faithfully worship and serve God. Ben Blatt was a driver for a large company. He worked hard, delivered his packages on time, was friendly with the customers, and met all the job requirements. Yet the company refused to permit him to take Saturdays off to accommodate his Sabbath observance. He was written up for refusing to work on Sabbath, and was eventually fired. When pressured by the federal government's civil rights agency, the EEOC, his employer agreed to put Ben back to work, but did not put him back as a driver. Instead, they made him unload the bulkiest, heaviest freight. This was the worst job in the company, and the lowest entry-level job. It was humiliating and backbreaking work. Even in this job, Ben was required to work Friday nights, with no accommodation for the fact that Sabbath begins at sundown on Friday.

Ben was out of work for more than three years. At first, companies refused to hire him because he had been fired from his previous job. Then, they wouldn't hire him because he had been out of work so long. His unemployment benefits ran out. He was unable to support his son in college, to make his car payments, or to contribute to the support of his wife, whose meager salary supported them both. He became depressed and despondent.

Eventually, Ben and His lawyer, Alan Reinach, prevailed in his court case and won a large out-of-court settlement on the eve of the trial. He decided to leave Los Angeles and move to Florida. Amazingly, ten days after settling near Tampa he found a good job where he is well liked, has good pay and benefits, and best of all, he doesn't have to work on Sabbath.

Ben is not alone, nor is he unique. He had the courage to stand up for God, like Esther, and to be faithful no matter what the consequences. He paid a high price. The enemy tried to discourage him, and succeeded for a time. He was out of work, out of money, but he was not out of God's love and care. God sustained Ben during this time, and brought him out of darkness and into the path of blessing. There are many Ben Blatts in this world, who endure suffering because of their faith. Around the world believers are still persecuted and subject to death for their faith in God. Even in America those who choose to follow God, no matter what, may suffer intense discrimination. But God does not abandon His children. You can trust God, no matter what!

TRADITIONS

Purim

The feast of Purim is a joyous occasion that celebrates God's deliverance as recorded in the book of Esther in the Bible. It is celebrated each year on the 14th and 15th days of the Hebrew month of Adar, which usually falls in February or March.

During Purim we eat a cookie called Hamantashen. Hamantashens are triangular in shape and are filled with jam. According to some traditions the triangle shape represents the shape of Haman's hat. Noisemakers called groggers are rattled in order to drown out the sound of Haman's name during the reading of the scroll, or megillah, of Esther. During Purim people usually dress up in costumes and have a lot of fun. Although we traditionally dress up in costumes, Purim is not a Jewish Halloween. Purim is about as different from Halloween as butterflies are from bats.

Purim is a celebration of yet another time in history when we allowed our walk with God to become too infrequent and impersonal; another time when the people of this world tried to destroy us; and another time when God intervened as we sought Him in prayer for deliverance. History repeats itself. Not much changes except the dates on the calendar and the names of the people God uses.

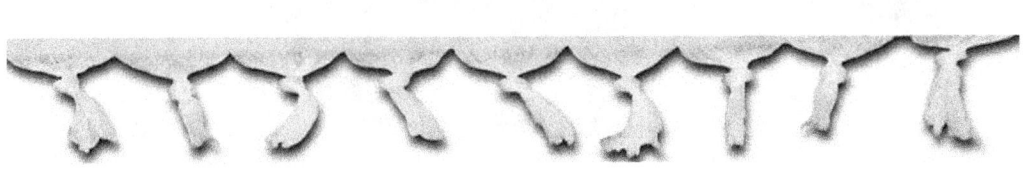

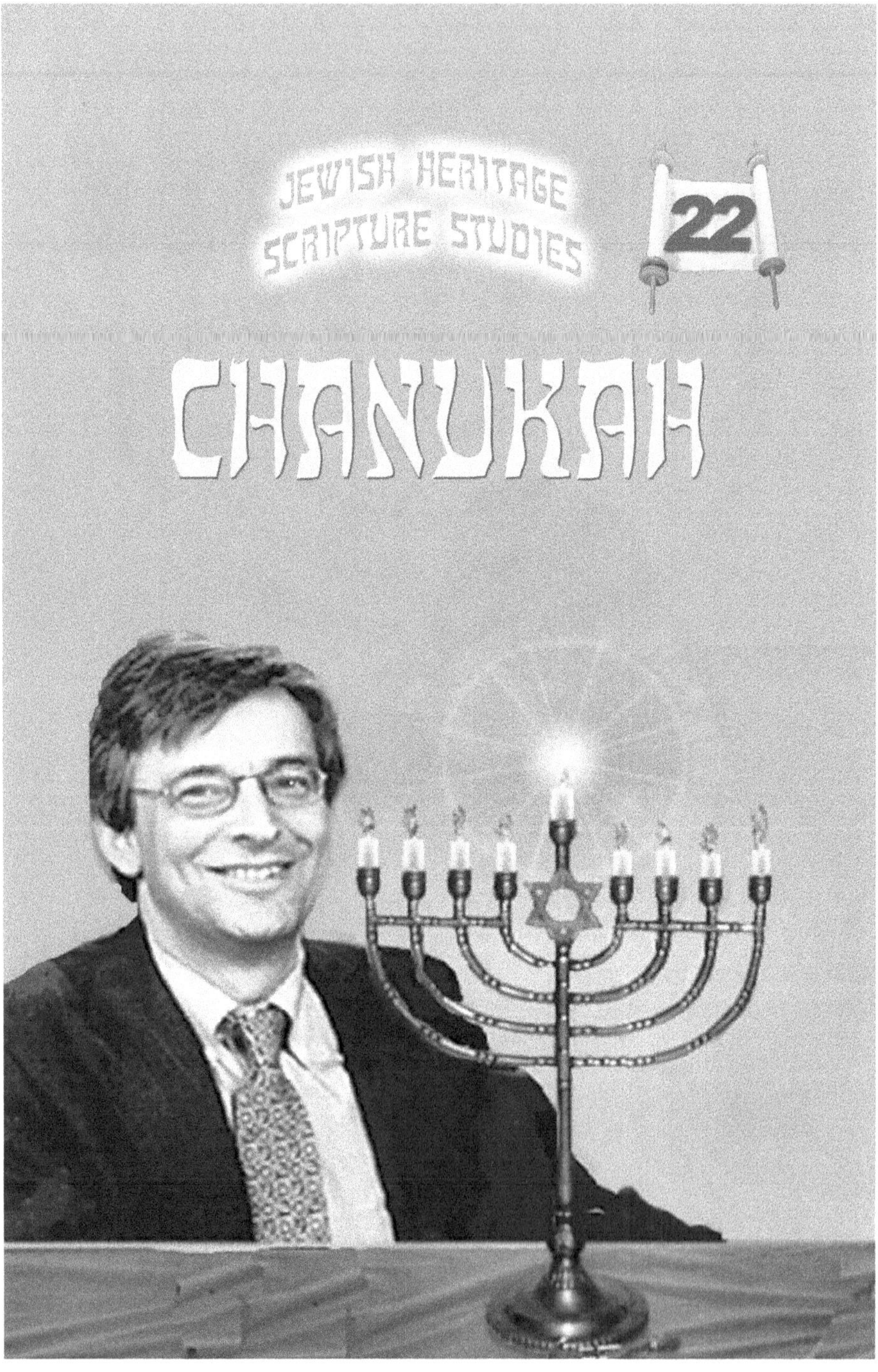
JEWISH HERITAGE
SCRIPTURE STUDIES
22
CHANUKAH

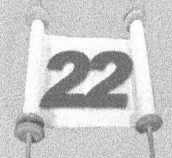

22. CHANUKAH

3. Why do some menorahs, like the one standing in front of the Knesset (parliament building) in Israel, have seven branches while the Chanukah menorah has nine branches?

    The seven-branched menorahs are reminiscent of the Sanctuary menorah that Elohim commanded should have seven branches on it. To answer why the Chanukah menorah has 9 branches we first need to answer the next question.

4. Why is Chanukah celebrated for eight days?

    The historical book 1 Maccabees states that they celebrated the dedication of the altar for eight days without specifically saying why they did it for eight days. The Talmud states that there was only enough oil to burn for one night, but that the oil in the menorah burned for eight nights.

The Talmud story may be true, but there is a biblical reason as well. The word Chanukah means dedication. They had re-dedicated the Temple, thus they celebrated the dedication, or chanukah. As we look in the Bible we see over and over again that eight days were used as the time period for dedicating, cleansing, or consecrating. A boy is dedicated and circumcised on the eighth day of his life (Genesis 17:12; Lev. 12:3.) Before a person with leprosy or a person with a discharge could be pronounced clean they had to wait eight days (Lev. 14:1-10; 15:13,14.) Animals had to be eight days old before they could be an offering to the LORD (Lev. 22:27, Ex. 22:30.) The first two Holy Days of the biblical calendar, Passover and the Feast of Unleavened Bread, combine to last eight days (Lev. 23:4,5). The last Holy Day of the biblical calendar, the Feast of Tabernacles, lasts eight days (Lev. 23:39). When Solomon dedicated the first permanent Jewish Temple the celebration lasted for eight days (2 chronicles 7:9.) In the vision given to Ezekiel of a temple of God's designing it was to be dedicated for eight days (Ezekiel 43:26,27). Thus, there is some precedent for the Maccabees wishing to dedicate the new altar and renewed Temple for eight days.

The Sanctuary menorah had seven branches because that is how God told us to make it. Chanukah is celebrated for eight days because dedications in the Bible often lasted eight days, especially in relation to dedicating the Sanctuary altar, and because of the story of the miracle of the oil lasting throughout the dedication period. But why does the Chanukah menorah have 9 candles? It traditionally has eight candles all at the same height and one candle that is either higher or stands apart from the others. This extra candle is called the shamash candle and is used to light the other candles. Shamash means servant, thus this candle that lights the other candles is the servant candle. Y'shua made some interesting statements that have application here. Y'shua said He came to serve, that He made Himself a servant. He also said He was the light of the world (John 8:1 and at another time He said those who believe in Him were the light of the world (Matthew 5:14). How can He be the light of the world and those who believe in Him also be the light of the world? Just as the shamash candle is the original light and is used to light the other candles, Y'shua is the original Servant and the original Light that came to serve us and to light us up with His love and power. We have no light of our own; we shine only because He lights us on fire for Him. (Matthew 20:28; 5:14; John 1:9; 8:12; 9:5; 12:46). The Chanukah menorah has 9 branches because the eight lower branches stand for the eight days of Chanukah and the ninth branch is for the shamash or servant candle which represents Y'shua the Messiah.

5. Where in the Bible is Chanukah mentioned?

Chanukah is not mentioned in the Torah or in the Tanak. It is mentioned once in the second part of the Bible in the Gospel of John 10:22,23. It says, *"It was the Feast of Dedication in Jerusalem, and it was winter. And Y'shua walked in the Temple, in Solomon's porch."* Complete Jewish Bible. The Feast of Dedication is the Feast of Chanukah. While Y'shua was standing in the Temple some people asked Him if He was the Messiah. He answered in the affirmative and said He and His Father were one. Some of the people who did not believe that He was the Messiah picked up stones to stone Him to death because the Torah states that is what was to be done to someone who blasphemed the name of the Lord by claiming to be equal with God or having the prerogatives of God, or by claiming to be God (Lev. 24:16). Stoning Y'shua was attempted several times but was never carried out. That is because He was not blaspheming the name of the Lord by claiming He was the Messiah and thus one with the Father. He was stating the truth. Y'shua was not stoned to death but He was hung from a wooden cross, from tree branches. The Torah states that is what was to be done to someone who becomes cursed (Deut. 21:23). Y'shua became cursed for us; He took our curse upon Himself as the Jewish prophet Isaiah stated: It is their punishment that he *bears . . . he bore the guilt of many and made intercession for sinners.* Isaiah 53:11,12

22. CHANUKAH

During the years of 1992 and 1993 in Billings, Montana there was a growing number of violent prejudice-related incidents and crimes committed against various minority groups. Then on December 2, 1993 "someone twisted by hate" (as the local newspaper referred to him) threw a brick through five-year-old Isaac Schnitzer's bedroom window, which had a Chanukah menorah decorating it. The glass shattered all over Isaac's bed, but fortunately he was in another room at the time. When Margaret MacDonald read about the act of violence in the newspaper she phoned her pastor and told him her idea of encouraging others to make paper menorahs to hang in their windows as a demonstration of their stand for freedom and against prejudice. Her pastor called several other pastors to enlist their support and by the end of the week there were hundreds of menorahs hanging in windows throughout the town. On December 7th The Billings Gazette published a picture of a menorah so people could cut it out and hang it in their windows. Local businesses passed out paper menorahs and one business put up a billboard demonstrating its stand against hate.

But the violence did not stop. Some of the churches and people that put up menorahs had their windows smashed or shot at. The violence only increased the resolutions of the people of Billings to stand against it. Soon there were 6,000 paper menorahs hanging on windows. The violence began to subside. Throughout 1994 solidarity with the Jewish people continued to be demonstrated by their non-Jewish friends and neighbors of Billings, Montana. May we, by God's power, be as resolute about standing against sin and evil in all of its forms and stand for truth and righteousness with love and mercy. *"Grace and truth have met together; justice and peace have kissed each other. Truth springs up from the earth, and justice looks down from heaven. Adonai will also grant prosperity: our land will yield its harvest. Justice will walk before him and make his footsteps a path."* Psalm 85:11-14 (CJB)

Fortunately, in many parts of the world today we have the liberty to worship God according to His Word. But an interesting thing is happening as in the days when the Greek rulers where trying to Hellenize the people with the Greek culture. Today, as then, some who have the opportunity and freedom to worship God are giving in to the secular culture of this age and neglecting the reading and following of the Holy Scriptures, the Word of Elohim. Today, as then, some take for granted the privilege we have to choose to follow God freely. History repeats itself and the Scriptures are clear that the freedoms we are experiencing today are fragile and will some day be taken from us. Now is the time to be absorbing God's Word while we have the ability to freely do so. Now is the time to be seeking God with all our heart, mind, and strength. Now is the time to accept Y'shua's substitution for our sins. Today is the day to allow the Spirit of God to fill our lives to empower us to live for Him. Let Y'shua, the shamash candle, light your life on fire with His love and zeal right now.

Beau, as he likes to be called, had a rough life. His full name is Mephibosheth Boruchschomer. His first name is the same as one of the grandson's of the first king of Israel, who became lame at the age of five when his nursemaid fell while holding him. The nursemaid was running for fear because she had just heard the news that Mephibosheth's father and grandfather had died together in battle. Eventually, the Mephibosheth of the Bible was invited to eat at King David's table all the days of his life.

Mephibosheth, in Hebrew, means dispeller of shame. Beau's last name, in Hebrew, means blessed keeper. In some ways Beau's life parallels the meaning of his names and that of the original Mephibosheth's.

Beau was adopted at birth. He never felt fully accepted or equal in his home. He was abused and felt like a second class citizen to his brother. When he became an adult he joined the military and fought in two Middle East wars. Over the years he went through over 25 surgeries and at times was lame, using leg braces, crutches, or a wheel chair. There were several times that doctors said he would not recover, but amazingly he did.

After serving in the military Beau met a young lady, fell in love, and married. Yet, just weeks after their marriage Beau was hospitalized again. While he was in one wing of the hospital his wife had to be hospitalized in another wing where she died without Beau's knowledge. Beau was devastated. For some time he wandered around questioning why he suffered so. He struggled to believe there was a God of love. He struggled to find purpose to life. Many times he just wanted to die.

Providentially Beau came in contact with the Beth-El Shalom congregation and he studied the very lessons you have just read. Over the years, slowly

22. CHANUKAH

at times and amid some set backs, his faith was strengthened and he found peace, purpose, and fulfillment in life. He became active in helping others and sharing God's love with others. The shame Beau experienced in his early life was dispelled and he became a blessed keeper of God's word.

After reading the amazing stories of individuals from Bible times until today who have experienced God's power in their lives you no doubt have been inspired to want to have a similar experience. Maybe you, like Beau, are struggling between what the Bible says on certain topics and what you have previously heard or believed. Like Beau you will find that putting God's Word first is always the best and safest course.

It is my sincere prayer that in discovering God's Word and God's plan for your life and for this world you have discovered true shalom, true peace. It is my prayer that your discovery is not just taking place in your mind but that it is also transforming your life and the lives of those around you.

Shalom alechem—Peace unto you.

More great books available from

JEWISH HERITAGE

visit www.Jewishheritage.net

Ulitmate Passover DVD:
This powerful docu-drama will take you on a journey from Egypt to the Promised land. Filmed on location the scenes cut from the first Passover in Egypt to a Jerusalem Passover 2,000 years ago to a modern Passover. 45 min. Many extras.

Source of Peace:
Has your well run dry? Are you looking for something better than what you have been experiencing in life. Found out about the never ending source of peace in this beautifully profound book.

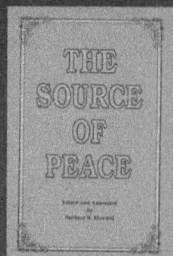

Isreal's Captivity and Restoration:
Travel through time with Israel from the time of King Solomon through to the greatest king of Israel. Many insights from our history will spring forth as we see them apply to today.

L'Chayim - To Life:
A stimulating book that will open new vistas, and bring exciting rewards. This book expands and deepens the principles learned in the Jewish Heritage Scriputre Studies. 451 pages

More great books available from
JEWISH HERITAGE

visit www.Jewishheritage.net

Steps to Shalom:
In our fast-paced lives, with its problems and stresses, we can find happiness, hope, and peace - shalom. This small, power-packed book will help lift you up and encourage you in your walk through life.

Twice Chosen:
Fifteen moving stories of faith. Personal stories of people on a spiritual journey. Find out what finally brought satisfaction and meaning to their Jewish Heritage.

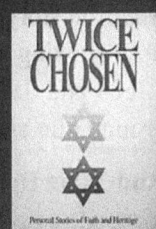

Persecution: Can it Happen Here?
We have lived as a persecuted people from the very beginning. Have times changed or will history repeat itself? Find out in this facinating book on what lies ahead and how to be ready for it.

Jewish Discoveries:
22 fascinating chapters of biblical history and lessons plus 25 rich Jewish tradition sections on 345 jam packed pages with close to 50 beautifully rendered artwork and over 20 powerful true modern stories. 345 pages

visit www.Jewishheritage.net
or write to :
Jewish Heritrage
P.O. Box 1238
New Port Richey Fl 34656

MORE GREAT BOOKS WORTH READING
Available at 1-800-765-6955

Flee the Captor: 373 pages

John Henry Weidner, a hero of the holocaust, saved the lives of 800 Jewish people. Weidner braved imprisonment and torture for his efforts.

The Clifford Goldstein Story: 92 pages

The story of a Jewish intellectual who refused to believe in God until one day the Lord touched his heart with love.

From Hollywood to Heaven: 128 pages

The true story of Steve Wohlberg, who started out as a happy, innocent little boy growing up in the Hollywood hills of Southern California during the 1960s and 1970s, but who slowly yielded to the tainted, deadly influences around him and then found a better way.

End Time Delusions: 220 pages

Steve Wohlberg clearly exposes false theories of last day events and plainly lays out what the Scriptures tell us will happen.

Secrets of Daniel: 192 pages

Jacques Doukhan re-creates the world of Babylon, explains obscure allusions, and finds hidden patterns within the prophecies, clarifying their meaning. His knowledge of the original languages makes this book a valuable asset.

Secrets of Revelation: 206 pages

The book of Revelation can only properly be understood with a thorough understanding of the Hebrew Scriptures. This book unveils the analogies and quotes from the Hebrew Scriptures that Revelation is filled with.

Jewish Discoveries: 345 pages

22 fascinating chapters of biblical history and lessons plus 29 rich Jewish tradition sections on 345 jam packed pages with close to 50 beautifully rendered professional works of art and over 25 powerful true modern stories.

We invite you to view the complete
selection of titles we publish at:

www.TEACHServices.com

Scan with your mobile
device to go directly
to our website.

Please write or email us your praises, reactions, or
thoughts about this or any other book we publish at:

TEACH Services, Inc.
P U B L I S H I N G
www.TEACHServices.com

P.O. Box 954
Ringgold, GA 30736

info@TEACHServices.com

TEACH Services, Inc., titles may be purchased in bulk for
educational, business, fund-raising, or sales promotional use.
For information, please e-mail

BulkSales@TEACHServices.com

Finally, if you are interested in seeing
your own book in print, please contact us at

publishing@teachservices.com

We would be happy to review your manuscript for free.

www.ingramcontent.com/pod-product-compliance
Lightning Source LLC
Chambersburg PA
CBHW050550170426
43201CB00011B/1646